REMEMBERING
SURVIVAL

REMEMBERING
SURVIVAL

INSIDE A NAZI SLAVE-LABOR CAMP

CHRISTOPHER R. BROWNING

W. W. NORTON & COMPANY

NEW YORK   LONDON

For information about permission to reproduce selections from this book,
write to Permissions, W. W. Norton & Company, Inc.,
500 Fifth Avenue, New York, NY 10110

For information about special discounts for bulk purchases, please contact
W. W. Norton Special Sales at specialsales@wwnorton.com or 800-233-4830

Manufacturing by Courier Westford
Book design by Chris Welch
Production manager: Julia Druskin

Library of Congress Cataloging-in-Publication Data

Browning, Christopher R.
Remembering survival : inside a Nazi slave-labor camp /
Christopher R. Browning.—1st ed.
p. cm.
Includes bibliographical references and index.
ISBN 978-0-393-07019-4 (hardcover)
1. World War, 1939–1945—Concentration camps—Poland—Starachowice.
2. Forced labor—Poland—Starachowice—History—20th century.
3. Holocaust, Jewish (1939–1945)—Poland—Starachowice. 4. Jews—Poland—
Starachowice—History—20th century. 5. Nazis—Poland—Starachowice—
History—20th century. 6. Wierzbnik (Starachowice, Poland)—History—
20th century. 7. Starachowice (Poland)—History—20th century. 8. Holocaust survivors—
Poland—Starachowice—Biography. 9. Wierzbnik (Starachowice, Poland)—Biography.
10. Starachowice (Poland)—Biography. I. Title.
D805.P7B76 2010
940.53'1853845—dc22
2009034202

W. W. Norton & Company, Inc.
500 Fifth Avenue, New York, N.Y. 10110
www.wwnorton.com

W. W. Norton & Company Ltd.
Castle House, 75/76 Wells Street, London W1T 3QT

1 2 3 4 5 6 7 8 9 0

FOR JENNI

CONTENTS

PART I

THE JEWS OF WIERZBNIK

PART II

THE DESTRUCTION OF THE WIERZBNIK GHETTO

PART III

TERROR AND TYPHUS: FALL 1942–SPRING 1943

PART IV

STABILIZATION

PART V
CONSOLIDATION, ESCAPE, EVACUATION

PART VI
AFTERMATH

LIST OF ILLUSTRATIONS

MAPS

Baltic Sea

LITHUANIA

EAST PRUSSIA

• Kaunas

• Vilnius

• Soldau

• Bialystok

• Poznań

• Płock

• Treblinka

• Warsaw

• Brest

Chelmno

Łódź

• Sobibor

Radom

• Kowel

• Lublin

• Starachowice

• Częstochowa • Ostrowiec

Kielce •

GENERAL GOVERNMENT

• Bełżec

GERMANY

• Katowice

• Cracow

Auschwitz-Birkenau

• Lwów

U.S.S.R.

SLOVAKIA

HUNGARY

ROMANIA

	Prewar boundary of Poland
	General Government boundary
	District boundary
	Gau boundary
	Incorporated Territories
	General Government
	Soviet-occupied Poland
	Soviet-occupied Poland in 1940; Galicia District of the General Government as of August 1941

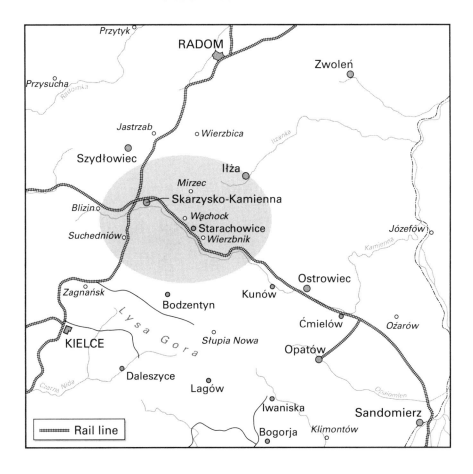

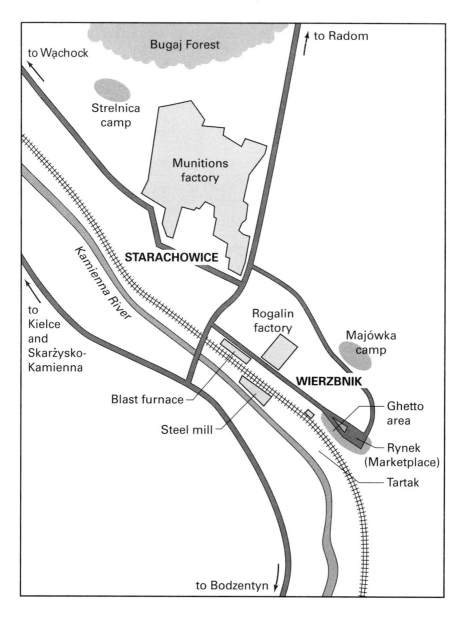

ACKNOWLEDGMENTS

This book could not have been written without the assistance and support of many people. First of all, I am indebted to the staffs of many archives, who helped in assembling and providing access to the sources on which this study is based: the Central Agency for the Investigation of National Socialist Crimes in Ludwigsburg, Germany; the Visual History Archive of the University of Southern California Shoah Foundation Institute; the United States Holocaust Memorial Museum; Yad Vashem; the Fortunoff Archive in the Sterling Library at Yale University; the Museum of Jewish Heritage in New York City; the National Archives, Washington, DC; the Holocaust Survivor Oral Testimonies collection of the University of Michigan–Dearborn, the Bundesarchiv Berlin, and the Starachowice branch of the Archivum Państwowe w Kielcach. The Visual History Archive was exceptionally helpful in providing early access to its collection of videotaped testimonies, and Yaacov Lozowick at the Yad Vashem Archives patiently answered many requests for copies of materials.

Numerous individuals provided me with important sources. Rachell Eisenberg sent me a copy of her sister Goldie Kalib's memoirs, and Phillip Eisenberg shared with me a copy of his father's account. Tova Pagi sent me a copy of her childhood memoirs, and Silvio Gryc sent me the relevant translated chapter from the Moskowicz memoirs.

Some of the sources were available only in languages I do not read.

These were made accessible to me by indispensable translations from Polish, Yiddish, and Hebrew by Ella Benson, Sylvia Noll, Barbara Kalabinski, Andrew Kos, and Nadav Davidai.

Indispensable financial support and release time for research and writing was provided to me as an Ina Levine Invited Scholar at the Center for Advanced Holocaust Studies at the U.S. Holocaust Memorial Museum (USHMM) in 2002–3 and a fellow of the National Humanities Center in 2006–7. Both the Center for Advanced Holocaust Studies at the USHMM and the National Humanities Center offer ideal environments for scholarship, and my year at each will always remain a cherished memory. My earlier academic home, Pacific Lutheran University in Tacoma, Washington, provided the initial help in developing this topic, and the Institute for Arts and Humanities at my current academic home, the University of North Carolina at Chapel Hill, allowed me to keep the momentum going at a crucial juncture.

The intellectual stimulus and support of colleagues is of course one of the great joys of the profession, and I have received much from many. In particular, Frank Bialystok, Nechama Tec, Sidney Bolkovsky, Douglas Greenberg, Sarah Bender, and Dick de Mildt have provided very important concrete assistance as well. Patrick Montague and Anita and Maciej Franciewicz made my visit to Wierzbnik-Starachowice both a memorable and a fruitful experience. Two of my graduate students, Michael Meng and Eric Steinhart, took time off from their own research to make archival forays on my behalf and procure vital documentation at key moments. Ewa Wymark has been generous in sharing various leads she has uncovered in her own research.

Above all, I am grateful to the fifteen survivors of the Starachowice factory slave-labor camps who agreed to meet with me and provided many hours of interviews, and especially to Howard Chandler, who helped arrange many of these interviews. As will be evident to an attentive reader of the footnotes, the magnitude of my debt to these interviewees is incalculable. Over the course of my research, I had assembled the written, transcribed, and/or taped accounts of 292 different survivor witnesses, and I initially conceived of these interviews as a useful supplement. In the course of my writing, however, it soon became apparent that their importance to my project was exponentially greater than I had originally expected, and the book would have been greatly impoverished without them. Given that different people experience the same events from different vantage points and remember the same events in different ways, the accounts of multiple witnesses invariably differ in both minor and major ways. Thus I fear that each of my invaluable interviewees will be somewhat disappointed when I have not accepted everything as they remember it. I hope for their understanding and remain deeply in their debt.

A NOTE ON NAMES

Dilemmas and choices abound concerning the use and spelling of names in this book. The first was which name to use in which circumstance, because many survivors went by different names in the period before 1945 and then subsequently in their new countries. In Israel and North America, where most of the survivors settled, their names were routinely hebraicized or anglicized. In the footnotes, I have used the names current at the time the testimonies were given, for this is how the testimonies are identified in the archival collections or court records. In some cases, the same person gave two different testimonies and listed his or her name somewhat differently each time, such as Abraham in one and Avraham in the other, or Najman in one and Naiman in the other.

When recounting the events of the 1940s, however, I found the use of hebraicized or anglicized names to be jarringly out of place in the text itself. Thus, whenever I have been able to ascertain the contemporary name, I have used it. Hence a footnote might refer to Henry or Morris and Chandler or Newman, but the text will refer to the same person as Chaim or Moshe, Wajchendler or Naiman. Likewise, for women married after the war, I refer to them in the text by their maiden names but in the footnotes by their married names, which they provided at the time they gave their testimonies.

Finally, there is a problem of alternative spellings. Yiddish names were spelled in the Hebrew alphabet and transliterated into the Latin alphabet for Polish, German, and English by different conventions. For instance, the person I refer to as Shlomo Einesman—an important member of the *Judenrat* and camp council—can be found as Szlama Ejnesman, Shloime Ehnesman, and Schlomo Enesman in different accounts. For names in which the conventional English spelling is common, such as Rubenstein, I have used that spelling rather than the prewar Polish transliteration of Rubinsztajn. For rarer names for which there is no common English spelling, I have rendered them by their prewar Polish transliteration.

Sometimes these different problems overlap. For instance, Rachmil Zynger in the text (as spelled during the war) is footnoted Rachmiel Zynger for his 1960s testimony, because that is how the German judicial interviewer spelled his name in the German court records. When writing a chapter for the community book in the postwar period, however, the same man identified himself as Jerahmiel Singer, an English transliteration of his hebraicized name.

If the reader finds all of this terribly confusing, he or she should be tolerant of the historian who dared to plunge into such records for the first time.

A Note on Pronounciation

| Starachowice | sta-RA-ko-VEE-tze |
| Wierzbnik | vee-ERZH-b'nik |

Remembering
Survival

Introduction

O n February 8, 1972, the seventy-five-year-old retired policeman Walther Becker awaited his verdict in a Hamburg courtroom. A veteran of World War I on both the eastern and the
western fronts, Becker made a career in the Criminal Police during the
Weimar Republic and joined the SPD (German Socialist Party) in 1930.
Briefly suspended and then restored to duty in 1933, Becker joined the
Nazi Party in 1937, but his application the same year to join the party's
elite organization, the *Schutzstaffel* (SS), was never approved. In 1940,
he was dispatched to the new Polish industrial town of Starachowice
and its adjoining old town of Wierzbnik in the Radom district, ninety-
five miles due south of Warsaw. From 1941 to 1945, he was in charge of
the branch office of the Security Police in that region. After the war, he
served as a policeman in Hamburg until his retirement in 1957.

He now stood trial for his role in the liquidation of the Jewish ghetto in
Wierzbnik on October 27, 1942—an action in which close to 4,000 Jews
were sent to their deaths in the gas chambers of Treblinka, some sixty
to eighty Jews were murdered on the spot, and about 1,600 Jews were
sent to three slave-labor camps in nearby Starachowice. By this time, the
ghetto-clearing campaign, underway since August in the Radom district, had a firmly established routine, one that had been documented in
numerous other trials in Germany. SS experts and an itinerant ghetto-
clearing squad of Baltic or Ukrainian auxiliaries sent from Radom coor-

dinated their activities with the local police forces, and the local police commander provided vital on-the-spot expertise of local conditions. In this particular case, a significant minority of the Jews from among those sent off to the work camps (instead of Treblinka) had managed to survive the Holocaust. For this reason, the prosecution could provide dozens of witnesses who gave testimony that Becker had been an extremely active and dominant presence that day. Some of these witnesses provided even more specific testimony that, pistol and club in hand, he personally had killed and beaten numerous Jews and ordered the killing of others. Becker's own account was that he knew nothing of the impending deportation action beforehand. Upon hearing word of it, he said, he had gone to observe the roundup on the marketplace and the loading of the train for forty-five minutes, during which time he neither participated nor gave orders, and then he left.

In the verdict, the presiding judge proclaimed, as a matter of principle, that eyewitness testimony was "the most unreliable form of evidence" with which the judicial process had to deal. In particular, the "ideal" witness had to be an "indifferent, attentive, intelligent observer" who observed events in a "disinterested" and "distanced" way, which none of the Jewish witnesses were. Not satisfied with this general disparagement, he proceeded methodically to discredit the testimony of each key Jewish witness individually, often with techniques of systematic doubt and tortuous reasoning that demanded a perfect consistency within and between testimonies nowhere to be found in the real world. Additionally, whole categories of testimony were deemed intrinsically flawed for one reason or another and dismissed as well. The judge then concluded that since Becker's account was not contradicted by any "reliable" evidence before the court, the defendant was acquitted. Becker walked out of court a free man.[1]

It was this egregious miscarriage of justice, amplified by the dismissal of the testimony of all Jewish witnesses when measured against a contrived and impossible standard of perfection, that first drew my attention to the Wierzbnik Jews and the Starachowice factory slave-labor camps. If Becker had escaped German justice, I felt that he at least could be given his appropriate place in historians' hell. As I looked further into the topic, however, my initial indignation over the Becker injustice gradually became less central to the project. Instead, I became increasingly fascinated with the methodological and historiographical challenge of how one could write a professionally respectable history of the relatively understudied phenomenon of the factory slave-labor camp through a case study of the Starachowice example that, by necessity, given the near total lack of surviving contemporary documents, would have to be based almost entirely on postwar eyewitness testimony. Indeed, except for a Wierzbnik-Starachowice community memorial book,[2] one English-language memoir,[3] one autobiographical pamphlet,[4] one auto-biographical article,[5] one chapter of a Yiddish memoir,[6] one chapter of an electronically posted memoir,[7] and one portion of a second-generation family study,[8] nothing had been published at all.[9]

The Nazi camp system, administered by the SS, was notorious for both its death camps and its concentration camps. The death camps—what Raul Hilberg, the dean of Holocaust scholars, called "killing centers"— were camps designed to kill incoming prisoners with poison gas on an assembly-line basis. The only permanent prisoners constituted a small workforce to empty the gas chambers, cremate the bodies, and sort the belongings of the victims. The principal single-purpose killing centers were Bełżec, Sobibor, Treblinka, and Chelmno. The concentration camps—modeled on the Dachau camp created in a suburb of Munich in the spring of 1933—were originally created for the incarceration of German political prisoners. Gradually they grew in number and size to hold those the Nazis deemed to be "asocials" (who engaged in a variety of nonconforming or unaesthetic behaviors) and then, after 1939, increasingly peoples from German-occupied territories. The concentration camps also spun off various subcamps and took on the task of exploiting prisoner labor. Two large camp complexes, Auschwitz and Majdanek, were composed of both base camps and extensive systems of satellite camps and combined all three functions of killing, incarceration, and labor exploitation. As the war progressed, the SS also established single-purpose forced-labor camps (in Nazi terminology, *Zwangsarbeitslager*, as opposed to *Konzentrationslager*), in which they established factories or contracted private businessmen to do so on their behalf within their own camps. Beyond the SS camp system, however, there were also literally hundreds of camps built on or near the premises of private businesses.

In this "privatization" of the camp system, those using uncompensated slave labor built, managed, and guarded the camps, while procuring their workers from the SS. The workers were slaves in the literal sense of the word: property owned by the SS who were "rented out" on a contractual basis.[10] The complex of three factory slave-labor camps in Starachowice constituted a medium-size example of this privatized camp system.

During the German occupation of World War II, central Poland was administered by a Nazi colonial regime known as the General Government, which was initially subdivided into four districts named for their respective district capital cities: Warsaw, Cracow, Lublin, and Radom. Starachowice was located within the Radom district, which, until recently, has been one of the regions of the Nazi empire most neglected in historical scholarship. Three noteworthy books—two available only in German—have now altered this situation. In 1996, Felicja Karay published *Death Comes in Yellow: Skarżysko-Kamienna Slave Labor Camp*.[11] This superb study of the largest factory slave-labor camp complex in the Radom district is to date not only the best but also the only significant study of this kind of camp. In 2006, Robert Seidel's *Deutsche Besatzungspolitik in Polen: Der Distrikt Radom 1939–1945* provided a detailed study of the German administration and its occupation policies of repression, exploitation, and destruction.[12] And in 2007, Jacek Andrzej Młynarczyk published *Judenmord in Zentralpolen: Der Distrikt Radom im Generalgouvernement 1939–1945*, which is noteworthy for its coverage not only of Nazi policies but also of Jewish and Polish perceptions and reactions.[13]

My research into the Starachowice factory slave-labor camps began in the pretrial interviews of witnesses for the Becker case and related investigations. Between 1962 and 1968, German judicial investigators assembled an impressive collection of 125 Starachowice survivor interviews. Of earlier testimonies of Starachowice survivors, taken between 1945 and 1948, there are only eleven—nine from the Jewish Historical Institute in Warsaw, one from London's Wiener Library, and one the transcription of a taped interview by the pioneering American psychologist David Boder.[14] Three of these early testimonies are exceptionally detailed and important, but most are very sketchy and brief. A third collection of testimonies is from those taken by Yad Vashem—in this case, three in the 1960s and six in the 1990s. The fourth major group of testimonies comprises those taped in the 1980s and 1990s, the vast majority by survivors residing in North America and speaking in English. By far the largest subgroup among these is that of the USC Shoah Foundation Institute Visual History Archive. From this collection I have used 123 testimonies taped between 1995 and 2001. Other collections containing testimonies of Starachowice survivors are found in the Museum of Jewish Heritage in New York (four), the Fortunoff Archive at Yale (six), the U.S. Holocaust Memorial Museum (six), and the University of Michigan at Dearborn (two). Finally, since 2000 I have conducted personal interviews with fifteen survivors, fourteen of whom were teenagers and one even younger when they were in the Starachowice camps. Altogether, including the testimonies of the community memorial book, I have eyewitness accounts from 292 survivors, some of whom have given multiple testimonies, taken over a span of sixty years from 1945 to 2008.[15]

Clearly in this particular case—unlike that of many small ghettos and camps for which there may be only a handful of survivors if any at all— the number of eyewitness accounts is not a problem. Aside from the community memorial book, almost all of these testimonies were given orally and recorded either in writing by someone else or on audio- or video- tape. Almost none involved the reflective process of writing and revising for publication. Among the survivors of the Starachowice camps, there is no Primo Levi or Elie Wiesel. The different ways in which their oral histories were recorded have both advantages and disadvantages, and ultimately it was beneficial to my project that I had a mix. The free-form testimonies, in which the survivors spoke without intervention or inter- ruption from the interviewer, allow us to see how they constructed their stories and narrated their memories without an intermediary. In some cases, the result was nonchronological and disjointed but reflective of the rupture and disorientation of their Holocaust experiences. Most survi- vors, however, strove spontaneously to provide a conventional chrono- logical narrative, though one often punctuated with thematically related anecdotes as well as moments of stress and struggle for composure.

The testimonies of the Visual History Archive, in contrast, were not free form but rather structured by prescribed format and an interven- tionist interviewer. Roughly one quarter of each interview was devoted to the prewar period and another quarter to the postwar, thereby

attempting to provide a "life story" rather than just a Holocaust experience. However, most of the prewar accounts were childhood memories
refracted through the horrible experiences that followed, so they were
extremely idealized and seldom captured the realities of Jewish life in
Poland in the 1930s, other than to affirm the pervasiveness of Polish anti-
Semitism. Overwhelmingly, the gist was that Jewish life in Poland was
wonderful except for the presence of the Poles.

On occasion, the interventionist interviewer was a positive factor.
I saw some interviews in which inarticulate survivors could not construct a narrative on their own; without the continued questioning of
the interviewer, there simply would have been no testimony. In one case,
a survivor had related his harrowing escape from Warsaw to the relative safety of a labor camp in Starachowice. He was then about to jump
immediately to the next peak experience—namely, the evacuation of the
Starachowice prisoners to Birkenau. Only because the interviewer broke
in and asked him about the intervening twenty-one months in Starachowice did he proceed to speak for thirty minutes on a topic that he
otherwise would have skipped entirely. On the other hand, there were
too many occasions when a survivor was slowly and indirectly broaching a topic of great interest and sensitivity when an impatient and clue-
less interviewer broke in and dragged the survivor away from what the
interviewer deemed an unimportant digression and back to the main
story line. Quite frankly, there were several occasions in which I wanted
to reach through the screen and strangle an interviewer who had just
shut down a survivor's seeming digression into a topic of vital interest
to me.

The German judicial interviews had a character of their own. The
investigators were looking for specific information about potential
crimes and potential criminals relevant to their case. No doubt in the
course of the interviews, survivors told them many things that would
have been of great interest to historians like me, but if they were not
relevant to judicial purposes, they were not recorded. Thus, from the
records of these interviews, we learn only incidentally—through contextual testimony tied to other questions—about the Jewish community
itself. However, the German judicial interviews have one undeniable
and tremendously important benefit. To obtain conviction for murder

or exceptional cases of accessory to murder, as defined by German law, the only Nazi crimes not beyond the statute of limitations at that time, German prosecutors had to prove that the killings stemmed from a base motive (such as race hatred) or were carried out cruelly or maliciously. Thus, they pressed the witnesses not only about the perpetrators' actions but also about any details that would be relevant to proving the perpetrators' state of mind. Telling their own stories, focusing on their own families and their own suffering, survivors usually provided few specifics about the German perpetrators. Many accounts, for instance, did not identify a single German by name. But the same witnesses, under targeted judicial questioning, were able to provide detailed information about the perpetrators. After all, they had lived face-to-face with these men for twenty-one months, and knowing the differences among individual Germans—who was "dangerous," who was "decent," and who could be bribed—had been vital to survival. The German judicial interviews, therefore, provided an indispensable dimension and focus missing from the other survivor accounts.

Scholars study Holocaust survivor testimony for many purposes, examining such diverse topics as trauma, narrative construction, and collective memory.[16] For the most part, the emphasis is upon the "authenticity" of survivor accounts. In contrast, the issue of "factual accuracy" in survivor accounts is generally deemphasized. Indeed, to intrude upon the survivors' memories with such a banal or mundane concern is deemed irrelevant and inappropriate, or even insensitive and disrespectful. For my current project, however, I am concerned not only with "authenticity" but also with "factual accuracy." My 292 witnesses all experienced the Starachowice camps from a different perspective, and each has remembered, refashioned, forgotten, and repressed aspects of this experience in his or her own way. In many cases, multiple perspectives on the same events are very illuminating, for they provide a fuller and more multifaceted understanding than could be obtained from a single witness. But invariably, I am also faced with conflicting and contradictory—in some cases, clearly mistaken—memories and testimonies. In some instances, differing memories and testimonies simply should not and cannot be reconciled, and critical judgments must be made.

Such critical judgment of eyewitness testimony is self-evident and commonplace for historians of other events, but it is emotionally freighted in the study of the Holocaust, where survivors have been transformed into "messengers from another world" who alone, it is claimed, can communicate the incommunicable about an ineffable experience. But what are the alternatives? Some historians, aware of the inevitable errors in factual accuracy and the limited vantage point—the equivalent of the view from the foxhole—in survivor testimony, minimize their use of it. For many topics that is possible. But in the case of the Starachowice factory slave-labor camps or, for instance, Jan Gross's study of Jedwabne,[17] that would mean foregoing any attempt to write their history at all. In my opinion, these are topics too important to be passed over simply to avoid the challenges of using survivor eyewitness evidence.

However, two public debacles have demonstrated the pitfalls concerning the use of survivor testimony when the emotional desire to believe has been allowed to eclipse the critical approach that should apply to any historical source.[18] The early lionization of the Wilkomirski pseudo-memoirs only slowly gave way to skeptical investigation and the embarrassing revelation that the author was not in fact a Holocaust survivor.[19] And the 1988 conviction of John Demjanjuk in an Israeli court as "Ivan the Terrible" of Treblinka, on the basis of the testimony of Treblinka survivors, had to be overturned by a courageous Israeli Supreme Court when documentation from Soviet archives indicated that he was instead "Ivan the Less Terrible" of Sobibor. I have no doubt that the Treblinka survivors sincerely believed in the truth of their testimonies. I suspect that even Wilkomirski was sincere albeit highly disturbed. But the historian needs accuracy, not just sincerity. Claiming that survivor testimony must be accorded a privileged position not subject to the same critical analysis and rules of evidence as other sources will merely discredit and undermine the reputation and integrity of Holocaust scholarship itself.

My methodology in this project, as it was in my study of Reserve Police Battalion 101, is to accumulate a sufficient critical mass of testimonies that can be tested against one another. In this regard, it is important to note expectations that I had about the project at the beginning that were not fulfilled. Since the Starachowice survivors clustered in three areas in the postwar period—Toronto, the northeastern United States, and Israel—I expected that as the survivors periodically met with one another regionally and retold their stories to one another, three geographically separate "memory communities" would take shape, increasingly homogenized within but increasingly divergent from one another. I also expected that as time passed, the survivors would speak less and less about sensitive topics, such as the roles of the "privileged" Jewish prisoners in the camp council and camp police, and increasingly cast their narratives in the less ambiguous terms of generic perpetrators and generic victims. These expectations were not fulfilled. I now share the counterintuitive conclusion of psychologist Henry Greenspan that the lack of differences between early and late survivor testimonies is "most noteworthy and remarkable."[20] In short, survivor memories proved to be more stable and less malleable than I had anticipated. And I found that two very sensitive topics—namely, rape and revenge killing—were broached more frequently and with greater candor in the later testimonies than in earlier ones. Again, the usual assumption that earlier testimonies are to be preferred as inherently more reliable and valuable than later ones is not always valid.

What emerges from a critical mass of testimony, I would argue, is a core memory that has remained basically stable despite the passage of time and the geographical dispersion of the survivor communities. With such a core memory, some reasonable judgments about plausibility can be made about various individual memories based on the overall credibility of the survivor's testimony, the vividness and detail of the particular events being recalled, the absence of contradiction with other plausible narratives, and—to be honest—the highly subjective intuition of the individual historian that gradually develops from prolonged immersion in the materials.

Having argued for the critical use of survivor eyewitness accounts in the writing of Holocaust history—especially when the number of survivor testimonies is sufficient, the vantage point of the survivor is apt, and surviving contemporary documentary is scant—I would now like to emphasize some of the pitfalls the historian is certain to encounter in the course of such a project. First, of course, is the problematic relationship between an event and the memory of that event, or, more precisely, the various layers of memory of that event. The deepest layer is "repressed" memory, in which the witness is not aware of what has been experienced but "repressed."

This is surely more prevalent when the events in question are especially traumatic and painful. Allow me a non-Holocaust-related example from my own family history. My uncle was a missionary in Singapore in 1942. Calculating that he could not return to his congregation later if he did not share their fate under the imminent Japanese occupation, he sent his wife and child on the last boat across the Indian Ocean but deliberately chose not to join their attempted escape. Of course, the fate that awaited him was utterly different from that of his primarily Chinese congregation. He was interned as an enemy alien, spent three and a half years in the notorious Changi Prison, and emerged at half his original body weight and barely alive. He also had no memory whatsoever of the decision he had made in early 1942 not to escape. It is doubtful that he could have survived if every day he had had to live with the constant awareness that his suffering had been avoidable except for his own naïve miscalculation. What would have been an utterly debilitating memory was mercifully repressed as a psychological defense mechanism crucial to survival. After liberation, he dug up the diary he had buried in his garden and only then became aware of the key decision that had determined the next three and a half years of his life.[21] I have no doubt that many Holocaust survivors have repressed, indeed *had* to repress, similar traumatic and potentially debilitating memories, which have never been recovered.

Second, there are "secret" memories that individuals still possess— systemic in the "choiceless choices" victims constantly faced—which are so searing and painful that they have never been shared with others. There are certain "confessional" points in some memoirs where such secrets are painfully revealed—the theft of a bunkmate's bread, the abandonment of a family member or friend, the elation that someone else was taken instead—but clearly such confessional moments are the visible tip of an iceberg that still remains mostly hidden.

Third, there are "communal" memories. These are shared and discussed among themselves by survivors from the same towns and camps. But there is a kind of tacit consensus that these are memories of events and behavior that outsiders might not understand and that hence dissemination could be potentially embarrassing or hurtful to certain members of the community. Thus it would be an inappropriate and antisocial act to bare these "communal" memories before others.

And finally there are "public" memories—those that are openly shared—that constitute the bulk of the survivor testimonies and eyewitness accounts upon which I am basing my study. The line that separates secret, communal, and public memory is not, of course, rigidly fixed—it can shift with time. As mentioned above, events of rape and revenge killing—obviously known to all Starachowice survivors but openly hinted at only by some and denied by others—began to become public memory some forty-five years after the event. But if the occurrences of rape and revenge killing are gradually becoming part of public memory, the identities of the victims of the first and the perpetrators of the second still remain within the confines of secret and communal memory.

Even within the realm of public memory, generally reliable witnesses whom I will cite frequently nonetheless provide obviously flawed and mistaken testimony on occasion. Most common in this regard are testimonies that incorporate iconic Holocaust tropes gained from postwar exposure to widespread representations in documentaries, movies, memoirs, and novels. My particular subject has a significant advantage in this regard. Since the Starachowice camps are so little known, memories of that experience remain relatively pristine and untouched by iconic tropes. This situation changes abruptly in some testimonies when the survivors end their accounts of Starachowice and relate their entry into Birkenau in the summer of 1944. One reason that there are a significant number of Starachowice survivors (including those who were children at the time) is that their transport—deemed a transfer of already-selected Jewish workers from another slave-labor camp rather than a cross section of Jewish population arriving from outside the camp system—entered Birkenau without the normal decimating selection on the ramp. Yet a number of testimonies nonetheless relate that the transport was subjected to selection on the ramp, with none other than the notorious Dr. Josef Mengele himself directing people to the right and the left. Both the memories of the majority concerning the very atypical entry into Birkenau (which could hardly have been invented and shared by so many if it had not happened) and the very survival of children who lived to testify because of that atypical entry provide convincing evidence that there was no such Mengele-led selection on the ramp immediately following arrival in Birkenau, the firmly held belief of other survivors notwithstanding.

Even if one does not go to the lengths of the Hamburg judge in his total rejection of eyewitness testimony as reliable evidence, the historian should concede that serious problems confront the use of such eyewitness accounts as a source. I would argue that the situation is even more problematic in the case of writing Holocaust history, because of the traumatic experiences of the witnesses, the understandable urge to treat less critically the testimony of those who have suffered so greatly, and widespread popular representation that has created iconic images and tropes that have been incorporated into subsequent memory. Nonetheless, other kinds of evidence are problematic in their own right, and if the historian must wait until he or she has perfect evidence, very little history would ever be written. The crucial issue in each case is that the problems of the evidence are recognized and taken into account, not that problematic evidence remains unused. Eighteen years ago, I published a study of a German killing unit, Reserve Police Battalion 101, based primarily on the postwar accounts of the perpetrators themselves. There was no question that the testimony of suspected killers—afflicted not only by the usual problems of forgetfulness and refashioning but also by a conscious, legally motivated manipulation, obfuscation, distortion, and mendacity—was highly problematic. Indeed, others have disagreed vociferously with the way in which I handled such evidence and the conclusions I reached. But no one has suggested that the attempt to write such a history should not have been made. Indeed, if one can attempt to write a history from sources in which the witnesses are mostly trying to lie, surely in the case of the Starachowice factory slave-labor camps I can try to write a history from sources in which the witnesses are mostly trying to tell the truth.

PART I

THE JEWS OF
WIERZBNIK

1

The Prewar Jewish Community of Wierzbnik-Starachowice

Wierzbnik-Starachowice is located in central Poland in the Kamienna River Valley, about twenty-eight miles south of Radom and ninety-five miles south of Warsaw. Before World War I, Jews concentrated in the old town of Wierzbnik. Here the Jewish population—which reached about 3,000 by 1939—pursued traditional occupations as cattle dealers, tailors, leatherworkers, shoemakers, upholsterers, hatmakers, carpenters, butchers, bakers, and blacksmiths as well as small-scale merchants and shopkeepers.[1] In typical Jewish families in Wierzbnik, mothers worked both in the family business and at home (often aided by a maid), and children attended public school in the morning and then received religious instruction in the afternoon. They lived in their own houses or apartments, with electricity installed shortly before the war but without running water or an indoor toilet. They spoke Yiddish at home and organized the rhythm of family life around the calendar of religious observances. For most survivors, prewar Wierzbnik was remembered quite simply as "a nice Jewish life."[2]

Located in a region rich in lumber as well as ore and clay deposits, the adjacent new town of Starachowice had the potential to grow into a small industrial city. Jews played an active role in the early stages of this development. In the late nineteenth century, the Rotvand family built a smelting furnace that was the beginning of the metallurgical industry in the area.[3] Also before the turn of the century, the four Lich-

tenstein brothers founded a plywood and veneer factory. After World
War I, the government of newly independent Poland decided to make
Starachowice the center of a government-owned armaments industry.
It took over the smelting furnace in the lower part of town and constructed a munitions factory in the upper town.[4] Few Jews lived in the
new town of Starachowice, and Jews were barred from employment in
the armaments factories of Starachowice in the prewar period. Many
even avoided walking past them for fear of being accused of espionage.[5]
But another Jewish business with international reach, owned by the Heller family, bought large tracts of forest land in the region and opened a
lumberyard and sawmill across the Kamienna River, just south of town.
The Lichtenstein and Heller firms were the major employers of Jewish
workers in Wierzbnik. Subsequently, the sawmill and lumberyard, the
smelting furnace, and the munitions factory were destined to become the
three central components using Jewish labor from the complex of Nazi
slave-labor camps founded in 1942.

World War I was traumatic for the Jews of Wierzbnik. The czar-
ist regime doubted the loyalty of its Jews, and as the German army
approached in 1915, the Jewish inhabitants of Wierzbnik were ordered
to evacuate the town with less than one hour's notice. Russian troops
exerted considerable force to drive the reluctant Jews north, first to Iłża
and then to Radom. There they spent two months living in utter desti-
tution before the German army swept through central Poland. In effect
rescued from exile by the German army, the evacuated Jews of Wierzbnik were then allowed to return home, only to find half the town razed
and the remaining homes totally pillaged. A typhus epidemic that swept
through town only increased the hardship.[6]

Getting a good sense of Jewish life in interwar Wierzbnik from post-
1945 testimonies is especially problematic for several reasons. First,
neither the immediate postwar testimonies of 1945–48 nor the 1960s
testimonies collected by German judicial investigators refer to the prewar period. Second, the videotaped testimonies—especially those of the
Visual History Archive of the USC Shoah Foundation Institute taken
in the late 1990s—do recall prewar life, but most of those are given by
survivors who were teenagers or in their early twenties in the camps and
thus either young children or teenagers in the 1930s.[7] Given what they

experienced immediately thereafter, their prewar memories are understandably idealized and nostalgic. Survivors continually refer to their "happy childhood." In the words of one survivor, "everything was beautiful."[8] According to the repeated assertions of another, "Everybody was happy."[9] Only two testimonies[10] even mention the economic hardships their parents experienced during the Great Depression—a theme that dominates the memories of non-Holocaust victims of that era.

As mentioned in the Introduction, distinct and diverging "memory communities" did not emerge among survivors who settled in Canada, the United States, and Israel in regard to war years. The prewar years, on the other hand, represent an important exception to that generalization. Contrasting portrayals of the Jewish community in Wierzbnik in the 1930s are found in the testimonies of the North American survivors and the accounts—overwhelmingly of Israeli survivors—compiled for *Wierzbnik-Starachowitz: A Memorial Book*, the *yizkor* or community memorial book published in 1973. In the accounts of those who settled in North America, the Wierzbnik Jewish community enjoyed a vibrant religious and associational life not untypical of prewar provincial Poland. There was one major synagogue in town, but also a number of prayer houses or *stiebel* to suit individual inclinations. Most Wierzbnikers were Yiddish-speaking at home and generally if not fanatically observant by orthodox-traditionalist standards. There were also followers of Ger Hassidism in Wierzbnik. The daughter of the Hassidic rabbi retrospectively characterized her family life as "more religious than God would like."[11] There was a network and tradition of social support and charitable giving (with funds for poor children's school fees, poor brides, a burial society, etc.), and a Yiddish theatre with visiting actors.

Alongside this depiction of a generally traditional Jewish life, there was little discussion of modern political involvement. Just one testimony mentioned the presence of the Bund—the Jewish, secular socialist labor party—in Wierzbnik.[12] This was a town of craftsmen, shopkeepers, and workers in the Jewish-owned lumber firms but not a Jewish factory proletariat, since Jews were not employed in the Starachowice factories. Many survivors subsequently identified themselves rather vaguely as both "religious" and "Zionist." But there is no reference to the ideological debates and hair-splitting among Zionist youth groups that characterized the memories of the urban Jewish intelligentsia.[13] Insofar as Wierzbnikers who settled in North America specified a particular kind of Zionism, they most often mentioned the right-wing, paramilitary Revisionist Zionists of Ze'ev Jabotinsky and its Betar youth group.[14] Also in the nearby town of Bodzentyn, with its Jewish community of some 1,000, Betar was the Zionist association "that offered the greatest inspiration" to the younger generation.[15] As evidence of at least some secularization and modernization in Jewish life of a less political kind, postwar testimony noted the existence of a Maccabi Sports Club, especially for soccer.

According to the testimonies in the community book, however, Zionism *was* a dominant feature of Jewish life in Wierzbnik. Only one account described the Jewish community as a typical Polish-Jewish town in which the Jews "filled their lives with religion and tradition."[16] More typically, another described Wierzbnik as "teeming with Zionist activity."[17] And according to yet another version, Judaism and Zionism were, for Wierzbnikers, "one and the same."[18] In this narrative, a Zionist awakening began after World War I, associated with a new influx of Jews, especially the notable community activist Symcha Mincberg, who married the daughter of one of the four Lichtenstein brothers who owned the plywood and veneer factory. In the first generation, there was not yet a sharp break between traditional religious sensibilities and modern Zionism. "Stemming from an extremely religious, traditional family," Mincberg wrote, "I made great efforts to ensure that the Zionist work would not be done contrary to religious outlooks." Indeed, the early Zionists created their own *minyan* or prayer group among the many such gatherings for religious observance in Wierzbnik.[19]

A second phase of Zionism followed that was decidedly more secular, political, and divided. Here one encounters an array of rival Zionist associations bewildering in its variety. On the right were both a religious-orthodox Zionist party (Mizrachi) and the militant and secular Revisionist Zionists, followers of Jabotinsky, who devoted themselves to hiking, physical training, and pre-military drill. For Revisionists, the appearance of Jabotinsky in nearby Ostrowiec was a memorable occasion. Middle-class Zionist Jews generally supported the mainstream Al HaMishmar of Yitzhak Gruenbaum, the longtime critic of assimilation and acerbic defender of minority rights against the Polish government, in opposition to the religious, non-Zionist Agudath Israel, dominant in the 1920s, which had supported the regime of Polish president Josef Pilsudski in return for communal autonomy in Jewish affairs. The moderate Labor Zionists (Poalei Zion Right) sought to bridge class divides by organizing night classes and improving conditions for the working poor. The radical Labor Zionists (Poalei Zion Left) "became a decidedly leftist movement" by Wierzbnik standards, and two Wierzbnikers associated with it were hard-core Communists who had to flee the country ahead of the Polish police to avoid arrest. Sports were not immune from the political and social fragmentation. The Maccabi Club was oriented to the middle and right of the spectrum, while the Gviazda club was founded to provide for the lower-class youth. However, in competition to recruit the best players, the clubs sometimes jumped class lines.

For some, Zionist youth activities were all-consuming. As Symcha Mincberg's daughter subsequently wrote, "Our childhood was wonderful . . . full of excitement. . . . Everything and everywhere was part of a boiling cauldron of gatherings and meetings."[20] Despite this bewildering array of associations, notably absent in Wierzbnik (though prominent elsewhere among Polish Jewry) were the secular, non-Zionist, socialist labor movement known as the Bund, and the Marxist Zionist youth movement Hashomer Hatzair.[21] As these were the two most prominent left-wing organizations in Jewish life in interwar Poland, their absence indicates that Wierzbnik was indeed more provincial and conservative than larger, more cosmopolitan Jewish urban communities.

This difference in memories of Zionism in Wierzbnik between the North American and the Israeli survivor communities can probably be attributed to two factors. One is self-selection, as prewar Zionist activists would have later immigrated from the displaced-persons camps to Israel in greater proportions than to North America and vice versa for non-Zionists. This tendency of self-selection would in turn have been reinforced by diverging "collective memories." Once the survivors were in Israel, the contemporary environment would have strengthened their desire to remember and emphasize their past as active Zionists rather than passive diaspora Jews, while the process of assimilation in North

America would have diminished the tendency to remember and emphasize earlier Zionist identities.

The emergence of a modern, Zionist-oriented element in Wierzbnik
society was reflected in both education and politics. At the core of the
modern trend was a more assimilated, economically better-off Jewish
elite in Wierzbnik. These heads of family generally were businessmen
and merchants rather than shopkeepers and artisans. They tended to
speak Polish rather than Yiddish at home. Some sought to send their
children to private schools rather than to the public schools in the morning, followed by traditional religious instruction (*heder*) in the afternoon.
As it became more difficult for Jews to get into elite private schools,
they founded a *tarbut* (modern, Hebrew-language, Zionist-oriented
secular school) in Wierzbnik as an alternative to the *heder*. By one estimate, some 80 percent of Jewish pupils attended the *heder* and 20 percent
the *tarbut*.[22] The religious Zionists in turn founded their own Hebrew-
language Hamizrachi school as well.[23]

In the early interwar period, the Jewish religious community or *Gmina*,
under the leadership of Szmul Isser, pursued an apolitical course. This was
in line with the governing style of Josef Pilsudski, who safeguarded the
autonomy of minorities in return for political quiescence. The craftsmen
of Wierzbnik organized to protect their economic interests but otherwise
"paid no heed to political issues" and supported Isser.[24] This apolitical
stance began to change in the 1930s, as the younger, modern Zionist faction became more assertive. Symcha Mincberg founded a Jewish bank so
that Jewish craftsmen and merchants would not be dependent on non-
Jews for credit. And Mincberg, his colleague Josef Dreksler, and others
began to run for and win positions on the town council, where the Jewish
delegation chaired by Mincberg sought more actively to protect Jewish
interests.[25] When the young novice lawyer Uri Shtramer arrived in Wierzbnik in 1937, he found the Jewish community divided between younger
Zionists and older members of the religious, non-Zionist Agudath Israel,
who kept out of public life and confined themselves to Jewish affairs.
However, financial mismanagement by the governing board of the *Gmina*,
in terms of failure to collect taxes and keep up Jewish institutions, led the
county government to dissolve the board and temporarily put Shtramer
in charge. With the support of the Zionists, he reorganized the tax system,

restored the crumbling synagogue, and then arranged for new elections to the board. The Zionists ran a united ticket and for the first time defeated the Isser-led traditional faction, which—in Shtramer's partisan character-ization—had "turned their back on their people" and passively accepted the edicts of the Polish authorities.[26]

There was one other area of divided memory concerning prewar Wierzbnik—namely, the factor of Polish anti-Semitism. A very dis-tinct minority of survivors remembered Poles and Jews as getting along fairly well, with Wierzbnik not as bad as other places in Poland.[27] Sev-eral noted explicitly that they experienced much more anti-Semitism during their army service than while living in Wierzbnik.[28] Accord-ing to Chuna Grynbaum's description of relations with Poles, "We got along with them beautifully. We had no problem with them. . . . Nobody bothered us. It was live and let live." This situation, he claimed, did not change until the war came, when suddenly Poles no longer acknowl-edged their former Jewish friends.[29] Others dated a sharp change to just before the outbreak of war.[30] Jerahmiel Singer (his Israeli name; in Poland he was known as Rachmil Zynger), in the account he wrote for the Wierzbnik community book was even more adamant in exempting Wierzbnik from the growing anti-Semitism fostered by Pilsudski's suc-cessors. He stated that government incitement against Jews "hardly had any effect on Wierzbnik, despite the efforts of outsider anti-Semites to organize boycotts, strikes, and so on. These attempts failed entirely, due to the disinterest of the Polish residents of Wierzbnik, who maintained their loyal relations with the Jewish population."[31]

Far more prevalent are bitter memories of a widespread anti-Semitism in Wierzbnik that escalated and intensified following the 1935 death of Pilsudski, whose relatively benign attitude toward minorities in Poland was supplanted by the militant and intolerant integral nationalism of his successors. As one survivor stated emphatically and bitterly: "We had a beautiful life . . . except for having Poles around, which was very unpleasant."[32] One prominent manifestation was the boycott movement, in which Poles either painted signs or stood in front of Jewish stores to deter customers from entering. The boycott was especially effective during Christmas shopping, according to one survivor.[33] Several people noted, however, that since virtually all the stores were owned by Jews,

Poles had nowhere else to shop and the economic impact was thus miti-
gated. Jews cautiously conducted business from the back doors of their
stores when either being boycotted or illegally transacting business on
Sundays.[34] Others remembered the constant sight of hateful graffiti on
fences and sidewalks and the shower of verbal abuse and rocks thrown
by "hooligans."[35]

Jewish boys had one gender-specific memory—namely, the problem
of fights and beatings at the hands of Polish boys, usually without any
recourse to protection from teachers or police.[36] Zvi Feldpicer remembered being beaten and kicked by Polish boys who got away with it
because Zvi was both a Jew and too weak to hit back.[37] Abramek Naiman
moved to Wierzbnik at the age of nine from a place where Jews and
Poles got along "quite nice" and was surprised that he had to fight with
Poles at his first school recess.[38] Jewish boys in Wierzbnik learned what
times and places were particularly dangerous. Boys had to be particularly careful to hide after class on Wednesdays, the day that the local
priest[39] visited the school, or risk being caught by their aroused Polish
schoolmates and either being beaten or having pork sausage rubbed on
their lips. They avoided swimming in the Kamienna River, for getting
to the beach was a particularly dangerous gauntlet.[40] Attending soccer
games, with their excited crowds, was also a high risk best avoided. At
least one young soccer enthusiast who went to games anyway nonetheless left early to avoid a predictable post-game beating.[41]

However strong the consensus among the bulk of Wierzbnik survivors concerning the breadth and nastiness of Polish anti-Semitism
there—particularly in the last four years before the war—such memories should be placed in perspective. Two other survivors of the Starachowice camps who came from a town that experienced a murderous
pogrom in 1936 offer prewar memories that provide a sobering comparison. When eleven-year-old Sara and fourteen-year-old Leah Rozenblitt
came home from school in the small town of Przytyk, fifteen miles west
of Radom, on March 9, 1936, a neighbor warned them that Jews were
being killed and they had best hide in their attic. When they were told it
was okay to come out, their uncle lay dead in the hallway, his head having been severed with a hatchet, and their aunt died from her injuries
two days later in a hospital in Radom. When their father, a cattle dealer,

tried to recover cattle that he had left with peasants for fattening, they refused and faced no repercussion. The Rozenblitts fled town, having lost everything. When pressed by her persistent interviewer to talk about the "happy times" of her youth, Leah replied bitterly that there had been no happy times.[42]

2

The Outbreak of War

The outbreak of war on September 1, 1939, posed a double threat to Wierzbnik's Jews. As inhabitants of a town in close proximity to the munitions and steel factories of Starachowice, they feared bombing. As Jews, they feared the Germans. The result was widespread panic and flight, though as Meir Ginosar put it, he was unsure whether his family fled as Poles or as Jews.[1] In fact, several patterns of flight emerged. Some indeed tried to escape the Germans by reaching Soviet-occupied territory (which, before the Soviet entry into eastern Poland on September 17, was much farther east than the subsequent demarcation line). Very few who attempted this trip actually made it, and among the few who did, some even subsequently changed their minds and returned. But most Wierzbnikers primarily feared the bombing. They fled to villages where they had friends or relatives, or even nearby forests, and returned home as soon as the German army swept past, leaving Wierzbnik-Starachowice occupied but no longer a potential military target. And a few Jews intentionally came to Wierzbnik from elsewhere because, in comparison to their hometowns, it seemed the safer refuge.

One week before the outbreak of war, the district inspector of police visited the main synagogue in Wierzbnik and asked for volunteers to dig defense trenches. Jews and Poles, he stressed, were now in the same boat. Many Jews volunteered and worked even on the Sabbath. With the outbreak of war, the Germans did not in fact try to destroy the Starachowice factories, which they hoped to capture intact. Nonetheless, the many planes flying overhead caused great fear, and stray bombs landed in the vicinity of Wierzbnik on each of the first two days of hostilities. This set in motion a widespread flight from the town, and by September 5, the mayor dismissed those who had stayed behind to dig trenches and advised them to leave as well.[2]

In most of the testimonies of survivors who briefly fled Wierzbnik, this episode is related quite simply. Their families packed their possessions in horse-drawn wagons and they made their way on crowded roads to not-too-distant villages where they had relatives or friends. After the Germans had arrived in both Wierzbnik-Starachowice and their places of refuge, they had nowhere else to go, and it made no sense to stay away any longer. Within a week or two, they returned to their homes in Wierzbnik from what one survivor labeled a "useless exercise."[3] Some returned home to find that none of their possessions had been touched.[4] The rabbi's family in particular was surprised to discover that a Polish woman they deemed an anti-Semite had protected their home from robbers.[5] More often, returning Jews found that their stores or homes had been looted,[6] or the family chickens taken.[7] One young woman returned to find her father and brother-in-law in hiding and the family grocery store being pillaged, as young Polish anti-Semites stood in front and signaled passing Germans that there was still something worth looting inside.[8] In the case of Wąchock, just three miles up the valley from Wierzbnik, those returning found most of the town had been razed in retaliation for a rooftop sniper attack on German troops.[9]

In Bodzentyn, fifteen miles south of Wierzbnik, the town's most prominent and "wealthiest" family, the Szachters, weighed the respective insecurities of remaining in town or trying to reach Soviet territory. After several days of hesitation, they opted for the latter. With two wagons, one loaded with possessions and the other with family members, they headed first for the estate of a wealthy Polish landowner with whom Mr. Szachter, a grain merchant and flour-mill owner, had maintained good business and personal relations. They were received cordially the first evening, but by the next day it was clear that they were no longer welcome, as the presence of a Jewish family on the estate was causing great unease. They headed back toward Wierzbnik and stayed a few days in a small village in the home of a wealthy Jewish grain merchant while they reconsidered their options. They decided once again to head east on crowded roads. When they became entangled with retreating units of Polish soldiers, who threatened to confiscate their horses, they turned off the main road and headed toward home on dirt tracks. After waiting a few additional days in a summer cottage they had often visited deep in the forest, they finally returned to Bodzentyn, "amazed" to find "everything exactly the way we had left it," even including American dollar bills left behind in the haste of departure.[10]

Even before the outbreak of war and out of fear of bombing, the Glatt family (father, mother, son, daughter-in-law, and three daughters) had already hired a horse and buggy for flight to the hometown of the father's parents. Within ten days, the German army had occupied the entire area. Father and son then traveled to the city of Ostrowiec to consult other family members. There they were challenged by a German soldier. The father halted but the son started to run and was immediately shot dead. He was the first Jew from Wierzbnik to be killed by the Germans.[11]

Ironically, while Wierzbnik Jews fled their town at the outbreak of war out of fear that the nearby factories would be bombed, once that fear proved unfounded it very quickly became a town that Jews fled *to*, not *from*. In the city of Tarnobrzeg, 3,400 Jews were rounded up by Germans, put on rafts for transport over the San River, and told to go to Russia. Once they were no longer under guard, one family opted to go west rather than east and made their way on foot to the home of a sister in Wierzbnik. As one daughter explained, at that point they did not know what would happen, and subsequently it was "too late" to change their fateful decision.[12]

A family that owned a lumberyard in Skarżysko-Kamienna fled that city at the outbreak of war and stayed away for two or three weeks. Knowing that they would be unable to hide lumber products, they decided to abandon the business. They returned to Skarżysko-Kamienna only to pick up personal possessions and joined the maternal grandparents in Wierzbnik.[13]

Fourteen-year-old Henyek Krystal from Sosnowiec was visiting his maternal grandparents in Bodzentyn when the war broke out, but his mother took him back to Sosnowiec as soon as it was possible to travel. Faced with labor roundups, Henyek's brother and then his father headed east and made their way to Soviet territory. On the presumption that younger boys were less endangered, Henyek was not allowed to undertake such a risky and arduous flight but instead was sent back to Bodzentyn with many of the family's possessions, to be rejoined by his mother later.[14]

In Łódź, the family of Guta Blass owned a textile factory that made uniforms for the army. In December 1939, before the ghetto was formed and before his factory had been seized, her father nonetheless sensed that it was getting too dangerous to remain in Łódź and decided to move to Wierzbnik, the hometown of his wife's family. They placed what belongings they could, especially a sewing machine, in one wagon. The father spoke fluent German, so they traveled as a family of mixed descent, not as Jews, and reached Wierzbnik despite heavy snow.[15] Another Łódźer, a salesman, made the same calculation in December 1939 that this city was becoming too dangerous and moved with his wife and three children to Wierzbnik because he had business contacts there.[16]

While some outsiders came to Wierzbnik for presumed greater safety, some Wierzbnikers decided to make an attempt to flee to the Soviet zone, once the partition of Poland, as prearranged in the Nazi-Soviet Non-Aggression Pact, had been completed.[17] Following the invasion of the Soviet army from the east on September 17, the closest crossing points of the new demarcation line were at Przemyśl on the San River (140 miles away) and Hrubieszów on the Bug River (160 miles away). One group of about twenty, including the prominent Dreksler family, must have taken the latter route. Having crossed the Vistula River by barge to avoid German sentries on the bridge there, they crossed over the Bug into the Soviet zone without being stopped and reached Luck. When asked by Soviet authorities to fill out a questionnaire as to where they ultimately intended to settle, they naively wrote *Palestine* instead of the *Soviet Union*. That landed them in a forest work camp near Archangel.[18] Pinchas Nudelman was among a group of young Jews from Wierzbnik who took the train to Przemyśl, where they paid a smuggler to get them across the river. The smuggler turned them over to a German patrol that robbed them before allowing them to proceed. Reaching Lwów, Pinchas was arrested and sent to a village of exiled Uzbeks near

Archangel.[19] They were not the only Wierzbnikers to end up felling trees near Archangel.[20]

Moshe Samet made one attempt to reach the border but was caught by a German patrol and interned in a POW camp because he had helped himself to abandoned Polish army clothing. After escaping from the camp, he returned to Wierzbnik and joined Yitzhak Kerbel in another attempt to reach the Soviet zone. Dumped by their Polish boatman in the middle of the San River, they reached the Soviet side soaking wet and made their way to Lwów. From there, they moved deeper into the Soviet Union, worked as coal miners in the Donbas, and eventually joined the Polish army that was being raised on Soviet territory.[21] Joining the Polish army in the Soviet Union was also the path to survival of at least one other Wierzbniker.[22]

In addition to working in the Arctic or serving in the military, some who reached the Soviet zone opted for a third alternative—namely, to return to their homes in the German zone. Abraham Rosenwald was among a group of young men who reached the Soviet zone near Przemyśl, but only after being robbed first by Germans and then by the Poles they had paid to smuggle them over the river. Finding himself with no food or warm winter clothing, he could not endure and decided to return.[23] Several people from towns near Wierzbnik-Starachowice, such as Opatów, Szydłowiec and Bodzentyn, who had made good their escape, also made the same decision. Three brothers fled Opatów five days after the outbreak of the war and successfully made their way to the Ukraine via roads filled with refugees and clogged with abandoned cars. Finding conditions there difficult and fearing that they, like many other refugees from Poland, would be sent deep into the interior to work in coal mines, they hired a guide to take them back over the Bug River and reached home in January 1940.[24] Another young man from Opatów, having been seized, briefly held as a male of military age, and then released, joined a group that made its way under fire across the Bug River. Learning that his father had been told that he had been shot and killed during the crossing, he made what he thought was a temporary return trip to Opatów to reassure his family. He never made it back to Soviet territory.[25] From Szydłowiec, one survivor's brother, among others, made good his escape to the Soviet zone. But he found life there "very hard" and since he had left behind a baby daughter, he returned.[26] Three of Goldie Szachter's uncles—two from Bodzentyn and one from the disintegrating Polish army—made good their escape to the Soviet zone and fortuitously met up in a breadline. After months on the Soviet side, they returned to Bodzentyn in the early spring of 1940. The entire family treated their return as a joyous event.[27] David Mangarten's brother and brother-in-law also made it to Soviet territory, returned to Wierzbnik to tell others that it was not so bad there, but then found themselves unable to cross back over the border again.[28]

In the memories of many Starachowice survivors, the first days of the war were a "crazy time"[29] of great uncertainty and panicked flight. For most, the immediate concern was to avoid the destruction of war, which in Wierzbnik was above all perceived as the threat of aerial bombing. But even for those who thought about escape eastward beyond the German reach, the speed of the German advance—passing through Starachowice on September 8—quickly rendered such plans hopeless for most. Thereafter, they began to trickle back to their homes to face not a short-term military threat but a long-term encounter with Nazi occupation policies.

3

The Early Months of German Occupation

The Jews of Wierzbnik remembered the early months of German occupation chiefly for the dizzying array of restrictions and humiliations showered upon them. As one survivor put it, "Every five minutes there was a new law."[1] In the words of another: "Every day brought a new edict, leading to complete chaos."[2] The first reality that faced every family with children was that young Jews could not return to their schools when they reopened. In nearby Bodzentyn, Jewish children were allowed to attend the reopened schools for a few days before they were banned in early October 1939.[3] But in Wierzbnik, the ban took place immediately.[4] Thus, a basic pattern of family life, fundamental to Jewish culture, was disrupted from the beginning. Other restrictions quickly followed. The Germans imposed a curfew that barred Jews from going out in the evening—after 6 p.m. in Wierzbnik and after 7 p.m. in Bodzentyn.[5] Jews were forbidden to possess radios.[6] They were barred from the use of public transportation, forced to take off their hats when encountering a German in uniform, and compelled to walk in the street rather than on the sidewalk.[7] Germans could search and pillage their homes and businesses with total impunity.[8] A young Rosalie Laks remembered a group of elegant German officers entering the family home and looking around for things. When one found something he liked, he politely told her mother: "This is beautiful, please wrap it for me."[9]

The German share of Poland was divided between the western "incorporated territories" annexed to the Third Reich and the central region that became a German colony known as the General Government. The latter in turn was divided into four districts: Warsaw, Cracow, Lublin, and Radom. Wierzbnik, in the district of Radom, had a total population of somewhat over three million people, of whom 375,000 were Jews.[10] In the four districts of the General Government, Jews were required to wear an armband with a Star of David on it. Perhaps because the provincial and mostly unassimilated Jews of Wierzbnik were already usually identifiable by virtue of their clothing, hairstyle, beard, language, and gestures, most of those who mentioned the armband requirement did so in a quite matter-of-fact manner.[11] Indeed, Sala Glatt was quite explicit that wearing the armband was "not the worst thing."[12] Only one survivor spoke emotionally of this particular German measure as "the most humiliating of all degrees," one that "branded" Jews with a "deep sense of shame."[13] And another deemed it "not a pleasant thing" to be singled out as a Jew in this way.[14]

More prominent in the memories of survivors was the burning of the Wierzbnik synagogue in late September 1939, close to Yom Kippur.[15] On Yom Kippur, the Germans also seized a clandestine *minyan* of Jews dressed in their religious finery. They forced them to unload coal from a train and then forced them to smear themselves with dirt and mud in order "to abase themselves even more."[16] German police also descended upon Rabbi Ben Zion Rabinowicz and demanded that he sign a declaration that the Jews had set the synagogue on fire, but he refused. Policemen soon returned looking for the rabbi, declaring that they had orders to shoot him, but the family successfully begged for his life. Subsequently, his daughter struggled to explain the unusual stay of execution: "I had the impression that these people were not yet accustomed to killing."[17]

Survivors' most vivid and searing memories of the early days of German occupation related less to German legal measures—which soon exceeded anyone's capacity to remember and enumerate—than the shock of German brutality that accompanied everyday encounters and the overwhelming sense of humiliation, vulnerability, and danger that such casual brutality inflicted. Many such incidents were tied to the random roundups of forced labor that the Germans carried out that fall, as men from their midteens to sixty years old were seized on the streets or taken from their homes to perform menial physical labor, such as working on roads, sweeping streets, shoveling snow, or carrying wood or water.[18] The men were frequently beaten and returned home "as cripples."[19] Forced to carry buckets of water, Henia Burman's uncle died of a heart attack.[20] Rosa Herling's father was forced to remove horse dung from the street while dressed in his prayer shawl.[21]

Particularly shocking for children was the sight of their parents being physically abused. When three policemen arrived at the apartment of Sesha Bromberger, the youngest of them slapped her mother, an experience that left Sesha with nightmares.[22] The Laks family, one of the most prominent Jewish families in Wierzbnik, was walking on the sidewalk and failed to step off into the street quickly enough when encountering a German. The German pushed Izak into the gutter and kicked him again and again, until his glasses were broken and his clothes ruined. This experience came as a shock not only to Izak—a man of German education and culture who had had many prewar business contacts with Germans without an inkling of such potential for violence—but also to his family. "This was the first time I understood what the war was all about," his daughter Rosalie recalled.[23]

One subject so often captured by German photographers of the Polish campaign and its aftermath was the cutting of beards of Jewish men as a particular ritual of degradation aimed at Jewish religious identity and manhood, demonstrating both a contempt for and the weakness of the victim. Among Wierzbnik survivors, this ritual was also one of the most frequently cited memories, as the sight of Jewish beards seemed to offer a particularly irresistible opportunity for abuse on the part of Germans stationed there.[24] The tormenters of Michulek Baranek's grandfather were especially creative, cutting off only half of his beard. Hurting from the "disgrace" but unwilling to cut the other half, he would only go out wearing a scarf to cover his face.[25]

The cumulative impact of these random roundups for menial and humiliating forced labor, physical beatings, plundering, and rituals of degradation such as beard-cutting paralyzed Jewish life in Wierzbnik in the early months of German occupation. Jews feared going into the streets, and men in particular hid as best they could. There could be no question of life returning to normal for Jews, but obtaining at least some measure of order, predictability, and mitigation was necessary just to cope. The German-imposed Jewish Council or *Judenrat* acted as an intermediary between the German occupiers and the Jews. It had the unenviable and difficult task of trying to find ways of satisfying the former while protecting the latter so that some semblance of life could return to the Jewish community.

4

The *Judenrat*

I n July 1939, the Nazi regime had transformed the central organization of Jews in Germany (*Reichsvertretung der Juden in Deutschland*)
into an institution of its own creation, the Reich Union of German
Jews (*Reichsvereinigung der deutschen Juden*). It was now responsible not
for representing German Jews but rather for carrying out the policies of
the Security Police. The policy of creating Jewish organizations to serve
German purposes was almost immediately imposed in conquered Poland
as well, by virtue of the order of Heinrich Himmler's deputy, Reinhard
Heydrich, on September 21, 1939. Accordingly, councils composed of
"Jewish elders" were to be established in each community; they were
to be "fully responsible in the literal sense of the word" for the execution of German orders.[1] The policy was reaffirmed in the November 28,
1939, decree issued by the new head of the General Government, Hans
Frank.[2] The imposition of the Jewish Council or *Judenrat* was a policy
that the German occupiers in Poland uniformly supported for several
reasons. The councils relieved the Germans of much of the burden of
managing the Jewish communities and thus spared them manpower.
And they served as lightning rods, attracting much of the hostility and
resentment of the downtrodden Jews. As the German manager of the
Warsaw ghetto, Hans Auerswald, cynically wrote: "When deficiencies
occur, the Jews direct the resentment against the Jewish administration
and not against the German supervisors."[3]

The Jewish councils, at least in the first generation of membership, were usually composed of traditional community leaders, though often they were those who had held only second-echelon positions before the war, as the most prominent leaders often had successfully fled.[4] These first-generation leaders conceived of their task as a dual one—not only to fulfill German demands in order to protect their communities from worse repercussions but also to devise strategies of mitigation and survival. Operating from a position of powerlessness vis-à-vis the German occupiers, they often faced what were—in scholar Lawrence Langer's memorable phrase—"choiceless choices." In some cases, individuals emerged from the councils as both dominant over the Jews and compliant toward the Germans. The most notorious examples of those who zealously adopted the Nazi principle of one-man authoritarian rule were Moshe Merin of East Upper Silesia and Chaim Rumkowski of Łódź.[5] In many Jewish communities, such as Wierzbnik (from which some of the most prominent prewar leaders had not fled), the leadership remained more collective and also struggled with a mixed record of success to protect the community while placating the Germans.

Immediately after the burning of the synagogue, Rabbi Rabinowicz, as the traditional religious leader of the community, was approached by the Germans to provide a list of candidates for the purpose of assembling the *Judenrat*.[6] Service on the council was not an attractive prospect. One lawyer who was approached refused.[7] Others begged the rabbi not to put their names on the list but then relented. Eventually the *Judenrat* was formed. It was supposed to have twenty-four members, but one surviving list of September 1940 distinguished between nineteen "members" and five "co-workers" or "staff." By occupation, there were five self-employed businessmen, one doctor, one dentist, two bookkeepers, four office workers, four artisans, and seven tradesmen. The oldest—the prewar community leader Szmul Isser—was fifty-nine; the youngest—the council secretary from Łódź, Moshe Adler—was thirty-three.[8] The *Judenrat* was also empowered to create a Jewish police force—the Order Service or *Ordnungsdienst*—which was formed before the end of 1939 under Commandant Kornblum.[9]

Among themselves, the members chose Symcha Mincberg as president.[10] He was a highly educated, cultured, cosmopolitan businessman and banker.[11] As a longtime activist and political leader of the community who defended Jewish interests vis-à-vis the Polish authorities in the interwar period, his election to this post must have been self-evident. Among those who served with him on the *Judenrat*, three names in particular were frequently recalled by survivors, perhaps because they were the only three on the council who subsequently held significant positions of influence on the camp council or *Lagerrat* of the Starachowice labor camps. They were the leather-goods dealer Shlomo Einesman, the draper Rachmil Wolfowicz, and Moshe Birenzweig. Moshe Adler from Łódź served as the council secretary. Moshe Birenzweig was vice president. Rachmil Wolfowicz was the council's liaison to the German police.[12]

From the outset, the *Judenrat* faced two major tasks. One, the collection of money and other valuables was imposed to meet German demands. Two, providing workers to meet German labor demands was undertaken at the council's own initiative. Concerning the first task, the German occupation authorities periodically demanded that the *Judenrat* collect sizable financial payments or make specific deliveries of gold, jewelry, furniture, fur coats, and other valuable items from the Jewish community. The unenviable task of the *Judenrat* was to apportion the obligation among the Jewish community by estimating each family's financial capacity to pay.[13]

Failure to make the required payments had drastic consequences at all levels. When Channah Glatt's father, owner of a textile business in the prewar period, received an assessment that he felt was based on a significant overestimate of his wealth and that he could not pay, he was arrested by the Jewish police and held in the city jail in Wierzbnik until his wife collected the required amount and turned it over to the *Judenrat*. Upon his release, he went into hiding with a peasant family in the countryside. When the next assessment was made and her mother did not pay, Channah herself was arrested and taken to jail. She was released three weeks later, only after her mother once more made the required payment.[14]

When the *Judenrat* failed to meet a number of petty demands from the German mayor, he wrote to the county administrator or *Kreishauptmann* in nearby Iłża, demanding punishment. In a rare surviving German document of November 16, 1940, the mayor accused the *Judenrat* of numerous transgressions. It had failed to make more than a perfunctory effort to demolish the ruins of the synagogue, which had burned down "through the events of war." It had not paid various debts it had accumulated. And it had failed in its responsibility to take care of the needy, as "the homeless and mentally retarded roamed the streets barefoot and in rags." He requested an "exemplary" punishment of the *Judenrat*, and specifically of "the chief culprits of this Jewish gang"—Mincberg, Birenzweig, and Adler. The *Kreishauptmann* imposed a fine of 1,000 złoty.[15]

More serious were the repercussions from failing to make a payment demanded by the police chief, Walther Becker. So-called SS men—understandably, on such occasions survivors can seldom identify German personnel or units with precision—arrived, stormed into the building of the *Judenrat*, and beat everyone in sight with their rifle butts. Many were badly injured, and at least one member of the *Judenrat* could not return to work for six weeks.[16]

Even more paralyzing to the community were the intensifying seizures of Jews for humiliating menial labor. Jewish males increasingly feared to walk the streets because of this threat, so they beseeched Mincberg to find a solution. He first approached the Polish mayor, Sokol, and begged for help. Though Sokol was the one Polish officeholder in Starachowice noted for his benevolent attitude toward the Jews, he proclaimed himself powerless in this matter. With trepidation, Mincberg then approached the German "commandant" and "with bitter heart explained to him the difficult situation the Jewish population was in because of the kidnapping for forced labor." He agreed that the Germans would "no longer grab Jews for work" if the Jews provided a quota of Jewish workers as requested by the Germans each day.[17] As a result, a Jewish labor division was established within the German Labor Office (*Arbeitsamt*). Izak Laks, Vienna-educated, fluent in German, and desirous of a "controlled atmosphere," was appointed as its head. He thus worked both for the *Judenrat* as well as for the head of the *Arbeitsamt*, an ethnic German named Niemczik. He was assisted by his eldest daughter, Chanka.[18]

The *Judenrat* was required to provide an exact count of male Jews in Wierzbnik between the ages of twelve and sixty, divided by profession

and capability. As of January 3, 1940, before the first major influx of
Jews from outside, the Jewish community had 828 male Jews capable of
work, divided into 462 unskilled workers, 357 artisans and craftsmen,
seven white-collar professionals, and two agricultural laborers.[19] It was
Laks's task to register all local Jews as well as newcomers capable of
work. Each one was obligated to perform forced labor once a week, but
"the people who had means also paid the poor people who were willing
to go to work in their place."[20] There were often more men lined up
each morning to serve as substitutes than were needed, as this was the
only means of livelihood for many.[21] This system had two clear benefits:
removing the fear of random seizure and providing income for poor
workers for otherwise-uncompensated forced labor. But it did have a
predictable social consequence. "Soon there were two groups: those who
were always sent out to work on the one hand, whilst the other group
comprised those who paid ransom money."[22] If some found this to be
a mutually beneficial arrangement, at least one survivor who identified himself as having been among the poor did not. "This is a tragic
moment in Jewish life, because it pitted one Jew against another. If you
had money and you could bribe a Jewish official, if you had sons, they
didn't go." In contrast, he worked at hard manual labor, breaking stones
and pushing wheelbarrows.[23]

In postwar memory, the survivors' assessment of the Wierzbnik *Judenrat* is mixed, though more are inclined toward a favorable rather than
an unfavorable evaluation. On the negative side, the daughter of Szmul
Isser, the more traditional prewar leader of the Jewish community, felt
that the younger men who followed her father were "not nice people."[24]
Another critic felt that in addition to prewar community leaders, people who were "simply opportunists" took advantage of their positions,
and "corruption set in immediately."[25] The most strident critic of the
Judenrat claimed that they were "hated" by everyone because "they got
rich from the Jews," keeping for themselves some of what was collected
for the Germans. "An honest Jew would not go to the *Judenrat*," she
claimed.[26] Others were more sympathetic. In the view of one survivor,
the Germans knew what they were doing when they forced the *Judenrat*
to collect money and put people to work, and thus she did not blame its
members. On the contrary, they anticipated the need to organize work

and took from the wealthy to pay the poor.[27] The *Judenrat* was composed of "decent" people, who did their best not to hurt others while trying to meet the constant demands and "outright blackmail" of the Germans, opined another survivor.[28] Mincberg in particular was viewed as "very intelligent,"[29] a "very fine man,"[30] and "not bad."[31] In contrast, the Jewish police of the Order Service were remembered less favorably. One survivor viewed them as more eager than they had to be in "collaborating" with the Germans.[32] Others noted cryptically: "Some good, mostly bad"[33] or "not too good."[34]

In nearby Bodzentyn, the *Judenrat* was even more clearly perceived by the Jews as a protector of the community vis-à-vis the Germans, and the price paid by its leader for failure to comply was more than a beating. When the elderly community leader was seen as unable to deal with the Germans, "the town elders deemed it wise to select, in his place, a younger man who would be better suited to cope with the expected difficult demands of the cruel occupation government." They turned to twenty-eight-year-old Froyim Szachter, who had voluntarily returned from the Soviet zone in the spring of 1940. Initially he sought to "mitigate" German demands for valuables by maintaining "a surface cordiality with the German authorities."[35] To lessen the horror of labor roundups, the Bodzentyn *Judenrat* also tried "increasingly to develop local work places so that the people wouldn't be sent away."[36] When the Germans demanded information on the whereabouts of a list of suspected black marketers, Szachter instead warned one of the suspects, who made good his escape. Szachter was arrested and taken to the Gestapo in Kielce for questioning. Various attempts to pay ransom for his release failed. He was eventually transferred to Auschwitz, where he perished.[37]

5

The German Occupiers in
Wierzbnik-Starachowice

The life of the Jewish community in Wierzbnik was deeply affected not only by the policies of the German occupation common throughout Poland but also by the individual personalities of the local Germans. In particular, a number of horrific local German policemen were vividly imprinted in survivor memories. The civil administration, Wehrmacht soldiers, and trustees of aryanized Jewish businesses were mentioned less often and portrayed less negatively than the most notorious policemen. Thus, unlike much recent scholarship, which has focused on the less-conspicuous complicity of the civil administration, military, and economic managers in imposing Nazi policies in the occupied territories, not surprisingly Jewish survivors remember best those who were their most visible and prominent tormentors, particularly among the police.

Because German judicial investigators in the 1960s sought information about specific crimes that the Wierzbnik survivors had witnessed, these judicial interviews have a structure and focus determined by the needs of German law, not spontaneous survivor memory and narrative. Under German law in the 1960s, manslaughter committed during the Nazi era had already passed the statute of limitations and could not be charged. Murder and accessory to murder were still within the statute of limitations, but by German penal code murder was defined as homicide committed under a number of specific conditions, including out of base motive (such as race hatred) or with cruelty, maliciousness, or deceit. When left to narrate their own stories without the structure imposed by targeted judicial questioning, survivors generally focused on their own families and experiences, not on individual Germans. But the German investigators needed eyewitness evidence not only about those who had killed but also about their mindset, motives, and mode of operation that were the necessary grounds for a murder indictment. Thus, the judicial testimonies of the 1960s provide an unusual focus on the German perpetrators and are the primary though not exclusive source for this chapter.

Concerning the Wehrmacht, one survivor opined that the German soldiers she initially encountered upon returning to Wierzbnik in the fall of 1939 were "not bad people." It was her conclusion that even when they were Germans, "soldiers are soldiers."[1] The wife of the Jewish dentist recalled that, despite her husband's providing treatment for many of the German occupiers, "the Germans nevertheless treated us very badly, with the exception of members of the Wehrmacht."[2] Another Wierzbnik survivor, Rachmil Najman, related the remarkable story of the soldier named "Joachim" from Austria, a "fine human being" who would take Rachmil home from work in his jeep after curfew on Friday nights. Then he would put away his weapon and stay while Rachmil's mother lit the Sabbath candles. He was in the army only because he was drafted, and he was opposed to Hitler, he confessed.[3]

Not every encounter with the Wehrmacht was benign, however. In Bodzentyn, Goldie Szachter recalled witnessing two frightening scenes involving German soldiers. Shortly after the 7 p.m. curfew was imposed in the fall of 1939, when it was still in fact broad daylight though past curfew, she saw from her balcony a young girl walking to the well where German soldiers were washing themselves. One soldier took a gun from his holster, aimed carefully and deliberately, and shot her dead. It was the first killing she had seen. On another occasion, she could see into the backyard of a neighboring house where a cousin was working, when two German soldiers entered and "began amusing themselves as they teasingly pulled hairs out of his beard." They continued to beat and torture him "until their sadistic urge had been sufficiently satiated."[4]

The behavior of the beneficiaries of "aryanization"—that is, the placing of Jewish property under the control of non-Jewish commissars or trustees—covered the spectrum. The family of Icek Guterman had scarcely reopened their store in September 1939 when a *Volksdeutscher* (ethnic German) who wanted their store and house arrived, accompanied by five policemen. They grabbed Icek's father and beat him until he managed to run out. The family was then given five minutes to leave both the house and the store, and the father was fined 20,000 złoty for fleeing.[5] A *Volksdeutscher* was also placed in charge of the leather-goods store of Moshe Neiman's parents. He allowed them to work on the premises, but he paid them virtually nothing, as he was singularly focused on how much he could extract from the business to send home.[6]

In Bodzentyn, the Szachters—the wealthiest family in town—experienced a more gradual economic strangulation. A *Volksdeutscher* moved into town and was appointed commissar in charge of overseeing and administering Jewish property. Initially, he was "courteous" and "friendly," and he and his wife even invited the Szachters for a social visit to see their Christmas decorations. Subsequently, when the Szachter family mill was sealed and Y'chiel Szachter was barred from the premises, the commissar "apologetically" explained that this had occurred on his superior's orders. Eventually the commissar was replaced, and his successor was "anything but friendly." He seized the grandfather's estate for his own residence and took over other remaining Szachter businesses as well.[7]

In Wierzbnik, the Issers owned a large, mechanized bakery that, after the occupation, had to supply the Starachowice factories that had been seized by the German state holding company and industrial conglomerate known as the Reichswerke Hermann Göring and run by its subsidiary, the Brauschweig Steel Works Corporation. The bakery was confiscated by the military administration (before the civil administration had taken over), and it installed Otto Bastian from Saarbrücken as its director. "Nonetheless we got along well with Bastian," Szmul Isser's daughter testified, "and I sought Bastian out in Saarbrücken after the war."[8] Apparently Bastian managed all the confiscated bakeries in town, for another bakery owner's family also felt they had been well treated by him.[9]

In two cases, men who would later play a significant role in saving

Jewish lives already distinguished themselves as sympathetic to the Jewish plight in the manner in which they managed Jewish-owned businesses. The German who took over the Tenzers' lumbermill took no money out of the business and allowed Jewish workers to stay there. He permitted the Tenzers to build a secret hiding place on the premises, in anticipation of the worst.[10] Similarly, Mordka Maslowicz owned a building materials and fuel business that was quickly "aryanized." However, the business was placed under the direction of a Polish engineer named Jacob, who was also head of the Evangelical orphanage and the Red Cross in Starachowice. He retained Mordka as an employee.[11]

Jews seldom came into contact with the German civil administration, so only a few individual survivors remembered those for whom they had performed some kind of service and from whom they had received advice or warning. Herszel Rubenstein's father owned a major butcher shop, which initially provided German officials—including the *Kreishauptmann* (or county chief), Hans Zettelmeyer—with meat. Eventually Rubenstein worked in the Zettelmeyers' house, shopping and doing errands for them as well as playing with their children. In 1941, Zettelmeyer advised Herszel to get a factory job.[12] Rachmil Zynger noted that Zettelmeyer was Catholic, and the Jews of Wierzbnik in general considered German Catholics to be somewhat "less dangerous." Within the city administration, Zynger also remembered a man named Huppert, a "decent man" who warned the Jews to flee to the Russian side, since "half of you are going to heaven."[13]

Far more prominent in survivor memories are members of the German police. Before delving into individual cases, therefore, some explanation of the organization of the German police forces in Poland is in order. The German police were divided into two main branches, the Order Police and the Security Police. In Germany, the former was charged primarily with everyday law enforcement, though its role was vastly expanded in occupied territories. It was divided into two sections, the rural police or *Gendarmerie* and the urban police or *Schutzpolizei* (Schupo). The Security Police was a more elite organization, composed of the Gestapo with jurisdiction over political crimes and the Criminal Police (*Kriminalpolizei* or Kripo), somewhat akin to the FBI in the United States, involved in special criminal investigations.

All of these branches of the German police were present in Starachowice. As Jewish survivors remembered, the Order Police were represented by some fifteen men of the *Gendarmerie*[14] as well as several members of the *Schutzpolizei* who supervised the blue-uniformed Polish municipal police.[15] Of the fifteen *Gendarmes*, all were known by sight but two were especially notorious: Ertel (or Ertl) and Schmidt.[16] Because of his "comical," small, crooked, upturned nose, Ertel was almost invariably referred to by his nickname—"nasal"[17] (*Näsel* or in Polish *Nosek* or in Yiddish *Neizel*). Survivors uniformly characterized him as "very feared." He patrolled the streets with a large dog that he incited to attack Jews.[18] Only one survivor claimed that Ertel set his dog on people by crying, "Bite the man," possibly conflating visual memories of Ertel and his dog with the notorious story of Kurt Franz of Treblinka and his dog Barry.[19] Ertel searched for "illegal" black-market goods and patrolled for those who had left the ghetto without permission, freely beating[20] or shooting[21] those he suspected of transgression. Ertel was termed a "sadist,"[22] "a terror of the Jews and also the non-Jews,"[23] and "the worst of all."[24] No Jew in Wierzbnik was sorry to learn that Ertel had been killed in a shootout with Poles in the nearby village of Michałów.[25]

Ertel's companion, Schmidt, was mentioned less often, though when either was on the streets, "Jews disappeared into their houses."[26] Most vividly, several survivors remember when Schmidt caught a seventeen-year-old boy of the Herblum family on a street outside the ghetto. He paraded the unfortunate Jew through the ghetto and into the forest beyond the town. He then returned to the *Judenrat* and told them where they would find the body that had to be removed and buried.[27]

Bodzentyn fell within the jurisdiction of a different *Gendarmerie* post, under the command of a man named Dumker. In his periodic visits to Bodzentyn, Dumker arrested various members of the intelligentsia—both Jews and non-Jews—who were never seen again. Sporadically, he also shot Jews "wherever and whenever the spirit moved him."[28]

The postwar German judicial investigation by the State Prosecutor's Office in Hamburg identified a number of *Gendarmerie* members who rotated through Starachowice at one time or another. But the three most notorious tormenters of the Jews—Ertel, Schmidt, and Dumker—were never listed as being among the commanding officers or even identified by name by anyone who was interrogated.[29]

The head of the *Schutzpolizei* that supervised the Polish "blue police" in Starachowice was Rudolf Angerer.[30] A large, well-muscled man of dark complexion, he was referred to as "Tarzan" by the young people who had seen the movie and "negro" (*Schwarzer*) by the older people who had not.[31] "Tarzan" was notorious for his beatings.[32] His propensity for inflicting physical abuse was finally his undoing. Under investigation for having beaten to death an ethnic German during interrogation and allegedly facing the prospect of being sent to Dachau, Angerer committed suicide in 1944.[33]

Within the other major branch of the German police, the Security Police or *Sicherheitspolizei*, in Starachowice, one name dominated both Jewish memory and postwar German judicial investigation—Walther Becker.[34] The branch office of the Security Police in Starachowice initially was under the Gestapo chief, Hans Soltau. However, Soltau and the Gestapo personnel were withdrawn in October 1941 as a manpower economy measure. Thereafter, all local Security Police matters were handled by Becker, who had been the head of the Criminal Police desk within Soltau's branch office since the summer of 1940.

Born the son of a master cabinetmaker in Hamburg in 1897, Walther Becker had joined the German army and fought on the eastern front in 1916 and 1917. Then he participated in major battles on the western front in 1918. He joined the Hamburg police in 1920 and gained civil-service status as a criminal investigator in 1924. Having joined the German Socialist Party (SPD) in 1930, he was temporarily suspended from duty when the Nazis came to power in 1933 but soon was restored to his position. He joined the Nazi Party in 1937 and attempted to join the SS at the same time, but his SS application was never approved. In the summer of 1940, he was transferred from Hamburg to Starachowice, given the rank equivalence of SS-*Untersturmführer* (second lieutenant) but not actual SS membership, and charged with setting up a Criminal Police desk within the Security Police branch office. In October 1941, with the transfer of Soltau and other Gestapo men, Becker remained as the ranking officer and thereafter handled all Security Police matters in Starachowice.

Before the departure of the Gestapo, two of its members were known to the Wierzbnik Jews for quite different reasons. On the one hand, there was Alfons Hayduk, who was on a first-name basis with Becker and frequently joined him in descending upon the Jewish community.[35] He was a "brutal puncher," and the screams of his victims could be heard throughout the Gestapo building. To the Jewish tailor who had to go there to make clothes for the Germans, he boasted of the men he had killed.[36] On the other hand, there was a young man named Dibber, who had lived in Tel Aviv and enjoyed the chance to speak Hebrew until Becker caught him fraternizing with a young Jewish woman one day.[37]

With the departure of Soltau and the Gestapo, Becker presided over a very small office. He had a deputy, Friedrich Labuhn, known to the Jews as "the man with the pipe," a chauffeur and adjutant named Franz Braun, and two ethnic German translators (Kunowalschik and Schütz). By his own claim, Becker supervised the work of some ten to fifteen Polish plainclothes policemen. Labuhn, like Ertel and Angerer, met a violent end. In 1944, he was shot by a fellow German in Starachowice during an argument.[38]

A frequent visitor to the Jewish quarter, Becker was particularly conspicuous and memorable on two accounts. First, he rode around in a motorcycle with a sidecar.[39] Second, he was insatiable in his relentless search for goods to confiscate.[40] Becker's obvious greed led the *Judenrat* to follow a conscious policy of bribery, procuring an endless list of items he had only to hint at in the hope that he would not want to destroy the source of his enrichment and thus spare the Jews from deportation.[41]

This ultimately mistaken calculation was based in part on overestimating Becker's importance. Over individual Jews in Wierzbnik he had the power of life and death, but in the larger scheme of the German occupation, he was a low-ranking nonentity who would not decide the fate of the community. It was also based in part on a misreading of Becker's character. In comparison with the most openly and consistently brutal Germans, Becker often seemed relatively restrained and not ostentatiously cruel—more greedy than bloodthirsty. Three Jewish girls who did cleaning for him had no complaint about any personal abuse.[42] In several other cases, he treated Jews decently or even intervened on their behalf. For instance, when one family was threatened by Becker's driver,

Braun, they successfully sought the help of the Polish police chief as an intermediary to Becker, and Braun did not bother them again.[43]

There were accounts of Becker both beating[44] and shooting[45] on the open street, but Becker's worst outrages of torture and execution were committed less visibly and far more often against Poles than Jews. Two Jews who worked inside Becker's police station—the tailor Rachmil Chaiton and a young boy sent to do menial chores, Jolek Arbeiter—have given harrowing accounts. Fifteen-year-old Jolek began working at the Gestapo in the spring of 1941 and continued working for Becker into the spring of 1942. Those brought in for questioning were kept in two cells under a stairwell that were too low to stand up in and that had barbed wire nailed to the floor to prevent prisoners from lying down. For interrogation, prisoners were taken to Labuhn's office, where they were tied into his special "torture chair." If they did not confess immediately, Labuhn began beating them with a horsewhip. Becker was present only for the "tough customers." If beating was insufficient, the prisoners were "served" a "hot meal"—that is, they were tortured with glowing iron rods taken directly from a fire that Arbeiter had to keep burning. After the interrogation had produced the desired confession, Becker made the decision: either "*Wegschicken*" (sent away) or "*Umlegen*" (put in Braun's car, driven away, and shot).[46] Arbeiter then cleaned up the blood. Becker whipped Arbeiter frequently, derided him as a *Ganef* (Yiddish for thief), and repeatedly threatened to kill him. One time, when Becker discovered some dust in the car Arbeiter had just cleaned, he beat him unconscious. Only then did the *Judenrat* arrange to have another worker sent in his place.[47] In Arbeiter's judgment, unlike so many Germans he saw kill others out of routine obedience and indifference, Becker was a true "sadist" for whom killing provided "pleasure."[48]

The tailor who occasionally had to visit Becker's office to make clothing for the Germans said that Becker generally did the office work and gave the orders but left the actual infliction of torture to others.[49] According to Nathan Gelbard, however, his brother was taken to Becker in late 1941 or early 1942. He had to undress and was beaten by Becker and one other man in a futile attempt to extract information that he did not have. When they finally released him, he was "totally battered." Bedridden and spitting blood, he never recovered.[50]

If most of Becker's worst cruelties were perpetrated out of sight, he did preside over one spectacular and memorable event that is mentioned by more Wierzbnik survivors than any other episode prior to the deportation—the public hanging of some sixteen or seventeen Poles in the marketplace or *rynek* sometime in 1941. As in any case in which there are thirty-three different witnesses offering testimony of the same incident, accounts inevitably vary according to date, cause, number of victims, and other details. But the vast majority of witnesses concur on the basics. Following an attack on German personnel in which the Polish attackers were not apprehended, Becker presided over retaliatory collective punishment in the form of a mass hanging of Poles. Crude gallows in the form of soccer goals were constructed in the marketplace square. On a Sunday morning after mass, the Germans surrounded the square and prevented the Poles exiting the church from leaving. The victims, including some women and at least one young girl, were then brought forth. They stood on stools and had ropes placed around their necks. Becker, who was clearly presiding, gave the orders. The stools were then kicked away, and the bodies were left hanging at least until the next day if not longer. The Germans forced young Jews wearing masks to carry out this public hanging of Poles.

From those testimonies that give the most specific and detailed accounts, the following additions to the "core memory" of this public mass hanging seem very credible. According to Peretz Cymerman, whose father ran a butcher shop, this was not the first time Jews had been forced into the role of hangmen on behalf of the Germans. Sometime earlier, Jewish police had come and fetched him, two brothers, and his brother-in-law. They were put in a horse-drawn wagon, along with a bag of ropes, and taken to Becker's office. The "man with the pipe" (Labuhn) told them that, as they were butchers by profession, they knew how to strangle cows with rope. They were to return at 5 a.m. the next day. Jewish police were stationed outside their house to make sure they did not flee. The next morning, the young Jewish butchers were taken by truck, along with eight prisoners—five men and three women—to a small town a two-hour drive from Wierzbnik, where they saw many German troops positioned on the rooftops. Becker went up to them and told them to do a good job or they would be next. The victims were placed on chairs, and ropes were put around their necks by Cymerman's brother, standing on a stepladder. The chairs were then kicked away.

It was all over in about four minutes. Everybody in the town looking out their windows knew who the young Jews were. Word got back to Wierzbnik about what they had been forced to do, even before they returned, and relatives were afraid to be seen with them for fear of Polish retaliation.[51]

Some months later, several Germans were fired on, raising imminent fear of similar German collective reprisal in Wierzbnik. Channah Glatt's brother-in-law was in prison at the time, for alleged sabotage while working at the factory. Desperately fearful that he would be included in the anticipated reprisal, her mother approached Shlomo Einesman of the *Judenrat* about the possibility of offering their remaining valuables as a bribe for his freedom. Einesman contacted Becker, and the young man was in fact released.[52]

The fear of collective reprisal was fully justified. The Germans demanded that the *Judenrat* provide ten executioners.[53] Young Jewish butchers were once again escorted by the Jewish police to Becker. They asked to be disguised and were allowed to wear "gypsy" clothing and to "paint" their faces. After the hanging, they were taken into a building where shots were fired to give the impression they had been executed too. Becker wanted them alive because he thought he would need them again.[54] The date of the Sunday hanging may well have been August 31 or September 7, 1941. A woman who gave birth to her first child on September 5 remembers that her husband took a great risk to fetch a Polish doctor despite the curfew in effect due to the hangings.[55]

The Wierzbnik survivors framed their memories of Becker's spectacular public hanging of Poles in different ways. For many, in response to the German judicial investigators' requests for eyewitness evidence pertaining to Becker, it was their most graphic memory of his criminality prior to the great deportation action that destroyed the Jewish community of Wierzbnik. What he did to Poles then foreshadowed what he would be capable of doing to Jews on a much larger scale later, and their testimony in this first regard gave credibility to their accusations in the second. For some, his scheme of forcing Jews to play the role of executioners added yet another insight into Becker's insidious and malignant character, for his behavior constituted the deliberate and transparent attempt to poison Polish attitudes toward Jews.[56]

Most unusual was the position taken by Peretz Cymerman, the only survivor who admitted to having been one of Becker's coerced hangmen. In his account, Cymerman declared that those who were hanged were "AK"—i.e., members of the *Armia Krajowa* or Home Army, a conservative nationalist underground movement that Cymerman viewed as a very anti-Semitic organization responsible for killing many Jews in hiding. Cymerman claimed that they were even more anti-Jewish than anti-German. Though acknowledging that he was "uncomfortable" about his role in the hangings, he nonetheless asserted, "I knew I hanged the right people." This justification chronologically reversed and telescoped his actions in 1941 with crimes that some AK members committed later (after Jews fled into hiding to evade deportation). Moreover, it was a rationalization that emphasized Polish guilt for anti-Semitism over German guilt for a horrific act of coercion against Jews on the one hand and murderous collective punishment against Poles on the other. Certainly Cymerman's perspective was not representative or typical. However, given in 1995 as part of the Shoah Foundation filming project rather than in the 1960s as part of a German judicial investigation, it reflects in extreme form a wider trend of the later testimonies in which the portrayal of Poles increasingly bordered on that of co-perpetrators and not just unsympathetic or hostile bystanders.[57]

6

Coping with Adversity
in Wierzbnik, 1940–1942

From early 1940, when the organization and survival strategies of the Jewish community in Wierzbnik began to take form, until October 1942, when the community was destroyed, the Jews struggled to cope with an intensifying adversity that took many shapes. The Jewish population grew exponentially from a large influx of newcomers, while space for housing shrank drastically through ghettoization. Labor, a source of livelihood for Jews and a reason for the Germans to keep them alive, had to be increased. At the same time, Jews had to be rescued from lethal work conditions and arbitrary arrest. While the Jewish leadership confronted these imperatives, individual Jews simply struggled to feed their families, educate their children, and—most difficult—without adequate resources, information, or alternatives, make decisions that would offer some hope of survival.

In addition to the flows of individual families to and from Wierzbnik in the early months of the German occupation, the community was the recipient of entire trainloads of Jews expelled by the Nazis from those regions of western Poland annexed directly to the Third Reich. When the Third Reich annexed these so-called incorporated territories of western Poland in the fall of 1939, the Nazi leaders envisaged expelling the entire population of some 7.5 million Poles and 500,000 Jews from these regions. They were to be repopulated with ethnic Germans repatriated from those parts of Eastern Europe surrendered to Stalin in the secret protocols of the Nazi-Soviet Non-Aggression Pact. These vast schemes of "ethnic cleansing" proved logistically impossible under the conditions of the continuing war. Nonetheless, if not all of the eight million unwanted Poles and Jews of western Poland were actually expelled, many hundreds of thousands were taken from their homes and deported into those regions of central Poland that had been turned into a German colony known as the General Government.

The first such trains to Wierzbnik carried 1,306 Jews from Łódź, with 483 arriving on March 2, 1940, and another 823 on March 13.[1] Although the Łódź Jews henceforth were a major component of both the Wierzbnik community and subsequently the prisoners of the Starachowice factory slave-labor camps, for no discernible reason and against all statistical probability, only two of the 292 survivor testimonies upon which this study is based were given by Jews forcefully relocated in these two transports. As this aspect of their persecution was not of immediate interest to the German investigators, neither testimony includes even the slightest description of the experience.[2] Nor do surviving German documents shed any additional light on these two transports.[3]

The second group of Jewish expellees to Wierzbnik arrived from the city of Płock in early March 1941. In contrast to the Łódź transports, no fewer than fifteen witnesses among the Starachowice survivors were among these expellees, and some gave quite detailed testimony concerning their expulsion. Located seventy-five miles west of Warsaw on the Vistula River, Płock in comparison to Wierzbnik was a "city," with a Jewish population between 10,000 and 15,000 concentrated in one part of the city.[4] The Bund and Zionist organizations were at the center of social life,[5] and discussion of politics was part of the "daily menu" for Polish Jews in Płock.[6] In venturing into other parts of the city, and particularly in daring to stay to the end of soccer games, Jews ran the risk of being beaten up.[7] In general, the Jews of Płock were a considerably more modern and cosmopolitan community than those of Wierzbnik, but they experienced the same pattern of growing anti-Semitism, boycotts, and exclusion from higher education in the prewar years.

Located close to the German border, Płock was quickly occupied in the first days of September 1939. As in Wierzbnik, the German occupation caused both an influx and an outflow of Jews. The Bromberger family, living even nearer the border amid a largely ethnic German population, fled immediately upon the outbreak of war and eventually managed to reach Płock with at least some of their clothing and valuables. Because of their blond hair and non-Jewish appearance, no one bothered them on their flight.[8] Several Jewish soldiers from the Polish army, released from German POW camps, also returned to their families in Płock.[9] In contrast, Tema Zylbersztejn's three older brothers fled Płock to Soviet territory. Although the family could conceive that the younger men needed to flee, they did not think that women, children, and older adults were in danger.[10] The older daughter of the Zylberberg family was encouraged to flee to Grodno in the Soviet zone with a neighboring family that had relatives there, but the rest of the family remained.[11] Likewise, the oldest of five brothers in Jolek Arbeiter's family fled east, but he could not convince his father—who still remembered the Germans from World War I as preferable to Russian Bolsheviks—to do likewise.[12] Others who wanted to leave could not do so for family reasons, such as Regina Rosenblatt, who would not desert her mother who was confined to a hospital and dying of cancer.[13]

As elsewhere in Poland, the Jews of Płock were quickly subjected to confiscation, marking, forced labor, and many other indignities. They were also "ghettoized," forced to reside in a delimited but unwalled section of town and forbidden to leave without a permit. As Płock was part of the "incorporated territories" of western Poland annexed to the Third Reich, the threat of total expulsion hung over Poles and Jews alike. The Jews paid a large bribe in mid-January 1941 to defer deportation until the winter weather had passed, but to no avail.[14] In a last flurry of expulsions in early 1941—before military claims on rail transportation in preparation for the invasion of the Soviet Union brought such expulsions to an end—the Jews of Płock were deported in late February. The first roundup took place on the night of February 21, when half the Jews were taken. The remaining Jews were expelled on March 1.[15]

The Jews of Płock were taken on a short trip northward to a transit camp at Soldau (now Działdowo), on the old Polish–East Prussian border. Memories differ starkly on the form of transportation: clearly, most remember traveling by truck,[16] but three individuals remember going by truck to the station and then by three distinctly different forms of rail travel—a passenger train,[17] a train packed so tightly that infants were crushed,[18] and an open train car in the midst of winter cold.[19] Soldau was a notorious camp, converted from an old army barracks that served not only as a transit camp for German expulsion measures but also as a minor killing center. Some 1,000 political prisoners and 1,558 mentally ill patients perished there, the latter in the improvised gas van of the itinerant "euthanasia" *Sonderkommando* (special commando) under Herbert Lange, on loan from Poznań. (This was the unit that subsequently founded the Chelmno death camp near Łódź).[20]

Conditions in Soldau were so unhygienic that, after a typhus epidemic killed six German guards, the camp was finally closed in the summer of 1941.[21] One Płock survivor judged Soldau "a very bad camp, worse than Auschwitz."[22] Particularly vivid in survivor memories were the toilet facilities at Soldau—namely, two big holes with a board across each, open in the middle of camp. Shocked by the calculated and humiliating lack of privacy, many of the expellees would not relieve themselves until after dark.[23] One survivor remembered the additional torment of older Jews being forced into the toilet pit and having to be cleaned off afterward.[24] Again, memories differ as to how long the Płock Jews were kept at Soldau, varying from two to three days to two weeks.[25] Thereafter, some of the Płock Jews were dispatched to Warsaw.[26] The remaining ones were sent to the Radom district, where some were assigned to be lodged in Wierzbnik and others were sent to small villages such as Bodzentyn and Suchedniów (just south of Skarżysko-Kamienna).[27]

The Płock Jews assigned to Bodzentyn were the least fortunate, for that community of 300 Jewish families was not able to absorb them, and the economy offered virtually no means of livelihood. Some could be taken into homes, and seventy young children were placed in an "orphanage" especially created by the community to care for them, but many adults were left to sleep on the floors of the synagogue or empty stores. Except for a few educated Płock Jews, who could be hired as tutors by propertied families—"we needed the education they had to offer"—most of them were unemployed, idle, and increasingly impoverished as they sold off whatever remaining valuables they had managed to carry with them. Starving and demoralized, they were the first to succumb to the typhus epidemic that struck Bodzentyn in the winter of 1941.[28]

Luckier Płock Jews were assigned housing in Wierzbnik, where they soon found work.[29] Others adroitly managed to avoid assignment to Bodzentyn and remain in Wierzbnik. Upon arrival in Starachowice, Regina Rosenblatt was afraid of being taken off in one of the horse carts to an even smaller village. Having brought 100-złoty notes hidden in her buttons, she purchased the local marking—an armband with the Star of David. She then removed from her jacket the yellow badge that would distinguish her as a Płock newcomer and found a family that would take her in.[30] Sesha Bromberger's family managed to find someone to hide them on the edge of town, while others were being taken on farther. After things settled down, they found one room to stay in among the "very religious Jews" of Wierzbnik.[31] Tema Zylbersztejn was separated from her family and sent to Bodzentyn, which she found to be "just more than a village." Once she found out where her parents and sister were staying in Wierzbnik, she joined them.[32] The Leibgott family found themselves in Suchedniów, which, like Bodzentyn, was much too small to offer any means of livelihood. The father left for Wierzbnik, found work as a tailor, and then had his family join him in early 1942.[33]

The housing problem posed by the influx of Jews from Łódź and Płock was soon intensified by the ghettoization of the Wierzbnik Jews on three days' notice on April 12, 1941.[34] The earliest ghettoization of Jewish communities had begun in late 1939; it reached Łódź in May 1940 and Warsaw in November 1940. The Jewish communities of southern Poland were generally spared until the spring of 1941, when a wave of ghettoization decrees in March and April engulfed the Jewish communities in the Cracow, Radom, and Lublin districts. The ghettoization of the Wierzbnik Jews was clearly part of this pattern, though untypical in one important regard. The ghettos of the Lublin district were largely "open"—that is, without walls or fences—while those in the Radom and Cracow districts were frequently "closed." Fortunately for the Jews of Wierzbnik, the ghetto there was "open," demarcated by signs but not physically sealed off by a wall or fence. Though Jews could not leave without permission, Poles could enter and sell goods.[35] According to one account, "Credit for this exceptional feat is apparently due to the Community leaders who succeeded in influencing and convincing the Germans" to create an "open" ghetto.[36] It is not known whether the Germans planned a "closed" ghetto but were dissuaded by bribes, or they merely took the money offered while carrying out their original intentions.

Although an "open" ghetto was clearly preferable to a "closed" one, ghettoization nonetheless imposed immense overcrowding, a problem that the *Judenrat* was left to solve.[37] In a community already saturated by the influx of Jews from Łódź and Płock, all Jews living outside the newly demarcated ghetto boundaries now had to move into an area restricted to some six to eight streets. Many families living in the older Jewish quarter had already taken in expellees. The Wajchendlers, for instance, took in a mother and two sons from Łódź, followed by a mother and two daughters from Płock.[38] Many families who had moved out of the old quarter into newer streets and nicer apartments now had to move back, making the overcrowding even more "unbearable." Two, three, and even four families squeezed into former one-family apartments.[39]

In addition to coping with the terrible lack of housing, finding an economic basis for subsistence living was the second great challenge facing Wierzbnik Jews. Craftsmen had an advantage over small business owners. In particular, those with tailoring skills continued to work their trade.[40] Some small business owners managed to hide their inventories with Polish friends and continue to sell their goods, at least for a while.[41] Others invented new businesses and trades. Icek Guterman's father went into an informal partnership with a Polish apothecary making and bottling vinegar.[42] Rachmil Najman discovered a new skill and found that he could get a job painting street signs for the Germans.[43] One entrepreneurial family had a Polish contact through whom they smuggled farmers' produce into the ghetto and resold it.[44] Children proved to be especially important intermediaries, especially those who characterized themselves as not particularly Jewish in appearance. They would leave the ghetto to sell possessions and buy food that they would smuggle back in.[45] Such ventures were not without grave risk, however. Israel Chaiton's twelve-year-old sister was shot when caught outside the ghetto without a permit.[46] At even greater risk were adults who left the ghetto to barter and smuggle. Naftula Korenwasser, who smuggled regularly, on one occasion was caught returning by two "older soldiers." He survived because his mother ran out and "kissed their boots," and they did not "feel like killing" and were "unsure" in front of one another.[47] In all such exchanges, within or outside the ghetto, Jews had to barter their possessions for food on very disadvantageous terms.[48]

However resourceful and inventive the Jews of Wierzbnik were in making a living, increasingly the factories of Starachowice—from which they had been barred from employment before the war—became the dominant economic factor in their lives. From the fall of 1939 to the spring of 1940, the paralyzing and capricious roundups for labor had been replaced by daily quotas of Jewish workers supplied by the Labor Office. At first this work was primarily menial, such as shoveling snow or sweeping streets, and the chief exploiters of Jewish labor were the municipal authorities, the German army, and the railway. According to German records, eighty to a hundred Jews were impressed into forced labor daily.[49] This pattern would continue to hold as long as Germans were winning quickly and easily, Polish labor was not in short supply, and the total expulsion of Polish Jews (first to the Lublin Reservation and subsequently to Madagascar) was expected soon. Under these conditions, the Germans had no incentive to integrate Jewish labor into the economy in any permanent manner.

By the spring of 1940, however, some Germans in Poland—including those in the business community—began to contemplate using Jewish labor in a more productive manner and to harness masses of Jewish workers for short-term, large-scale projects. The big change in Wierzbnik came on May 6, 1940, when the Germans ordered a mustering of all male Jews between sixteen and forty-five, from which 300 to 400 were chosen for unloading work at an iron mine about seven miles from town. The hard physical labor, to which they were not accustomed, "left them in a state of shock."[50] Thereafter, the Labor Office began to receive demands for large contingents of Jewish workers for outdoor work at the local factories, mostly loading and unloading.[51] By mid-June, daily demand for Jewish labor on the part of industry exceeded that of the communal authorities, railway, and army by 430 to 180.[52] The fate of the Wierzbnik Jews had begun to intertwine with the productivity and profits of local factories confiscated by the Germans.

In July 1940, demands for Jewish labor increased dramatically. Numerous contractors in the Lublin district, engaged in water-control and road-construction projects, were filling their work camps with Jews.

At the same time, the SS and police leader in Lublin, Odilo Globocnik, began conducting roundups to fill labor camps with Jews to work on constructing defensive fortifications, especially antitank ditches, along the border with the Soviet zone. Opposed by the civil administration— which did not want its attempts at a rational assignment of Jewish labor to be disrupted by SS roundups—Globocnik appealed to the other districts of the General Government to provide large contingents of Jewish workers.[53] Wierzbnik was one of the towns targeted for this purpose, and the Germans placed their demand on the *Judenrat*, which in turn provided one portion of the contingent of Jews from the Radom district who were seized for this purpose. On the holiday of Tisha Be'Av (in August 1940), these men of Wierzbnik—carrying their own blankets and backpacks—were taken to the train station and sent to the Lublin district.[54]

Thereafter, witness accounts differ in significant ways. One version has the Wierzbnik contingent consisting of 120 men, another of between 300 and 500.[55] According to three accounts, the destination was the camp of Bełżec (still a labor camp for the construction of border fortifications, not yet a death camp).[56] Three other accounts specify the destination as the labor camp at Lipowa 17 in the city of Lublin.[57] The distraught community did not know where the men had been taken, but the *Judenrat* discovered through contacts in Radom that they had been sent to the Lublin district. At least several accounts credit the *Judenrat* with successfully obtaining the return of the married men in four weeks by bribing officials in Radom for special papers for their release.[58] Symcha Mincberg's account implies that all the men, not just the married ones, were released. In this version, he led a small delegation of men from Wierzbnik to Lublin, where they were caught in a police raid and temporarily incarcerated at Lipowa 17. Once their own release had been obtained through the intervention of Lublin Jews, they eventually procured the release of the other men from Wierzbnik and returned home by train.[59] Yet another account complicates this story further. In this version, people were reluctant to give the money to the *Judenrat* because of a lack of trust, so the funds were raised by a private individual and then funneled through the *Judenrat* to the corrupt officials to obtain the false papers.[60] At least several survivors testify that the release of other individuals was also obtained through direct bribery by family members.[61] One abducted worker escaped from the Lublin work camp on his own.[62] Some Jews taken for work in the Lublin district never made it back to Wierzbnik.[63]

The account of Robert Seidel, in his recent comprehensive study of German occupation policy in the Radom district, indicates that different survivors remembered different parts of the overall story. In Seidel's account, based on surviving documents, more than 100 men were sent from Wierzbnik to the Lipowa camp in Lublin in the latter half of August as part of a districtwide contingent that Seidel estimates at more than 10,000. From Lipowa, Jewish workers were distributed to various camps for water-control and border-fortification projects. Among the latter was the labor camp at Bełżec, so a number of Wierzbnikers could have been sent there. In September 1940, *Kreishauptmann* Hans Zettelmeyer complained to the Labor Office in Radom that, contrary to his knowledge, a number of married Jewish men had been taken, and he needed them back for his own purposes. This was among a number of interventions from the Radom district, and the married Wierzbnik men were released and returned that month. Most but not all of the remaining men from the Radom district returned in October or November.[64] Since German records never acknowledge that corrupt German officials were acting in response to Jewish bribes, that aspect of the story is of course dependent solely on Jewish testimony.

The extortionate arrest of individuals who were held until ransomed was a common occurrence in Wierzbnik.[65] Sometimes ransom money was paid by the desperate family, but the prisoner was not released and died in German custody.[66] There were at least two other episodes of mass arrest and ransom through concerted effort, though certainly not on the scale of the Lublin rescue. In 1939, twenty Jews were arrested, taken to Kielce for eight days, and then released upon payment of ransom.[67] In 1940, a Polish engineer suspected of helping the Germans put the munitions factory back into production order was assassinated by the Polish resistance. In addition to the arrest of many Poles, twenty-eight Jewish men, many of them among the more prominent propertied members of the Wierzbnik community, were arrested and imprisoned in Radom. When sixteen-year-old Beniek Zukerman dared to go to the police and inquire about the whereabouts of his arrested father, he was arrested and placed in the hostage pool as well. In the prison, the guards amused themselves with daily beatings of their prisoners. Once again money was collected for the hostages' release, in one account priced at an exorbitant 20,000 złoty per person. The better-off families paid their own ransom and less-well-off families had to get help from others. The ransomed Jews returned to Wierzbnik after three or four weeks.[68]

As privation intensified for the Jews and labor shortage intensified for the Germans, employment not only for occasional work outside the factories but also for regular work within the factories gradually assumed central importance in the economic life of the Wierzbnik Jews. Though some members of each family still tried to make a living in the traditional manner, despite the constrictions of ghettoization and con-fiscation, at least some members, even in the most well-to-do families, eventually sought work in the factories, while others were grabbed off the street for factory work and given no choice.[69] Deprived of any future as merchants and craftsmen, the Jews were increasingly being trans-formed into an industrial proletariat.

Because the conditions of work were constantly changing—from the early roundups and Labor Office quotas through early factory employ-ment to the slave-labor camps—survivor memories of the working con-ditions in the factories prior to the slave-labor-camp phase are mixed and contradictory. For instance, some do not remember being paid even during the initial period, though they were fed.[70] Others, in contrast, state that they were paid initially.[71] Prior to ghettoization, they could go to work as individuals. After ghettoization, they went from the ghetto to the factories in groups.[72]

Despite the great stress and radical change to which the Jewish com-munity of Wierzbnik was being subjected in these years, traditional val-ues and behavior patterns asserted themselves in many ways. With no chance for their children to go to school, many parents hired private tutors to continue their education.[73] Given the demands on parents to work, a number of young people opened kindergartens and nurseries for child care.[74] Especially following the influx of new arrivals, commu-nity kitchens were organized to provide food for those in need.[75] People were hungry in Wierzbnik, but they did not starve. The vast influx of refugees from Łódź and Płock—who, in the eyes of the provincial Wierzbnikers, "belonged to the intellectual circles"[76]—now had to live cheek by jowl with those whom they in turn saw as "the very religious" Jews of Wierzbnik.[77] Given the extremely difficult circumstances, it is astonishing that relations between the uprooted urban Jews of western Poland and the beleaguered traditional Jews of south-central Poland remained extraordinarily supportive and harmonious. Snide or resentful comments about one another's communities are totally absent from the postwar testimonies.[78]

PART II

THE DESTRUCTION OF THE WIERZBNIK GHETTO

7

Wierzbnik on the Eve of Destruction

On June 22, 1941, German forces launched the invasion of the Soviet Union. In the two following months, Nazi policy rapidly evolved from the widespread but selective mass murder of adult male Jews, especially those in leadership positions, to the systematic mass murder of all Soviet Jews who fell into their grasp in the territories conquered by the invading forces of Operation Barbarossa. In the fall of 1941, the scope of killing expanded beyond Soviet territory, as the old vision of creating a Nazi-dominated Europe free of Jews through expulsion or "ethnic cleansing" (accompanied in practice, needless to say, by unfettered violence and high loss of life) gave way to a new vision of attaining this goal through the systematic and deliberate murder of every last Jew—man, woman, and child—caught within the Nazi sphere of domination. In order to turn this fantastic vision into reality, the Nazis experimented with new technologies of mass killing. They tested a new-model gas van using diverted engine exhaust instead of cylinders of pure carbon monoxide as well as stationary gas chambers using either engine exhaust or the highly toxic fumigant Zyklon B. By November, a fleet of thirty gas vans was on order, and construction of death camps was underway at Chelmno in the Warthegau (near Łódź) and Bełżec in the Lublin district of the General Government.[1]

Implementation of the new policy of total and systematic mass murder—what the Nazis called the "Final Solution"—in the General

Government began in mid-March 1942. Over a four-week period, Nazi ghetto-clearing forces rounded up the 40,000 inhabitants of the Lublin ghetto and deported some 36,000 of them to Bełżec, where they perished in the camp's primitive gas chambers. Their bodies were dumped into mass graves that had been dug behind the camp. That this operation was a trial run for the fate that would engulf all Polish Jews was clear to the Nazis at the time. On March 28, 1942, less than two weeks into the Lublin-ghetto liquidation, a jubilant local Nazi proclaimed: "The Jewish resettlement has proven, therefore, that such an action even on a large scale can be carried out for the entire General Government."[2] Just one day earlier, Minister of Propaganda Joseph Goebbels had noted in his diary: "The Jews in the General Government, beginning in Lublin, are now being evacuated to the east. This is a pretty barbaric procedure, not to be described here more precisely, and of the Jews themselves not much will remain."[3]

In reality, the small prototype death camp at Bełżec was quickly overwhelmed by the dimensions of its murderous task.[4] Even before a second death camp, at Sobibor, came on line in early May 1942 to receive additional transports of Jews from the districts of Lublin and Galicia, construction of considerably enlarged gas chambers took place in Bełżec. More fatefully, construction of yet a third death camp for the Jews of the General Government began at Treblinka, northeast of Warsaw.[5] In early June, the ghetto-liquidation campaign spread to the district of Cracow. German administrators in the districts of Warsaw and Radom eagerly awaited their turn, which—after a brief delay occasioned by the military demands on all rail transport in preparation for the summer offensive in the Soviet Union—finally came with the opening of the Treblinka death camp in late July.

Shortly after deportations from Warsaw to Treblinka began on July 23, the ghetto-clearers struck in the Radom district as well. In three brutal deportation *Aktionen* between August 4 and 18, nearly 24,000 Jews of the Radom ghetto were deported to Treblinka or shot on the spot.[6] Between August 19 and 25, another three *Aktionen* dispatched some 21,000 Jews from the Kielce ghetto to the gas chambers of Treblinka. So many Jews were shot that Polish peasants with horse carts had to be hired to collect the many hundreds of corpses strewn about the ghetto and along the march route to the train station.[7]

It had taken the Germans a month to clear the Lublin ghetto the previous spring. But the Germans almost entirely liquidated the two large
Jewish communities of Radom and Kielce in three one-day actions in
each city because Nazi authorities in the district had developed what
was perhaps the most efficient and destructive ghetto-clearing organization of the entire General Government. The SS and police leader
of the Radom district, *Oberführer* Dr. Herbert Böttcher, operated with
an extremely small staff to coordinate the joint operations of different
SS units in the district. Ghetto-clearing was, of course, one such joint
operation. His key subordinate in this regard was *Untersturmführer*
Erich Kapke, who created and led an itinerant unit of police auxiliaries
recruited from the Eastern European borderlands occupied by the Soviet
Union after September 1939 and by Germany after June 1941. Heading
the Jewish desk of the Gestapo in Radom was *Hauptsturmführer* Adolf
Feucht, who formed a *Sonderkommando* of twelve German policemen.
Their chief tasks were to plan the entire deportation program and then
to provide experienced experts throughout the district to help local
authorities carry it out. In each city and town with a Jewish community
targeted for deportation, the local chief of police met beforehand with
the experts. He was placed in charge of local arrangements and left to
perform the "major work" of the *Aktion*.[8]

As in the case of Bełżec earlier, the massive simultaneous deportations from the Warsaw and Radom districts—reaching 10,500 deportees
arriving each day in late August—logistically overwhelmed Treblinka's
killing capacity. The trainloads of incoming Jews could not be gassed
immediately upon arrival. Waiting trains lined up and unburied bodies piled up. The camp was temporarily shut down for reorganization
under a new commandant, Franz Stangl, and construction of additional gas chambers.[9] Deportations from Warsaw resumed quickly, but
in the Radom district only in mid-September. By the end of the month,
another 56,000 Jews had been deported from various ghettos within
the Radom district, such as Jędrzejów, Włoszczowa, Wodzisław,
Skarżysko-Kamienna, Suchedniów, Szydłowiec, Kozienice, and
Zwoleń.[10] But by far the biggest *Aktion*, beginning in late September
and running into early October, was the clearing of Częstochowa. It
was the largest ghetto in the Radom district, containing more than

50,000 Jews by the summer of 1942. Beginning on September 22, the day after Yom Kippur, and ending on October 5, seven or eight immensely long and overloaded trains carried 45,000 Jews from Częstochowa to Treblinka.[11]

Throughout October, itinerant ghetto-clearing units continued to cut their destructive swath through the Radom district, destroying large ghettos, such as Piotrków, Chmielnik, Opatów, and Ostrowiec, as well as many smaller ones. The deportations from nearby Szydłowiec and Skarżysko-Kamienna to the northwest and Opatów and Ostrowiec to the southeast brought the ghetto-clearers ever closer to Wierzbnik.[12] The deportation of the Jews of Bodzentyn on September 21–22 and those of other small towns in the immediate region—such as the 2,000 Jews of Iłża just a few miles to the north on October 22—clearly signaled that the remaining life of the Wierzbnik ghetto was numbered in days, not weeks or months.[13]

The Jews of Wierzbnik viewed this ominous chain of events that began with the clearing of the Lublin ghetto in March 1942 with both imperfect knowledge and growing alarm. They sought answers to a number of crucial questions. What was happening to the Jews of the General Government, and particularly what was the fate of those Jews who had been cleared from ghettos and allegedly sent to labor camps "in the east" but then seemed to have disappeared without a trace? Would the same fate befall the Wierzbnik ghetto, and what if anything could they do in the face of such a looming threat? And as the inevitability of ghetto liquidation became increasingly accepted, when exactly would that occur and what last-minute steps could still be taken to mitigate its effects?

For a historian working with testimonies given at a much later date rather than contemporary letters and diaries, perhaps nothing is more uncertain than the attempt to reconstruct the actual state of mind and awareness with which most Wierzbnikers lived through the last six months of the ghetto's existence. Two biases in the sources are probable. First, it is highly likely that those who most pessimistically and realistically assessed German intentions survived disproportionately in comparison with those who lived in denial and clung to unrealistic hope. Thus, the considerable number of survivors who claimed in postwar testimony to have perceived the truth behind deportation before the ghetto liquidation should not be taken as representative for the ghetto population as a whole. Second, these claims are subject to the usual vagaries of all reconstructed memory, not just that of Holocaust survivors, in which chronological sequence is often confused, different events are often telescoped, and knowledge obtained later is not infrequently incorporated into recollection of past awareness. Fully aware, therefore, of the uncertainty of any conclusions reached, what can a historian say about what Wierzbnikers knew shortly before their ghetto was destroyed?

According to Jerahmiel Singer, some Wierzbnikers began receiving crucial information at a very early date. During Passover in the spring of 1942, a relative of Symcha Mincberg who had escaped the Lublin deportation reached Wierzbnik and told of how Lublin's entire Jewish population had been taken off in "an unknown direction." Subsequently, there were rumors from the Polish side that Polish railway men drove Jewish transports into a specific region of the Lublin district and were briefly replaced by German engineers, who then returned with the empty cars. Moreover, "over the whole region hung a sickly smell of corpses." Unfortunately, Singer concluded, "very few took these stories seriously and put them down as pure fantasy."[14]

Jolek Arbeiter, the errand boy in Walther Becker's Starachowice headquarters, remembers being told by Becker's chauffeur, the Sudeten German Franz Braun, that "we Jews would all be killed." When Jolek asked him how that would be possible, the latter replied that the Jews would be put on ships and sunk at sea. Jolek discussed what he had learned with his family, who did not find it credible.[15]

Rosalie Laks, then sixteen years old, remembers how in August 1942 a young man—perhaps a year or two older than she was at the time—came out of the bushes behind her house. He was utterly filthy and disheveled, but even more noticeably he was terribly frightened and had the "wild look" of someone who had had a shocking or traumatic experience. He told the story of how he had arrived in Treblinka with his parents but was immediately separated from them and put to work on unloading the belongings that had been brought to the camp. He had escaped by getting under a train car and suspending himself over the axle. Rosalie took him inside to feed him and told her parents that this "crazy" guy was telling "unbelievable" stories. They promptly sent her away before she could hear more from this strange visitor.[16]

Rachmil Zynger noted explicitly that, "in contrast to many other Jews I judged the situation realistically." A Polish railway official sought him out and told him that the Jews from other cities had been sent to Treblinka and Majdanek, and that in these regions "the air from the smoke was so bad" that the Poles fled. This official then urged Zynger to turn over certain things to him, and Zynger initially thought he was telling him tales in order to enrich himself at Zynger's expense. As he thought more about it, however, he concluded that it was at least possible that "the Germans wanted to kill us Jews."[17]

Zvi Faigenbaum talked with Poles about what they had heard on radio broadcasts from London. He then read an underground newsletter that listed the many towns from which the entire Jewish populations had been deported to Sobibor and never heard from again. When he "linked" this prior information with news of deportations from nearby towns, "I no longer had any doubts about the terrible, tragic meaning of these shipments."[18]

Aside from these accounts, which are unusual in their specificity about their sources of information, there are many references in the testimonies simply to "rumors" that were circulating in Wierzbnik. And as the destructive swath of ghetto liquidation came "closer and closer," according to Henyek Krystal, "the idea that they were killing them was, was talked about a lot."[19] But what was concluded from these rumors and discussions varied greatly from individual to individual. The assertion of one survivor that at this time 90 percent of the Jews knew of the gas chambers,[20] or of another that it was "quite generally known in the city that innocent human beings were being sent to the gas chambers,"[21] are undoubtedly exaggerated. Nonetheless, it is clear that many Wierzbnikers, even without full knowledge of specifics, were assessing German intentions correctly.

By mid-1942, according to Goldie Szachter, her father "had concluded that all this could only be part of a master plan aimed at the total destruction of Polish Jewry."[22] Others focused on the more immediate fate that awaited the Jews of Wierzbnik. Zvi Feldpicer had heard "rumors" of "gas chambers" (though not specifically of Treblinka), and had "no doubt" that these rumors were true.[23] Some had heard of Treblinka as a destination of deported Jews but not specifically of gas chambers.[24] For Dora Kaminer, the "extermination" of Jews transported to Treblinka "was already somewhat known."[25] For Abraham Shiner, the name Treblinka was already current, and he knew that deportation "would amount to the murder of Jews," but "naturally the extent and horror of this crime" were inconceivable.[26] Beniek Zukerman likewise knew that deported Jews were sent to Treblinka. "We did not know exactly what happened there, but we were convinced that the deportees were somehow killed there."[27] Perhaps Regina Rosenblatt captured most aptly the uncertainty concerning the Treblinka rumors. "We knew it was not good but not how much it was not good."[28] For many others who did not mention either gas chambers or Treblinka specifically, there was nonetheless a general conviction that deportation meant death.[29]

Many others who heard the same rumors, however, dismissed them either as not credible in general or not valid for Wierzbnik in particular. The most constant refrain among those who did not credit the rumors was that such rumors were inherently "exaggerated" and "we couldn't believe" them.[30] Abramek Naiman admitted that the rumors were not believed "because above all we did not want to believe stories of this kind."[31] Some at least tried to base their disbelief in rational calculation, not just denial. Three survivors noted that their parents explicitly harkened back to the decent behavior of "civilized" German soldiers in World War I that stood in such favorable contrast to the behavior of Russian soldiers.[32] Others thought that Wierzbnik would not suffer the fate of the surrounding Jewish communities because of the importance of Jewish labor in the Starachowice factories.[33] Abraham Rosenwald noted: "Although we had already heard about the extermination of the Jews in other places," because of the factories in Starachowice, "we thought it wouldn't happen to us."[34] Clearly, a great deal of wishful thinking was involved.[35] Michulek Baranek provided a harsh but simple retrospective analysis: "We lied to ourselves."[36]

For many Jews in nearby towns that did not have factories producing for the German war effort, the need to make a decision came earlier than for the Wierzbnikers. In Szydłowiec, some twenty-three miles to the northwest, the large Jewish population—swelled by expellees from the territories incorporated into the Third Reich—watched the approaching catastrophe with alarm. Isachar Salek, a refugee from Łódź, had frequently been taken out of Szydłowiec for forced labor. Having heard that one could volunteer to work in the munitions factory in Starachowice and live in Wierzbnik without the threat of being grabbed out of bed at night, he moved there.[37] Ruth Rosengarten, who had fled Warsaw to Szydłowiec, moved on to Starachowice to join family members there.[38] Nachela Szczesliwa's father returned home one day in September 1942 and told her to pack. The family had considerable means, so she and three siblings went to Starachowice in a hired car. They were joined by an older sister, Hanka Szczesliwa, who had obtained "Aryan papers" and traveled by train. They paid a "Jewish Macher" 300 American dollars for work permits.[39]

Several refugees from Szydłowiec explained in more detail the important role played by Leopold Rudolf Schwertner, the head of non-German personnel in the Starachowice factories, for Jews seeking work there. Born in the Sudetenland in 1911 and a salesman by profession, he took up his key position in the Starachowice factories in May 1942.[40] In the summer of 1942, Yaacov Shafshevitz, his brother, and a group of friends decided "to try our luck" with work in Starachowice. Once there, they gave Schwertner "a pair of tanned calf skins" to send a truck back to Szydłowiec and bring another thirty young Jews for factory work.[41] Joseph Tauber made a harrowing escape from Warsaw after the deportations were well underway there. He made his way to Szydłowiec but was not there long when a "German civilian" came from Starachowice to recruit Jewish workers.[42] Jack Pomeranz "made a deal for money," paying 300 złoty to a German who arranged for a truck ride to Starachowice in early September 1942.[43] Josef Friedenson, having heard rumors of Treblinka and gassing, followed his father's advice to register for factory work. Through intermediaries, he paid for a German truck to come and take him, his wife, and his mother-in-law to Starachowice. The man who came with the truck was Schwertner. Once the truck arrived in Wierzbnik, Schwertner was interested only in Josef, not the women, as workers. Josef had to pay yet again to obtain a work card for his wife as well.[44] Forewarned of the imminent deportation, Anna Perel's uncle paid a German a lot of money to take him and her to Starachowice on the night before the ghetto liquidation, while her father and two sisters went into hiding.[45]

The Nazi ghetto-clearers struck Szydłowiec on September 22–23, 1942, and sent 10,000 Jews to Treblinka. In the process, yet more Jewish workers were seized and selected for work in the Starachowice factories.[46] In one account, all children and those over forty were sent away, while younger Jews were placed on trucks, driven to Starachowice, given work permits, dumped into the ghetto, and told to report to the factory in the morning. Having no place to sleep, Macha Wajchendler, her brother, and her two sisters looked up a distant relative. The relative already had thirty people sleeping in two rooms but told them they could stay if they could find space.[47] According to another witness, Schwertner was present when they were selected and taken from Szydłowiec at this time.[48] Even then, the influx of Jews from Szydłowiec to Starachowice did not end. Jakob Binstock and three friends managed to hide in a false wall during the *Aktion* there. After Poles coming to loot the seemingly empty ghetto nearly discovered their hideout, they slipped away after dark, stayed in the barn of a helpful Polish peasant for three nights, made their way to Starachowice because of its factories, and obtained work.[49] Anna Perel, who had left her father and two sisters in hiding when she fled Szydłowiec on the night before the liquidation, found someone to take them to Starachowice as well.[50]

In Ostrowiec, just twenty miles southeast of Starachowice, the ghetto was liquidated on October 12, 1942, but many young Jewish males were held back from the transport. Some 800 were taken off to work in the local factory that produced railway freight cars. Late in the afternoon, a German from Starachowice arrived and asked for 110 workers. Barek Blumenstock volunteered but was rejected as "too small." Nonetheless, after his two brothers were chosen, he managed to slip into the group that was subsequently placed on trucks and driven through the dark, arriving in Starachowice just before midnight. Here they were placed in barracks in a camp that was surrounded by barbed wire but not yet occupied by local Jews from Wierzbnik.[51]

In Opatów, thirty-two miles southeast of Wierzbnik, Moshe Pinczewski heard "rumors" from the Polish underground of mass killings in camps such as Treblinka and decided that only those working in industries important to the war effort had "a chance of survival." He returned to Starachowice, from where he had moved to Opatów in 1938, and procured a work place. "I even had to pay something for it," he noted. He had a permit that allowed him to return to Opatów on weekends until the ghetto there was liquidated on October 20.[52] The Sztajman family, sensing the "obviously imminent resettlement in Opatów," fled together to Starachowice one week before the deportation and reported for factory work.[53] Members of the Czernikowski family took the heartbreaking decision to separate in order to increase the chances that someone might survive. After dividing up the family money and jewelry, Josef "paid" for a place in a truck that took him to Starachowice, while his brother Majer headed for Sandomierz. He remembered passing through the already emptied and desolate Ostrowiec on the way.[54] Though she was already noticeably pregnant when the ubiquitous Leopold Schwertner came to Opatów several weeks before the *Aktion* there, Toba Weisfeld and her husband paid him 4,000 złoty for the trip to Starachowice. However, as had happened with Josef Friedenson's family from Szydłowiec, Schwertner provided a work permit only to her husband.[55] In the village of Klimontów, just south of Opatów, a German truck arrived in October, offering transportation to Starachowice for forty American dollars per person. Leib Feintuch and his sister purchased their seats, leaving behind the rest of their family but joining a brother already there.[56]

On September 21, the Jews of the village of Bodzentyn were transferred to a collection point at Suchedniów, from which 4,000 Jews were sent to Treblinka on September 22, one day before the *Aktion* in Szydłowiec on September 23.[57] However, some Jews from Bodzentyn escaped to Wierzbnik-Starachowice beforehand. The head of the prominent and wealthy Szachter family worked through an intermediary—in this case, a childhood friend of Y'chiel Szachter and key member of the Wierzbnik *Judenrat*, Shlomo Einesman—to arrange for transport on Schwertner's trucks. Before departing, they buried some of their jewelry and gold in different places in the garden and hid money in their shoes. Then, "Schwertner himself arrived by truck in front of our courtyard to transport our entire family. . . . In two trips, all twenty-two members of our family were to be transported." Once in Wierzbnik, further meetings with Einesman led to the purchase of work cards for all family members over twelve years of age.[58] Ruth and Hannah Ehrlich, whose mother was a Szachter, also reached Wierzbnik in one of the German trucks. When work cards had been procured for the entire family, they sent for their parents and younger sister, but it was already too late to rescue them from the Bodzentyn *Aktion*.[59]

Some of the other Bodzentyn Jews without the same means of the Szachter family also found their way to Wierzbnik. Henyek Krystal remembers passing up an initial opportunity for a seat on a truck to Wierzbnik because he did not want to separate from his mother. "And my mother, the first day when I didn't go, she became completely frantic. She became practically berserk that I should go. . . . So the second day I did go. . . . As we were leaving I was looking down and my mother was standing there just dissolving in tears, knowing that this is a goodbye, you know, forever."[60] The Sztarkman family in Bodzentyn also realized they could not stay there any longer. Chava's father and sister went to Starachowice to pay someone for work cards. Then, a few at a time, they slipped out of town, taking virtually nothing, and walked through the forest to the ghetto in Wierzbnik, where a room had been found.[61] The most unusual account was that of a young woman whose family had already moved from the village of Słupia Nowa to Bodzentyn after her father and uncle had been killed. An "older German policeman" who liked them warned of the impending deportation and told them to grab anything they could. Her mother would not leave the grandparents, but the German policeman drove her and her sister to Starachowice in his jeep.[62]

In the last days of October, the influx into Wierzbnik came from towns even closer. Iłża, the seat of the county administration or *Kreis-hauptmannschaft* just fifteen miles to the northeast, was cleared on Thursday, October 22.[63] On Friday, October 23, the Jews of Wąchock—a village just three miles west of Starachowice—were rounded up. Some already had work cards and had been working in the steel works. Others were selected and taken directly to the munitions factory. The rest were moved into the Wierzbnik ghetto.[64] To Symcha Mincberg, the arrival of 700 Jews from Wąchock in the midst of Sabbath prayers "served as a sign that the liquidation was advancing."[65] On the same Friday, in a nearby mining camp connected with the steel works, Jewish laborers who were sick or injured were told to report for medical examinations in order to be sent home for "rest and recovery." This was "a trap," for in reality, those deemed hindered in their ability to work were marched under guard to the Wierzbnik ghetto.[66]

The deluge of rumors, the news of ever-nearer ghetto liquidations, and the influx of Jews seeking work in the Starachowice factories convinced virtually every Jew in Wierzbnik that the end of their ghetto was both inevitable and imminent. Few Jews, and only young men at that, seriously considered flight to the forest, a course of action for which the urban Jews were unprepared as well as one that exposed them to denunciation.[67] There were other considerations, of course. One former soldier in the Polish army felt he himself would have had no trouble going to the forest, but life would not have been worth living if he survived and his wife did not because he had abandoned her.[68] Thus, none of the surviving Jews who later gave testimony attempted to hide in the forest at this time. Three survivors admitted that they had undertaken the construction of special hiding places, though in the end they did not use them.[69] Fourteen-year-old Mania Isser planned to live on the "Aryan side" with false papers, along with her seventeen-year-old cousin. Both were blond and not "Jewish-looking." But she spoke with a Yiddish accent and could not conceal her typically Jewish gestures. Her father became "hysterical" and ripped up her false papers to prevent her from leaving.[70] False papers were effective in at least one case, however. An old college friend approached Rachmil Zynger and freely gave him "Aryan papers," after which he successfully hid his wife and two sisters with Polish families.[71]

Most Wierzbnikers made the same calculation as those who were flocking to the Starachowice factories from elsewhere—namely, that the best chance for survival lay in obtaining employment crucial to the German war industry. Indeed, why would Jews in Wierzbnik try to escape from the very factory town that so many other Jews were desperately attempting to reach? Thus began, for those who had not already done so, what Jerahmiel Singer called "the Witch Dance around Work Permits."[72]

The procurement of work cards had both a macro- and a micro-economic aspect, though what was common to both was that increasingly desperate Jews bought their way into their subsequent slavery as the best alternative to deportation and death. According to Symcha Mincberg, the head of the *Judenrat*, in anticipation of the coming deportation he obtained approval from the SS and police leader in Radom, Herbert Böttcher, for the construction of work camps next to the factories, where working Jews would be kept rather than sent away.[73] The *Judenrat* in turn paid Schwertner to fill these camps with as many Jews as possible.[74] Other Jewish communities allegedly gave Schwertner money to create work places as well.[75] Schwertner could do this at no risk to himself because the employment of Jewish workers was still permissible within the General Government under very specific conditions dictated by SS chief Heinrich Himmler, who was in charge of implementing the Nazi "Final Solution."

Himmler was ever-suspicious of the claims of German entrepreneurs that Jewish labor was indispensable. They were, he felt, merely trying to enrich themselves at the expense of implementing Nazi racial policy and making the Final Solution truly final. Yet wartime economic exigencies could not be totally ignored. Thus, in the fall of 1942, Himmler stipulated strict conditions for the employment of Jewish labor that would temporarily spare a few of them deportation to the death camps, though he made it clear that "there as well the Jews shall disappear some day in accordance with the wish of the *Führer*."[76] Himmler's three key conditions were: (1) Jewish labor had to be working directly, not just indirectly, in essential war production. The steel and munitions industries of Starachowice clearly qualified in this regard. (2) At their own expense, the employers of Jewish labor had to construct and guard camps where their *Arbeitsjuden* or "work Jews" would be kept in total isolation from the rest of the population once the nonworking Jews had been deported and the ghettos liquidated. The Braunschweig Steel Works Corporation, the Reichswerke Hermann Göring subsidiary in Starachowice, complied in this regard. (3) The inmates of these camps would be property of the SS rented to the employers on a per head (5 złoty per male, 4 złoty per female) per day basis. In short, the "work Jews" would quite literally be slaves of the SS, rented to and exploited by factory owners, who would pay the slaveholders (the SS), not the slaves themselves, for labor extracted.[77]

Within these wider parameters, however, there was a microeconomic "black market" in work permits on the unofficial side of Nazi policy vis-à-vis Jewish workers that determined which individual Jews would obtain the coveted document. Here, Schwertner and others were free to enrich themselves. According to Singer, "all kinds of agents appeared overnight who led a brisk trade with these permits which were sold at exorbitant prices," and many "permits sold were fictitious."[78] But aside from the tricksters selling phony work cards, valid work cards were sold as well. As with Jews brought in from outside Starachowice, the Wierzbnikers most commonly named Schwertner in this regard.[79] According to one survivor, he paid a gold watch and gold chain to procure just one work card from Schwertner for his fifty-eight-year-old father.[80] But Schwertner was not alone in extorting the terrified Jews. Through a Jewish tailor who made clothes for many of the Germans, the Glatt family was put in contact with a factory foreman named Molender (or, alternatively, Molenda). For a diamond ring and other valuables, he provided "precious" work cards for the mother and three daughters.[81] According to another survivor, Molender—a "half-Pole/half-Silesian" foreman—took money and gifts to register her entire family for work. In her words, Molender became a "millionaire" through this business.[82] Only one German was spoken of favorably in terms of work-card procurement. The German engineer Willi Frania visited the family of Rabbi Rabinowicz. He sat at their table, speaking "very friendly," while he increased the ages of the three daughters on the documents and put the youngest on the night shift so that she would already be at the factory and thus less likely to be subjected to document examination and selection during the anticipated early-morning roundup.[83]

The "Witch Dance around Work Permits" clearly had a class, gender, and age bias. Elderly Jews, female Jews, and poor Jews were far less likely to be able to procure work cards than younger, male, and more propertied Jews. Infants and children twelve or younger were another highly endangered group excluded from the protection of work cards. Some parents together, mothers alone, or grandparents resigned themselves to staying with the younger children while seeking the protection of the older children, and hence the survival of a remnant of the family, by purchasing work cards for them. Others who had succeeded in pur-

chasing cards for everyone in the family over twelve years of age made
the desperate decision, if they had the means and connections, to hide
their infants and young children with Polish families.

In addition to money and connections, several other factors—gender
and appearance—played a role in the ability of Jews to find hiding places
with Poles. The danger of discovery posed by circumcision made girls
easier to place than boys,[84] though some young boys nonetheless were
also successfully hidden.[85] And children with lighter complexion, blond
hair, and/or blue eyes were easier to place than those who looked stereo-
typically Jewish. The Szachter family tried to place their two youngest
daughters in hiding. Even though the older of the two, Rachela, was
thirteen and had a work card, she looked very young for her age. However, in comparison to ten-year-old Goldie, who was blonde, Rachela
was dark, with a "big nose," and "looked too Jewish." A Polish peasant
woman with whom the family had made arrangements agreed to take
Goldie in return for 50 percent of future earnings of the family flour
mill, if they survived the war. She was supported by her young nephew,
a Communist activist, but the rest of the family was merely told that
Goldie was a niece from Cracow. But the family that was to take Rachela
changed their minds when they saw how "characteristically Jewish" she
looked.[86]

Nine-year-old Tobcia Lustman also had "fair hair and blue eyes."
Weeks in advance, she was prepared by her parents for separation and
hiding, but she could not accept the reality until it actually happened.
When deportation was imminent and no further delay could be risked,
a "Christian woman" fetched her from the ghetto at night. With a small
bag of valuables tied around her neck, Tobcia and the woman walked
several hours in the dark to her new home, where she was presented as
a visiting "cousin."[87]

All too frequently, attempts to hide children ended in tragedy. Pola
Zynger helped place her sister's two-month-old daughter with a Polish
family with the promise of money to help support her. They later heard
that the infant had been placed in a nursery and had died.[88] Another
family paid a Polish family to hide their nine-year-old daughter, but
the Polish family turned the little Jewish girl out during the ghetto
liquidation.[89] The Wajchendlers intended to place both their youngest

sons—eleven and thirteen—with Polish families on Thursday, October 29. When the deportation came two days earlier, the younger boy slipped away to his Polish family as planned. But much to the surprise of his thirteen-year-old brother, Chaim, the younger boy appeared on the marketplace during the selection and was taken off to Treblinka. Chaim never learned whether it was his younger brother or the Polish family who had had a change of heart.[90] The oldest daughter of the Glatt family, Perl, had a two-year-old daughter whom a Polish woman agreed to take. However, when the child was actually taken away, Perl fainted. Her younger sister ran after the Polish woman and brought the child back. Both mother and child were sent to Treblinka.[91] Regina Milman's mother kept her eleven-year-old daughter with her but gave a Polish woman a "fortune" to hide her younger brother and two younger sisters, ages five to nine. The family later learned that the children had been kept just two days and then killed.[92] Regina Rosenblatt cared for the three children of a former bakery owner's family, who were relatively well treated by the new "Aryan" owner, Otto Bastian. Arrangements were made that the children would be taken to a Polish family before the deportation, which they also had been misinformed would occur on Thursday, October 29. When it happened two days earlier, Bastian hid the children in the basement during the *Aktion* and then transferred them to a Polish contact the following night. Shortly thereafter, the children were walking out of town to the village of the Polish contact's grandfather when they were detected by German police and shot dead in the street.[93] Gutta T. relates that her baby daughter was given to a nanny, but Gutta—thinking she would join the child later—could not stand to leave her husband and family before liquidation of the ghetto. Incarceration in a labor camp intervened, and she never saw the child again.[94]

Jews who had purchased work cards for family members but were not sure the cards would be honored during the anticipated selection—either because the recipients were very young, elderly, or even just women who did not appear strong physically—made one other desperate calculation. They had learned from the refugees who flocked into Wierzbnik from communities that had already been deported that the ghetto-clearers invariably struck early in the morning, assembled the Jews in the marketplace, and conducted a selection of workers before forcing the vast majority into the freight cars of the waiting train. Thus, Jews already working the night shift at the factory and not in the ghetto during the roundup might be automatically included among the "work Jews" and thus avoid being subjected to an examination of work cards and selection. At least some Jews, therefore, strove to get the most vulnerable family members onto the night shift.[95]

Wierzbnikers knew that deportation was truly imminent when Germans demanded the return of goods they had left for repair with Jewish craftsmen as well as goods they had custom-ordered, whether finished or not.[96] Pinchas Isenberg's father, a furnituremaker and upholsterer, was working on a large order for the police chief in Radom. On October 26, the SS arrived with a truck and took all the materials as well as ten workers back to Radom. There the ten abducted Wierzbnikers worked in a special camp for skilled craftsmen until 1944.[97] Clearly, some Germans spread specific but false information that the long-expected clearing of the Wierzbnik ghetto would occur on Wednesday or Thursday, October 28 or 29, or even later.[98] Some Jews acted accordingly, particularly those not wanting to part with children they hoped to hide until the very last moment, with tragic consequences. At least a few Jews in Wierzbnik had more accurate information, however. On the eve of the deportation, the skilled craftsmen whom the Germans intended to keep in Starachowice were told of the impending deportation but assured that they and their families would be spared. Thus, they were to move tools into a special work hall being prepared for them.[99] On the night before the deportation, a Wierzbnik dentist and his wife were taken into one of the camps, and he was designated "camp dentist."[100] At least some members of the *Judenrat* (such as Moshe Birenzweig and Shlomo Einesman) moved their children into one of the factory camps beforehand. Einesman's only surviving daughter—then eight years old—remembers riding to the camp in a wagon just before the ghetto was liquidated.[101] Others (such as Symcha Mincberg's family) remained in the ghetto and had not been warned ahead of time.[102]

On the evening before the deportation, the Jewish police were summoned to the building of the *Judenrat* and told that all the Jews of the ghetto had to be assembled on the marketplace by 7 o'clock the next morning. Just how late in the evening they received this information is unclear.[103] But Hershel Pancer was on his way to the night shift when he was halted by a family friend and ghetto policeman, Jeremiah Wilczek. Wilczek asked him to attend the imminent wedding of his daughter. Since Wilczek already knew that the town was "doomed," he preferred that his daughter and prospective son-in-law face their fate as a married rather than an engaged couple.[104]

At least some other Jews in Wierzbnik were also informed the night beforehand.[105] But they were the exception. For most Wierzbnik Jews, fear, tension, and uncertainty reigned. They sewed money and valuables into their clothing.[106] They had small "bundles" or "backpacks" of personal belongings all prepared in order to be able to depart on a moment's notice without going emptyhanded.[107] Sensing imminent disaster, "we slept with our clothes on."[108] That the fateful blow would fall was certain, but "we did not know only the hour and day."[109]

8

The *Aktion*,
October 27, 1942

O ctober 27, 1942, would turn into a warm, sunny autumn day in southern Poland,[1] a day whose natural beauty would stand in stark contrast to the manmade horrors that played out on the streets of Wierzbnik. But it was still dark when Wierzbnikers got their first confirmation that this was the day of the *Aktion* that would liquidate their ghetto and destroy their community. Those up first that morning were workers who tried to leave the ghetto in order to begin their 7 a.m. shift at one of the factories. Invariably they encountered unknown armed and uniformed men blocking the streets out of the ghetto; they were told to return home or go directly to the marketplace or *rynek*.[2] It was clear that the ghetto was surrounded.

A number of people attempted unsuccessfully to slip through the cordon and were shot.[3] At least six people did escape the ghetto that morning, however. From his window, Pinchas Heldstein saw *Judenrat* member Moshe Birenzweig in the street early in the morning. When Birenzweig confirmed that the ghetto was surrounded, Heldstein took his wife and three daughters through backyard gardens to a Polish family, where he left them in hiding. Trusting in his own usefulness to the Germans as a bootmaker, he then reported to his place of work. The German in charge accompanied him back to the marketplace, however, since any Jew found outside the ghetto was liable to be shot on sight.[4] Eighteen-year-old Chaim Wolgroch had earlier escaped from Warsaw to Starachowice, where he briefly hid in a Catholic mission devoted to the conversion of Jews. When he declined conversion, he had to leave and went into the Wierzbnik ghetto. This morning, he made his way back to the mission, but when still faced with the requirement of conversion in order to stay, he went to the marketplace.[5] Fifteen-year-old Mania Isser, whose fearful father had earlier torn up her false papers, took off her armband and put on a Polish scarf. This time, without telling her parents, she slipped out of the ghetto around 4 a.m., when it was still dark. On the outskirts of the city, she hid in a woodshed, from which she could hear the screams and shots coming from the ghetto.[6]

Most Jews in the Wierzbnik ghetto first learned of the impending *Aktion* from the Jewish police. Nathan Gelbard, the only surviving ghetto policeman who gave a postwar account, testified: "On the morning of that day, I went through the houses with the other members of the Jewish *Ordnungsdienst* [Order Service], in order to inform people that they had to present themselves on the market place for resettlement."[7] And indeed, many survivors confirm that they first heard the summons to the marketplace from the Jewish police, not from the Germans or their auxiliaries.[8] When Syma Dawidowicz attempted to hide and was discovered by a Jewish policeman, he bluntly warned her that the SS would conduct a subsequent search and shoot anyone still found in an apartment.[9] Apparently at least some Polish municipal police were involved in this stage of the roundup as well, for the daughter of the head of the *Judenrat* remembers that as soon as her father had left their apartment, the Polish police commandant Chmielewski and two other Polish policemen arrived at the door and warned her family to leave for the marketplace within five minutes.[10]

The order to depart for the marketplace immediately, accompanied by the warning that noncompliers would be shot, posed an excruciating dilemma to those Wierzbnikers who lived in extended families with elderly parents who were either immobile or simply unwilling to leave their homes. In the Mincberg household, Riwka's grandfather, Moses Pinchas Lichtenstein, one of the four brothers who had founded the veneer and plywood factory in Wierzbnik, was too ill and weak to stand up, much less run to the marketplace. According to one account, with considerable effort she persuaded her mother not to remain with him;

in another account, she pulled her mother outside "forcefully." In either case, they left him behind alone in his bed.[11] Moshe Kumec had been beaten so badly in an earlier encounter with German police that he could not rise from his bed and was left behind.[12] Witnesses from six other families also reported having left one or two grandparents behind when they departed for the marketplace. In all these cases, the surviving family members later learned from the burial commando that the elderly and sick people they had left behind had been found shot in their beds.[13]

Others did not have to wait to have their worst fears confirmed. They saw the killing of elderly family members firsthand, as the impatient ghetto-clearers murdered those whose immobility threatened to slow the *Aktion*. The Winograd family had not yet left their apartment when German policemen broke in and dragged the grandmother, Gitl Winograd, into the courtyard, where they shot her in front of the family. Then they chased the rest of them onto the street.[14] Rywka Slomowicz's grandmother refused to leave her family home. "She preferred to die in this place rather than to be deported." An "SS man" obliged.[15] Regina Crujecki's fifty-year-old father was killed in their apartment before her eyes.[16] Szajndla Herblum's two aunts and uncles, who lived next door, were shot down on the doorstep of their apartment because they were unable to leave quickly enough.[17] Rachmil Najman saw his aunt and uncle gunned down on the front step as well.[18] Chuna Grynbaum's uncle, dressed and praying, was shot on the spot.[19]

As people rushed onto the streets and streamed toward the marketplace, the air was filled with the sounds of banging on doors, the repeated call of "*Raus, raus,*" screams, and shooting. The ghetto-clearers hurried people along with whips, dogs, and shots into the air, as Jews were "chased" and "driven" to the *rynek*.[20] Once again, those whose immobility was deemed a hindrance to the swift completion of the *Aktion* were marked for immediate murder. These killings now took place in full daylight, not in the dark or early dawn, and before many assembled witnesses on or near the marketplace, not in individual apartments and courtyards. Varying accounts of the same event thus increasingly appear in the postwar testimonies.

Two killing sites in particular were mentioned in numerous testimonies. One major road in the ghetto, the Kolejowa, ran from the train station past the *Judenrat* building and parallel to the length of the marketplace, from which it was separated by one row of buildings. Providing a passageway through this row of buildings to the marketplace and serving as a shortcut was a series of steps up to a narrow corridor or covered alleyway. As Jews streamed up the Kolejowa past the *Judenrat*, a cluster of ghetto-clearers was stationed by and on the stairway. Here a number of Jews, especially those who appeared elderly and slow-moving, were pulled out of the crowd and shot.[21] As the Wierzbnik Jews assembled on the marketplace, the killing shifted to a gateway and courtyard of a building that had belonged to the Korenwasser family. Jews were pulled out of the lines of five that were being formed on the marketplace, led to the gateway, and shot either out of sight in the courtyard or sometimes even in full view while still in the entryway.[22]

In addition to the elderly, the physically handicapped were especially victimized that morning. Rachmil Najman's neighbor, a polio victim with a lame foot and hand, was shot on his doorstep.[23] Adam Kogut's uncle, Pinchas Gottlieb, partially paralyzed on one side, could move only slowly with the help of a crutch. He was shot in the narrow corridor between Kolejowa and the marketplace.[24] The watchmaker Moshe Najman, who moved awkwardly due to a shortened leg, was shot outside his home.[25] The first dead person in the street that Abramek Naiman saw on the way back to his house, after he had been turned back from going to work, was apparently crippled.[26] Even those who, despite their handicap, made it to the marketplace were not spared. A man with one leg,[27] a man with a pronounced limp,[28] and a man with a heavily bandaged foot[29] were all shot there.

Amid all the havoc and slaughter, three killings in particular remained prominently lodged in the memories of numerous survivors. Many people specifically remembered the shooting of Shlomo "Szkop" Zagdanski, a teacher at the Jewish school, as he entered the marketplace at one corner.[30] Even more vividly, people remembered the killing of the Biederman couple. Elegantly dressed in their best *Shabbath* clothes (and he particularly conspicuous in his white prayer shawl), the elderly and frail couple ever so slowly made their way up the street to the marketplace before they were intercepted by their killers and shot.[31] But accounts differed as to exactly where—at the corner of the marketplace or at the entryway to the courtyard off the marketplace—and by whom they were killed.

The third killing mentioned in numerous accounts was that of a young woman, Esther Manela. According to her sister, Esther "had repeatedly said beforehand, that under no circumstances would she go into the camp." As the family reached the steps leading to the marketplace, Esther said she had left something in the apartment and turned back. "A short time later we heard a shot from our apartment."[32] If one accepts the sister's account as the most reliable, then none of the other survivors actually witnessed her killing. But the story of a young woman who clearly had a good chance of being selected for labor and who nonetheless refused to go to the marketplace stuck in many people's memories and was included in their accounts as a story they had heard from others.[33] There was also a tendency to incorporate such hearsay into presumed memory. One person claimed to have seen Esther's body on the street.[34] Another related a heroic account of Esther's death on the marketplace. "Esther Manela was standing not far from me. She stepped out of the row and went to police chief Walther Becker. I heard how she said to Becker that she did not want to go to the camp. Becker ordered her to step back into line. She did not do that. Becker drew his pistol and then shot her."[35] In yet another heroic account, the site of Esther's defiance and death shifted to the waiting train. There she refused to mount the freight car, stating that she preferred to die in her hometown. She was promptly shot by a German, and her dying words were, "I beat you."[36]

In addition to general references to indiscriminate mass killing both during the roundup and on the marketplace—such as, "People fell like leaves from a tree"[37]—numerous other individual killings were described by different individual witnesses as well.[38] The systematic killing of the elderly, the handicapped, and those who did not follow orders was clearly standard operating procedure for the ghetto-clearers. Although the exact number of Jews killed during the *Aktion* that day cannot be ascertained with certainty, some approximation can be made. According to Leib Herblum, a survivor of the "cleanup commando" that was charged with burying the dead, he and his comrades dug "two graves, a separate one for the men and one for the women" in the Jewish cemetery. On the first day, they counted the bodies of twenty-six men and twenty-two women. Over the next few days, other bodies were brought for burial. In the end, he simply lost count. "Too numerous were the victims I was ordered to bury. . . ."[39] According to Jerahmiel Singer, writing for the community memory book, forty-two "old and sick" people who had remained in their homes had been killed there.[40] Another survivor placed the number of Jews killed on the marketplace at thirty-six.[41] A number of others gave a rough total of around sixty.[42] Given the traumatic nature of that day, it is perhaps surprising that so few other witnesses offered only modestly higher, probably somewhat exaggerated estimates.[43]

The identity of the killers can also be ascertained only approximately. There is quite persuasive testimony that the Jewish ghetto police played an initial role in summoning Jews to the marketplace. And Nathan Gelbard, the surviving Jewish policeman, likewise testified that they played a role on the marketplace in keeping order. "My task was limited to watching out that people remained standing in the column."[44] A number of survivors also testified to the presence of Polish police, either in surrounding the ghetto or keeping order on the marketplace.[45] But no one suggested that either the Jewish or the Polish police were involved in killing. There was also agreement on the presence of the factory security force or *Werkschutz*, composed of Ukrainians "whom we knew." They would play a key role in herding those selected as workers from the marketplace to one of the labor camps but not in the roundup and killing.[46] They were dressed in dark blue uniforms.[47]

The German Gendarmerie, the Schupo, and Becker's Security Police, who were normally stationed in Starachowice, were certainly present that day.[48] But crucial additional manpower for the roundup and killing of Wierzbnik Jews were "other people"[49] whose precise identity was unknown but who had been "sent only for this purpose."[50] Though referred to as Ukrainians in some testimonies, in the more discerning testimonies they were thought—because of their "language"—to be "probably" either Latvian or Lithuanian,[51] "in any case from the Baltic."[52] The other distinguishing memory held by survivors about these strangers was that they were "drunk," a practice that no doubt helped them to carry out the "dirty work" that the Germans assigned to them.[53]

Survivor memories in this regard are consistent with the conclusions reached by German judicial investigations of other ghetto-clearing operations in the General Government, which established a common pattern of employing outside itinerant units of Eastern European auxiliaries as a crucial component of manpower. These auxiliaries were euphemistically referred to by the Nazis as *Hiwis* (short for *Hilfswilligen* or "volunteers"). For the most part, the *Hiwis* had been recruited out of prisoner-of-war camps and trained at a special SS facility in the town of Trawniki in the Lublin district. This training center provided such manpower not only for itinerant ghetto-clearing units but also for the guard detachments of the death camps of Bełżec, Sobibor, and Treblinka. By ethnic origin, the Trawniki men were Ukrainian, Lithuanian, Latvian, and *Volksdeutsche*. For the obvious reason of common language, the Ukrainians, Lithuanians, and Latvians were organized into separate units. *Volksdeutsche* or ethnic Germans, who knew the relevant language of the rank and file, usually served as noncommissioned officers. But the judicial investigation of the Trawniki camp staff examined the dispatch of Trawniki men as ghetto-clearers only for the Lublin district and the Warsaw ghetto, not for the Radom district.[54]

Various individual investigations of ghetto liquidations in the Radom district confirmed the existence of a notorious, itinerant *Judenvernichtungsbatallion* or "Jewish destruction battalion," made up of Eastern European auxiliaries and commanded by *Hauptsturmführer* Adolf Feucht and his assistant, *Sturmscharführer* Walter Schildt. But these investigations did not confirm either the unit's ethnic makeup or its Trawniki origins. In different investigations, the Hiwis in this unit were identified variously as Latvians, Lithuanians, and/or Ukrainians, or more generically as Baltic or "ethnically alien" (*fremdvölkischen*) auxiliaries.[55] According to *Untersturmführer* Erich Kapke, who commanded detachments of this unit in various ghetto-clearing actions in the Radom district, the manpower was both Ukrainian and Baltic in origin.[56]

If not even the ethnic origin, to say nothing of the individual identities, of the *Hiwis* sent to clear the Wierzbnik ghetto can be precisely established, command responsibility for the ghetto-clearing operation was no mystery to the Jews of Wierzbnik gathered on the marketplace that morning. Other postwar investigations of ghetto-clearing operations in the Radom district once again established a common pattern, in which the SS staff in Radom scheduled the sequence of operations and coordinated the arrival of outside manpower and trains, but the actual on-the-spot conduct of the ghetto-clearing was placed in the hands of those with the most expertise in local conditions.[57] In the case of Wierzbnik, this was Walther Becker. The pretrial investigation of Walther Becker, initiated by the Central Agency for the Investigation of National Socialist Crimes in Ludwigsburg and then taken over by the Office of the State Prosecutor in Hamburg, led to the large collection of eyewitness testimonies in the 1960s that constitute one of the major sources for this study.

There was virtual unanimity among the survivors about several aspects of Becker's appearance and role that day. First, they agreed that he was present. Indeed, from the testimony it is clear that he was the single most conspicuous and consistently recognized German there.[58] Virtually everyone described the same vivid image of Becker running around with a drawn pistol in one hand and a whip or club in the other. Furthermore, most witnesses testified that he was obviously the man in command. He ran around giving orders, and others went to him for instructions. No one saw him taking instructions from anyone else.[59] As one survivor put it, Becker was "the man of the day."[60]

Numerous witnesses went even further and described him as a man possessed or run amok. Especially to those on the *Judenrat*, who had earlier perceived Becker as a corrupt rather than a sadistic German and thus cultivated him through gifts, this came as a great surprise. The daughter of the head of the *Judenrat* noted: "Before the resettlement I had not thought that Becker could behave so wildly. . . . We had even placed a certain hope in him. Specifically he frequently came to the *Judenrat* and had himself presented with gifts, especially from Wolfowicz, so that one could assume he would attempt to spare us from resettlement."[61] Wolfowicz's niece affirmed that previously Becker had made "a calm impression" but not on the day of the *Aktion*.[62]

Time and again, survivors resorted to the same images and vocabulary in trying to capture Becker's dominant and terrifying presence and absolutely frenetic behavior on the marketplace that day. He "ran" or "raced back and forth like a mad man."[63] (*lief/rannte wie ein Verrückter hin und her*). He made an "excited" or "wild impression."[64] (*erregten/*

wilden Eindruck). He ran about "like an animal," "a wild animal," or "a tiger."[65]

Some witnesses provided very general testimony, devoid of specific details, that they saw Becker beating with his whip and shooting with his pistol. Several described instances of beating quite specifically. Mendel Mincberg, son of the head of the *Judenrat*, had to run the gauntlet past Becker to reach the marketplace. "I saw exactly that it was Becker who struck me. As a result of this blow I almost fell to the ground, but my brother supported me. I forced myself to run further, because it was clear to me that I would be shot if I fell down."[66] Another man testified: "On this day Becker carried a leather whip, in which a lead or in any case a metal ball was braided into the end, and which was about 1 or 1.2 meters long. . . . I saw that he struck my friend standing next to me— Godel Kadiszewicz—over the head. My friend suffered a wound that bled so severely that afterwards his clothing was entirely soaked with blood. . . . I remember that for many days after this blow with the whip Kadiszewicz cried all night long like a little child."[67]

More important, no fewer than twenty-eight witnesses testified to particular shootings by Becker in which he killed one or more people. Some of these killings had multiple witnesses. Five identified Becker as the killer of the elderly Biederman couple.[68] Three identified him as the killer of the Jewish schoolteacher, Shlomo "Szkop" Zagdanski.[69] Three testified to Becker's beating to the ground and killing an old man on the steps leading up from Kolejowa to the marketplace.[70] Two testified that he killed a man named Henoch Kaufman.[71] None of the other descriptions of alleged Becker killings converged to provide multiple testimonies of the same event, however. And some of the accusations, such as the claim by two witnesses that they saw Becker shoot Esther Manela on the marketplace, are contradicted by other, more persuasive testimony. And just one witness testified to seeing Becker grab a small child by the feet and smash its head against the wall next to the courtyard entrance off the marketplace.[72] Given that this is an archetypal Holocaust image, which poses a greater likelihood of being incorporated into memory later, and that despite Becker's notoriety no other witness remembers what surely would have been the single most horrifying and indelible scene on the marketplace that day, this particular accusation cannot be deemed credible either.

The testimony about Walther Becker demonstrates the possibility but also the problems in writing history from postwar testimony. In light of the overwhelming consensus among the witnesses, there can be no reasonable doubt that Walther Becker was present at and in tactical command of the ghetto-clearing operation in Wierzbnik on October 27, 1942. There can be no reasonable doubt that he played a tremendously active and zealous, not reticent or minimal, role in discharging his duties. There can be little if any doubt that he personally beat and shot people that day as well. But each particular act of beating and murder for which there were multiple accounts was remembered and described somewhat differently by each witness. And in some cases, the testimonies against Becker were either uncorroborated or contradicted by other testimonies. These uncorroborated and contradicted accusations suggest the possibility that at least some of the witnesses, frustrated at being unable to identify the many anonymous perpetrators who killed that day, may have tended to name the notorious Becker by default.

The Jews who crowded onto the marketplace stayed together as families. As the roundup was completed in the packed marketplace, the Germans conducted a series of selections. First, the men with work cards were called out and sent to the so-called long side or south side of the marketplace. Next, women with work cards were likewise summoned. The Germans then conducted three further selections. They inspected those who answered the call for work-card holders and sent back those whom they deemed too young or unfit. They scoured the rows of five into which the nonselected Jews had been formed to take out anyone who looked young and healthy enough to work, even if they did not have a work card. Finally, they grabbed additional Jews to compose a "cleanup commando" that would remain in the ghetto for the next several months rather than being sent immediately to the work camps for factory labor. The remaining Jews were marched to a sidetrack of the rail line and packed into waiting train cars.

As a result of the *Aktion* in Wierzbnik, the Germans sent approximately 1,600 Jews—1,200 men and 400 women—to work camps and deported nearly 4,000 Jews to the gas chambers of Treblinka.[73] The fact that more than 25 percent of the Jews rounded up in Wierzbnik were not sent immediately to their deaths stands in sharp contrast to the fate of other communities in the Radom district, where the deportation rate during ghetto-liquidation actions routinely stood at 90 to 95 percent.[74] This is one of several crucial contingent factors that accounts for the unusual cluster of Wierzbnik survivors upon whose postwar testimonies this study is based. What was seared into the memories of the survivors, of course, was not that more than 25 percent of the community had survived but that these selections posed terrible choices, ruthlessly tore apart virtually every family, and left many survivors with never-healed feelings of loss and guilt.

Goldie Szachter Kalib, who was already in hiding and not present at the marketplace that day, nonetheless described the scene based on what she subsequently learned from others about the selections that day.

What chaos ensued! What confusion! Sounds of shouting and crying were heard coming from all directions, as people with and without workers' cards struggled, competed, shoved, and pushed with all their strength in a desperate effort to land in the group selected for work. Germans were shouting orders, cursing, and beating and shooting Jews who failed to jump quickly enough to their commands. Families cried for mercy as they were torn apart. . . . young children were torn from their young parents to be condemned. Heartbreaking good-byes were heard and seen everywhere. In some families, quarrels erupted over which parent should go with the children. For the most part, mothers chose to go with their beloved offspring. Many men fought their way into the lines of the workers, abandoning wives and children, but there were others who chose to go along with their wives and children. . . . many in the workers' lines who had abandoned their families began to feel pangs of guilt. How could they in good conscience have spared their own lives while allowing their dear ones to go to their deaths? On the other hand, what would they have accomplished by not having saved their own lives? Could they have prevented the slaughter of their loved ones? Of course not. . . . Then why torture oneself with self-inflicting blame? Yet despite all logic, such feelings of self-reproach and guilt haunted many and deepened their agony even more.[75]

One survivor succinctly summed up the "choiceless choices"[76] that so many faced that day: "Many people were given the option, either to go into the camp and thereby abandon their children or remain together with their children in the great mass on the market place."[77] Another survivor related the staggering tragedy of a family of six—husband and wife, two teenage children, and two infants—faced with such a choice. The parents and older children all had work cards. During the selection, the parents sent their teenage children over to join the workers. The parents then left their infants to join their teenagers among the workers. In the meantime, the teenagers had left the workers to rejoin their family. In the end, all four children were deported and the parents were taken to the work camps, "alive" but in "hell."[78] Such horrific stories could be narrated about others, but survivors telling their own stories of the selection had simply reached the human limit as to what was possible to remember and tell about the tragedy of such "choiceless choices." Such a narrative was simply too unbearable, and they usually adopted one of three narrative models, each of which neutralized the role of agonizing choice on their own part in the tragedy of separation. I do not mean to imply that the public memories of the survivors are untrue in this case, but rather that repressed and secret memories play a greater role in affecting what and how much can be told about the experiences of this particular day than for any other aspect of the Starachowice testimonies.

One such narrative model employed brief, matter-of-fact description, usually in the passive voice, in which the Jews were without agency and simply acted upon. Once at the marketplace, "the men capable of work were immediately separated from the rest."[79] "After some time a kind of selection was carried out, in which they sought out the younger and stronger people and sent them over to the other side of the market place."[80] "Some people were summoned and placed with the workers. . . . In that way our family was separated."[81] One survivor "lost contact" with her mother and three sisters, who were sent to Treblinka.[82] Another said that his family was "separated" because some were chased to the right and others to the left. "We just sort of parted, separated by force. They were screaming something, I was screaming something."[83] And finally: "After some time I suddenly found myself, without being able to say how it came about, in the rows of those selected for work in the factories."[84]

A second model was a narrative of resistance to separation overcome by force. According to Mendel Mincberg, "After some time the possessors of work cards were requested to step out. But only a portion of the people complied." Thus, Schwertner had to go through the columns, choosing the young and strong regardless of whether they had work cards.[85] The community memory book provides the same scenario: "People with work permits refused to part from their dear ones, relinquishing thereby voluntarily the opportunity to be exempt from expulsion, but the Germans took them by force. . . ."[86]

Many individual narratives follow this scenario of thwarted self-sacrifice. Abraham Rosenwald was planning to flee with his mother when a German "tore me out of the line in which I stood and sent me with drawn pistol to the workers."[87] Syma Dawidowicz "had no work card and also wanted to go with my parents, because I saw no hope of survival." But a German placed her with the workers "against my will" because she was young and strong.[88] Chaja Weisblum had a job at the lumberyard, and her supervisor tried to persuade her to join the workers. "Because I had both of my children with me, I could not bring myself to go with the other lumber yard workers." But Becker appeared, struck her with his whip, and had one of his Ukrainians take her to the other side. "I wanted to return to my children, but was prevented by force."[89] Szmul Erlichson was chosen for work but "I did not want to be separated from my wife and my two children, as well as my parents." Thus, he asked if he could take his wife and children with him over to the workers' side. "I was simply sent over to the others with a kick of the foot."[90] Natan Wajchendler heard the call for those with work cards: "My father held me back and said to me, that we—that is he and I—should stay with my mother." But an SS man beckoned him out, clubbed him over the head, and sent him to the workers.[91] Abraham Frymerman did not step out when those holding work cards were "ordered" to do so, because "I did not want to separate from my wife. However, I was pulled out of line by a SS man who struck me with a club."[92]

The third separation narrative is that of other family members rejecting the offer of family solidarity for the sake of individual survival. When Beniek Zukerman heard the call for work-card holders, "my sister and I at first wanted to remain with our family. But my father persuaded us to comply with the order. He thought that we might then perhaps remain alive. . . ."[93] Pesia Kumec said that when women with work cards were summoned, "My mother pushed my sister and me out of the line."[94] Peretz Cymerman said he wanted to stay with the family but his father told him to go to work. "We kissed goodbye. That's it."[95] Nacha Baum's parents had purchased work cards for her and her brothers. Thus, when the selection began, "my parents pushed me to go."[96] Chil Leibgott said that when the Germans called for workers, "I really didn't want to go," but his father "actually pushed me out from the line."[97] Rosha Kogut likewise said her mother "pushed her out" when the selection began.[98]

Some narratives combined the elements of familial urging with German force. Tauba Wolfowicz was already employed at the factory but did not want to leave her family when work-card holders were summoned. "I wanted to stay with my mother. But she could not bear that." Thus, she "announced that I had a work card, and I was led away by the collar by a Latvian."[99] Toba Steiman told how, when she tried to stay with her parents, her father "pushed her away" and told her to stay alive. Then someone grabbed her, beat her on the head, and shoved her into the workers' group.[100] Chemia Reichzeig related that when the workers were told to step out, "My wife said go, go, she pushed me." The Germans saw this, grabbed him by the collar, and sent him to the workers.[101] Dvora Rubenstein was standing in line with her parents when her husband, accompanied by a German, came and pointed her out. The German struck her, and her parents begged her to step out and save herself, since she had successfully hidden her child, who would need her later.[102] Icek Guterman and his mother were on the factory night shift, but his father and three sisters were sent to the marketplace. His father had been a business partner of *Judenrat* member Moshe Birenzweig, who asked Becker to place him with the workers. When his father rejected Becker's offer, the latter became infuriated. "You Jew, I get gold and diamonds for bringing over people and I tell you to go and you do not want to go." Becker pulled his pistol, but one of Icek's sisters pushed her father out of line and he crossed over. Guterman added that, having lost three daughters on the marketplace while the parents survived, "My father could never talk about it and my mother could never talk about it. There was not a day they did not remember what had happened. It was very difficult for them to live."[103]

Gender clearly had considerable impact on the selection to and composition of the workers' group. As we have seen, even prior to the liquidation of the ghetto, Schwertner—although willing to sell seats in his trucks to both men and women to take them to Starachowice—was more inclined to provide work permits to men than to women. And witnesses tell of only one man—Rabbi Rabinowicz—whose work permit was not honored on the marketplace, but there are numerous accounts of women who had their work cards rejected.[104] According to one male witness (who was separated from his wife and three children that day), women with work cards—unlike men—were not forced to join the workers' group if they had children.[105] But two female witnesses were emphatic that women were also forcibly torn from their children.[106] The collected testimonies of that day suggest three conclusions. First, men selected for work outnumbered women by a large margin—around 1,200 to 400. When families were separated, those fated for deportation were overwhelmingly mothers and their young children and the elderly. Second, there was no single, uniform German policy concerning women with children, and the fate of individual mothers was often decided by the selector they encountered.[107] Third, at least on some occasions Jewish mothers themselves made the fateful decision as to whether they would remain with their younger children.

One witness went to the marketplace with his wife, son, and daughter. Having worked at the sawmill, he was chosen to join that group of workers. But his son was not, "because he was at that time still too young." The son, left by his father, nevertheless managed to slip into another group of workers, saved himself, and was eventually reunited with his father. The fate of the women in the family was quite different. "My wife had also been designated for work in the saw mill. Because in this case she would have had to leave our daughter alone, she refused to go to the camp. My wife and daughter were then sent to Treblinka."[108]

The tailor Rachmil Chaiton had already been promised that the skilled craftsmen like himself would remain with their entire families—in his case, a wife and child. Thus, when the call for those with work cards went out, he approached Becker on the marketplace for permission to take his wife and child with him. Becker said he could take his wife but not "the little shit" (*die kleine Scheisse*), indicating the child. "We naturally did not want to separate from our child. I was forced to join the row of Jews chosen for work, while my wife remained with the child and . . . was deported."[109]

Much rarer is the story of a mother who chose to separate from her children in order to survive. In one account, a survivor went to the marketplace with one of his sisters, who had a work card but also a four-year-old child. In order to join the women workers' group, she persuaded her child to join her mother, another sister, and two young nieces. The little girl screamed at first but calmed down when she saw her cousins. A brother and one sister joined the workers. The mother, second sister, and three children were all sent to Treblinka.[110]

A frantic desire to be among the workers, even when it involved heartbreaking separation from family, was not absent that day, even though subsequent narratives of reluctance overcome only by brute force or familial urging are understandably more prevalent among the testimonies. Fully consistent with the flood of desperate refugees into Wierzbnik and the "witches' dance" for work permits, one survivor admitted candidly: "On the market place itself everyone had very great fear, and each wanted to be in the rows of those who were selected for work, because it appeared to those affected as salvation."[111] Thus, another standard narrative among the survivor testimonies is that of making it successfully into the ranks of the workers. These accounts are cast, however, less as stories of separation and tragedy—leaving family behind on the marketplace—and more as stories of survival and triumph, of outwitting the Germans in order to rejoin their families.

Goldie Szachter's father had arranged for the entire immediate family to work on the night shift precisely in order to increase their chances of avoiding the roundup and selection altogether. But her thirteen-year-old sister, Rachela, had balked at going to work that particular night, and her father had stayed with her. They were both caught in the roundup the next morning. Her father would not let Rachela depart for the marketplace with her aunts and their small children. Instead, he held back and arrived at the marketplace alone with his daughter. He instructed her that when those with work cards were called out and he had to leave her, she must do everything in her power to sneak over and join the workers. This she managed to do after several attempts, and several women then hid her between them.[112] Although Rachela's immediate family remained intact that day, through her father's perspicacity and her ingenuity, ten members of the extended family were lost, including the aunts and nieces she did not join on the marketplace.[113]

Chaim Wajchendler was only thirteen years old but had a work card. When work-card holders were summoned, Chaim crossed over to the other side of the marketplace but was intercepted by Schwertner, who asked him his age. Chaim gave the improbable answer of sixteen. Fortunately for Chaim, Moshe Birenzweig was nearby, and Schwertner asked him for confirmation. Birenzweig vouched for both his age and his ability as a worker, and Schwertner let him pass. Subsequently, Chaim could see Schwertner ripping up the work cards of other boys his age and size and sending them back. Schwertner also scanned the line of workers as if he was having second thoughts about Chaim, who hid in a doorway out of Schwertner's sight. Though he lost his mother, sister, and younger brother that day, he was able to join his father and older brother in the camps.[114]

On the marketplace, twelve-year-old Michulek Baranek's parents were selected for work, but Michulek's card was ripped up. He and his ten-year-old brother were left with their grandparents. As the mass of Jews moved from the marketplace toward the rail line, Michulek decided to attempt an escape. He gave his water bottle (with a double bottom containing coins) to his younger brother, threw away his coat, and, on the last corner before they reached the train, just walked away, hoping he would not be noticed. He hid in now-empty Jewish houses until dark and then stole into the sawmill and lumberyard, where he was reunited with his mother.[115]

In the memories of the survivors concerning the desperate attempt to cross over to be with the workers, the fates of two individuals in particular are mentioned in multiple testimonies. The first is that of Rabbi Rabinowicz. He had procured work cards for himself and his children, and several of his daughters were working the night shift and thus were spared the scene on the marketplace. When the rabbi answered the summons for possessors of work cards, he was intercepted and, despite his work card, he was turned back. His wife, however, who had no work card, was selected for work.[116] According to one witness, it was Becker himself who sent the rabbi back.[117] According to another witness, the rabbi was also struck on the head by a Ukrainian auxiliary.[118]

When men with work cards were first summoned, Abramek Naiman and his father joined the column of workers. When the women with work cards were summoned, however, Abramek's mother, Stefa, was turned back, her work card notwithstanding. When she then tried to sneak over to the column of women workers, Becker spotted her. He knocked her to the ground, beat her with his whip, and then set a dog on her. Before he and his father were marched away, Abramek saw her limp body being carried by Jewish police and placed on a pile of corpses at the end of the marketplace. But his mother was in fact still alive. She washed off the blood from her wounds in the nearby well, managed on her next attempt to join the column of women workers, and was eventually reunited with her family in the camp.[119] The terrible scene of Becker beating her and the dog tearing at her was apparently so grotesque, even among the other horrors of the marketplace, that it was described and Stefa Naiman identified by name in no fewer than four other testimonies given decades later.[120]

We have no direct testimony about the fate of the nearly 4,000 Wierzbnik Jews who were not selected for work but instead were loaded onto the waiting cattle cars that day. There was not one single survivor from this group. We do know that many of them were robbed of their possessions either on the marketplace or as they were pushed into the cattle cars.[121] And, like all other transports from the Radom district, the train carried them to Treblinka, where they were murdered in gas chambers immediately upon arrival.[122]

9

Into the Camps

E ven before the many Jews fated for deportation were marched to the train siding and loaded into the waiting cattle cars destined for Treblinka, the work Jews were marched away from the marketplace to one of two sites. One was the sawmill and lumberyard complex, formerly the Jewish-owned Heller lumber business until it was "aryanized" in 1939. In most survivor accounts, it was referred to simply as Tartak. It was fairly close, just beyond the railway tracks and the Kamienna River to the south of Wierzbnik. Many of the original Jewish employees had continued to work there, and many other Jewish workers had been added under what was deemed to be a relatively benign "aryanization" management. On the marketplace that morning, the assistant manager at Tartak, a man named Piatek, not only sought out his workers but added others as well. As one such survivor noted: "Piatek was the right hand of the director of the saw mill. He saved many Jews, myself included."[1]

The column destined for Tartak left around midday, guarded by Ukrainians from the factory security force (*Werkschutz*) and supervised by Schmidt and Schulz, two German policemen from the Gendarmerie. The column was hurried along at a run by shots and dogs, but no one was killed during the forced march.[2] Upon arrival, the prisoners were assembled and told to surrender their valuables. In the course of collecting valuables, the German policemen searched two young men from

Płock, about twenty years old, found a few złoty in their pockets, and shot them.[3] At this point, another tragedy unfolded. A young couple, the Tenenbaums, had smuggled their three-month-old infant into the lumberyard in a small backpack and had hidden it in a woodpile. However, Fräulein Lutz, the secretary to the sawmill and lumberyard manager, heard the baby's cries. Unable to locate the baby, she informed the two policemen. They then threatened to shoot twenty prisoners unless the mother came forward. Pressured by the other prisoners, she did so and led the policemen to the baby's hiding place. According to one account, mother and infant were then shot.[4] According to two other accounts, the mother and infant were taken to the nearby train that had not yet departed.[5] Whatever the immediate fate of the Tenenbaum mother and infant, Fräulein Lutz had claimed her first victims. They were not to be her last.

At least two additional Jews joined the prisoners at Tartak shortly thereafter. Michulek Baranek, who had slipped away from the column marching to the train and hid in empty Jewish houses, made his way after dark to Tartak, where he found his mother. Piatek took a bribe, and Michulek was allowed to stay. The next day, however, Walther Becker arrived, held a roll call, and immediately spotted the twelve-year-old Michulek, who was short even for that age. Becker grabbed him by the throat and asked his age and how long he had worked there. Michulek said he was fifteen and had worked there three months. The "decent" Piatek, who knew he was lying, vouched that he was indeed fifteen and a good worker.[6]

Chaja Weisblum, already a worker at Tartak, had been urged by Piatek on the marketplace to join his group of workers. Reluctant to leave her children, she was separated by force. Her oldest son also managed to slip away before reaching the train cars and hid with one of the family's "numerous Polish friends." After several days, he too reached the gate at Tartak but could not get in. Chaja went to Piatek, who admitted her son. Once again, Becker, controlling for "illegals" at a roll call, wanted to remove him, but the "very decent and friendly" Piatek vouched that "this little boy could work as much as a man," and he was allowed to stay.[7]

The second destination of workers marched from the marketplace was the Strelnica or "shooting range" beyond the munitions factory, formerly a low, flat field shielded by raised banks on two sides where ammunition produced at the factory had been tested. Located diagonally across town, on the northwest edge of Starachowice, it was much farther from the Wierzbnik marketplace than Tartak. The long forced march of some four to five miles, uphill from the Kamienna River Valley to the far edge of town bordering the Bugaj Forest, was far more traumatic than the short march to Tartak. It also took part in stages—starting around midday, different groups left the marketplace for Strelnica.

The first group to depart for Strelnica was composed of some 500 men.[8] It was followed closely by the women, who could see what was happening ahead better than the men in the front of the first group, who could not see what was happening behind them. All testimonies agree that the columns of workers were forced to run, as the Ukrainian guards freely wielded clubs and rifle butts. It was an unusually warm late October day, and most Jews were wearing extra layers of clothing and carrying their backpacks or bundles of essential possessions that they had prepared in advance.[9] As the grueling pace continued, many struggling Jews threw down whatever they were carrying.[10] According to three testimonies, Poles lined the streets through which the Jews ran. Not only did they rejoice at the Jews' misfortune and pick up whatever they could lay their hands on, but they also applauded, spit, and threw stones.[11]

Though some witnesses spoke generally about the guards firing blindly into the columns and killing many Jews on the way to Strelnica, more specific and detailed accounts render a somewhat different, though still lethal, picture. According to several testimonies, the guards shot into the ground at the feet of the Jews to cause panic and make them run faster. As a result of flying stone splinters from such shooting, a number of people arrived at the camp with leg wounds.[12]

Two men in the first group—Josef Rosenberg and Leib Szpagat—refused to drop the baggage they were carrying and fell increasingly behind. The women at the front of the following group saw what happened to the unfortunate stragglers. One survivor recounted: "On the way to the Strelnica camp I ran at the front of the group of women. I saw how a straggler from the men running in front of us was shot. A piece of the bullet struck through my left leg. The man murdered was named Josef Rosenberg; the murderer was a Ukrainian guard."[13] Another woman survivor recounted: "On the way a man named Spagat [sic] was shot near me, because he was carrying a packet. He fell down to the left of me. The shot was taken by a Ukrainian."[14] Leib Szpagat's son, Moszek, and his sister had worked the night shift and thus were not with him on the marketplace. Moszek later learned that his father had tried to carry the prepared packages of essentials for himself and his two children and had fallen behind when he refused to throw them down.[15]

As for the second group of men taken from the marketplace to Strelnica, there is a different story. One survivor—a skilled shoemaker—recounted: "Already at the beginning of my stay on the market place I got in contact with the leader of the Ukrainian guard. I told him that he and his comrades had nothing to gain if they shot Jews. If he brought our column to the camp without shooting and also if his comrades did not molest us, he would receive a pair of ski boots from me. He threatened to shoot me if I did not keep my promise. . . . Thus it was that the column to which I belonged marched from the market place to the camp without anyone being shot."[16]

Many testimonies name Rosenberg and Szpagat—and *only* these two specifically—among the "many" Jews who were said to have been shot on the march to Strelnica. No women were specifically named. Thus it would seem, upon close examination of the evidence but contrary to the widely held impression of many survivors, that Rosenberg and Szpagat were the only fatalities of the march to Strelnica. Given the trauma of killing and separation on the marketplace that they had just experienced, followed by the frantic run to the camp, it should not be surprising that so many survivors remembered that latter event as one of random and widespread killing. Moreover, that was not yet the end of the killing that day.

The columns that reached Strelnica discovered a fully prepared camp of six barracks on the higher levels above a lower field with an assembly ground and other buildings. They were not the first inmates of the camp. Jews from Ostrowiec, brought to Starachowice after the liquidation of the ghetto there, had constructed the camp, putting up the barracks and wire fence.[17] Other Jews from neighboring areas who fled to Starachowice for employment had also then lodged there.[18] And finally, some Jews—skilled craftsmen, the dentist, and selected members of the *Judenrat* whom the Germans kept safe from the selection—had been allowed to move in with their families the night before.[19]

Having been forced to go to the camp on the run, the prisoners were now made to wait a long time.[20] Key German personnel were presumably busy loading the train for Treblinka before they were able to make their way to Strelnica. A group of German officers eventually arrived, including Becker by most accounts. Indeed, if the SS was turning over Jewish slaves to the factory management, it is highly likely that Becker—as the highest-ranked SS officer in town—would have been present for what followed—namely, the collection of valuables that the SS still considered its own property. By some accounts it was Becker, but by most accounts it was another man, Willi Althoff, whom the prisoners were seeing for the first time, who climbed up on a stool or table and addressed them. Althoff was the chief of the factory security force and now also the first commandant of the factory slave-labor camps in Starachowice. Althoff rather than Becker would be at the center of survivor memories of events that occurred over the next six months.

Althoff emphatically told the prisoners that they must give up all their valuables, and he threatened that anyone caught trying to hide valuables would be summarily shot. In some accounts, a man was thereupon arbitrarily pulled from a row of Jews and shot on the spot "as a frightening example" or "for demonstration purposes" to "intimidate" the rest to give up all their valuables.[21] In other accounts, a young man was shot after he had been searched and found trying to hide money.[22] There was an even more memorable killing, mentioned in no fewer than ten accounts. At the end of a traumatic and exhausting day, a pious young man, Abe Kumec, suffered a nervous breakdown. In one account, "Kumec began suddenly to scream and cry to God. Althof [sic] approached him, pulled him out of the row and shot him in front of all of us."[23] Another witness gave a nearly identical description. "About this time one of the Jews among us lost his composure and began to scream. Althoff approached him, hit him in the face. Thereupon the man screamed even louder. Althoff drew his pistol and shot him."[24]

A different version of Kumec's death—one cast as heroic defiance— appears in the Wierzbnik community book. In this version, Kumec did not break down but rather had "the courage to start swearing at the Germans," and "his fury made his last words an incoherent babble." Initially there was no reaction by either Jews or Germans, "since the scene was too surreal." However, Althoff then quickly recovered and proceeded to shoot the "brave man."[25]

The Jews at Strelnica were presented with yet one more intimidating example. The butcher Jankiel Rubenstein—a big, strong man—was assigned to take over the camp kitchen. Before he left for his duties, he was ordered to turn over any valuables and then searched. He was found hiding valuables. Althoff gave him a beating that would have killed a smaller person, but he survived. "The incident was sufficient for all the others who started to dig deep into their pockets and other hiding places and handed all that was left them."[26]

The demand for valuables posed to every Jew in Strelnica yet another terrible choice—to give up hidden valuables that could be lifesaving in the future or to keep them at the risk of search, discovery, and immediate death. For some, the fear and risk were too great. When they passed by the large boxes into which they were to throw their valuables, they gave up everything they had except their extra layers of clothing, which were not considered valuables by the Germans in any case but were nonetheless very significant for the prisoners.[27] Others emptied their pockets but gambled on keeping gold pieces that were well hidden, such as in the heels of their shoes or boots.[28] Some thought incredibly quickly and took a chance. Thirteen-year-old Rachela Szachter rolled up the money her father had given her, wrapped it with paper, and substituted it for the cork in her water bottle. "I opted not to give in, I think it was the first time I became mature," she recounted.[29] Some got rid of their valuables out of fear, only to discover that another member of the family had taken the risk and made it through without doing so.[30] One young boy turned over his valuables, only to discover later a 100-złoty note that, unknown to him, his mother had sewn into a seam of his clothing.[31] In general, it seems that women, perhaps correctly calculating a lesser chance of search, took more frequent risks in keeping their valuables than men.

For many of the Jews marched into the Strelnica camp, their journey was not yet over. It was merely a transit point at which their entry into the Starachowice factory slave-labor camp system was processed. Either that evening or the following day, they were transferred to yet another camp in Starachowice called Majówka.[32] It was located back on the east side of Starachowice, on a stone bluff overlooking the Kamienna River Valley.

Two other small groups yet remained to be absorbed into the camp system. One consisted of the Jews who had been working on the night shift when the *Aktion* began. The other was the group of workers held back from the march to the camps to serve in a *Reinigungskommando* or "cleanup commando" in Wierzbnik in the wake of the destruction of the ghetto.

Many Jews had sought work on the night shift in the hope that they would not be subjected to the expected ghetto roundup, which, according to incoming refugees from other towns, invariably began in the early morning hours. This calculation proved correct. By 6 a.m., it was clear to those on the night shift that the morning shift of Jewish workers was not arriving. Moreover, they were not allowed to leave their factories to return home. Polish workers did arrive for the morning shift, however, and immediately told them that the Jewish quarter in Wierzbnik was surrounded and the roundup was already underway.[33] According to several witnesses, the Poles were "very happy" and "gloated" about what was taking place.[34] Some of those working in either the blast furnace of the steel works or in the Rogalin brick factory—both located along the railway tracks in the river valley—were able to catch glimpses of the train being loaded if they were briefly allowed to find a proper vantage point.[35] Thus they saw what none of those marched off to the camps were able to witness—namely, the loading of the transport to Treblinka, composed of fifty or more cattle cars and two passenger cars that began around 2 p.m. and was completed around 5 p.m. Some of the Jewish night-shift workers were taken into either Strelnica or Majówka late that afternoon or evening.[36] Others remained for yet another night at their factory before entering one of the camps the following day.[37] Some were not sent to the same camp as other family members, so they often did not learn for days who among their family had survived.

Schwertner and Piatek were on the marketplace that day to ensure that sufficient numbers of workers were selected for their respective enterprises. It would appear that no one had been assigned the task of forming a cleanup commando, and that only at the last moment were additional Jews taken out of the mass of people destined for deportation to staff such a group. Some Jewish policemen who had stayed on the marketplace until the end to help keep order were therefore assigned, along with some members of their families.[38] It would also appear that the chief of the Jewish ghetto police, Commandant Kornblum, as well as other policemen, were given considerable latitude in choosing others who would be given a last-minute reprieve in this manner. Leib Herblum was already on the march to the train when he was removed from the column and ordered to stay.[39] Yechiel Eisenberg had not been selected for factory work but was recognized by the two Jewish policemen who had brought him to Starachowice from the nearby mines several days earlier. They asked him if he wanted to do "town work," to which he readily agreed.[40] Guta Blass's father and mother were brought over to join her in the Tartak group by her father's very good friend, Kornblum. He then also chose her brother and young nephew for the cleanup commando.[41] Altogether, sixty to seventy people were assigned for cleanup duty, among them a small group of six to nine young girls.[42]

The very first task of the cleanup crew was to take care of the bodies of the many people killed that day. Some of the men were sent to the cemetery to prepare two large graves, separate for men and women. Others were given horses and wagons and sent street to street and house to house to pick up the dead and take them to the cemetery. Leib Herblum, in his testimony about grave-digging at the cemetery, introduced a macabre specter that haunts many testimonies of Starachowice survivors. In his account, a young Jewish man suffered a broken leg while digging. He was shot in the head, but the bullet only pierced his mouth, leaving him alive and fully conscious. His horrified coworkers were then ordered to bury him alive, and only at the last moment were they allowed to take him back to the lodgings, where he was shot the next morning.[43] As we shall see, this haunting image of being buried alive will reappear time and again in the testimonies.

Following burial detail, the cleanup commando turned to cleaning out the houses of the deported Jews. They boarded up the houses, many of which had already been at least partially looted by Poles, and then collected clothing, linens, household goods, and furniture. The women did the sorting. The commando was under the supervision of the Schupo, not Becker's Gestapo, and members of the Schupo helped themselves to the best pieces. An auction was then held, in which the Polish population of Starachowice could buy the property of their former Jewish neighbors. The remainder was packed into large boxes and trucked away.[44] Having easy access to food, clothing, and even money found in the empty homes, the cleanup workers lived well while the work lasted.[45]

Gradually the commando was reduced, with some of its members being sent elsewhere—such as the policeman Nathan Gelbard's father— and never heard from again. Others were kept doing sorting and packing or other odd jobs, such as tearing down dilapidated buildings, and then after several months were sent to one of the Starachowice camps.[46] There they gave many prisoners the news that confirmed for the first time the deaths of family members who had remained in their beds when others had departed for the marketplace on the morning of October 27.

PART III

TERROR AND TYPHUS

FALL 1942–SPRING 1943

10

Personalities and Structures

The experience of the Jewish prisoner community now enslaved in the factory camps of Starachowice would be determined by two sets of personalities: the German factory and camp managers and guards on the one hand and the "privileged" Jewish prisoners whom the Germans empowered to control the internal affairs of the camps on the other. These personalities operated within the typical structures of German factories and labor camps in the occupied territories of the Nazi empire but nonetheless left their own indelible imprints. Two names dominate the memory of Starachowice survivors as symbols of what shaped the particular experience, camp culture, and social hierarchy of their prisoner community. They are Ralf Alois "Willi" Althoff, the first commander of factory security, and Jeremiah Wilczek, the head of the Jewish camp police or *Lagerpolizei*.

In September 1939, the steel works and munitions factory in Starachowice, previously owned by the Polish government, had been taken over by the Reichswerke Hermann Göring. A state holding company that had been established by Göring in his capacity as plenipotentiary for German economic mobilization for war and facilitated both his self-enrichment and the Nazi regime's penetration and manipulation of the German economy, it proved particularly adept at profiting from German expansion. Particularly with the absorption of Austria and the Czech provinces of Bohemia and Moravia (the so-called Protectorate),

the Reichswerke gained a controlling position over coal, steel, and armaments production in these newly acquired territories. After the conquest
of Poland, the Reichswerke quickly confiscated the various factories of
the Polish State Armaments Works as well.[1] Among these were the Starachowice steel and munitions factories, which in turn were operated by
a Reichswerke subsidiary known as the Braunschweig Steel Works Corporation (Stahlwerke Braunschweig GmbH). While the Reichswerke
Hermann Göring also took over factories in Ostrowiec and Warsaw,
it seems that the Starachowice factories were the "crown jewel" of its
Polish acquisitions, for the overall director of its Polish operations, Fritz
Hofmann, and the personnel director, Franz Köhler, were both head-
quartered in Starachowice.[2]

The protection of these confiscated Starachowice factories against
possible sabotage or partisan attack was in the hands of the deputy for
security (*Abwehrbeauftragter*), Althoff. He had under his jurisdiction
a factory guard or *Werkschutz* commanded by a SS-*Unterscharführer*
Meyer.[3] The *Werkschutz* consisted of approximately ten Germans and
some 80 to 100 Ukrainians[4]—young men from Lwów and Kowel,[5] in the
eastern region of prewar Poland that had fallen to Soviet occupation in
September 1939. Though a few survivors referred to them as ethnic Germans from the Ukraine, this is unlikely. A Jewish prisoner from Lwów,
who conversed in Ukrainian with guards from her hometown,[6] as well
as most other survivors, identified them as Ukrainian. Indeed, many
Ukrainians fled the Soviet occupation during the population exchange
permitted under the terms of the Nazi-Soviet Non-Aggression Pact by
claiming to be ethnic Germans, who had the right to be repatriated to the
Nazi sphere. When their claims were subsequently disallowed by German racial screeners, these Ukrainians were not sent back but instead
were employed by the Germans in various types of guard duty that
would maximize their usefulness to the German occupiers but minimize
their contact with the Polish population. Most likely, the Starachowice
Werkschutz comprised such men. Their primary impact on the Jewish
prisoners was in guarding the perimeter of the camps and escorting the
workers from the camps to their workplaces and back.

The Strelnica and Majówka camps, which were hastily constructed
by the factory management as the condition for retaining their Jewish

workers, fell under Althoff's jurisdiction, as he added the function of camp commandant to his duties. Little is known about Althoff's background, since after the war he lived under the false name of Ralf Matthias Bracke until his death and therefore was never subjected to judicial investigation. His original family name, in fact, had been Jaworek, which he legally changed to the less Polish and more German-sounding Althoff in 1938.[7] Born on March 1, 1909, in Ratibor in Upper Silesia, he had joined the Nazi Party in 1930, left for unspecified reasons, and rejoined in January 1933.[8] According to several witnesses, Althoff was also a member of the SA (*Sturmabteilung*) or "Brownshirts."[9]

First encountered by the prisoners when they entered Strelnica after the run from the marketplace, he was known to the prisoners as "Willi" Althoff.[10] He was indelibly imprinted on the memories of survivors who subsequently experienced Auschwitz-Birkenau, many notorious camps in Germany, and the death marches. Comparatively speaking, Althoff was "the worst of all,"[11] "worse than all others,"[12] "the worst animal,"[13] "the worst of all camp commandants that I experienced,"[14] and "the most horrible man in the world."[15] He was "a beast,"[16] "a cannibal" (*Menschenfresser*),[17] "the ultimate of sadism,"[18] a man who killed with "obvious pleasure,"[19] "to amuse himself,"[20] "for fun,"[21] and "for sport."[22] In his early thirties, Althoff was a good-looking young man,[23] obviously concerned about his appearance. Shunning anything as commonplace as a regular uniform, he wore a three-quarter-length leather jacket lined and trimmed in white fur, tall leather boots, and white leather gloves.[24] When he came to camp for major killing actions, however, he wore rubber coat, boots, and gloves to keep his fine clothing from being spattered with the blood of his victims.[25] Among the prisoners, it was widely rumored that he came from a circus background.[26] This rumor was reinforced by bizarre aspects of his behavior, such as jumping and leaping about like an acrobat,[27] or making prisoners run in circles around him while he whipped them as if he were a circus animal trainer.[28] Many of his killings were theatrically staged, and he occasionally invited "guests" to attend his productions.[29] His behavior was so outlandish that several survivors assumed that he was a drug addict, who "fell in and out of a sadistic trance."[30]

Even the Germans in Starachowice, who in postwar interrogations routinely vouched for one another as proper, sober, orderly, and humane gentlemen, did not include Althoff in this mendacious ritual of mutual whitewashing. According to the head of personnel, Althoff was a "coarse" and "unstable ruffian" (*rüder . . . haltloser Kerl*).[31] According to the factory production manager, who subsequently also took over Althoff's job as deputy for security, he was "very impulsive and hot-tempered" (*sehr impulsiv und jähzornig*).[32] The deputy head of accounting referred to Althoff as a "swine" who was "extremely unpopular" (*äusserst unbeliebt*) with the entire German staff.[33] And the factory director noted contemptuously, "Despite his manly appearance, Althoff was a feminine type. He ran around scented." (*Althoff trotz seiner männlichen Erscheinung ein femininer Typ war. Er lief parfümiert herum.*)[34]

While Althoff and Meyer would make frequent visits to Strelnica and Majówka, all too often with lethal consequences, the day-to-day management of the camps was in other hands. The chief camp administrator was a Sudeten German named Waschek, who worked out of an office within the Strelnica camp. His deputy in Majówka was a man named Pohl.[35] Nothing further is known about Pohl, but Waschek was remembered on several accounts. First, as a Sudeten German, he spoke Czech and could understand Polish.[36] And second, though he was notoriously foulmouthed and verbally abusive, in sharp contrast to Althoff he was remembered as being "very decent," "good to us," and "the only one who had a heart."[37] With certain exceptions,[38] he was remembered as someone who neither beat nor killed and occasionally even protected Jewish prisoners. He was alleged to have proclaimed in vain that the Ukrainian guards had no right to beat "my Jews."[39]

From the very beginning of the Nazi dictatorship in 1933, when Theodore Eicke—the innovative commandant of the Dachau concentration camp and subsequently head of the SS Concentration Camp Inspectorate—developed the "Dachau model" on which the subsequent concentration-camp system would be based, prisoner life was dominated not only by the camp administration and guards but also by the infamous *kapo* system. Long before Jews constituted a significant portion of the camp population, the Nazis had already perfected an insidious mechanism of prisoner manipulation through "divide and control." The Starachowice slave-labor camps—though run by factory managers rather than the SS—were no exception in this regard. The two key institutions for internal prisoner control were the camp council or *Lagerrat* on the one hand and the camp police or *Lagerpolizei* on the other.

The entire membership of the camp council is not known, and only one source even mentions the number of members as seven.[40] It was not merely a replica of the Wierzbnik *Judenrat*, for its chairman, Symcha Mincberg, seems to have been totally marginalized. Not a single testimony attributes any significant role in the camps to him. But three names of former *Judenrat* members often surface in the survivor testimony about the *Lagerrat*—Shlomo Einesman, Moshe Birenzweig, and Rachmil Wolfowicz. Of the three, Einesman was the only one to enjoy a decent reputation.[41] Birenzweig was characterized as "not nice."[42] And Wolfowicz was clearly the most detested, as an "unpleasant,"[43] "corrupt," and "spoiled"[44] man who turned his back on his prewar friends.[45] According to one account, he was even cursed by his own mother for not doing good things when he was in a position to do so.[46]

The privileges enjoyed by the prisoner elite were considerable. They lived in separate housing with their wives and in some cases with their children, whom they had been allowed to bring into camp.[47] They were able to maintain contact with people outside camp and even visit them in town, in order to conduct business or have access to valuables hidden with friends.[48] They controlled the access to food and clothing and thus ate and dressed relatively well, while normal prisoners in the camp went hungry and dressed in rags.[49] They could allocate jobs, above all assigning coveted jobs in the kitchen to family and friends.[50]

Alongside the camp council was a second internal camp institution—the camp police—whose commander, Jeremiah Wilczek, soon eclipsed all the other privileged prisoners in importance and notoriety. Wilczek already had a dubious reputation even before the war, having served time in jail. His rumored offenses included running prostitution and dabbling in counterfeiting.[51] Released from jail at the outbreak of war, he knew how to make himself useful to the German police. According to Wilczek's daughter, Walther Becker frequently visited her father's cigarette shop before the deportation.[52] According to another survivor, Wilczek served as the bag man for the extortion arrests of Jews made by the feared Gendarme Schmidt.[53]

When the Jews arrived at Strelnica on the afternoon of October 27, 1942, the Germans had already placed Wilczek in his new position of authority. He joined Althoff in demanding that the Jews surrender their valuables.[54] He then organized a work group of prisoners to fetch water that afternoon.[55] And the following morning, it was Wilczek who ordered the prisoners out of their barracks for work.[56]

Described as "a quite ordinary man"[57] and "just a short, little Jewish man,"[58] Wilczek was most often judged by survivors simply and cryptically as "not a nice person" and "not a good man." Wilczek had more influence than any other Jew in camp to affect the fate of individual prisoners, but for a period of twenty-one months of incarceration in the Starachowice camps, only four witnesses attested to occasions on which he warned, helped, or saved them.[59] Wilczek had a few other defenders who argued that he did not actually hurt or kill anyone[60] and that he "was also tortured the same as we were."[61] After nearly a year in camp, he was severely beaten by Althoff's successor.[62] And before that, Althoff did publicly humiliate Wilczek in front of the other prisoners for his own amusement. On one occasion, he poured liquor into Wilczek's mouth until he could not breathe.[63] On another, he staged one of his degrading theatrical performances, forcing Wilczek and other members of the *Lagerrat* to run through camp on skis (there was no snow) while he fired off shots.[64] Althoff had proclaimed in front of others: "All Jews will perish but you, Wilczek, will be the last in line."[65] However, to others Wilczek often bragged that Althoff had assured him he would kill every Jew but him.[66] Apparently denial of reality and delusional hope were part of what drove him. In any case, Wilczek certainly knew that his pact with Althoff—however humiliating on occasion—involved sacrificing others in order to save or at least prolong his own life.

Among the overwhelming majority of survivors, the postwar memories and verdicts on Wilczek were quite negative. Three survivors did make the explicit accusation that either Wilczek individually or the Jewish leadership collectively participated with the Germans in the lethal process of selecting who would die.[67] More generally, Wilczek and the other most privileged Jews were seen as the cause and beneficiaries of a camp culture of corruption, favoritism, bribery, hierarchy, and inequality that was distinctly more pervasive in Starachowice than in other camps the prisoners experienced.[68]

Wilczek commanded a small force of camp police whose main tasks were to assemble prisoners for the march to work and to keep order inside the camps, which on occasion meant assisting with German barracks searches and selections. Since most of the Jewish ghetto police of the previous period had remained with the cleanup commando in town, after which many of them were sent elsewhere, Wilczek's camp police were for the most part newly appointed.[69] Some were selected primarily for nepotistic reasons, such as Wilczek's eighteen-year-old son, Abraham. (Wilczek's second son, Chil, apparently too young to be a policeman, was named a *Blockälteste* or barracks supervisor.) Wilczek's nineteen-year-old son-in-law, Chaim Kogut, likewise became a policeman, though his sister also attributed his appointment to the fact that the family was well off and had handed over a lot of money.[70] But Wilczek also recruited others without such connections. On the first day in Strelnica, he approached Rachmil Najman and offered him a rubber club and a position as policeman, promising him better rations and a chance to help his family. Rachmil handed back the club and turned down the offer after his wife warned him that if he took the club he would undoubtedly have to hit people with it.[71]

Several survivors bitterly and hyperbolically characterized the camp police as "worse than the Germans."[72] Others took a more differentiated view, noting that some of the police were nice and "a few" were not,[73] "some were bastards and some were good,"[74] and "at least some were not unkind" while others "degenerated" and "abused their power unnecessarily."[75] This last phrase about the *unnecessary* abuse of power is significant. This same survivor expressed a quite representative view: "The general feeling in the camp was that a genuinely fine person did not become a policeman for the Germans for any reason."[76] Yet, paradoxically, the few survivors who spoke about individually identified Jewish policemen performed an act of disassociation, judging them by particular acts of kindness and decency that they performed out of their own volition rather than by the hated functions they performed on behalf of the Germans by virtue of the position they held.

Altogether, the names of ten of Wilczek's policemen are known. Szmul

Szczesliwy and Chaim Kogut were classified as "not nice" by some[77] but were viewed favorably by others.[78] Ezra Linzon, Otto Hilf, Moshe Herblum, Goldfarb, and Turek were spoken of positively.[79] Manek Tenzer was deemed an "angel."[80] Only one policeman, Szaja Langleben, was universally and unequivocally condemned. Not one witness credited him with even a single act of helping, warning, or saving another prisoner in the entire twenty-one months of incarceration in Starachowice. One survivor characterized him as a "dark type" who was a devoted servant of the Germans and an informer.[81] Another described him as a "ferocious" and "disgusting animal."[82]

The most controversial policeman discussed in the postwar testimonies—and the most problematic for a historian trying to work his way through contradictory claims and views—was Jeremiah Wilczek's older son, Abraham.[83] According to one survivor, he was—like his father—an agent of the German police in the ghetto before the deportation, who even advised his masters concerning whom to beat to get the information they wanted.[84] From the first day in camp, the newly appointed teenage policeman was openly rude and disrespectful of the adult men and women over whom he now suddenly held authority.[85] Several accused Abraham of responsibility for a beating received or for not saving a family member whom he was in a position to save.[86] But even a survivor who said he could never forgive Abraham Wilczek admitted that over time he "mellowed."[87] One man who considered Abraham's father "not a good man" nonetheless conceded that in contrast Abraham "helped us a lot."[88] Others noted specific occasions when Abraham had saved people from beatings or death.[89] In the end, Abraham took a lead in attempting to organize resistance within the camp, escaped, survived in hiding, and then provided significant help to many survivors returning through Łódź in the postwar period. In short, Abraham Wilczek seems to have been a resentful teenager growing up in the shadow of a dubious father who, under the most unfavorable and potentially corrupting conditions, matured into a quite different person.

11

The Typhus Epidemic

The camps at Strelnica and Majówka had been hastily thrown up in the weeks before the liquidation of the Wierzbnik ghetto. One consequence of their hasty construction, at minimal expense by people inexperienced in either building or managing camps, was the total lack of adequate hygiene facilities. The toilets were nothing more than boards with holes over an open trench that was emptied periodically by the prisoners.[1] Water came from a few spigots.[2] There were no showers or baths in camp, and the only opportunities to bathe were provided by rare visits to the former Jewish baths in town. One survivor remembered making the trip once per month, another just once every three months, and yet another just once in two years.[3] The prisoners had only the clothes they wore or carried into camp, for which they likewise lacked washing facilities and soap. Further aggravating the systemic uncleanliness was the nature of the work; people returned each day from the factories very dirty from the smoke, oil, and heat.[4] The inevitable result was that Strelnica and Majówka were utterly filthy places to live, where no one could cope with what one survivor called the "impossible dirt."[5] In terms of comparison, survivors were emphatic that, measured against the Starachowice camps, Płaszów and Auschwitz-Birkenau were much cleaner.[6] None was more emphatic than Icek Guterman, who described his response to going through the shower and disinfection procedures at Birkenau after two years of unremitting filth in Majówka: "I thought there is a God, I am clean."[7]

The "impossible dirt" of Strelnica and Majówka was matched by yet another condition of misery—infestation. The phrase that appears time and again in the testimonies is that the vermin "ate us alive."[8] "Huge lice"[9] could be picked off the prisoners' clothing by the "handful,"[10] though they invariably returned. And at night, the moment the lights were turned out, masses of bedbugs "descended" or "parachuted" down from the woodwork upon the beleaguered prisoners.[11] The overcrowding of people into lice-infested barracks without the possibility of washing either their bodies or their clothing could have only one result in the environment of wartime Eastern Europe—the outbreak of a devastating epidemic of typhus.

Exanthematic typhus—what the Germans called spotted fever or *Fleckfieber*—is caused by a rickettsia carried by body lice.[12] It was a public-health threat that Germans encountered not in Germany itself but primarily during their military forays into Eastern Europe in both World War I and World War II. Many German public-health officials studied the medical data concerning typhus epidemics through the prism of race as a biological reality rather than as a social construct.[13] Noting the prevalence of typhus outbreaks among the impoverished and overcrowded populations of urban Jews in Eastern Europe, they mistook correlation for causality, ignored the obvious environmental factors, and attributed the spread of typhus to alleged Jewish cultural and genetic defects. In a 1940 article on "spotted fever and ethnic identity," the German chief of public health in Nazi-occupied Poland, Dr. Jost Walbaum, proclaimed: "The Jews are overwhelmingly the carriers and disseminators of the infection. Spotted fever endures most persistently in the regions heavily populated by Jews, with their low cultural level, their uncleanliness, and the infestation of lice unavoidably connected with this." One of his associates, Dr. Erich Weizenegger, similarly argued: "The sickness occurs . . . especially among the Jewish population. This is caused by the fact that the Jew totally lacks any concept of hygiene."[14] German doctors were also generally convinced that typhus, if it spread among the German population, would have a far higher fatality rate than among the Jews, who had developed greater resistance to it.[15]

The response of German public-health officials in Nazi-occupied

Poland to the typhus threat was consistent with their warped perceptions. They advocated that the Jews, as natural carriers and disseminators, should be quarantined in ghettos. The result was an entirely predictable self-fulfilling prophecy. Forced into vastly overcrowded ghettos, without adequate food, medicine, and hygiene facilities, the Jews sealed up in the major ghettos experienced the very outbreak of typhus epidemics the Germans feared.[16] Wierzbnik, as an unsealed small ghetto in which conditions did not deteriorate to the level of Warsaw or Łódź, experienced some cases of typhus but not an epidemic. When the Jews selected for labor were incarcerated in the squalid and lice-infested camps of Strelnica and Majówka, however, the inevitable occurred. In December 1942, a typhus epidemic broke out, and the disease swept through the prisoner population with incredible ferocity.

Those afflicted experienced extremely high fevers of 105 or 106 degrees and throbbing headaches. This lasted for up to two weeks, with the climax usually coming around the eleventh or twelfth day. At that point, the typhus victim was usually delirious and hallucinating if not unconscious. Even after the fever broke and the crisis was over, the person recovering was weak and debilitated for up to three months.[17] For people who were kept alive only for their labor, typhus posed a twofold danger—from the disease itself and from the Germans.

From those who survived both typhus and the Germans to give post-war testimony, one theme occurs over and over in their accounts of the ordeal—that they could not have survived alone and without help. Since many of those who entered the Starachowice camps did so through the purchase of work permits as a family strategy of survival, they were in the camps with other family members. Usually they came down with typhus not simultaneously but one after another. As a result, family members cared for one another in succession.[18] Those who had had typhus earlier and were now immune were especially important as caregivers.[19] Some without family connections were fortunate enough to have friends who helped.[20] Insofar as family or friends had managed to smuggle money and valuables into camp, they purchased medicines.[21] Insofar as patients could eat, family and friends brought food—usually soup or tea, since those stricken with typhus could eat little else during the worst days.[22] If this had been a camp in which individual prisoners had been thrown together randomly rather than a family camp from a particular community, the fatality rate from the typhus epidemic clearly would have been much higher. As it was, the lesser danger was dying from typhus itself. During the first wave of the epidemic, from December 1942 into March 1943, the far greater danger came from the Germans.

12

The Althoff Massacres

Although the complex of Starachowice factory slave-labor camps was in existence for a period of twenty-one months (October 27, 1942, to July 28, 1944), the vast majority of Jews who died there were murdered either by or at the behest of Willi Althoff in a three-month period from early December 1942 to early March 1943. Althoff's murderous predilections were evident very soon. Just a few days after the prisoners arrived in the camps, Althoff reportedly lined up three or four Jews against a wall and shot them for no discernible reason other than that he disliked them.[1] He also began to prowl the camp kitchens on a fairly regular basis, looking for unauthorized people to shoot and even killing some who had been assigned to work there.[2] And in early December, after several prisoners escaped, he staged a theatrical "deterrent" killing. Althoff descended upon the camp in the middle of the night and selected ten prisoners, who were blindfolded and placed against a wall illuminated by truck headlights. Althoff then carried out target practice until they were all dead.[3] He also staged a Christmas Eve "play" of "death and humiliation," when he forced everyone to run around camp on a "bright moonlit night."[4]

Althoff's killing spree escalated when the typhus epidemic broke out, and he became obsessed with identifying and eliminating those prisoners who were temporarily incapacitated by the disease and desperately trying to hide their affliction. Althoff's first tactic was to arrive in camp at night and order all the prisoners out of the barracks. Those who could not get out of bed were then shot.[5] As prisoners became aware of how important it was to drag themselves out of bed and out of the barracks—both to go to work and to escape the nighttime barracks searches, even if it meant being literally carried out of the barracks by comrades—Althoff intensified his methods. Strelnica had a natural obstacle especially daunting for those dizzy from high fever: steps that separated the barracks of the upper camp from the assembly grounds of the lower camp. Sick prisoners who could not rush down the steps without wobbling or staggering were pulled aside and shot.[6] This method netted Althoff at least twenty or thirty murdered prisoners on one evening.[7] Another variation was to make the prisoners quickly walk a long, straight board or balance beam, which those dizzy from high fever could not do.[8] On other occasions, both in Strelnica and Majówka, Althoff made prisoners run in circles—what was cynically referred to as *Runde machen* or "making the rounds"—to sort out those who did not have the stamina to keep up.[9]

The murderous attrition of Althoff's frequent nighttime selections and killings was not sufficient to keep up with the rate at which prisoners fell sick with typhus. While the prisoners of both Strelnica and Majówka experienced Althoff's murderous nocturnal visits, the larger and more unsanitary Strelnica was also the site of a series of large-scale killing actions.

Shortly after the typhus epidemic had broken out in Strelnica, Althoff ordered those who were too sick to work to be moved into Block 5, which was then referred to as the isolation barracks or sick barracks (*Krankenbaracke*). The block was quickly filled to overflowing, so Althoff arrived in the night and killed every patient but one—sixteen-year-old Jolek Arbeiter, the former cleaning boy for Walther Becker—who managed to escape.[10] According to Jolek, who was luckily lying on the top bunk in the very back corner of the barracks, Jeremiah Wilczek entered and ordered the Jews to stand, because Commandant Althoff, who was standing in the doorway, wanted to inspect and count them. As those patients who could rise from their bunks staggered toward the doorway, Althoff opened fire on them with his submachine gun. Jolek managed to open the window at the back of the block but saw an armed German standing guard there. However, when no more patients would or could come forward and Althoff prepared to enter the block to shoot them as well, the German guard left to join him. Jolek jumped out the window and, between sweeps of a searchlight, made it back to his barracks. Friends hid him and threatened the block supervisor with death if he betrayed him. According to Jolek, he was the only one of eighty-six Jews to survive the *Krankenbaracke* massacre that night.

Following the massacre in Block 5, Althoff and two Ukrainian guards fetched some more typhus suspects and lined them up front-to-back to see how many could be killed with the fewest bullets. One witness in the women's barracks clearly heard the sound of Althoff's submachine gun—quite distinct from the sound made by the carbines of the Ukrainian guards—amid the screams. The women fled from their barracks window and covered their ears.[11] According to another witness, Althoff returned to Strelnica the next day, heavily perfumed, without showing the slightest sign of remorse.[12]

Thereafter, the sick barracks was filled and then emptied "several times"[13] through Althoff's infamous "visits to the sick"[14] (*Krankenbesuchen*). One witness estimated that these occurred about every four weeks.[15] However, the exact number of such massacres cannot be established, since it is unclear when the rare survivors of them were relating the same or different events. In any case, there are four additional accounts by those who narrowly escaped the attacks and two more by hearsay. According to one survivor, he was in the sick barracks after the first massacre when his father heard that a second Althoff visit was imminent; the father rescued his son just before Althoff killed another fifty typhus patients.[16] Jakob Sztajman was in the sick barracks with sixty to seventy other typhus-stricken Jews when Althoff arrived. He chased away the Jewish attendant and began shooting the sick. Only Jakob and two or three others managed to escape out the back window.[17] On one night in which Althoff shot fifty typhus-stricken Jews, one young man from Opatów survived. Though hit in the ear, he was not discovered and shot again, because other bodies had fallen over him.[18] Chaim Flancbaum and one other boy likewise escaped an Althoff killing of fifty sick people in the isolation barracks.[19] Chaim Wolgroch was also in the sick bay filled with fifty patients when

Althoff arrived and demanded that the sick Jews stand up. When no one could, he went from bunk to bunk, shooting each one in the head. On a top bunk, Chaim managed to push aside a board, make an opening in the ceiling, and slip into the crawl space. He was followed by two others. Althoff shot randomly into the ceiling, wounding him in the arm.[20] And on one occasion, Althoff ordered fifty Jews who were well on the way to recovery to report to a "convalescent barrack." The next day, he shot them all, with the exception of Szymszon Gutwil, who escaped out the window.[21]

Not all the killing took place inside the camps. Strelnica backed up against the Bugaj Forest, which offered convenient space and privacy for both killing and mass burial. More than once, prisoners from Strelnica were taken on trucks into the forest and killed in large numbers. As in the case of the *Krankenbaracke* killings, we cannot ascertain the total number of times this occurred, nor the total number of victims. But at least two such *Aktionen* can be clearly identified—one in December 1942 and one in early March 1943. After Jolek Arbeiter had escaped from the first Block 5 massacre and been hidden in the barracks, he was still too sick to go to work. The camp policeman Abraham Wilczek sent him back to the now-empty Block 5 with the promise that he would reassign him to work as soon as he had the strength. Block 5 began to refill, and rumor spread of a selection. Wilczek checked Jolek out of the sick barracks, and that night his friends literally carried him to work on their shoulders, while others filled his quota at work. When the night shift returned in the morning, they learned a selection had indeed taken place, through Althoff's infamous running of the Strelnica steps, and many Jews had been taken to the forest.[22]

Twelve-year-old Hersz Unger had been caught stealing food for his sick sister and was severely beaten. Since he was disabled from the beating, not from typhus, Jeremiah Wilczek told him not to go to the sick barracks. That was the day before all the patients there were shot. "A few days later," however, the weakened boy faced the ordeal of Althoff's selection run. He stumbled over someone who fell in front of him. He was sent to a truck but slipped off the back side and successfully hid until it left for the forest, but he lost his uncle that day.[23] Fourteen-year-old Abramek Naiman had become separated from his parents, remaining in the Strelnica camp utterly alone after they had been transferred to Majówka. Without parental help, he was very soon demoralized, covered with lice, and bedraggled in appearance. An easy target for selection, he found himself on the truck alongside another young boy who turned out to be the nephew of the Jewish policeman Manek Tenzer. When Tenzer arrived to rescue his nephew, Abramek jumped off the truck as well and made it to safety.[24] Several others also remember family members or acquaintances being "taken to the forest" before March.[25]

The climax of the Althoff terror occurred on March 3 or 5, 1943.[26] One day, Althoff had demanded a workforce of twenty men, who were sent into the forest with shovels.[27] The work party came from Majówka rather than Strelnica.[28] Four days later, in a daylight visit rather than the usual nighttime one, Althoff and Meyer and his Ukrainians arrived in camp with two trucks.[29] According to three witnesses, Becker was also present.[30] According to others, there was also a squad of Gendarmerie led by Schmidt.[31] In any case, it was a far larger group of Germans and guards than for other killing actions, so clearly an *Aktion* of considerable proportions had been planned in advance. Both the presence of Becker, representing the SS, and parallel killings in other camps at this time, indicate that this particular massacre was the product of an order from Berlin to reduce the number of "work Jews" in Poland and not merely one of Althoff's lethal whims.[32]

Since few if any Jews still reported to the sick barracks, Althoff conducted a "run" to select his victims.[33] Knowing their fate, some did not go quietly. One man leaped down from a truck and protested that he was still strong. Althoff shot him on the spot.[34] Althoff also shot two teenage girls from Szydłowicc near the trucks.[35] At least several killings were done for amusement. During the run, some of the Ukrainian guards tormented an elderly cobbler, then shot him and dragged his body around by the feet, to much laughter.[36] Chanka Laks served as Waschek's secretary and file clerk in Strelnica. In charge of listing the names of those selected for the trucks, she pleaded with a guard to release a friend. Instead, before her eyes the guard shot the girl she was trying to save.[37]

The victim who was most clearly remembered and most often cited in the testimony about that day was the wife of Rabbi Rabinowicz.[38] Recovering from typhus but still very weak, she could not keep up in the run and was sent to the trucks. One of her daughters approached Althoff and gave him a gold tobacco box that she had smuggled into camp and saved for a desperate occasion such as this. She asked that her mother be spared. Althoff took the gift but did not let the mother climb down. Instead, the daughter received a blow on the head for stepping out of line.[39]

Several other rescue attempts were more successful. When Rachela Szachter, who had smuggled in money wrapped up as a bottle stopper, was selected and taken to the trucks, her mother joined her. The father then went to his friend Shlomo Einesman (apparently the entire *Lager-rat* was in attendance for the occasion as part of Althoff's entourage) and asked for his help. Einesman advised Althoff that a woman who was not sick (the mother) had gone to the trucks. Althoff authorized Einesman to get her off, which he accomplished through the Jewish policeman Szmul Szczesliwy. Szczesliwy then returned and surreptitiously rescued Rachela as well.[40] Szczesliwy was also credited with getting Jakob Sztaj-man's brother Max off the trucks.[41]

The trucks then drove out of camp and into the Bugaj Forest. The prisoners subsequently learned what happened there from the sole escapee, a young man named Binsztok. He was in the work group of twenty young men from Majówka camp sent four days earlier into the forest to dig a mass grave. At the burial site, Althoff and Meyer personally shot not only the 120 Jews selected for their weakness but also the remaining nineteen of the work party. Having nowhere else to go, Binsztok joined a column of workers during a change of shift, reentered camp, and told his story to a number of other prisoners.[42]

The horror of the Bugaj Forest *Aktion* was intensified by news relayed from Polish workers at the factory who visited the mass grave site. They described how for days afterward the ground above the mass grave still moved, and how hands and legs stuck out of the earth.[43] Not knowing about the effects of bodies decomposing in shallow, inadequately covered graves (a phenomenon the German killers encountered repeatedly), the prisoners imagined the most terrible explanation: that many of the victims had been wounded and buried alive, that they had struggled for days to work their way out.[44] The fearful specter of being buried alive continued thereafter to haunt the scarred and traumatized imaginations of the Starachowice prisoners.

The Bugaj Forest massacre was the last for the lethal team of Althoff and Meyer. On March 22, 1943, Meyer died of typhus—ironically, the very disease that had been the pretext for murdering so many of his victims.[45] Then, in a crucial turn of events, Althoff disappeared,[46] and one of the German authorities appeared and announced a revolution in German policy. We have three different versions of this important moment. According to one witness, Leopold Schwertner arrived in Strelnica and promised "that now the sick would no longer be killed."[47] A second witness said that it was Becker and Waschek who came and announced: "You dogs have nothing to fear anymore. The sick will no longer be shot, and the camp will be closed until the epidemic is over." More food was also promised.[48] According to a third and most frequently corroborated version, the crucial announcement was made by Kurt Otto Baumgarten, one of the factory managers. According to one witness from Strelnica, "Baumgarten made a beautiful speech when Althoff left, when he came into camp, he said there will be no more shooting, if you work you will be treated correctly, just no sabotage."[49] According to another, an "engineer" from the factory (subsequently identified as Baumgarten) made a speech at Strelnica that "Jews will no longer be shot, sick ones get medicine, but you must work." The witness continued: "We thought an Angel had come. After this things got a little easier."[50] Yet another witness confirmed that Baumgarten had told the prisoners that things were not going to be the way they had been.[51]

If the name of the announcer of the policy change is in dispute, the change in policy itself is certain. Both the reason for this crucial change in policy and its timing are connected to another event—the arrival of the first transfer of Jewish prisoners from outside into the Starachowice camps. The wanton killing of typhus-stricken Jews had apparently so decimated the workforce that replacements were needed. One hundred twenty Jews were sent from Kielce and twenty Jewish women from Bodzechów (thirty-five miles southwest and twenty-six miles southeast of Starachowice, respectively). According to one of four from Kielce who survived and provided postwar testimony, the Kielce contingent arrived sometime in March 1943, but *after* Althoff had already left.[52] According to another, they were to replace workers who had died in the typhus epidemic.[53] However, upon arrival in the lice-infested Starachowice camps, the Kielce Jews immediately contracted typhus as well. Apparently having less immunity or resistance to typhus than native Wierzbnikers, seventy of the 120 died within the first month.[54] The Bodzechów contingent likewise arrived in the spring of 1943 *after* Althoff had left. They too found the Starachowice camps completely infested with lice and quickly contracted typhus.[55]

The spring of 1943 was also the period during which the Nazis in the General Government were carrying out a second sweep, eliminating "remnant ghettos" whose Jewish inhabitants had hitherto escaped deportation as well as work camps not deemed essential to the war economy. The German factory managers in Starachowice were thus facing a self-induced labor shortage in their own camps caused by the profligate killing of sick Jews, at the very time when the replacement of those Jewish workers was becoming increasingly difficult. Something had to give.

In the memories of the survivors, understandably, the obvious bloodlust and sadism of Althoff is most salient. But it is difficult to escape the conclusion that his murderous rampage against the typhus-stricken occurred with the full sanction of Althoff's employer, the management of the Braunschweig Steel Works, because it coincided with their "bottom line" economic calculations. Sick Jews could not work, and even if they recovered from typhus, they were weak and less productive for a long period of time. Yet management had to continue paying to the SS the fixed daily fee for each Jewish worker, whether or not he or she was productive. Killing sick Jews not only coincided with the ideological agenda of the SS, from whom they were renting their slave labor, but it also reduced the labor costs that management had to pay out. Once the labor shortage became more critical and the difficulty of replacing killed workers more evident, the economic calculations of the factory management changed. Murdered Jewish workers could not be replaced easily, but sick Jewish workers could eventually recover and return to productive labor. The economic rationale of killing typhus-stricken Jews no longer made sense, and Althoff—the instrument of that policy—was removed. The SS's ideological goal of total extermination (and hence of eliminating all use of Jewish labor as soon as possible) no longer coincided with the Starachowice factory management's economic goal of exploiting and preserving irreplaceable Jewish labor for war production and company profit.

This basic economic rationale was not lost upon the prisoners themselves. As one of them explained succinctly: "In 1943 the Germans were very short of laborers and needed us to supply their army with weapons. So, they treated us a little better than before. In the past sick Jews were routinely murdered; now many were allowed to recuperate and then sent back to work."[56] The Althoff terror was over, and a new period of relative stability set in.

Up to this point, the ability of the enslaved Jews to affect their own fate through activism and reciprocal aid was fairly limited. As we have seen, the Jewish prisoners nursed the sick through typhus and became increasingly adept at shielding them from Althoff's assaults. Some prisoners hauled others out of the barracks during the inspections and supported them during the forced runs.[57] Sick prisoners were carried to work by their family and comrades, and their quotas were filled by others doing their work.[58] Those too sick to move were hidden.[59] Usually, in desperation, the sick were simply covered with straw in the hope that the barracks inspection would be superficial, but occasionally the hiding was quite ingenious. During one selection, David Mangarten was tied to the chimney on the barracks roof and his mouth was stuffed so he could not cry out and give himself away.[60] Sometimes those saved knew who had rescued them. Anna Freilich from Szydłowiec remembered that it was her fellow townsman, the policeman Szczesliwy, who dressed her, helped her down the steps at Strelnica, and then made fellow townsmen carry her to work.[61] Rosalie Laks did not learn until years later that when she was too sick and delirious to leave her barracks, it was Pinchas Hochmic who covered her with straw and saved her.[62] Chaim Kleinberg never learned who picked him up out of the snow, where he had collapsed, and carried him back to his barracks before he could be found and shot—an event he could only describe as a "miracle."[63]

With the German change of policy in March 1943, the Jewish strategy of survival through labor—seemingly so hopeless during the Althoff reign of terror—was viable once again. Jewish agency—basically confined to individuals trying to save themselves, their families, and their closest comrades from the twin threats of typhus and selection during the Althoff era—now could be exercised more collectively and systematically. A new era in the life of the Jewish slave-labor community in the Starachowice camps could begin.

13

Tartak

While most of the Jews selected for labor on the day the Wierzbnik ghetto was liquidated were sent to either Strelnica or Majówka, a smaller contingent of Jews had been assigned to work in the sawmill and lumberyard called Tartak. An even smaller group of eighty-four Jews was temporarily kept at work in the electricity works (Zeork), where they already had been living before the deportation. Neither Tartak nor Zeork was administered by the Braunschweig Steel Works Corporation. They were thus spared the murderous visits of Althoff and Meyer, but as German-run businesses using Jewish labor, they fell under the more distant supervision and occasional inspection of the local police chief, Walther Becker.

The electricity plant, which backed up against Tartak in the lowlands of the Kamienna River Valley, was supervised by a German named Stricker,[1] Stroeker,[2] or Starker.[3] On November 3, 1942, Becker arrived to "control" Zeork for "illegals" who might have managed to evade the roundup and find refuge there. One "illegal," Hersz Faigenbaum, managed to slip undetected into the group of authorized workers while the roll call was being taken. Another, Abraham Rosenwald, who had been visiting from nearby Tartak to recover valuables he had hidden there earlier, was caught. He managed to bribe a Pole to fetch Piatek, the deputy at Tartak, who had expanded the workforce there to provide a haven for many Jews. Piatek intervened on Rosenwald's behalf and saved him.

Becker had to content himself with having just one person shot that day—a sixteen-year-old boy named Adler with a broken leg.[4]

Some of the workers at Zeork were transferred to Szydłowiec, which had been reopened as a remnant ghetto and proclaimed a legal haven for Jews in order to entice them out of hiding. Hersz Faigenbaum was among those transferred, and in Szydłowiec he had the good fortune to be reunited with his only surviving daughter, Chava, who had arrived there via a different camp. On January 13, 1943, however, the trap was sprung, and the Szydłowiec Jews were rounded up once again for deportation. Three days earlier, the Jewish workers at Zeork had also been rounded up. Both groups were sent eastward on the same train. Near Łuków in the Lublin district, just sixty-five miles south of Treblinka, Hersz Faigenbaum and his daughter managed to slip through an opening in the cattle car that some of the prisoners had made and escaped the train. They entered the nearby remnant ghetto of Łuków, where they remained until its last inhabitants were rounded up in early May. Placed again on a train to Treblinka, they jumped once more. After twenty-one days walking cross country, they reached Starachowice, slipped into the labor camp, and informed others of the direction in which their deportation train had gone, though not its ultimate destination.[5]

Tartak was a prewar Jewish lumber business named after its absentee owner, Heller. It had been "aryanized"—taken over and placed under a German manager named Fiedler (also referred to as Fittler or Fickler). He was described by his grateful workers as "decent" (*anständig*),[6] "a nice man,"[7] an "angel,"[8] and "a very good man" who "cared for us well"[9] and was "good to us."[10] The only negative survivor comments about Fiedler were that he took bribes, embezzled worker provisions for himself, and slept with his secretary, producing an illegitimate son[11]—rather trivial though very common vices among the German occupation personnel in Eastern Europe. Fiedler's deputy, the likewise highly esteemed Piatek, at some undetermined point left Tartak for military service.[12] The ethnic German foreman Novak was deemed "not so good"[13] and "cruel,"[14] but he was certainly not the chief symbol of evil at Tartak in survivor memories. That dubious position was unquestionably held by Fiedler's secretary, Fräulein Lutz. She was uniformly remembered and judged to be "an evil person"[15] and a "sadist."[16] She was "feared"[17] and "very dangerous."[18]

Under the Fiedler-Piatek management team, Tartak produced ammunition crates and other wood products for the German military. It also became an extraordinarily unusual and highly desirable haven and refuge for Jews. In Tartak, the Jewish workers were fed and clothed better and lived in a much cleaner environment than in Strelnica and Majówka.[19] They were given the day off from work on Yom Kippur, and in the spring of 1944 they were provided with flour to make matzos for Passover.[20] Fiedler warned of imminent inspections and advised that the children in camp be hidden.[21] A number of workers there, through a combination of bribery on the one hand and the helpful support of Fiedler and Piatek on the other, were able to bring family members from one of the other camps to Tartak and effect unification of the remaining family.[22] But more important than any of these factors was the single most basic difference from Strelnica and Majówka: in Tartak the Jews did not live in constant fear of being shot.[23]

As a result, Tartak had no barbed-wire fences and armed guards.[24] That was unnecessary, because it was far more dangerous for Jews outside Tartak than on the inside. In an early and rare escape attempt in November 1942, one of the three escapees returned to camp voluntarily after several days. The other two did not survive.[25] Moreover, Fiedler assured his Jewish workers that as long as he was there, nothing would happen to them. According to Josef Kohs, who provided a very detailed and important early testimony in 1948, Fiedler had told them: "If he were to leave, we could do as we wanted. In this regard, he always referred to the lack of any guard."[26]

Despite the relatively enviable position Jewish workers held in Tartak in comparison to the Strelnica and Majówka camps, they did not entirely escape the twin scourge of typhus and terror. In January 1943, Fiedler was away on vacation, and Fräulein Lutz wielded much greater power in his absence. Despite the better sanitary conditions in Tartak, some prisoners there had nonetheless contracted typhus. But this potentially lethal information initially was kept hidden from the camp management. However, when Lutz became aware that some of the workers were ill, she summoned a Polish doctor, Cirkowicz, who diagnosed four men with typhus.[27] Fräulein Lutz then telephoned the police.[28] The prisoners were ordered to prepare four stretchers and were assured that the sick men would be taken to the hospital.[29]

On one crucial point accounts differ on the subsequent events—namely, whether Walther Becker himself came and personally gave the orders for what followed or merely sent some of his men to kill on his behalf.[30] Whatever the case concerning Becker's personal involvement, there is no dispute over what happened thereafter. The German police arrived at Tartak and ordered eight stretcher bearers to carry the four sick men out the front gate. The column did not turn toward the hospital but instead took the road to the Jewish cemetery. The stretcher bearers included Moshe Zucker carrying his son and Chaim Asch carrying his brother, as well as Abraham Rosenwald, and Naftula Korenwasser.[31] At the cemetery, the bearers were ordered to tip the stretchers over, so that the men they had been carrying were dumped facedown on the ground. The German police then stepped up behind their victims, revolvers drawn, and killed them with "neck shots." The bodies were thrown into a trench and covered.[32] According to Rosenwald, some of the victims were "not quite dead" when buried.[33] According to Korenwasser, there was detectable rattling in the throats of the victims when they were covered.[34] According to Asch, the German police carried out the execution "fully cold-blooded," as if they were slaughtering cattle.[35]

Though at least three Jewish women were also infected with typhus at Tartak, they escaped execution at the hands of the German police. One was successfully vouched for by Dr. Blum, a Jewish prisoner in camp, and removed from the group of four that was taken to the cemetery, though she in fact did have typhus.[36] One was dressed and sent off to work without being detected.[37] A third was successfully hidden in the laundry.[38] Once again, prisoner initiative was able to protect at least some potential victims from imminent death.

Between the first day at Tartak, when those caught trying to smuggle valuables or an infant into the camp were shot, and the last day, twenty-one months later, when many were killed trying to escape the final evacuation of the camp, these were the only shootings at Tartak. This event, therefore, was therefore indelibly imprinted on the memories of the Tartak survivors, even if the scale of typhus and terror at Tartak was small in comparison to that of Strelnica and Majówka.

PART IV

STABILIZATION

14

The Kolditz Era:
Summer–Fall 1943

Following the death of Meyer and the sudden departure of Althoff in the spring of 1943, the "mood was calm" in the Strelnica camp. Immediate improvements were felt, especially in that a clinic was set up to actually help the sick, and flour was smuggled into the camp to bake matzos for Passover.[1] In terms of the administrative history of the camps, there was a brief interlude on which neither subsequent German judicial investigations nor postwar survivor testimonies have shed much light. For several months, one of the investigators of the factory security department, Heribert von Merfort, held an interim appointment filling Althoff's position as *Abwehrbeauftragter* or deputy for security.[2] Meyer's position as head of the *Werkschutz* was temporarily held by a man named Rode or Roderich.[3] Waschek remained in charge of the day-to-day management of the camps. Then, in the summer of 1943, major changes took place. The factory division manager in charge of grenade production, Kurt Otto Baumgarten, took on the additional task of deputy for security. Walter Kolditz, a security employee of the Reichswerke Hermann Göring operations in Ostrowiec, was brought in as the new head of the *Werkschutz*, and Waschek was transferred to Ostrowiec. The hopelessly unsanitary camp at Strelnica was closed down, and its prisoners were moved to newly built barracks in an enlarged camp at Majówka. Additional groups of prisoners were brought into Majówka from more distant labor camps. And the SS in Radom—that is, the actual slaveholders who were renting their Jewish workers to the Braunschweig Steel Works in Starachowice—made a rare intervention from outside and imposed another massive selection on the camp population. It was this conjuncture of events that shaped the lives of the Starachowice slave laborers during the summer and fall of 1943.

The new deputy for security, Baumgarten, was born in Alsace in 1908 to German nationalist parents. The family was "expelled" in 1919 from territory returned to France by the Treaty of Versailles and moved to Thuringia, where Baumgarten took up an apprenticeship as a factory electrician. Working one-quarter time in 1932 at the height of the Great Depression, he joined the Nazi Party and the SA "Brownshirts." He served as an auxiliary policeman (wearing a *Hilfspolizei* armband) during the dissolution of the labor unions in the spring of 1933, and that same year he quit the more plebeian SA and joined the elite SS. He prospered professionally, and by 1940 he had been given responsibilities for factory security and had taken a training course in grenade production. At that point, one of his former employers, Franz Köhler, invited him to take over the division for grenade production at the munitions factory of the Braunschweig Steel Works in Starachowice, where he began work on August 1, 1941. Two years later, he added the responsibilities of *Abwehrbeauftrager* to his duties.[4]

Baumgarten was visually remembered by the Jewish slave laborers for his summer costume of leather shorts (*Lederhosen*) and Tyrolean hat.[5] He also could not help but be remembered somewhat positively in light of his predecessor. Compared to Althoff, Baumgarten was "not at all as bad,"[6] "more decent,"[7] and "not as feared."[8] Most important, Baumgarten was fundamentally different in terms of his relationship with the Jews, especially the camp elite. While Althoff was "feared" and "dangerous," Baumgarten was approachable, pragmatic, and greedy—in short, quite corruptible. The pragmatism he expressed to postwar judicial investigators was not entirely mendacious. In addition to the "humanitarian reasons" that allegedly moved him, Baumgarten noted that "it was in the interest of the factory to sustain the workforce and raise productivity."[9] Furthermore, he noted, "The factory had to make a fixed payment to the police for each Jew. For this reason and also other reasons, it was interested that the Jews remain able to work."[10]

By his own admission, Baumgarten met with the Jewish camp leadership nearly every other day, listened to their grievances, and addressed their concerns when possible. In his own self-serving postwar account, he emphasized the improvements that occurred after he took up his new post. The camp food allotment was brought directly from the supplier to the camp rather than through the factory, where it had been regularly pilfered before delivery. A camp bakery was constructed. Sanitation and housing conditions were improved. He tolerated the presence of children in the camp and even warned of imminent inspections, so they could be hidden. He permitted the camp leaders to live with their wives in private quarters and provided them with passes to go into town and conduct business. He sharply limited authorized entry into the camp, leaving internal affairs in the hands of the Jewish *Lagerrat* and *Lagerpolizei* and keeping the Ukrainian guards outside the fence.[11]

All of this was at least partially true but far from the whole truth. Baumgarten had realized that by negotiating with and extorting rather than killing his Jewish workers, he could increase factory production as well as line his own pockets. As Jeremiah Wilczek's son Abraham testified later, Baumgarten took little interest in the day-to-day running of the camp. "He negotiated over work issues and other matters again and again with the Jewish council and also had himself paid a constant flow of bribes."[12] According to Chanka Laks, the camp clerk, Baumgarten was seldom in camp. "I remember, however, that repeatedly collections of money, etc., were carried out for Baumgarten."[13] Baumgarten's insatiable greed for bribes was well known even among prisoners without connections to the camp leadership.[14]

One upshot of the symbiotic relationship developing between Baumgarten and the Jewish leadership was the departure of Waschek without replacement. His functions were largely taken over by the *Lagerrat*, symbolized most visibly by the fact that it now took custody of his keys, particularly those to the supply room. Abraham Wilczek surmised that the camp leadership wanted Waschek removed without replacement because he had posed difficulties for their emerging black market or underground economic operations.[15] Baumgarten, in contrast, had little concern for what happened inside the camp as long as order was kept, the Jewish workers were productive, and he received his bribes.

Baumgarten's empowering of the camp elite in return for personal enrichment and an intensified but utilitarian exploitation of Jewish labor set the parameters within which camp culture developed over the following year. The Jewish workers experienced marginally better living conditions and were far more secure against the threat of arbitrary killing. But they were forced to work very hard, and the highly nonegalitarian and hierarchical social structure within the prisoner community became even more pronounced. All prisoners benefited to some degree from the new system—certainly by comparison with the Althoff regime of terror—but the benefits were not shared equally. Growing tensions and resentments within the prisoner community were one inevitable result.

If the distant figure of Baumgarten hovered over and shaped camp life for the next year, the summer and fall months of 1943 were more immediately dominated by the closer presence of another German, Walter Kolditz. Born in 1911, he joined the Nazi Party and the SA in 1930. In 1932, he left the SA and entered the SS. A butcher and slaughterer by trade, he also picked up work as a factory watchman in Braunschweig.[16] It was presumably through this latter job that he was recruited to become a security guard for the Braunschweig Steel Works in Ostrowiec. In the summer of 1943, he was appointed the new head of the *Werkschutz* for the company's operations in Starachowice.

Many witnesses who later commented about Kolditz could not help but note his most striking physical characteristic—namely, his extreme obesity. According to one survivor, he was "so fat" one could not even see the motorcycle he rode into camp.[17] Kolditz presided over the closure of the irredeemably squalid camp at Strelnica and the transfer of its prisoners to newly built barracks in an enlarged camp at Majówka. For the former inmates of Strelnica, Majówka was clearly a "better" camp—more spacious in its layout and less restrictive in its regulations.[18] With a single wire separating the men's and women's barracks, people could easily mingle and visit after work.[19] In summer, prisoners could also sleep outside on the ground to escape the bedbugs.[20]

Kolditz also made clear to the prisoners his determination to keep the camp clean, in a vain attempt to combat the threat of typhus. Indeed, he wanted Majówka to be a "model of cleanliness."[21] To this end, Kolditz assembled all the prisoners and kept them outside for several days in September while the barracks were fumigated. He also ordered that everything left in the barracks—including whatever possessions the prisoners had managed to amass but had not carried with them—be collected and burned.[22] Intended as a measure to end recurrent outbreaks of typhus whenever new shipments of prisoners not yet immune to the disease arrived in camp, it was unsuccessful. Inadequate washing facilities and lack of clean clothing precluded successful elimination of the lice that carried the typhus rickettsia.

Five new groups of prisoners arrived in Starachowice during the Kolditz regime: 156 from Wolanów near Radom on July 17; sixty-six from Tomaszów-Mazowiecki on September 5; sixty-eight from Mokoszyn near Sandomierz on September 16; eighty-nine from Radom on October 15; and ninety-four from Cracow on November 18, 1943.[23] The prisoners from Wolanów had been constructing barracks for a German army training facility to be built on the site of a former prisoner-of-war camp where virtually all the Soviet prisoners had died of starvation and disease. When their construction work was finished in July 1943, the camp was liquidated and its workers were split up and sent as reinforcements to work camps in Bliżyn and Starachowice.[24] The Jews from Tomaszów-Mazowiecki had worked there as a cleanup commando following the liquidation of the ghetto, and they were transferred to Starachowice when that task was done.[25] Mokoszyn was an SS-run agricultural estate where a small number of Jews from Sandomierz had found refuge, until it was closed and its workers transferred to Starachowice.[26] The Cracow prisoners were transferred from the concentration camp at Płaszów under the notorious commandant Amon Göth.[27]

Four themes are repeated in the testimonies of the newcomers concerning their transfer to the Majówka camp in Starachowice. First, they found that the physical labor in the factories was extremely hard and exhausting.[28] Second, the old prisoners appeared to them to be poorly fed and dressed in dirty rags.[29] Third, the camp was lice-infested, and the new contingents from Mokoszyn and Płaszów in particular were immediately swept by a renewed outbreak of typhus.[30] Fourth, their initial encounter with the Jewish camp police and camp administration was very negative.

Two prisoners noted that en route to Starachowice, the Ukrainian guard tried to rob them of their valuables.[31] But no fewer than four witnesses said it was the Jewish camp authorities who tried to strip them of all their possessions upon arrival. A newcomer from Wolanów noted that when his group arrived, they were told to put everything they had on a table.[32] Another newcomer from Wolanów described how they were met by a Jewish policeman who asked them to hand over their money for safekeeping.[33] And Mendel Kac, perhaps the most trenchant critic of the Starachowice camp elite vis-à-vis the strict but more egalitarian regime of the Jewish leadership in Wolanów, described how they were met by Rachmil Wolfowicz upon arrival and asked to turn over all their possessions for cleaning and storage. They were then introduced to Szaja Langleben, the most hated camp policeman, as their new "boss."[34] One newcomer from Tomaszów-Mazowiecki judged that while the Ukrainians were bad, the Jewish police were even worse. "They robbed from you. They stole from you. They took everything you had. . . . It's a shame to say it, but it's true."[35]

Prisoners transferred from the Płaszów concentration camp run by the notorious Amon Göth had a somewhat different standard of comparison. They had no property to be taken, but they were "amazed" to find privileged Jews living in separate quarters with their families still intact. For them, the chief benefit of the transfer to Starachowice—despite the unsanitary conditions, hard work, inadequate rations, and inequality vis-à-vis the privileged and local prisoners—was the noticeable "absence of terror." Moreover, the Ukrainian guards "never interfered with our lives inside the camp." And the camp leadership could intercede with the factory director to stop excessive abuse and arrange for "better treatment" of Jewish workers at the factory.[36]

Four other newcomers all noted explicitly that they had been extremely lucky to have had some kind of connection with one of the camp elite—in this case, Wilczek, Einesman, or Rubenstein—and how important this had been for their receiving an easier work assignment or extra food.[37] And a few newcomer families entered the camp with children and apparently possessed the resources to purchase the right to live together with their children in the family barracks of the camp elite.[38] The bulk of the newcomers, in contrast, had no such connections or resources. They found themselves at the bottom of the camp hierarchy and felt greatly disadvantaged.

The single most traumatic and tragic event of the Kolditz era was unquestionably the great camp selection of November 8, 1943, in which as many as 160 prisoners lost their lives. As in the case of the Bugaj Forest selection and massacre in early March 1943, this selection seems also to have been imposed by SS authorities in Radom and thus was impervious to mitigation through bribery and economic self-interest. From the beginning of the implementation of the Final Solution, Heinrich Himmler and his deputy Reinhard Heydrich had been skeptical about the claims of businessmen producing for the war economy concerning the indispensability of Jewish labor. As Heydrich had noted, even as early as October 1941: "There is in any case the danger that above all, those in the economic sector will in numerous cases claim their Jewish workers as indispensable and no one will make the effort to replace them with other workers. But this would undo the plan for a total resettlement of the Jews from the territories occupied by us."[39] Himmler remained intensely suspicious of the ideological purity of those valuing Jewish labor. He threatened harsh consequences for anyone who opposed him "with alleged armaments interests" but "in reality merely wanted to support the Jews and their business."[40] When Himmler ordered the liquidation of the remnant ghettos of the General Government in the spring of 1943, many desperate Jews turned increasingly to resistance, however hopeless. With the Warsaw ghetto uprising in April/May, increased Jewish flight to the partisan resistance in the forests, and the Treblinka death-camp breakout in early August 1943, Himmler's animus against the exploitation of Jewish labor was increasingly aggravated by his paranoia about Jews as the source of anti-Nazi resistance.

Himmler's response was to begin the systematic liquidation of the Jewish slave-labor camps under his control. The road-construction camps of eastern Galicia were liquidated between late June and late July 1943, and the work camps in the eastern Cracow district were closed in early September. Himmler's murderous assault on Jewish slave labor climaxed with the horrific *Erntefest* ("harvest festival") massacres of November 3–4, 1943. Following the breakout at the Sobibor death camp in the Lublin district in mid-October, and apparently not trusting even

local SS camp managers to overcome their vested interest in the exploitation of Jewish labor, Himmler summoned SS and police units from
all over the General Government, and even as far away as Czech territory. These units massacred 42,000 Jewish workers in the Lublin district
camps (especially Majdanek, Trawniki, and Poniatowa) in two days—
the single largest shooting action of the Final Solution, exceeding even
that at Babi Yar by nearly 10,000 victims.[41]

The factory slave-labor camps of the Radom district just to the west
escaped total liquidation at this time but did not emerge unscathed. Early
on November 8, 1943,[42] before the night shift had returned to camp,[43]
Kolditz, another German officer of the *Werkschutz* named Willi Schroth,[44]
the Ukrainian guards, and by some accounts Baumgarten,[45] descended
upon Majówka, accompanied by at least two large trucks.[46] The Ukrainian guards surrounded the camp and set up machine guns.[47] All prisoners
were ordered out of the barracks for a selection.

Accounts differ on just how the selection was conducted. According
to one version, prisoners filed past Kolditz and he pulled aside some
older men but especially concentrated on older women and children.[48]
According to a second version, Kolditz and his helpers sought out the
weak among the assembled prisoners.[49] According to a third account,
Jeremiah Wilczek passed on a German order that all children, elderly,
and sick had to separate.[50] And in yet another version, a list proposed by
the *Lagerrat* was read out that included older men, women, children,
and weaker people. They were joined by mothers who would not be
separated from their children.[51]

Those selected were placed in a barbed-wire enclosure to keep them
separate from the other prisoners before they were loaded onto the waiting trucks.[52] Kolditz then entered the hospital barracks and called for
everyone who could get up to do so. Those who were well enough to
dress and walk out were allowed to leave.[53] The others were either taken
to the trucks or, if too weak even to move, were shot on the spot.[54]

As before on such occasions, some Jewish prisoners found ingenious
ways to save themselves or family members or were rescued through the
intervention of others. Those not so fortunate were faced with excruciating choices concerning family separation and survival. Eleven-year-old
Goldie Szachter—just recovering from typhus—and her forty-one-year-

old mother were prime targets for this selection. They both put on rouge and lipstick to hide the paleness of their faces, and Goldie wore high-heeled shoes for added height. Kolditz looked past both of them.[55] Meir Lewental knew his younger brother had no assigned job and was thus on the "black list" for deportation. He took his brother with him to his construction job and thereby saved him.[56] Sesha Bromberger and her sister worked as knitters in the barracks for skilled craftsmen and had managed to get their father placed with them as a tailor, though he had no such skills. On the day of the selection, she was unsuccessful in hiding him, but she was successful in persuading the Jewish policeman who found him that he belonged with the skilled craftsmen and he was released.[57] Ten-year-old Rachel Waksberg had been transferred from Wolanów along with her mother and older and younger brothers. On the day of the November selection, her younger brother hid successfully, but she was found and put on the truck. The Jewish policeman Turek advised her to jump and run, but she was intercepted by a Ukrainian guard and put back on the truck. Turek then intervened and got her released. Only later did she discover that her forty-five-year-old mother had been taken.[58] Thirteen-year-old Eva Mangarten and her mother were both selected by Kolditz, but a Jewish policeman vouched to Kolditz for her claim to be sixteen, and she was released. When her mother jumped down from the truck as well, Kolditz struck her and forced her back on.[59] When Rachel Borman's seven-year-old youngest sister was found and taken, her middle sister joined her. But Rachel—trying to save at least one family member—told a Jewish policeman that the middle sister worked in the factory, and he took her off the truck. The youngest sister went to her death alone.[60]

Several young women who tried to join their mothers were stopped from doing so on the grounds that they were still capable of work.[61] Abramek Naiman's mother had never fully recovered from the savage mauling she had suffered on the marketplace one year earlier. Then, three days before the selection, she had suffered an injury to her hand and received permission to remain in the barracks for a few days rather than go to work. When she was selected, she called from behind the wire to her son to go to Wilczek, but he told young Abramek he could do nothing. When Abramek then tried to join his mother, he was kicked and beaten senseless. Only when he recovered did he learn that his father—a debilitated typhus patient in the hospital barracks who had been shot on the spot—was also dead, and he was now an orphan.[62]

Aside from the shootings in the hospital barracks (and several other individual shootings for which there are only single testimonies),[63] there was one additional killing inside the camp so memorable that it was mentioned by many survivors. After the prisoners had been summoned from the barracks and the Jewish police had searched and certified that the barracks were all empty, a Jewish woman was nonetheless discovered hiding. The Jewish policeman responsible for the search of that barracks was Jeremiah Wilczek's son-in-law, Chaim Kogut (who had married his daughter just the night before the ghetto liquidation).[64] Kolditz personally shot Kogut in front of many witnesses, and accounts of the unique event—the very first killing of a Jewish policeman—quickly spread among other prisoners.

There was apparently more behind the Kolditz killing of Kogut than the latter's failure to uncover the hidden woman. When Kolditz arrived in Starachowice, he brought with him two Jewish policemen from Ostrowiec with whom he had worked.[65] As no further mention of these two men is found in the testimonies, apparently they proved to be inconsequential and did not provide Kolditz with control over the camp police. Sometime thereafter, Kolditz replaced Jeremiah Wilczek as commander of the Jewish police with a Jew from Szydłowiec, Abraham Finkler. For what followed, we have only the testimonies of Finkler and his future wife.[66] According to their account, following his appointment as the new head of camp police, Finkler was put in charge of improving the drainage system at Majówka. Rather than obligating anyone to compulsory labor, he offered extra bread rations to those who volunteered to do the additional physical work after they returned from their factory jobs. The extra rations produced many eager volunteers, and the job was completed in two weeks. Finkler was then denounced by the *Lagerrat* for "wasting" bread, summoned by Baumgarten's two security investigators, Heribert von Merfort and Gerhard Kaschmieder, and threatened with a firing squad. However, the decent von Merfort blocked Kaschmieder's rush to summary execution and accepted Finkler's explanation. He was spared but was stripped of his new position after just three weeks. Wilczek then resumed his previous position.

In the Finklers' interpretation, this event simply demonstrated the evil machinations of the corrupt *Lagerrat* and explained why "in principle no decent man" would ever want to be head of the camp police. But there was probably another dimension to the event beyond the *Lagerrat*'s defending its privileges against an outsider by undermining Wilczek's temporary successor. Wilczek and the *Lagerrat* were allied with Baumgarten in a cozy and corrupt arrangement that impeded Kolditz's own attempt to gain total control over the camp by putting his own minions into key positions. As one perceptive eyewitness to the Kolditz murder of Kogut observed, "It is possible—so I heard at the time—that Kolditz wanted to revenge himself on the chief of the Jewish camp police Wilczek, whom he did not like, by killing his son-in-law."[67]

Whatever the hidden agenda behind Kolditz's unprecedented shooting of a Jewish policeman, it did not alter the terrible fate awaiting the 150 to 160 Jews, mostly older women and children, loaded onto the trucks. They were driven away to Firlej, near Radom, accompanied by Kolditz, Schroth, and some Ukrainian guards.[68] The Jews were forced out of the trucks and marched between armed SS men standing every six feet through a gate that opened onto a field with a tent and a stone building with a smoking chimney. There were also other trucks unloading Jews. Schroth assumed that Jews had been brought in from all over and that they were going to be gassed. But he did not admit to witnessing their actual fate.[69]

The Jews in Majówka had their worst fears confirmed in two ways. First, the clothing of the victims was quickly returned to camp for redistribution, and at least one prisoner soon saw another prisoner wearing her mother's familiar coat.[70] From other sources they heard that the Jews who had been taken away in the trucks had been killed. Most accounts assumed they had been shot, but there were also rumors that they had been gassed,[71] blown up,[72] or buried alive.[73]

In the Firlej *Aktion*, the victims were taken from Starachowice, joined with victims from other camps in a coordinated operation, and killed by SS executioners at a distant site. And this happened within a week of the great *Erntefest* killings in the nearby Lublin district. Every indication points to this as being a killing action planned and ordered by the SS in Radom, not a local initiative of the Starachowice factory managers.[74] The German industrialists using Jewish slave labor in the Radom district may have been able to prevent the total extermination of their Jewish workforce, but it would appear that Himmler exacted a grievous price in terms of the systematic selection and murder of Jews who were deemed less productive or nonproductive.

Even if the initiative came from elsewhere, the killings at Firlej unleashed a sadistic bloodlust in Kolditz. Apparently one woman, Mrs. Schwarzman, managed to escape the killing field at Firlej and, having nowhere else to go, made her way back to Majówka. There her presence was "betrayed," and she was beaten and shot by Kolditz.[75] Ten days after the Firlej selection, the contingent of Cracow Jews arrived from Płaszów. Two brothers tried to escape the camp to rejoin their sister and were caught. For the amusement of Kolditz and the Ukrainian guard, one brother was ordered to beat the other with a multitailed whip, which he did. When one brother was then ordered to kill the other, he refused. On Kolditz's order, a Ukrainian guard then shot both brothers.[76] These torture-killings were the last murders perpetrated by the increasingly unhinged Kolditz. Like Althoff before him, he was dismissed, in this case largely for his growing conflict with Baumgarten.

Kolditz already had a reputation among fellow Germans for drunkenness, womanizing with local Poles, and being difficult to work with.[77] Baumgarten presumably perceived the shooting of Kogut as a challenge to his own position, for he responded by barring Kolditz from entering the Majówka camp, though he continued to allow Kolditz's subordinate, Willi Schroth, to do so.[78] Schroth's willingness to move against his direct superior, Kolditz, and ally with Baumgarten, was clear from another episode. According to Schroth, he was invited to Kolditz's apartment. Upon arrival, he found Kolditz dressed only in his shirt with two Polish women, one of whom Kolditz offered to him while he busied himself with the other. Unable to reach climax, Kolditz ordered Schroth to take both women to the forest and shoot them. Instead, Schroth went to Kaschmieder and informed on his boss.[79] Suspended from his duties, the enraged Kolditz approached Baumgarten in the factory canteen and hit him.[80] Baumgarten arranged for a disciplinary transfer to Warsaw,[81] and the Kolditz era came to an abrupt end.

15

Jewish Work

The actual place of Jewish work in Nazi ideology and policy has been a matter of dispute. Seizing on the phrase "destruction through labor" or *Vernichtung durch Arbeit*,[1] some have portrayed Jewish work as merely instrumental to the Nazi ideological goal of extermination. In one such formulation, Jewish work was not only a method for the destruction of Jewish life but also an additional means for the gratuitous torment of Jewish victims and the gratification of German perpetrators through the systematic infliction of economically wasteful suffering. The purpose of Jewish work was punishment, torture, and debilitation, not economic production.[2] Others have dismissed Nazi ideology as "propaganda" or "rhetoric" and characterized the Nazi persecution and mass murder of the Jews as the by-product of economically motivated and calculated decisions and priorities.[3] The position for which I am arguing, and which is joined by several other historians who have recently published on the subject,[4] is that the German use of Jewish slave labor was not a matter of consensus and varied so much according to time and place that no single phrase (such as "destruction through labor") can capture some presumed consistency and essence of Nazi policy. Thus, even during the period of systematic extermination, when ideological goals enjoyed their greatest priority over utilitarian considerations, there always were exceptions. Indeed, one justification for a case study like this one of a single complex of factory slave-labor camps is that it can provide a detailed look at one historically demonstrated variant of the productive use of Jewish slave labor within the parameters set by an ideologically driven policy of extermination.

Jewish work in the Starachowice camps can be divided into two basic categories: primary work for factory production of munitions and ancillary work for camp maintenance. Work in the factories was, of course, the very reason for the existence of the camps in the first place. Factory production in turn had two components: the blast furnace and smelter in the lower factory in the Kamienna River Valley for the production of steel, and the higher-up munitions factory near the Bugaj Forest for the manufacture of shell and grenade casings. These products were then packed in wooden crates produced by the workers at Tartak. The explosives for the munitions were produced in the factories in nearby Skarżysko-Kamienna.[5]

The Radom district was home to additional munitions production sites in Radom, Kielce, Ostrowiec, Radomsko, and Częstochowa as well as Starachowice and Skarżysko-Kamienna. On June 30, 1943, the Radom district munitions plants employed more than 52,000 workers, of whom more than 14,000 were Jewish slave laborers. In Starachowice, 1,239 Jewish workers (not including those at Tartak) constituted nearly 10 percent of a total factory workforce of 12,449.[6] Since the Jewish workers did not have the same high degree of absenteeism that characterized the Polish workers, they were responsible for an even higher percentage of production. And by the spring of 1944, the production of ammunition in the Radom district provided one-third of the needs of the German infantry.[7] Jewish work here was clearly not contrived as a gratuitous means of torment but rather was an essential contribution to the German war effort. This in turn explains why even Himmler could not extend his murderous and maniacal campaign of systematic Jewish labor-camp liquidation into the Radom district after the *Erntefest* operation had been completed in the neighboring Lublin district. It also explains why in this particular case the Jewish strategy of survival through labor was not entirely illusory.

If military and economic exigency preserved the existence of the Jewish slave laborers in Starachowice, it also provided the spur for the hyperintensive exploitation of that labor. Work was organized into both three

eight-hour and two twelve-hour shifts, depending upon how strenuous the jobs were.[8] Added to these eight- and twelve-hour workdays, of
course, was the time needed for the march from the camp to the factories
and back. The most physically difficult jobs were of three kinds: first,
those that involved working in tremendous heat in very close proximity
to the factory furnaces;[9] second, those that involved hard lifting, such as
loading and pushing carts of coal or scrap metal to the smelter or stacking
heavy shells;[10] and third, those that involved working with the acid baths
for newly produced casings.[11] Jobs that were somewhat less physically
taxing were highly desired. Assigned to a controller's job, one survivor
remarked that relative to others, "I had it good."[12] Another survivor hurt
his hand in an industrial accident but had the good fortune to be working for a foreman who had been a prewar customer in his mother's shop,
so the manager reassigned him to the warehouse. There he was able to
set up a smuggling business, "so that I was living pretty well."[13]

The pace of work was set by very high quotas that had to be met,
and factory foreman imposed such quotas brutally to pressure Jewish workers for higher productivity. Years later, many survivors could
still remember precisely the daunting quotas they raced to meet.[14] For
instance, when Jewish women replaced Polish women in the section producing bomb fuses, the daily quota was immediately doubled from 250
to 500.[15] The sanctions for not meeting quotas were compelling: being
kept at work through the following shift, beating, or even accusation
of sabotage.[16] The ultimate sanction, of course, was the danger of being
listed as *arbeitsunfähig* or "incapable of work," with lethal consequences
if a selection were held.

The job assignment directly affected each slave laborer's "quality
of life" in camp and ultimate fate. The same people who staffed the
Jewish labor division within the German labor office in Starachowice,
Izak Laks and his daughter Chanka, kept the index-card files of workers in Majówka and Strelnica, respectively. They received instructions
from the camp council, which in turn relayed from the German factory
managers the numbers of workers that needed to be allotted to various
tasks each day.[17] At least several survivors were convinced that they had
received especially difficult work assignments for being in the bad graces
of the camp council or the camp police.[18]

The work experience was shaped not only by the job assigned but also by the nature of the Polish foreman and the German supervisor to whom one was assigned. Some Polish foremen took advantage of their position to abuse Jewish workers.[19] Others were strict but not vicious.[20] At least one had the reputation of screaming and kicking when there was a German present but otherwise was not harsh.[21] Some were simply extortionate and corrupt. They tormented their Jewish workers until they were given gifts or payments and then provided easier jobs for those who paid up. For instance, Chaim Flancbaum gave his Polish foreman cigarettes and vodka and was then assigned indoor rather than outdoor work in the middle of winter.[22] Some Jewish workers remembered significant differences among their Polish supervisors. Leo Bach, who worked at the physically taxing job of pushing carts of ore to the smelter, said that the weighmasters were "good Polish individuals" who, "out of sympathy for us," overlooked incorrect loads, but two of the Polish supervisors went out of their way to make life miserable for their Jewish workers.[23]

Among the German supervisors, von Schwarzer, who was in charge of the blast furnace, was "cruel" and notorious for making his Jewish laborers work double shifts.[24] In contrast, Tempel in the shell division was deemed "very decent."[25] Willi Frania at the new press had a reputation as "proper" and "decent."[26] But the most preferred German supervisor was Bruno Pappe at the small forge. He treated his 120 Jewish workers decently and even allowed the establishment of a separate eating room—a so-called *Judenstube*—where they did not have to wait until Polish workers were finished eating to get whatever was left. He pronounced separate eating space for his Jewish workers as being "in line with our ideology." He also allowed the baking of matzos there. He permitted his Jewish interpreter, Josef Friedenson, to arrange for more workers than were needed, including women, but especially those who were endangered and needed a place safe from mistreatment and harassment. When Kolditz insisted that Symcha Mincberg, the former head of the *Judenrat*, work at the factory, the camp council placed him with Pappe. The same arrangement was made for some older Talmudic scholars who arrived in camp with the Cracow transport. There was, in short, a "different atmosphere" in Pappe's small forge than elsewhere in the factories.[27]

Since factory production of munitions was the labor camps' reason for being, the vast majority of inmates clearly worked for that purpose. But the existence of the camps in turn created the need for camp maintenance and thus required a number of internal jobs as well. Many of these—the camp council, camp police, and barracks supervisors (*Blockältesten*)— were held by members of the camp's male elite. Jews who supervised other Jews through the camp administration were spared factory labor.

But there were also two other types of internal camp jobs. One kind was for providing special services to the Germans. Most important in this regard were the skilled artisans and craftsmen, such as tailors and shoemakers. Even before the liquidation of the Wierzbnik ghetto, the Germans had confiscated some items such as sewing machines and had set up a workshop of skilled craftsmen known as the *Konsum*.[28] It was supervised by a man named Otto von Ribbeck, who was considered "not bad." Of his two assistants, Neuman and Wunderlich, however, the latter was "very feared" for the frequent use of his ox whip.[29] When the ghetto was liquidated, the skilled craftsmen were moved into their own barracks in Majówka, some accompanied by their wives and children. They had their own kitchen, received more food, and were dressed "like humans" rather than in rags.[30] The craftsmen of the *Konsum* produced uniforms, boots, and other such items highly desired by the Germans. Several entrepreneurial women who engaged in dressmaking for the Germans on the side were given nondemanding cover jobs as well.[31] One man found himself occupying a special niche as personal barber to Kolditz and the Ukrainian guards. The camp council was instructed to provide him with decent clothing once he had been assigned this job.[32]

The other internal jobs, in the camp kitchen and the camp laundry, were held more frequently—though not exclusively—by women. Assignment to these coveted jobs was usually obtained in one of four ways. One was through connections. The relatives of the camp elite often had positions in the kitchen.[33] Another was through payment. Nacha Baum was a short and skinny girl of seventeen. Before her parents were taken away, her father not only procured her a work card but also arranged for her to have a job peeling potatoes in the camp kitchen. After six months, with no further help from her parents, she lost that job and was sent off to heavy labor.[34] Rachela Szachter and her mother soon found the factory work dangerously exhausting. Rachela's younger sister subsequently wrote:

> Father was able to arrange through Shloime Ehnesman, now a member of the Judenrat, for Mother and Rachela to work in the camp laundry. Favors such as these were by no means had for the asking. While it is true that Father and Shloime Ehnesman were boyhood friends, and that Shloime may have been more inclined to extend a favor to Father than to other Jews even without payment, special treatment was gained for a price. *Lapowka* (bribery) was a byword, a way of life in camp. Father paid off Ehnesman hand-somely for the countless acts of intervention on behalf of our family, though not necessarily for each one.[35]

In addition to connections and payment, however, sometimes people seem to have been assigned to the kitchen and laundry simply out of mercy. Mirjam and Halina Zylberberg, two teenage sisters from Płock, found themselves alone in Strelnica when their father, working the night shift, was sent to Majówka and the rest of the family was deported to Treblinka. Without any connections or financial means, they were none-theless given jobs in the kitchen and laundry, respectively.[36] A weaken-ing Salek Benedikt, on a doctor's recommendation, was allowed to work for one week in the kitchen, where he could regain a little strength by working less and eating more.[37] And finally, some worked in the kitchen or laundry on overtime, peeling potatoes and washing clothing for oth-ers who had the means to hire them as substitutes.[38]

Jewish work at Starachowice was a serious matter of economic utility and military exigency to the Germans. For the Jewish slave laborers, it was a matter of life and death, both in justifying their continuing exis-tence in spite of the German goal of total extermination and in affecting if and how they survived the conditions under which they were enslaved. This latter issue of surviving camp conditions was closely related not only to work but also to two other key factors—namely, food and the camp's underground economy.

16

Food, Property, and the Underground Economy

Even when German employers valued Jewish labor and wanted it to be productive, and furthermore understood that starving Jews were less productive than adequately nourished ones, they invariably encountered a systemic problem within the Nazi empire. The ravages and demands of war had created a general food shortage that reached crisis proportions by 1942. Among all the populations of Nazi-occupied Europe whose claims on an inadequate food supply were being weighed and prioritized, Jews invariably were placed last in line.[1] Thus, even though the Jewish factory slave-labor camps in the Radom district were not liquidated, the prisoners remained undernourished. As one Starachowice survivor noted, the Jews there did not die from how little the Germans fed them but they could not live from it either.[2] A Jewish strategy of survival through labor, therefore, was burdened with terrible ironies. It depended not only on Jews buying their own enslavement through the purchase of work permits and providing labor indispensable to the war effort, thereby prolonging German rule, but also to no small extent on supplementing the inadequate German food supply through their own ingenuity and efforts.

In the early months of camp life, typhus and the Althoff terror understandably eclipsed concerns about food. At that time, the prisoners received only two meals per day—imitation coffee and a piece of bread in the morning and watery soup and a piece of bread in the evening. When the German factory management ended the Althoff policy of killing the sick, they also improved the food supply. A third meal of soup and bread was added at midshift on the factory premises.[3] In his postwar defense, Kurt Otto Baumgarten took full credit for this improvement, claiming that he arranged for the direct delivery of supplies to the camp council rather than through the factory (where the Jewish allotment had been regularly pilfered) and for the construction of a bakery in Majówka to prepare the bread ration on the spot.[4] As virtually all accounts agree that living conditions improved at this point, and an improvement in food supply was consistent with Baumgarten's interests at the time, this is a rare case where self-serving postwar German testimony seems credible.

The camp soup, which alongside bread was the mainstay of the prisoner diet, was a watery brew flavored with potato peels, turnips, cabbage, or rutabaga. A little marmalade was occasionally added for the morning bread or a little horsemeat to the evening soup. The watery soup was so foul in taste and smell that two prisoners testified that, despite the hunger, they went through the entire twenty-one months in the Starachowice camps unable to eat it.[5] The factory soup, according to one witness, was marginally better, made with vegetables and fish.[6]

Everyone sought to supplement these meager rations. Some prisoners mentioned that they survived by virtue of charity or connections. A number of survivors offered testimony that at least some Poles gave away food at the factory "out of pity" or "sympathy."[7] More noted that they had relatives or friends working in the camp kitchen who provided them with extra rations.[8] For example, Eliahu Koslowski described how he sometimes worked a second shift, substituting for Moniek Rubenstein. In exchange, the latter would exploit his relationship with his uncle, Jankiel Rubenstein, who was in charge of the camp kitchen, to procure meat and potatoes. "If you had influence, you could survive," Koslowski concluded.[9]

For the vast majority of prisoners, however, the most common way of supplementing the food supply was simply through purchase. Sometimes this was done directly in camp. According to Mendel Kac, scarce items such as meat and sugar, which had been distributed equally to all prisoners when available in Wolanów, were hoarded and sold to those with means by the camp council in Majówka. The kitchen was controlled by relatives of the camp council, so there were no witnesses to their stealing, Kac charged.[10] Another newcomer from Wolanów was equally indignant and accusatory at finding even prepared food for sale in the camp. "So how did they get it? Well, they stole from the kitchen, they cooked and they sold to people. So if you had enough money, you could buy. . . . They had like two restaurants in the camp. Our Jews, our Jews could do it. . . . it was really bad."[11]

The main market for food, however, was not between privileged and wealthy Jews inside the camp but between Jews and Poles outside the camp. The initial resources for this exchange were twofold: the valuables that at least some of the prisoners had brought into camp at considerable risk in defiance of the German demand to surrender them, and the clothing they were wearing or carried in their bundles. One survivor had worn a new topcoat to the marketplace and into camp, despite the warm weather. He subsequently bartered it for bread.[12] A prisoner transferred from Płaszów sold the good pair of boots he was wearing to buy food.[13] A refugee from Płock had refused to turn in her wedding ring and she had an extra dress. Both were bartered for bread.[14] Those who had more resources to begin with, and had prepared ahead of time, were somewhat better off. Goldie Szachter's father had carefully hidden valuables in the family's shoe heels and clothing that they wore into camp. They did not go hungry.[15] Channah Glatt had likewise kept her nerve and not surrendered the diamonds and gold she had carried to camp. Little by little, these were traded for bread.[16]

Exchanges between Jews and Poles usually took place at the factories. Ruth Rabinowicz had the task of carrying soup kettles from the factory kitchen to the mess hall. She would carry money with her and buy extra bread directly from the kitchen personnel.[17] If there was extra soup, the factory kitchen also sold it at one złoty per bowl. Groups of workers would also band together to buy loaves of bread that Polish workers brought to the factory.[18] Eli Chaim Oberman met each day with the same Polish worker, who brought him a bottle of goat's milk that he drank on the spot.[19] For many, buying potatoes at the factories was particularly convenient, because they could be cooked in no time by placing them near one of the furnaces.[20]

Exchanges took place elsewhere as well. Those who had Polish friends in town could buy from them during the march to or from work. As the column went around a corner and those behind the front guard were briefly out of sight of the rear guard, quick exchanges could be made between marching prisoners and those standing on the side of the road.[21] A person with means, Y'chiel Szachter, "arranged for himself to work outside the factory," collecting scrap iron for the smelter. "He had sought this position for himself . . . because this particular situation better enabled him to remain in contact with Poles," from whom he "bought food and other items."[22] As the camp regime became more relaxed, Poles even came to the fence to sell. They would take orders for delivery and set a time for the subsequent meeting and exchange.[23]

The valuables and clothing that individual Jews brought into camp initially, even for those most prepared and well stocked, were clearly exhaustible resources that did not suffice to continue buying supplementary food over a period of twenty-one months. For the continued importation of food, an underground camp economy had to be created and financed; for this, new sources of income had to be found or generated.

One major source of new funds was the property many of the interned Jews had left with Polish friends before the liquidation of the ghetto. Accessing such property was the key, and it was especially difficult for those not from Wierzbnik. One refugee from Szydłowiec had given her suitcase full of the possessions she had brought with her to "a very nice Polish guy." He subsequently brought bread and other items to her.[24] Another family from Szydłowiec had buried their gold and silver. They revealed the location to someone they trusted, who subsequently brought bread to them every so often.[25] The wealthy Szachter family from Bodzentyn had carefully buried many valuables whose locations were noted on a closely guarded treasure map. When funds were needed, they too placed their trust in a Pole and gave him the map with an agreement to split the proceeds. The Pole, a young Communist who was subsequently caught and executed for his underground activities, delivered the sack of gold and silver coins as agreed.[26]

Many native Wierzbnikers depended on the goodwill of friends, neighbors, and business associates with whom they had left property to deliver food or money periodically to the factory. Most Poles with whom property had been left proved to be "decent" and "honorable" in this regard.[27] In contrast to postwar attempts to recover property, there were surprisingly few complaints about Poles who were given property by Jewish friends and then refused to help while the Jews remained as workers in Starachowice. At certain times, it was much more practical and tempting for native Wierzbnikers to risk leaving camp in order to access their nearby valuables personally. For two groups, this involved little danger. At the unguarded and unfenced Tartak, people simply slipped out at night, went to their nearby homes, and gradually brought things back to the camp.[28] And the camp elite in Strelnica and Majówka could get passes to leave and visit town to conduct business.

For most prisoners, however, leaving camp and making contact with Poles to recover property or conduct business was both less frequent and more dangerous. These ventures outside of camp were thus remembered with particular vividness by those who undertook them. Fourteen-year-old Chaim Wajchendler made two such journeys. On the first occasion, he sneaked out of camp to the home of the woman with whom his younger brother was to have been hidden and who therefore had been given many of the family's possessions. She denied she had anything belonging to the Wajchendlers, but since Chaim had helped deliver the items in question, he knew where they were located. He simply grabbed a bolt of cloth and ran back to a point where he could join a column of workers returning to camp. On a second occasion, he went to the secretary of his father's lawyer, who gave him 200 złoty and three shirts. Caught by a Ukrainian guard trying to sneak back into camp, he was beaten and then let go.[29]

Icek Guterman bribed a Ukrainian guard to leave camp, visited a woman with whom the family had left possessions, and returned with a pillow, blanket, bread, sugar, flour, and beets. Before he was caught and beaten, he threw his booty over the fence to his waiting brother.[30] Nacha Baum slipped away from a column of workers marching to the factory, went to the man with whom her father had left his inventory of shoes from the family business, and presented him with a list of needs before rejoining her group of workers. On the march back to camp, she repeated the procedure, picking up the requested items. However, when she visited a Polish woman with whom the family had left other possessions, the latter threatened to call the police. Nacha grabbed one item she recognized and fled.[31]

Rosha Kogut persuaded a lenient Ukrainian guard to let her leave camp on the promise that she would return quickly. She went to former neighbors with whom her family had left furs and jewelry. They were terribly frightened by her presence, gave her a hot meal, wrapped up some things, and told her to leave quickly. Her father then traded her retrieved items at the factory.[32] Desperate for food, Josef Kaufman urged his teenage daughter to risk visiting the family with whom he had left property. She slipped out when a "decent" guard "looked away" and picked up bags of rice and farina from the family. Upon her return, she discovered the "decent" guard had been replaced, and she had to slip into camp under the wire.[33]

Abramek Naiman's mother had left two fur coats with one family. She slipped out, and they sheltered her for two nights while she arranged for the sale of the furs. Another family with whom they had left possessions, however, refused to give anything back. When his father fell ill, Abramek sneaked out of camp and begged an apothecary for medicine. Though he had no money, the apothecary gave him some medicine.[34] When her sister fell ill, Sala Glatt waited for the right guard to be on duty and then walked out of camp. She procured aspirin and other medicine from family friends, but she had to sneak back into camp upon return when she discovered the guard had changed.[35]

As in virtually every camp within the Nazi empire, the most enterprising prisoners sought to "organize"—to create some kind of private business or source of income to enhance their chances for survival. This was particularly urgent for prisoners from the outside, who did not have the same opportunity as native Wierzbnikers had to tap into reserves of hidden property. Salek Benedikt from Szydłowiec collected pieces of old clothing, which he took to his friend, a skilled hatmaker. Salek then sold the hats to Poles at work for potatoes, and in turn sold the potatoes to other prisoners.[36] Regina Rosenblatt from Płock made brooms and her brother-in-law made caps from blankets. On the days when "good" Ukrainian guards were on duty, these items were smuggled out of camp for sale.[37] Chaim Klajman had been assigned to a job in the warehouse and made the most of his opportunity. First he stole materials that he sold to shoemakers in camp. Then he arranged to be paid by someone on the outside to mark barrels in which he would place vodka from the warehouse supply for the Poles' vodka ration. "So I was living pretty well," he concluded.[38]

In addition to individual and small-group entrepreneurship in Majówka, more extensive production for the underground camp economy was also "organized." The skilled craftsmen of the *Konsum* produced not only high-quality customized products for the Germans on demand but also an array of consumer goods for sale to Poles on the black market. To be effective, this operation needed not only craftsmen but large numbers of scroungers to keep the craftsmen supplied with raw materials and smugglers to transport and sell the finished products. Eli Chaim Oberman from Kielce said he "had to do something" to survive. Knowing where leather belts from obsolete machinery had been stored in the warehouse, he cut off pieces and sold them to the camp shoemakers whenever he had the chance. In the other direction, he smuggled repaired shoes and clothing from the camp to the factory to sell to Poles.[39] Jakob Binstock from Szydłowiec smuggled products from the tailors and shoemakers to sell to Poles in the factory, then smuggled food bought from Poles back into camp.[40] Halina Firstenberg from Płock bought blouses that were sewn by girls in the camp and took them to the kitchen in the factory. There she exchanged the blouses for bread, which she took back to the girls who were sewing.[41] Jacob Szapszewicz from Szydłowiec sold caps made by camp tailors to Poles in the factory and then bought bread and potatoes, which he resold in camp for a profit.[42] It can be no mere coincidence that most of those smuggling the goods produced by the camp craftsmen were not native Wierzbnikers but rather outsiders who had to undertake such activities because they had no other economic resources on which to fall back.

Given wartime shortages, there was no lack of demand from the Polish side for goods produced in the camp. But an adequate supply of raw materials for *Konsum* production for that black market was clearly a problem that threatened the viability of the whole project. Here the camp council exercised its power on behalf of sustaining production for the black market (from which it clearly profited) rather than on behalf of internal distribution to alleviate the distress of ill-clad and ill-shod camp inmates. In the most notorious example, some 2,000 pairs of shoes arrived at Majówka from Majdanek. Most prisoners were desperate for new footwear to replace the worn-out shoes with which they had come to camp, but only about 100 pairs were distributed to those in favor. The rest were cut up and used to make shoe tops for wooden clogs and sold to Poles on the black market. The critical Mendel Kac was convinced that the camp council gave a cut to the craftsmen but kept most of the profits for itself.[43] The confiscated possessions of newcomers to the camp presumably served the same purpose. And when the clothing of Abramek Naiman's parents was shipped back from Firlej, he did not receive it as his property or inheritance. Rather, it was sold on the black market.[44]

The underground economy in Majówka was crucial in supplementing the inadequate food supply and financing the systematic bribing of German officials such as Baumgarten. In these ways, all prisoners in the camp benefited to some degree, even if they did not benefit equally. But the extent and nature of the underground economy also intensified the pervasive inequality within the prisoner community. Camp society was already divided between privileged and ordinary prisoners. Sharp differences in economic standing created a second division. Native Wierzbnikers with access to valuables that had been hidden with Poles had access to resources that outsiders and newcomers—with a few exceptions like the Szachters from Bodzentyn, who had both hidden wealth and ties to Einesman—did not have. As one survivor noted, the non-Wierzbnikers were in effect "double strangers," in that they were both part of a Jewish minority amid a Polish majority and outsiders and newcomers amid the native Wierzbnik Jews.[45] Lacking both outside resources and outside contacts, they faced a far greater challenge in coping with hardship and insinuating themselves into the camp's underground economy. Economic disadvantage was of course compounded by a sense of exclusion from, and indeed exploitation by, the privileged Jews of the camp elite, in a system in which the dispensing of favors from above invariably required the payment of bribes from below. As Leo Bach from Cracow and Płaszów put it: "One of the unpleasant experiences for me in that camp was the strong feeling of sectionalism among the inmates. [The] Great majority of the people there were the locals. . . . We from Krakow were treated as intruders, unwanted guests. . . ."[46] The Jews from Łódź and Płock at least had some time to integrate into the community, and those from places such as Bodzentyn and Szydłowiec who had relatives or contacts within the Wierzbnik community seemed also to cope relatively well. But the later newcomers from Kielce, Wolanów, Radom, Tomaszów-Mazowiecki, and Płaszów, who were brought directly into Majówka from other camps, were especially vulnerable and often bitter and resentful at their fall to the bottom of their new camp's social hierarchy.

17

The Ukrainian Guards

The underground camp economy, with its widespread smuggling between camp and factory and the movement of at least some prisoners in and out of camp, raises important questions about the Ukrainian *Werkschutz* and their functions. The agreement between Jeremiah Wilczek and Kurt Otto Baumgarten had restricted the Ukrainian guards to the outside perimeter of the camp, leaving internal camp affairs in the hands of the Jewish camp council and camp police. In addition to guarding the camp perimeter, the Ukrainians performed the major function of marching the prisoners from the camp to the factories and back. Even excluded from the internal affairs of the camp, the Ukrainians were thus in a position to interdict exchange and strangle the camp underground economy, yet clearly this did not happen.

For most aspects of the Jewish experience in Starachowice, there is consistency between earlier and later survivor testimonies. However, the portrayal of the Ukrainian guards is one exception to this generalization. The testimonies given to the German judicial investigators in the 1960s create a uniform image of the Ukrainians as brutal anti-Semites who beat and killed Jews viciously and gladly. In the words of one survivor, the Ukrainians were "plain murderers."[1] A few of the Ukrainian guards were known by name: Hanusevich, Koszak, Mrosowicz, Kosc, Soltau, Domeshsky, Grenjani, and Pryet.[2] Others were known by nicknames: the "shooter,"[3] the "businessman,"[4] the "Hebrew commandant"

1. Kurt Otto Baumgarten.
A division manager in the
Braunschweig Steel Works
in Starachowice 1941–44, and
deputy in charge of factory
security 1943–44. *Bundesarchiv
(former BDC), ZK, Kurt Otto
Baumgarten, 17.7.1908*

2. Walter Kolditz. Commander
of the Braunschweig Steel Works
Werkschutz (factory guard) in
Starachowice, summer/fall 1943.
*Bundesarchiv (former BDC), RS,
Walter Kolditz, 11.4.1911*

3. Gerhard Kaschmieder. Chief detective for factory security of the Braunschweig Steel Works in Starachowice, 1942–44. *Bundesarchiv (former BDC), RS, Gerhard Kaschmieder, 16.7.1912.*

4. Leopold Schwertner. In charge of non-German workers at the Branschweig Steel Works in Starachowice, 1941–43. *Bundesarchiv (former BDC), SM, Leopold Schwertner, 7.12.1911*

5. Deportation of Jews from Plock, February 1941, some of whom were sent to Wierzbnik and Bodzentyn. *USHMM, CD #122, W/S #79083, Desig #483.16 (public domain)*

6. Deportation of Jews from Sydlowiece, September 1942, during which some Jews were selected for labor in Starachowice. *USHMM, CD #0244, W/S #83868, Desig #483.19 (Yad Vashem Photo Archives)*

7. Tartak: main building of the sawmill. *Maciej and Anita Franciewicz, Starachowice*

8. Tartak: lumber yard. *Maciej and Anita Franciewicz, Starachowice*

9 and 10. Tartak: unidentified workers. *Maciej and Anita Franciewicz, Starachowice*

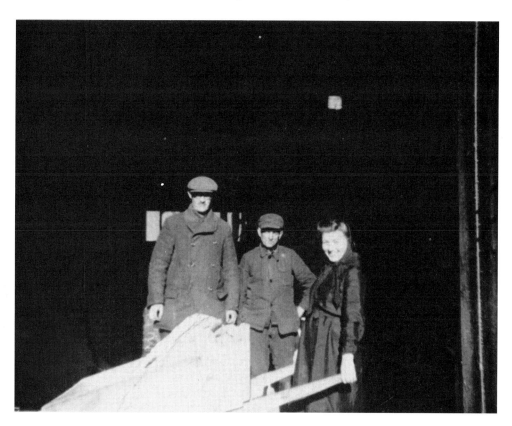

11. Group of workers in front of the Starachowice blast furnace. *With permission of the Wierzbniker Landsmannschaft, Toronto, Canada*

12. Group of workers in front of Tartak. *Courtesy of Martin Baranek, who generously made the photograph available to the author*

13. The Laks family sisters (Chanka/Anna, Rosalie/Rozalia, Renia) from Wierzbnik. *USHMM, courtesy of Miles and Chris Laks Lerman*

14. The Arbeiter family brothers (Yosef/Josef, Aaron, Srulek (Jolek), Matek, and Elek) from Plock. *USHMM, courtesy of Israel Arbeiter*

(because he could call out the marching count in Hebrew going to and from work),[5] and the "one-hand man" or "the incapacitated one."[6] The most frequently mentioned guard was known as "Thunder" or *Pjorun*, because he screamed so loudly at the Jewish prisoners, and in the early testimonies he was accused of the same misdeeds of killing and beating as other guards.

In the testimonies beginning in the late 1980s, a more differentiated and nuanced portrayal of the Ukrainian guards emerges. They are still accused of killing and beating, which undoubtedly took place. But they were also capable of other kinds of behavior. Two different survivors noted that Ukrainian guards, one characterized as a "nice" boy, spotted them hiding in the barracks sick with typhus during inspection, but they saved their lives by not reporting them.[7] Another time, a Ukrainian guard hid his outside work party of Jewish women from an approaching group of aroused Germans attending the funeral of a fallen comrade "because he felt sorry for us." Some of the Ukrainians, the same witness noted, were surprisingly lenient and well behaved.[8] Two child survivors, both of whom described themselves as blond and blue-eyed and not typically Jewish in appearance, said that Ukrainian guards developed a fondness for them and helped them.[9] Jews who spoke Ukrainian and could converse with the guards in their native language also enjoyed better relations with them.[10] The Ukrainians occasionally played soccer with Jewish prisoners, until the Germans put a stop to it.[11] And Ukrainians listened appreciatively to Jewish singing in the camp or even joined in.[12]

A very different picture of Pjorun in particular emerged in the late testimonies. His streams of verbal abuse were now characterized as cover for the fact that he did not beat and kill prisoners. He was, a number of witnesses now said, a Jew successfully passing as a Ukrainian guard, something no one knew until he registered with the Jewish community after the war.[13] According to Abramek Naiman, when he jumped from the truck that was supposed to take him to his death in the Bugaj Forest, Pjorun kicked him in the pants and told him to hide in the barracks.[14] David Mangarten, summoned to the camp office for a beating for hiding during inspection, placed a folded blanket inside his pants. When the thirty-five lashes cut his pants to shreds, exposing the blanket, Pjorun told him he was "a real Jew, so smart," and gave him a ration of bread.[15]

There were at least rumors of another Ukrainian guard who was also a passing Jew.[16]

Prisoners came to know the individual personalities of the Ukrainian guards after a while.[17] This was important, as a number of prisoners noted that they could approach particular guards known to be lenient, who would allow them to leave camp when their backs were turned. The problem was that those who left never knew which guard would be on duty when they returned, so they often encountered trouble when trying to reenter.[18] The Jewish policeman Manek Tenzer was viewed by some prisoners as an "angel" because he would regularly warn in Yiddish which guards were at the gate when prisoners returning from work were about to reenter the camp.[19]

For those who needed to reduce uncertainty when smuggling themselves or goods in and out of camp, financial arrangements could be made. Some guards would let prisoners go into town or even accompany them for safety in return for a share of whatever the prisoners brought back.[20] Others took bribes to let goods pass through the gate.[21] Indeed, the beatings that some guards inflicted on prisoners whom they caught returning may have been a punishment not so much for infringing the rules by leaving camp as for trying to move goods without paying the guards their expected bribes and not making the appropriate financial arrangements ahead of time.

The Ukrainian *Werkschutz* was a key manpower source for the Germans in managing the factory slave-labor camps in Starachowice. Clearly, many of these guards committed numerous killings and beatings on behalf of their German masters and often did so with great personal pleasure as well. Even when kept outside the camp, they remained the masters of the march to work. Here they could assert themselves without limitation. They forced the Jews to march in perfectly straight lines and to sing, and were free to punish the slightest infraction—even talking on the way to work—with beatings.[22]

But the *Werkschutz* was not a homogeneous unit of crazed killers and sadists. The prisoners came to know some of them as lenient and approachable and others as at least corruptible. As the focal point in German policy toward the Jewish prisoners switched from killing under Willi Althoff to exploitation under Kurt Otto Baumgarten, it is not surprising that many Ukrainian guards adapted to the new atmosphere for their own benefit as well. Thus the Ukrainian perimeter guard around Majówka was an extremely porous cordon riddled with laxness and corruption. These were essential conditions for the viability of the underground camp economy.

18

Poles and Jews

In describing their prewar life in Wierzbnik, most Jews testified to widespread Polish anti-Semitism even before 1939. They experienced this hostile environment not only in the boycott of Jewish businesses but also in the insecurity they felt from random acts of vituperation and violence, all suffered without recourse to protection of the law. Only a minority testified that a dramatic rise in Polish anti-Semitism occurred only after the outbreak of war and the arrival of the Germans. From that point on, a negative portrayal of Polish-Jewish relations was a matter of general consensus.

Three specific accusations of misbehavior occur frequently in the postwar testimonies. The first is that Poles openly displayed their joy at the suffering and humiliation of the Jews. As noted earlier, according to three testimonies, during the march from the marketplace to Strelnica, Poles lined the streets through which the Jews ran. They not only rejoiced at the Jews' misfortune and picked up whatever they could lay their hands on, but applauded, spit, and threw stones.[1] According to yet another witness, the occasional march from the camps through town to the baths also took place along streets lined with unsympathetic spectators, a deeply humiliating experience.[2] Jews also remembered acts of torment at the workplace, in the form of verbal or physical assault as well as the discriminatory actions of Polish foremen who could assign the worst jobs to Jewish workers.[3] In its most extreme form, this accusation alleged undisguised Polish satisfaction that Hitler and the Germans were exterminating the Jews.[4]

A second frequent accusation was that Poles made no attempt to help Jews, even when such help could have been provided at no risk and little cost. A number of survivors noted that it would have been easy to leave a piece of bread at the workplace (such as one survivor experienced later at Buna) or throw a piece of bread or potato to Jews on the march.[5] The most uncompromising of these accusatory accounts alleges that "not one Pole" performed such a simple "good deed" in Starachowice.[6]

The third frequent accusation was that Poles identified and pointed out Jews to the Germans, who otherwise would not have been able to distinguish between Poles and Jews. The Germans alone could not have enforced the requirement of wearing the Jewish star if Poles, able to recognize Jews by nuances of accent, gesture, and appearance, had not stood ready to point them out. Jews would have been far more willing to risk fleeing to the forest, going into hiding, or trying to live on false papers, if that did not mean living under the constant threat of denunciation from Polish informers eager to turn them in to the Germans.[7] One survivor even classified the Poles as "the greater enemy."[8] Expressing her deep sense of betrayal, another survivor—an assimilated, fluent Polish-speaker and former admirer of Polish culture from Płock—emphasized that she hated the Poles "more than the Germans because they were my neighbors."[9]

In sharp contrast to these blanket accusations, three survivors explicitly emphasized the crucial help they had received from Poles. When Josef Czernikowski learned that his sister was still alive in a labor camp in Sandomierz, he resolved to join her. A Polish friend from work promised to help. When Josef escaped from camp, the Polish friend bought him food and a train ticket. He then escorted him to the camp gate in Sandomierz and helped make arrangements for his entry.[10] Abramek Naiman saluted his "three Polish angels"—first, a Pole who took him from Strelnica to Majówka to be reunited with his parents; second, the family who hid his mother's fur coats and then hid her for two nights while she arranged for their sale; and third, a Pole who stopped others from beating him at work.[11] Esther Stern emphasized that Stefan, whom she married after the war, brought food, money, and clean clothing to her in Tartak, and that the Polish mechanic Janek saved her by warning her to hide when her name appeared on a list of prisoners to be transferred. "If not [for] the Poles, I would be already dead," she said. "I can say nothing bad about them."[12] The last two, it should be noted, juxtaposed their atypical praise of their Polish saviors with atypically harsh criticism of the Jewish camp elites.

Between sweeping accusations of Polish misbehavior and the rare invocation of Polish saviors, many survivors compartmentalized disparate experiences and memories. They acknowledged or took for granted the generally hostile and anti-Semitic environment in which they had lived but could not tell their stories without including the mention of individual Polish friends and benefactors. Contrary to the sweeping accusation that "not one Pole" gave food to Jews, a number of survivors explicitly mentioned receiving gifts of food, especially at work.[13] The most nuanced analysis was by Chaim Kleinberg. He noted that one had to be "lucky" to have Polish coworkers who would "share" their food, because they were not well off either. However, "there were a lot of good Poles who had sympathy," he asserted.[14] A number of other survivors also noted favorable relations with Poles at work, at least in some cases.[15]

Those most frequently mentioned, as well as most important, were the Polish friends, neighbors, and business associates with whom the families of survivors had left property for safekeeping. With a few exceptions,[16] these arrangements were honored, and as long as they remained in Starachowice, most Jews were able to access the property they had left with Poles either through transactions in the factories or through occasional visits from camp.[17] Returning after the war to reclaim property, long after the Polish holders of Jewish property had presumed the original owners to be dead, Wierzbnik Jews would have a very different experience.

Concerning Poles with whom property was left, some of the testimonies use the precise term of Polish or Christian "friends."[18] Others refer to a "wonderful Polish family,"[19] "neighbors" whom the family knew "well,"[20] or a "nice Polish guy."[21] Some testimonies imply somewhat more distant, less personal relations, referring to Polish "neighbors,"[22] a former Polish landlady,[23] a Polish family,[24] or "the gentile to whom we gave our jewels."[25] In Wierzbnik, where many Poles and Jews lived in mixed apartments and neighborhoods prior to ghettoization, and Jewish retailers and craftsmen had many Polish clients and customers, clearly there was frequent contact between Poles and Jews. As a result, friendships as well as cordial business relationships were not uncommon. No testimony suggested that any Jewish family in Wierzbnik had not left property with Poles simply because they knew no one with whom they could enter into such a relationship. They stood in sharp contrast to the Jews from Łódź and Płock, who could not avail themselves of such relationships.[26]

Polish friends and acquaintances were individual people and could be identified as such; the Polish population at large, however, was anonymous and faceless, and beleaguered Jews could not distinguish who among them was a potential informer or predator. As a composite, Poles represented a grave and unknown danger to any Jew risking hiding, escape, or even brief business transactions outside the camp. Thus, Jews who could speak positively of individual Polish friends and acquaintances with whom they left property and from whom they received help could simultaneously speak of "the Poles" or even "the Polacks" as anti-Semites and collaborators in German persecution. Individual Polish friends and helpers on the one hand and "the Poles" as a source of hostility and danger on the other were simply experienced, remembered, and spoken about in a compartmentalized manner by survivors.

19

Children in the Camps

Though only Jewish workers capable of factory labor vital to the German war effort were supposed to be interned in the Starachowice camps and rented from the SS as slaves, in fact many children twelve years old and younger lived in the camps through a combination of German laxity, favoritism, and corruption on the one hand and Jewish ingenuity and solidarity on the other. By one estimate, as many as fifty children who were not yet teenagers entered the Starachowice camps at various times.[1] The postwar testimonies of sixteen such children who managed to survive not only Strelnica, Majówka, and Tartak but also the ordeal of subsequent camps and relocations illuminate a highly unusual aspect of life in the Starachowice factory slave-labor camps. Though some of these testimonies are composed of quite fragmentary memories of particularly vivid moments, others provide surprisingly coherent and sustained narratives.

Children came into the camps in a number of ways. First, there were the children whose presence was permitted by the Germans as a calculated concession to the privileged prisoners. Second, there were children who successfully falsified their age in procuring work permits, who were selected on the Wierzbnik marketplace for labor despite their age, or who evaded deportation and sneaked into camp following the liquidation of the ghetto. Third, there were children who survived in hiding with gentile families during the deadly Althoff era and who were subsequently smuggled into camp when conditions inside the Starachowice camps seemed safer than the growing risks of continued hiding on the outside. Fourth, there were a few children among the new contingents of Jews transferred into Starachowice from Bodzechów, Wolanów, Tomaszów-Mazowiecki, Mokoszyn, and Radom in 1943.

Concerning the children of privileged Jews, Shlomo Einesman brought into camp one son, Noah, and two daughters, Rozia and Leah.[2] Rachmil Wolfowicz had in camp his two children, seven and nine.[3] Moshe Birenzweig was alleged to have had his children in camp as well as his lover's son.[4] Among Jews in the *Konsum*, shoemaker Pinchas Heldstein by his own account had initially hidden his wife and children on the morning of the deportation.[5] By other accounts, his one son and two daughters were in the camp,[6] so they may have joined him at some point after the deportation. Of the children of privileged Jews in the camps, two gave postwar testimony. One was Yankiel Feldpicer, son of the head of the tailoring section in the *Konsum*, Meir Feldpicer. Born in December 1930, Yankiel was still only eleven years old when he entered the camp. He slept in the same family quarters with his parents (though not with an older brother who worked in one of the factories) and stayed with his parents in the tailoring section of the *Konsum* during the day. He was free to run around unless there were Germans in camp, at which point he hid out of sight under the cutting table in the tailoring section.[7]

The other surviving child of the privileged was Einesman's daughter Rozia, born in 1933. She remembers that in Strelnica her father and others were subjected to a mock execution in front of their families—a very plausible memory, given Althoff's predilection for staging theatrical "amusements." She also remembers the family waiting at the camp gate for the return of her father, who had been sent for one day of hard labor at the blast furnace as a punishment. After moving from Strelnica to Majówka, the Einesman and Wolfowicz families each had a separate cabin, so she did not live in the family barracks with the other privileged Jews and their children. In her private cabin, she was exempt from selections, so she does not remember having had to hide. Nor does she remember associating with the other children in camp. She was uncomfortably aware of her privileged status, kept to herself, and had "no life" in camp.[8]

Three twelve-year-olds had a precarious legal status in camp. Eva Zukier's father had paid the required bribe for her work permit. Eva (born in March 1930) was on her way to her first day of work on the morning of October 27, 1942, when she was turned back and sent to the marketplace. Despite her age, her work permit was honored. She was working with her mother in the kitchen on the night shift in Strelnica when Althoff made one of his notorious night visits there and shot a young man from Opatów. Eva remembered having to clean the blood off the potatoes. She and her mother survived the run for the Bugaj Forest selection in March 1943, though she was still weak from typhus. However, the following November, when she and her mother filed past Kolditz during the Firlej selection, they were both sent to the trucks. A Jewish policeman vouched to Kolditz that she was sixteen years old and she, though not her mother, was spared. Thereafter, she did strenuous labor unloading sand (in which shell casings hot out of the furnace were cooled).[9]

Hersz Unger (born in July 1930) was selected for labor on the market-place along with his father and older brother. When questioned about his age, he claimed to be eighteen.[10] David Mangarten (born in March 1930) was selected for labor along with the rest of his family, but he does not mention whether or not he had a work permit. His father and one brother were kept for the cleanup commando but never arrived in camp. His sisters were in Majówka, but one managed to get into Strelnica and nurse him when he was stricken with typhus. He survived selection at the height of his illness when other prisoners tied him to the chimney on the barracks roof, and his mother subsequently bribed a Ukrainian guard to procure medicine for him. He survived the Firlej selection—when the Germans were specifically searching for thirteen- and fourteen-year-olds as well as women over forty—by hiding in the factory and not returning to camp with his shift.[11]

Michulek Baranek (born in August 1930) did have a work permit even though he had not actually worked. When his card was rejected on the marketplace, he was sent with his grandmother and younger brother to the waiting train. He ran, hid, and then made his way to Tartak, where his mother arranged with Piatek for his entry into the camp. From Majówka, his father joined the family in Tartak after paying a large bribe. Michulek worked a regular shift carrying wood products from one machine to the next.[12] Two or three other younger children were said to have survived Tartak as well, living in a carefully constructed hideout inside a double wall.[13]

Jacob Kaufman (born in October 1931) had just turned eleven when the Wierzbnik ghetto was liquidated. A German engineer at the factory valued his father's work and thus provided the son with a work permit despite his young age. When his mother and two sisters were taken to the train, he and his brother and father entered the camp. At the factory, he was given a relatively easy physical job as a sweeper. While most young survivors remembered the ordeal of the selections most vividly, Jacob remembered that his father—having incurred the dislike of an unnamed Jewish policeman—was switched to heavy shell production. Through ties to his own German supervisor (unnamed, but circumstances indicate once again Bruno Pappe), young Jacob was able to get his father reassigned. Since his father had left merchandise with Poles and was now in a position that allowed frequent contact with Polish workers, the family enjoyed an ample supply of food from the outside.[14]

Two young girls—eleven-year-old Goldie Szachter (born in December 1931) and nine-year-old Tobcia Lustman (born in August 1933)—were successfully hidden with Polish families before the liquidation of the ghetto and then smuggled into Majówka many months later. Goldie stayed with a peasant woman in a village just three miles from her hometown of Bodzentyn. Over time, various people either recognized her or at least suspected her Jewish origins. On two occasions, she was sent elsewhere for weeks or months in the hope that suspicions would diminish or be forgotten, but without success.

Finally, in September 1943, her father decided it would be safer for Goldie to reunite with the family in Majówka than to continue risking denunciation on the outside. He bribed a Jewish policeman to arrange for a morning "overcount" in a small, lightly guarded work party being sent to outside labor in the quarry near Majówka. The peasant woman brought Goldie to the quarry, where she managed to mingle inconspicuously with the workers. Goldie then marched with them back through the camp gate, where the total in the work party now matched the number recorded. In Majówka, she joined her mother and sister Rachela, working in the camp laundry. Even though she observed the inexorable deterioration in the health of her parents, the family remained intact throughout its internment in Starachowice.[15]

Tobcia Lustman was placed with a Polish family and posed as a visiting cousin. Though fair-haired and blue-eyed, her knowledge of Christianity was tested by suspicious neighbor children with whom she played—to the point that her "aunt" decided she must remain hidden inside. Kept in a closet or pantry whenever there were visitors, she had to relieve herself in the family sewage bucket without privacy, while others crudely commented on the "size" of her "share." At night, she could hear members of the family whispering that they had to get rid of the Jew.

After nearly one year of hiding Tobcia, the increasingly frightened "aunt" arranged to return Tobcia to her mother at a designated meeting place outside of camp. A Ukrainian guard had been bribed, and Tobcia was able to mingle with a column of returning workers and enter Majówka. She remained in camp during the day while her mother and sister went to work. One Ukrainian guard who grew fond of the pretty blonde child brought her extra food. She was also befriended by the Jewish policeman Abraham Wilczek. On the day of the Firlej selection, she ran to the building of the Jewish police in the hope that her sister's friend, whom she described as a policeman from another town (thus presumably Szmul Szczesliwy from Szydłowiec), would help her. This he did by placing her in an attic hiding place with other children. She was narrowly missed when a Ukrainian guard fired into the ceiling.[16]

There is one other example of a child about seven or eight years old being smuggled back into camp by his father from an endangered hiding place—in this case, even during the murderous Althoff period. Unfortunately, his parents did not survive. He was cared for by other prisoners and, incredibly, survived the camps even without his parents. Just recently, he has begun to contact other Starachowice survivors to learn about his own past, about which he has little or no memory.[17]

Tobcia Lustman and Rozia Einesman seem to have been the youngest native Wierzbnikers to survive the Starachowice camps and testify about it after the war. But seven other children from elsewhere, some even younger, also survived to testify about their internment in Starachowice. Two were from families from Ostrowiec who entered Starachowice with their mothers when the Bodzechów camp was closed down in the spring of 1943. Ruth Muschkies (born 1934) had no specific memories of Starachowice but had vivid fragmentary memories of several harrowing episodes. In particular, her mother was among 180 people, including two children, transferred from Starachowice to a new camp in Ostrowiec. She remembers that, upon arrival, the commandant in Ostrowiec did not want to accept the two children and the driver refused to take them back with him. Ruth sat on the ground outside the gate while the two adults discussed whether she should be shot. Finally the driver convinced the commandant that the children could be useful as messengers or kitchen help, and she was admitted.[18]

Yankiel Rosenberg (born in 1935) likewise entered Starachowice with his mother when Bodzechów was closed. His mother had a common friend with Jeremiah Wilczek, so she could speak with him. His father in Warsaw made arrangements to get his family out, but when the day came, Yankiel had come down with typhus and was too sick to travel. His mother departed, while he remained in the care of Wilczek's wife. As a blond, blue-eyed child, Yankiel also attracted the favor of a Ukrainian guard, who gave him extra food. When he finally recovered from typhus, he was smuggled out to Warsaw.[19]

A number of children entered Majówka from Wolanów in July 1943, including Rachel Waksberg (born in December 1932) and Abraham Malach (born in May 1935). Rachel was part of a larger family from whom she got food, even though she and her younger brother did not work. She and her brother both tried to hide when the Ukrainian guards summoned everyone out of the barracks for the Firlej selection. Her brother remained successfully hidden, but she was found and put on one of the trucks, as was her forty-five-year-old mother. However, Rachel was rescued by the policeman Turek. Abraham Wilczek found the suddenly motherless Rachel and her brother wandering around camp the following day and took them to join the children of the privileged Jews. Turek then arranged for her to have a factory job cleaning pieces for bomb assembly, and he even paid a Polish foreman to watch over her and to let her sleep when she had the night shift.[20]

Abraham Malach's father had made a small fortune in the leather-goods business, which provided him with the means to help his family

through bribery in the following years. When the family was transferred from Wolanów to Starachowice in July 1943, Abraham's father
must have made a substantial payment to someone, for they were taken
into the quarters of the privileged Jews and slept together as a family.
Unusual among children's testimonies, he made no mention of how
he survived the Firlej selection, which took so many children from the
camp. As an eight-year-old, he did not work in the factory but made
himself "productive"—something he learned that was very important in
camp—through cleaning the family barracks and carrying messages.[21]

Bronia Karafiol (born in April 1932) arrived in Starachowice from
the small or remnant ghetto in Radom. Though only eleven years old,
she worked in the factory sorting and polishing bullets. She also remembered leaving camp to smuggle in food.[22]

Two even younger children, Rutga Grynszpan (born in June 1937)
and Tola Grossman (born in September 1938), arrived in the transport
of prisoners from Tomaszów-Mazowiecki on September 5, 1943. Rutga
was aware, when giving her testimony, that she could not clearly distinguish among what her own actual memories were, what she had learned
from her parents, and what she read after the war. But she did have a
distinct memory that her family was tipped off that the children were
about to be taken, and that she was quickly thrown up into a hiding place
in the ceiling. The guards shot into the ceiling, but she "sensed" that they
had been bribed to miss.[23] According to her mother's testimony, when
the families learned that the children were to be taken away, the fathers
constructed a hiding place inside a double roof. She in fact stayed with
the children in the hiding place to keep them quiet.[24] Neither mother
nor daughter said so explicitly, but it can be inferred that they too were
living in the family quarters where Tobcia Lustman was hidden by the
Jewish policeman.

Tola Grossman entered Starachowice with her parents, and they also
lived together in one corner of the family barracks. Her parents left each
day for work, but she and other children in the barracks were cared for
by a "pregnant woman." They moved about in gangs and played violent
games, such as "You're a Jew, I'm a Nazi." Her mother did not attempt
to shield or protect her from the danger of the situation. Instead, she
went out of her way to tell Tola what the parents knew, including the

rumors of Auschwitz and gassing. One day her father barged into the room and warned, "Hide her." She and her mother were both shoved into the hiding place in the double ceiling, and her father covered it up behind them. Through cracks she could see children with whom she had played being placed on the trucks. She called this event the "children's selection" and said that thereafter all her friends were gone. She was never again allowed to go outside the barracks and play, or even to stand by the window.[25]

It is clear that some Germans had taken bribes permitting the admission of the children of privileged Jews into the camps at the very beginning. Others came into camp in 1943 with the full knowledge of the German authorities. The lists of the transfers from Radom and Tomaszów-Mazowiecki, found after the war and reprinted in the Wierzbnik community book, list entering children separately, and the list for Wolanów also openly includes the post-1930 birth years of a number of transferred prisoners.[26] The known and tolerated presence of some children obviously facilitated the presence of "illegal" children as well, making them less conspicuous. The Firlej selection aimed specifically at older women and children, but it had been dictated by SS officials in Radom, not local Germans who had accepted bribes to overlook the children in camp.

After the war, Kurt Otto Baumgarten claimed not only that he had permitted children in camp but also that he had provided warnings when they had to be hidden—that is, when he could not protect them, such as during the Firlej selection.[27] The testimony of some survivors corroborates that the parents living with their children had been tipped off, knew a children's selection was imminent, and thus prepared a hiding place ahead of time in a double ceiling in the family barracks. At least some of the nonprivileged Jews living in the regular barracks also had heard that such a selection was imminent, and they took what measures they could to increase their chances for survival. Among these, at least several were rescued by the Jewish police.

Kolditz's killing of the Jewish policeman Chaim Kogut during the Firlej selection, when someone was found hiding in a barracks for which he was responsible, thus once again fits into the wider picture of a mutually beneficial alliance between Baumgarten and the camp council and camp police. Kolditz was trying to exploit the selection ordered from Radom to shatter that alliance and take control of the Majówka camp. The parents and children who survived had reason to be grateful, especially those who were rescued through help from Jewish policemen. For those who lost family members, however, the Firlej selection was a great source of resentment and bitterness. One young man who had grown up on the same street in Wierzbnik as the Wilczeks, and played with their two sons, lost his younger sister during the Firlej selection. Why had the police not protected his sister, a neighbor since childhood, when the children of some newcomers—strangers and outsiders—had been protected and survived but could have been sent in his sister's place? he asked.[28] Some of those who lost family in the Firlej selection, alongside unpropertied newcomers who felt very disadvantaged and discriminated against, remained among the staunchest critics of the Wilczek regime.

20

Childbirth, Abortion, Sex, and Rape

The bulk of survivor testimonies about the Starachowice camps were given either before German judicial investigators in the 1960s or before a videotape camera in the 1990s. The latter were often given for family posterity, and the largest single videotape collection—testimonies taken for the Visual History Archive of the Shoah Foundation Institute—almost invariably ended with a family gathering of children and grandchildren. Thus, certain aspects of life that were central to prisoners' experiences in the camps—childbirth, infanticide, abortion, sex, and rape—were understandably topics that many survivors did not deem appropriate for open discussion either with German interviewers or for a family audience. Nor were they topics that I felt comfortable broaching in interviews, particularly with female survivors many years my senior. This chapter, therefore, is in many ways a chapter that cannot be adequately written. What follows is, by necessity, often based on fragmentary evidence and remains speculative.

At least six women gave birth in the Starachowice camps. Four survived to give their own accounts. Two others are known only through the testimony of others. On two central facts all accounts agree. In line with the German policy of temporarily sparing working Jews but not others, birth mothers were spared but newborns were killed immediately. But the testimonies differ on precisely who killed the newborns and how.

Three witnesses agree on one birth in Tartak. In one account, Esther Richter gave birth when the aryanized sawmill and lumberyard's German owner, Fiedler, was away. His much-feared secretary, Fräulein Lutz, summoned Walther Becker, who beat the father and ordered that a grave be dug. But this witness did not know how the killing of the newborn occurred.[1] In a second account, Becker was summoned to Tartak on account of an escape, but during the inspection he heard a baby crying. After demanding to know why a newborn was still alive, he then went into the room accompanied by Dr. Blum, who tried to assure him the baby would not survive in any case. The baby was killed, and the father and the witness buried the body.[2] In a third account, Becker ordered the Jewish doctor to do the killing.[3]

In Majówka, an unnamed woman gave birth with the assistance of Mrs. Glatt. Althoff entered the room accompanied by a guard, asked where the baby was, and ordered the guard to shoot it. Crushed by what she had witnessed, Mrs. Glatt—in the accounts of her daughters—died of a "broken heart" in March 1943.[4]

Two women, Toba Jadek and Toba Steiman, arrived in Strelnica six months pregnant and gave birth on the same night in January 1943. In her 1966 testimony, Toba Jadek said that a Jewish policeman took the child, and she was told it had been "buried alive." The very night after her child was taken, her husband was shot in the back of the head by Althoff while trying to escape out the back window of the sick barracks during one of Althoff's night visits to liquidate the typhus patients.[5] In her 1995 testimony, Toba Jadek identified the Jewish policeman who took her baby as Jeremiah Wilczek.[6]

In her 1968 testimony, Toba Steiman said that Pjorun came and said to her husband Jacob that both mother and child would be shot if the baby did not disappear. She "only knew" that her husband took the newborn away, and she never saw it again.[7] In the 1995 testimony of Toba Steiman, both the Jewish manager of the camp (i.e., Wilczek) and the Ukrainian guard who turned out to be a Jew (i.e., Pjorun)—she did not want to name either—showed up while she was still in labor. Wilczek's sarcastic comments on a Jewish woman giving birth scared her so much the baby finally came out. Wilczek then demanded that the husband hand over the baby or he would take his wife as well.[8]

Leonia Kurta, who had attended both women during their labors, subsequently gave birth herself. The newborn was taken and "likewise buried alive." Who took her newborn she did not know, because the midwife, Toni Weinberg, had held her head and she had closed her eyes.[9]

Regina Rosenblatt did not yet know she was pregnant when she entered Strelnica. When she began to "show" in early 1943, she was given a position caring for the ten-year-old daughter of Pinchas Heldstein in the *Konsum*, since he could provide protection for her. Her husband had been sent to work in Majówka but arranged to return to Strelnica several months before she was due to deliver. Attended by the midwife, Toni Weinberg, Regina gave birth to a baby girl on May 22, 1943. Althoff had by then been transferred, and apparently in the new circumstances there was some delay in deciding the infant's fate. However, on the third day the newborn was taken away. In her husband Rachmil's account, the Germans did not know about the birth, and Wilczek sent a Jew to take the baby.[10] In her accounts, the baby was taken by a German or a Ukrainian.[11]

In summary, it clearly was not policy in the Starachowice camps to murder women simply because they were pregnant. In six cases during the first seven months—at the peak of the killing period—women were allowed to give birth. However, it clearly was policy that newborns were to be killed, and this happened in each of these six cases. The key difference in the testimonies concerns who did the killing—ranging from infanticide carried out on the direct orders of Althoff and Becker in the respective cases of Majówka and Tartak to the Ukrainian guard, Jewish police, or even the unfortunate father in Strelnica. Among these, the Jewish police are the most frequently mentioned. And once again, the nightmare image of being "buried alive" emerges in several accounts.

All of these women had entered the camps already pregnant. After the departure of Althoff and the closing of Strelnica, by all accounts camp life in the newly enlarged Majówka was more relaxed. The barracks for privileged families aside, men and women still lived in separate barracks, but now they could mingle and visit with one another after work. Some of this visiting was more than just social. One survivor delicately noted that when husbands and wives met, there was the possibility for "romance."[12]

With rare frankness, Lucyna Berkowicz explained that she and her husband, Daniel—both transferred from Wolanów—were young and enjoyed sex. In Majówka they met after work each day, and soon she was pregnant. When she began to "show" in her fifth month, and fearing that a pregnant woman would not be allowed to survive, she decided to have an abortion. As an outsider, she had to rely on information from women from Wierzbnik. They knew of a Polish gynecologist who would perform an abortion, if Lucyna could pay for it. She sold both a ring and her beautiful wool coat to raise the funds. As a native of Lwów, she spoke Ukrainian and got along well with the guards. They took her to the home of the doctor, who initially refused to perform an abortion in the fifth month, insisting it was too dangerous. She pleaded that the Germans would kill her anyway, so the risk had to be taken. With two men holding her down, she had the abortion without anesthesia. The Ukrainians carried her on a stretcher back to camp, where she stayed two days in the sick barracks. Warned of the looming danger, she left the sick barracks just before the Firlej selection.[13] Given that the Firlej selection occurred less than four months after the arrival of the Wolanów contingent, she must in fact have conceived in Wolanów rather than in Majówka if the abortion in early November came in her fifth month. But clearly Lucyna remembered Majówka as a place where she and her husband could meet and have sex frequently and without difficulty.

Only four women referred to menstruation in their testimonies. One stated flatly that "no women" menstruated in camp in Starachowice.[14] The three others, in contrast, explicitly noted that they did not cease menstruation until they reached Auschwitz.[15] One woman implied that there was little sexual activity in camp, since there was no place for privacy and no one got pregnant.[16] Another said that there was "casual mixing" and some "pairing off" of boys and girls, but it was "not serious."[17] There were, in fact, references to two additional camp pregnancies beyond that of Lucyna Berkowicz. One "pregnant woman" served as the nanny for the children of the family barracks before the Firlej selection.[18] And another woman became pregnant in Starachowice and gave birth after the evacuation to Auschwitz-Birkenau.[19]

In her extraordinary book *Death Comes in Yellow: Skarżysko-Kamienna Slave Labor Camp*, survivor and historian Felicja Karay describes the permissive atmosphere that developed within another complex of munitions factories and camps quite close to Starachowice in the Radom district. Lonely and young, many people paired off. But above all, Karay emphasized that women seeking protection and support formed unequal partnerships with well-positioned and influential male prisoners—the *Prominenten* of the camp. Men and women who paired off in such extra-marital sexual relationships were euphemistically referred to as "cousins." Particularly in the latter period of camp life in Skarżysko-Kamienna—what Karay refers to as the "liberal" period—such arrangements were so "common" that "no one thought anything of it anymore," and "love-life flowered."[20]

None of the oral testimonies about the Starachowice camps portray a similar phenomenon there, but the one written memoir—Goldie Szachter Kalib's *The Last Selection: A Child's Journey Through the Holocaust*—explicitly describes the same situation, though from the disapproving perspective of her parents' generation and their futile attempts to protect their impressionable young daughter.

> Boys and girls would take an occasional stroll on the campgrounds outside the barracks. They would be seen promenading, necking, and making love. At night, young men would come into the women's barracks, ascend one of the tiers, and lie down beside a girl friend. Sometimes they would make love, openly engaging in intercourse.
>
> Mother would attempt to block our view of such goings-on, exhorting us, "Go to sleep, children, go to sleep." Her efforts, however, were in vain. On the one hand, it was impossible for her to totally prevent our awareness of the actions themselves. Moreover, all the women were fully aware of what was taking place and commented freely and critically. In general, they held in contempt any girls willing to let themselves be so used—or, who were "visited by cousins," as the procedure was described in cover-up jargon—and considered such girls tramps and prostitutes.[21]

And in another memoir with a brief chapter devoted to Starachowice, the author noted that men returning to camp from their factory shift "look around and vanish rapidly in the women [sic] barracks. They are attracted by the forbidden love play that runs as the water in the hills."[22] Clearly this topic was easier to address when mediated through the written word than in oral testimony. In any case, it should not be surprising if young people—living under a sentence of death with only the date of execution still pending and seeming to have no prospect of ever experiencing the normal family life of their parents' generation—increasingly discarded traditional attitudes about modesty and restraint and lived for the moment, whatever the disapproval of the older generation.

Kalib's account differs from Karay's in one important regard. She does not emphasize the same dynamic of privileged male prisoners or *Prominenten* using their power and influence to extract sexual favors that Karay does. However, several other testimonies do refer to such a phenomenon in Starachowice as well. In one account, Rachmil Wolfowicz—who was described by this witness as "a little spoiled" and "a little corrupted"—sought "sexual favors."[23] More explicit and detailed is an accusation against Wilczek. According to Regina Rosenblatt, Wilczek "became the rooster of the camp" and had lots of girls available to him. But he "fell in love" with Regina and made repeated passes that she rejected. When he finally tried to put an arm around her, she warned him, "Don't touch me," and he left her alone thereafter.[24]

The rape of Jewish women by Germans is another phenomenon that most survivors have difficulty confronting or discussing in their testimonies. According to Karay, it was a frequent phenomenon in the much larger camp complex of Skarżysko-Kamienna.[25] And there is convincing testimony that there were incidents of rape by Germans in Wolanów, including a holiday celebration gang rape in December 1942, before that camp was closed and the prisoners transferred elsewhere.[26] Testimony concerning rape in Starachowice is more fragmentary. According to one account, the Germans did not touch Jewish women but had no qualms about sending in the Ukrainians, and the resulting "cries and screams" at night were "unbelieveable."[27] There is, however, no corroborating testimony concerning such sexual assault by the Ukrainian guards. Soon the danger of typhus in the infested barracks and then the Wilczek-Baumgarten agreement to keep the Ukrainian guards outside the camp would have made such a practice difficult in any case.

One woman, Guta Blass, a noted beauty in Tartak, related two incidents in which Germans attempted to rape her. On one occasion, Piatek—normally "nice, mild," and "basically decent"—invited her into his room and pushed her down on his bed. When she resisted, he immediately had second thoughts and released her. On another occasion, she was briefly sent to help deal with the new outbreak of typhus in Majówka in the late summer of 1943, where a German officer of the *Werkschutz*, Willi Schroth, saw her for the first time. Later he came to Tartak waving a gun and screaming for her. He had cornered Guta in the upstairs women's sleeping quarters and tried to kiss her when Piatek intervened and got him to leave.[28]

In the collected testimonies concerning Starachowice, there is only one incident concerning rape for which there are multiple accounts—not written or on videotape but given in interviews with me. As one of the interviewees noted, everyone knew about it but no one wanted to discuss it, since the victim was still alive. Though differing in minor detail, three accounts taken together indicate that Kolditz carried out an exhibitionist rape in the Majówka camp. He forced a young woman with whom he had become obsessed to submit to him in plain sight of the other prisoners through threatening the lives of her family members.[29] An act of violent domination over the powerless victim, this rape was also a ritual of humiliation aimed at degrading the entire camp population, which was forced to stand by and witness helplessly. While some aspects of the Starachowice experience have moved from the realm of communal to public memory, and after many decades are now spoken about openly, this incident remains in the realm of those horrors that survivors cannot forget but also cannot find the words to speak about.

21

The Schroth Era:
Winter–Spring 1944

In survivor memory, the phases of camp life were associated with the most visible and notorious German of each era. The prisoners referred to them as "commandants," though that was not their official German title. In this succession, Willi Althoff and Walter Kolditz were followed by Willi Schroth, who was the most visible German presence in camp life in the first seven months of 1944.

Schroth was born in 1905 in the town of Langenbielau in Silesia. He left school at fourteen, initially apprenticed to follow in his father's footsteps as a horse slaughterer, and then—allegedly against the will of his unpleasant and authoritarian father—became a dyer. Married in 1931, he rapidly fathered eight daughters. His wife died during her ninth pregnancy in 1939. After the sixth daughter had been born and his wife had received the *Mutterkreuz* (Mother's Cross), he joined the Nazi Party in 1937, allegedly in order to receive more ample housing for his rapidly growing family. Schroth remarried in 1941. He was drafted into the army but was soon released from service as a "father of many children" (*kinderreicher Vater*). In September 1942, the local Labor Office found him work with the *Werkschutz* of the German factories in Starachowice, where, for the first time in his life, he escaped from relative poverty and began receiving a handsome salary.[1]

Originally supervising Ukrainian guards at one of the factory gates, Schroth claimed that he was not involved in marching Jews from the

Wierzbnik marketplace to Strelnica on October 27, 1942. Clearly he had become involved in the guarding of Jewish prisoners at some point. Possibly in May 1943 he killed his first Jew. A worker's legs had been crushed in an industrial accident, and the victim—screaming in pain—was being attended to by the Jewish physician in camp, Dr. Kramarz. Schroth arrived, surveyed the situation briefly, then drew his pistol and shot the injured worker in the head. The man gasped that he was still alive. Schroth's failure to kill his first victim with an initial shot at point-blank range perhaps indicated his nervousness on the occasion. Schroth then killed the man on his second try, with a shot to the heart.[2] In the summer of 1943, according to three witnesses, Schroth urinated into the open mass grave of Jewish typhus victims, remarking sarcastically that the dead Jews should "drink up."[3] Urinating on Jewish corpses was apparently a common ritual of degradation on the part of Germans in Starachowice, as two others were accused of performing the same debasing act on other occasions.[4]

By his own admission, Schroth accompanied Kolditz during the selection of November 8, 1943, witnessed his shooting of the Jewish policeman (Wilczek's son-in-law, Chaim Kogut), and accompanied the selected victims as they were taken by truck to the execution grounds in Firlej.[5] Several weeks later, after Kolditz had amused himself tormenting the two brothers recently arrived from Cracow who had tried to escape, Schroth was in charge of the execution squad of Ukrainian guards that ordered the two brothers to run and then shot them down from behind.[6]

During the Kolditz era, Schroth was one of three Germans in the *Werkschutz* who supervised the Ukrainian camp guards in rotation. The others were the Sudeten German Alois Schleser and a man named Wolf. Of the three, Schroth—whom many prisoners assumed to be Ukrainian or an ethnic German from Eastern Europe (*Volksdeutsch*) rather than German[7]—was the most memorable, since he was clearly trying to distinguish himself.[8] Indeed, it was Schroth who provided Kurt Otto Baumgarten with the information concerning Kolditz's illicit womanizing with Poles that helped Baumgarten get him sacked.[9] The great hypocrisy here was that Schroth himself was openly living with a Polish woman who had already borne him a child. But Schroth was protected by the new commander of the *Werkschutz*, a sixty-year-old former army man named Schumann. Other Germans in the *Werkschutz* could not understand this obvious favoritism of Schumann toward Schroth, since they were such opposites. Simply put, Schumann was very intelligent, while Schroth was just plain "dumb."[10] But Schroth's protected position presumably had a higher source than Schumann. Schroth's ultimate reward for siding with Baumgarten against Kolditz came after the New Year, when Baumgarten ended the system of rotating German supervisors at Majówka and named Schroth permanent commander of the camp guard.[11]

Kolditz was not the only German deeply involved with the exploitation of Jewish slave labor who suddenly disappeared from Starachowice at the end of 1943. On December 13, 1943, Leopold Rudolf Schwertner—who was in charge of recruiting non-German workers for the Braunschweig Steel Works in Starachowice and who had profited handsomely from selling work cards to desperate Jews before the liquidation of the Wierzbnik ghetto—was summoned to the office of the factory director, Fritz Hofmann. There he was accused of taking bribes from Jews and was placed under arrest by Walther Becker. His apartment was searched, uncovering silverware he had received from Jews. Schwertner claimed after the war that he had received the silverware in order to purchase medications that were to be smuggled into the camp through Otto von Ribbeck of the *Konsum*. The German engineer Willi Frania—who, like Schwertner, had earlier been quite active in selling work permits to desperate Jews—was arrested on the same charge that same day. They were both taken to Radom and held under arrest until April 17, 1944. Schwertner and Frania were then released but forbidden to remain in the General Government, on the grounds that their behavior there had damaged German "prestige." Without his exemption for performing work vital to the war economy, Schwertner was soon drafted into military service.[12]

That Kolditz could be removed at least in part for womanizing with Poles, based on the testimony of Schroth who was openly living with a Polish woman and their child, and Schwertner and Frania could be removed for accepting Jewish bribes, while Baumgarten and Becker were notorious in this regard, indicates that sexual and monetary improprieties were not the real reasons for these dismissals. Taking Jewish bribes and consorting with Polish women were blatantly pervasive practices among the occupying Germans, but these "offenses" could be used conveniently and selectively to get rid of rivals.

One other figure associated with the factory management also disappeared during this period, though in very different circumstances. Major Lemberger was a former officer in the Austrian army who had been taken into the Wehrmacht following the German absorption of Austria. In Starachowice, he served as the military liaison for munitions production. When it was discovered that he was a Jew, he was arrested. He allegedly then took his own life.[13]

After his appointment as permanent commander of the camp guard, Schroth was almost constantly at Majówka. He emulated his patron Baumgarten in his willingness to take bribes. As Wilczek's surviving son testified, "He was corruptible and could be used by the Jewish council for its own goals. Schroth was at the camp leaders' beck and call."[14] According to another prisoner, Schroth committed many atrocities but he also "turned a blind eye" to various happenings in the camp, particularly concerning the hiding of children.[15] Schroth even claimed that in cooperation with the Jewish camp leadership he checked out the children's hiding place they had constructed to ensure it would not be discovered by visiting inspectors from Radom and that on Baumgarten's instructions he warned when such inspections were imminent.[16] Given his limited intellect and the unimaginative nature and transparent mendacity of the lies that he did tell during postwar interrogations, he was probably telling the truth in this case. After all, the discovery that children were still in the camp in 1944 would have threatened not only Baumgarten's and Schroth's continued income from bribery but also their comfortable positions—safe from the war.

Schroth was basically a primitive nonentity whom one prisoner called "a nothing and a nobody."[17] But his unpredictability made him dangerous. He could smile and be "friendly" and "a little human" at one moment.[18] He could become "rabid" and kill "for pleasure" the next.[19] Precisely because the Baumgarten-Schroth era was the "quietest" in the history of the camp,[20] and killing was no longer an "everyday" event,[21] three subsequent killing actions by Schroth were remembered in vivid detail by numerous witnesses. There is no consensus, however, concerning either the approximate dates or even the chronological order of these killings.

Szmul Wajsblum was a wealthy miller from Opatów.[22] He was accompanied to the labor camp in Starachowice by his beautiful daughter Tobka, who was described as having blonde hair and "sky-blue" eyes.[23] Before they left Opatów, they allegedly hid their considerable wealth. Szmul apparently had access to at least some of his hidden wealth, for on one occasion he paid off Becker for the rare return of prisoners from a grave-digging detail when such an assignment usually meant the disappearance of the grave diggers as well as those for whom the graves were dug.[24] In late 1943, Tobka Wajsblum offered Becker hidden money if he would take her out of the camp.[25] Chanka Laks, the prisoner clerk at the camp office, was struck by how obligingly Becker treated her when he fetched her from the camp in his automobile.[26] After Tobka returned to the camp, needless to say, the rumor soon spread that more was involved in her relationship to Becker than a monetary transaction.[27] Some two months later, Becker arrived and fetched Tobka once again. This time he was not so polite, and this time she did not return.[28] After the war, survivors learned from local Poles where they had found and buried her body. She had been killed by a shot to the head.[29]

Shortly after Tobka's disappearance, her father, Szmul, had returned from his work shift and was sitting in front of his barracks, reading the bible. Jeremiah Wilczek appeared and ordered Szmul to dig a grave outside the camp wire. Szmul said such work should be given to a younger person, not a fifty-year-old like him. Wilczek said he had been specifically instructed by Schroth to fetch "the old Wajsblum," and the latter left carrying a shovel. Nonetheless, even his nephew was not particularly alarmed.[30] Wajsblum began digging just outside the fence, fully visible from the back side of the camp. Some people who had been watching suddenly ran through camp, shouting that Schroth was shooting old Wajsblum. Thus there were many witnesses when Schroth shot the old man as he stood in his freshly dug grave. Wilczek sent Wajsblum's nephew to collect his coat and boots.[31]

On May 15, 1944, two women in their thirties, Mala Szuch from Opatów and Jadwiga Feldman from Skarżysko-Kamienna, were summoned by Schroth and taken out the back gate of the camp to roughly the same spot where Szmul Wajsblum had been shot and buried.[32] According to numerous witness accounts, the women had refused to go to work that day.[33] Feldman was resigned to her fate and went quietly. But Szuch screamed at Schroth, resisted, and spat on him. Schroth pulled her by the hair the entire way and then shot both of the women outside the wire, in plain sight of the prisoners.[34]

The two Lewkowicz sisters from Łódź, Malwina and Romana, blonde- and red-haired beauties, were renowned in camp for their artistic brilliance. They recited poetry from memory, composed their own poems, and sang songs.[35] They were, in short, memorable figures in the cultural life of the camp. As closure of the camp loomed, they decided to escape but were caught. In one version, they paid a gentile to provide them with false papers, but they were betrayed, and the false papers were discovered.[36] In another version, they were caught outside camp trying to make good their escape.[37] In any case, they were clearly planning an escape, and the Germans decided to make an intimidating example as a deterrent against the growing wave of such attempts. The women prisoners were assembled to witness the execution.[38] Schroth shot one sister. Then his pistol jammed when he tried to shoot the other. She begged for her life and kissed his boots, but he procured another pistol and shot her as well.[39] The bodies of the two sisters were then thrown into the drainage ditch of the camp latrine.[40]

There were two other memorable killing actions, but they centered on Baumgarten and Kaschmieder. Baumgarten was a much more distant figure than Schroth, meeting regularly with the Jewish leadership but not often appearing in camp. A number of survivors noted that in comparison with other Germans, Baumgarten was "not so bad,"[41] "not so feared,"[42] and even relatively "decent."[43] Several survivors perceptively noted, however, that while Baumgarten never shot anyone personally, he clearly had given orders for or induced shooting by others.[44] The most memorable case involved a Jewish worker named Brenner. One day Baumgarten assembled a number of workers, before whom he accused Brenner of sabotage and announced the death sentence. Some workers were forced to watch as Brenner dug his grave and, on Baumgarten's orders, was shot by a Ukrainian guard on the factory grounds.[45]

After the war, Baumgarten claimed that a Jew whom he had appointed as a foreman, Moishe Weinberg, had told him of Brenner's inattention to faulty production, and said that Brenner had been repeatedly warned. On the fourth occasion, Baumgarten telephoned the Security Police in Radom. A police official from Radom arrived and ordered Brenner's execution for sabotage, which was carried out by a Ukrainian guard in front of some twenty assembled workers. Baumgarten dated this event to the spring of 1944.[46] Moishe Weinberg admitted that he had been appointed to a supervisory position by Baumgarten because of his good German but he vehemently denied ever having informed on Brenner.[47]

Kaschmieder's killing was connected to a key turning point in the history of the Starachowice factory slave-labor camps that occurred in April 1944, when a transport arrived from the concentration camp of Majdanek in Lublin carrying 150 to 200 Jewish prisoners. The survivors of numerous *Aktionen* and selections as well as the horrific *Erntefest* massacre, they were literally the remnant of a remnant of a remnant—a handful of Jews in the Lublin district still alive in the spring of 1944 against all imaginable odds. Because of the large letters "KL" (for *Konzentrationslager*) painted on their clothing, they were referred to as "Klneks," or alternatively as the "Lubliners." In the typical black humor of camp life, the initials KL were said to stand for *kein Leben* or "no life."[48]

Of the six Lubliners who gave postwar testimony, five talked about the incredible odysseys that took them to Starachowice.[49] Moishe Burman was born in Pinsk in 1915. Drafted into the Polish army, he was taken prisoner in 1939. Initially kept in a German *Stalag* near Königsberg, he was transferred to a labor camp in Biała Podlaska in the northern Lublin district in October 1940. He escaped to the Międzyrzec Podlaski ghetto in January 1942. He survived the first great deportation *Aktion* there, August 21–22, 1942.[50] Eventually caught and put on a train for Treblinka, he pried off a door board with a knife that he had kept in his boot and jumped. Finding survival in the forest impossible, he insinuated himself into a workforce of some fifty Jewish artisans and mechanics being kept alive by the Gestapo in Biała Podlaska. In the spring of 1944, these skilled Jewish workers were sent to Majdanek, kept there for one week, and then put on the train to Starachowice.[51]

Chaim Ehrlich was born in Międzyrzec in 1924. He survived a stint in a work camp in Osowa in 1940, digging a canal between the Vistula and Bug Rivers. By hiding in a bunker his family had prepared, he also survived the first great deportation from Międzyrzec. Finding a position as a skilled worker in the workshop of the military commandant, he managed to survive all the additional Międzyrzec roundups as well, hiding in a prepared bunker at the crucial moments. He too then joined the Gestapo's small private camp of skilled Jewish workers in Biała Podlaska, from where the prisoners were sent to Majdanek in March 1944 and then on to Starachowice.[52]

Szmul Chaim Wolfowicz was born in Nowogródek near Baranowicz (now in Belarus) in 1914, served in the Polish army, was captured, and eventually was sent with other Jewish POWs to the labor camp in Biała Podlaska. He escaped from that camp, found various jobs, and evaded various roundups, but he was finally arrested and taken to the Gestapo, which put him to work until the transport to Majdanek in the spring of 1944.[53]

Daniel Goldfarb was born in Krasnik in 1926 and moved to Warsaw in 1937. When the ghetto was created there, part of his family returned to Krasnik. He survived the first great deportation there in October 1942 but was caught in the second and sent to the concentration camp at Budzyń. These Budzyń Jews worked in a Heinkel aircraft factory and also produced items for the particular needs of the Lublin SS and police. They were thus spared during the *Erntefest* massacre of November 1943. From Budzyń, Goldfarb was shipped to Majdanek for two weeks in the spring of 1944, and then on to Starachowice.[54]

Abram Goldman was born in Włocławek in 1924 and fled to Warsaw in 1939. Working as a courier for the Resistance, he was caught, spent two weeks in the Pawiak prison in Warsaw, and in March 1943 was sent on to the Poniatowa camp in the Lublin district, where he was soon joined by other survivors of the Warsaw ghetto uprising. In October 1943, shortly before the Poniatowa camp was liquidated in the *Erntefest* massacre, Abram was among 1,000 men and 200 women sent to Zamość for airfield construction. By the time the airfield was completed in the spring of 1944, this contingent of Jewish workers had shrunk to a mere seventy-five men and five women. Taken by train to Majdanek, they worked there for three weeks before they joined the transport to Starachowice in April.[55]

The Lubliners were not a homogenous group before arriving in Starachowice. They were either natives of the Lublin district, captured Jewish soldiers of the Polish army sent to the labor camp in Biała Podlaska,
or prisoners sent to the Lublin district in connection with the repression
of the Warsaw ghetto uprising. They survived the near-total destruction of all Jews in the Lublin district by virtue of one of three protected
niches: the Budzyń concentration camp, the skilled workers camp of
the Biała Podlaska Gestapo, or the contingent of airfield construction
workers sent to Zamość. In the context of their insertion into the prisoner community in Majówka, however, they appeared very much as a
single, homogeneous group of distinct (and, in some survivors' views,
disruptive) "outsiders."

The arrival of the Lubliners in Starachowice set off shock waves in
numerous directions. First, they brought with them direct and credible
information about the course of the Final Solution in the Lublin district in general and the gas chambers at Majdanek and Treblinka in
particular.[56] The earlier waves of Jews entering the Starachowice camps
had seen their work in the German war economy as the best chance for
survival, and, with a few exceptions, Jews generally had tried to get *into*
these camps as havens, not *escape* from them. The shocking confirmation of the existence of gas chambers, combined with the foreseeable
approach of the Soviet army (which had already caused the Lubliners'
evacuation westward from Majdanek), made clear to many now that
the safe haven offered by the Starachowice camps would not last much
longer. Escape became a rational choice and a valid alternative to placing continued faith in the German need for their labor. As a result, the
quiescence and seeming stability of the Schroth era came to an end, and
the number of escape attempts rose precipitously.

At the forefront of the escape attempts were the Lubliners themselves.
They had no illusions about the stability of their position in Starachowice, and in comparison to their previous places of incarceration, the
relatively lax camp security virtually invited escape attempts. While the
Zamość contingent had been sent off as a separate group to construct
new barracks on the factory grounds of the munitions plant,[57] many of
the other Lubliners—like so many waves of newcomers before them
lacking connections and *protekcya*—were assigned to work in the stifling

heat of the blast furnace. Ten Lubliners from one blast-furnace shift promptly escaped as a group.

The German response to such an unprecedented mass escape was twofold. First, the camp commander or *Lagerführer* gave a speech to the assembled prisoners. From the context of the entire testimony, the key witness was referring here to Baumgarten, not Schroth. He addressed the "talk" about crematoria and the extermination of the Jews and said these were all a "big lie" made up from "A to Z." The crematoria did not exist, and those spreading such rumors, he threatened, would be severely punished.[58]

Second, the Germans carried out the largest killing action since the Firlej massacre of the previous November. In addition to the Ukrainian guards and their German officers, two German detectives had been attached to the *Werkschutz* to investigate cases of sabotage, spying, and theft at the factories. They dealt primarily with Polish, not Jewish, workers. On occasions requiring investigation, however, such as the camp-council accusation against Abraham Finkler as temporary head of the camp police under Kolditz in the fall of 1943, the two detectives— Heribert von Merfort and Gerhard Kaschmieder—had become involved in camp affairs. Von Merfort was drafted into military service at the end of 1943.[59] The task of dealing with the escape of the ten Lubliners fell to Gerhard Kaschmieder alone.

Born in 1912, Kaschmieder was from Silesia, like so many of the other Germans in Starachowice. He trained to become a cabinetmaker but switched to truck-driving in 1934. After a brief stint in the SA in 1933–34 (which he left in a timely manner in mid-June 1934, just weeks before the "Blood Purge" of the SA leadership), he joined the Nazi Party and SS in 1937. Following two years of service in the army, he became a driver for the Gestapo in Troppau in 1940. He was then sent to police school as a detective candidate in training but failed the exam. He returned to Troppau reluctantly and thus applied for a position with the *Werkschutz* in Starachowice, where he arrived in mid-November 1942.[60] If his boss, Baumgarten, was remembered by Jewish survivors for his summer costume of *Lederhosen*, Kaschmieder was remembered for wearing knickerbockers.[61]

The day after the escape of the ten Lubliners, Kaschmieder—dressed on this occasion in his SS uniform rather than knickers—appeared in Majówka. Even before the mass escape by the ten prisoners, the Germans had tried to deter the increase in escape attempts through collective responsibility. Through written announcements posted on the barracks, they warned that in case of further escapes, members of the same work groups from which such Jews escaped would be shot. Kaschmieder now made good on that threat. Calling out some thirty Lubliners who worked at the blast furnace, he selected ten by pointing with his whip. Negotiating desperately, Shlomo Einesman persuaded Kaschmieder to substitute two terminally ill Jews from the sick barracks for two of the selected workers. The ten victims, including the two sick Jews carried on stretchers, were marched out the back gate, accompanied by four Ukrainian guards and members of the camp police. There they were forced to dig their own graves. One young Jew, Moishe Zemelman, desperately flexed his muscles for Kaschmieder to demonstrate that he was a valuable worker, but in vain. Lying face down on the ground, the ten Jews were shot by Ukrainians from behind.[62] After the shooting, Kaschmieder performed the ritual urination on the bodies.[63]

News of this rising epidemic of escape attempts apparently reached the Radom SS. On the night of June 5–6, 1944, Schroth ordered the former head of the Jewish council, Symcha Mincberg, to report to the camp's guard station. There he was taken into custody by two Gestapo men, incarcerated in the Wierzbnik jail for the rest of the night, and early the next morning taken by train to Radom. At SS headquarters in Radom, he was subjected to three days of intense interrogation and torture about how many Jews were actually in the camp at Majówka and who was planning to run away. Mincberg replied that he did not know, for if anyone were planning to escape, he would surely keep it a secret. Mincberg then languished in the Radom prison under the continuous torment of a vicious jailer for five weeks, until he was shipped via the Gross Rosen concentration camp to its satellite camp at Fünf Teichen.[64] The fact that the Radom SS would select Symcha Mincberg, the once-prominent head of the Wierzbnik *Judenrat* but since October 1942 totally marginalized by the new power structure of Wilczek and his coterie, as the target of their interrogation indicates how little they were aware of what was actually going on between Baumgarten and Wilczek within Majówka.

The arrival of the Lubliners also affected the dynamic of the prisoner community and the hitherto-unchallenged position of the camp elite. After their harrowing experiences in the Lublin district, the newcomers were astonished to discover that a place like Starachowice, where Jewish families—men, women, and children—were still together, even existed.[65] As one later noted,

> That I would never believe. I saw a few thousand Jews . . . women and men, and they had everything there. They had food. They had stores, you could have bought food for money, for anything. And it was like a different kind of world. . . . We were surprised. . . . Some of the eldest of the Jews, the *machers*, they were living very good. They were getting nice civil dress . . . they had their own women and they had everything there. . . . The *Judenrat* of the *ganzen Ding*, they lived in nice houses and the leader had a car at his disposition.[66]

Astonishment soon gave way to resentment and challenge. As one earlier newcomer from Wolanów testified:

> And the people from Majdanek came to us, to Starachowice. And when they came in and when they went into the kitchen, and you know, staying in line for the soup, and when they seen what came in the soup, they said you can't feed people like this, you are not going to feed us like this, you're going to give food, where is all the food you getting. We are from Majdanek, we are already trained, and you better give us food. And for the short time they were with us, there was no hunger, no hunger, plain and simple. There was no hunger.[67]

Another witness concurred that thereafter the elite's "stealing" from the common food supply was not as open as before, since they were now afraid of the consequences.[68]

But the Lubliners wanted more than just a more equitable distribution of food. They challenged for a share of power in the camp. According to Mendel Kac's detailed 1945 testimony, one of the Lubliners, a man named Zyg, was temporarily made a member of the camp council and proved to be a good organizer, but it did not last. "The money won," Kac cryptically noted, presumably referring to bribes paid by the old guard to Baumgarten to restore their former position.[69]

Opinion about the Lubliners among the earlier prisoners was mixed. To some of those who had entered Starachowice in 1943 from camps such as Wolanów, the Lubliners were seen as champions of the disadvantaged newcomers who successfully curtailed some of the most blatant abuses perpetrated by the camp elite. But some of the original Wierzbnikers also admired them. One deemed them the "very strongest" and "best" people.[70] To another, they included intelligent and educated Jews from Warsaw, and they were strong, young men "made out of iron."[71] To Rachela Szachter, whose father was a close friend of Einesman on the camp council, however, the Lubliners were "troublemakers from the beginning" whose past experiences had made them "immune to violence."[72] According to Josef Friedenson from Łódź, this "gang" from Lublin had "a lot of chutzpah" to come with "demands" that they should be "privileged." Though there were some assimilated Jews from Warsaw among them, most of them in his view were "primitive."[73] To others, such as Henyek Krystal, the Lubliners were simply aloof and incommunicative. "I never got to talk to them and they never, they were not willing to just talk."[74]

The arrival of the Lubliners in April 1944 marked the end of a period of relative stability and quiet in the Starachowice camps. Thereafter, the prisoner community could no longer view the camps as a safe haven and rely on the hitherto relatively successful strategies of survival through labor and bribery as offering the best chance for the future. Whatever the future might hold, they knew for certain that the current situation would not last long. Once again, with too little information upon which to make decisions and too little power to control their own lives, they would face a series of "choiceless choices" that would help determine their fate.

PART V

CONSOLIDATION, ESCAPE, EVACUATION

22

Closing Majówka and
Tartak

As spring turned to summer, tensions among the Jewish slave
laborers in Starachowice rose precipitously. The Zamość contingent of construction workers among the Lubliners had been
building barracks for an entirely new camp on the factory grounds of the
munitions plant. The prisoners of Majówka were transferred there in
early July.[1] This relocation was a response at least in part to the increasingly brazen attacks by partisan forces on the guards marching the prisoners to work. These attacks had been aimed, of course, not at liberating
the prisoners but at seizing weapons from the Ukrainian guards, who
had become increasingly uninterested in fighting. Indeed, in June 1944
the partisans had even staged a direct attack on the guardhouse outside
the factory, making off with both weapons and cash.[2]

The prisoners "felt that the ground was burning under their feet"[3]
or that "doomsday" was approaching.[4] Indeed, there were a number of
indications that their stay in the new camp would be short. Work at the
factories shifted from producing munitions to dismantling equipment,
which clearly signaled the end of the camp in the not too distant future.[5]
As the machinery was loaded, most work ceased and the Jewish workers increasingly sat idle.[6] The prisoners were kept apprised of the Soviet
approach and the German retreat. In July 1944, Red Army forces crossed
over the 1939 demarcation line in central Poland that had been the starting point of the German invasion in June 1941. Some credited this infor-

mation to Polish contacts.[7] One witness claimed access to a secret radio.[8]
There was also contact with the Jewish Resistance (allegedly a remnant
of the Jewish Fighting Organization or ZOB, which had been the prime
mover behind the Warsaw ghetto uprising) on the outside. It offered to
create false documents if photographs could be provided, but it primarily
urged escape as the best course to follow.[9] When some of the Lubliners,
who upon their arrival that spring had already confirmed the existence
of gas chambers, recognized Majdanek personnel among a visiting SS
commission, the sense of panic intensified among the prisoners.[10]

The new camp posed both challenges and opportunities for the prisoners. It was surrounded by a double fence—the first of barbed wire
and the second of wood planks—and two watchtowers.[11] Yet it was just
about 100 yards from the forest; once outside the fences, a quick sprint
could take an escapee to terrain where Germans and Ukrainians were
by now afraid to follow.[12] The forest also offered cover for partisans to
approach the camp, if contact and cooperation could be established.

According to several survivors, however, there was no organization or
leadership to incite or plan escape.[13] But others claim that small groups
of young prisoners began to meet and talk about an uprising and mass
escape.[14] Because of fear of denunciation, such planning was kept very
secret.[15] Those initiated were told explicitly not to talk to others.[16] At
least two such groups can be identified. One was a small group of young
men—"camp brothers"—from Płock, who planned to smuggle large
wire cutters into camp. It was hoped that during the night an advance
group could cut the fence in the corner where the searchlights were
weakest. If they managed to get through the fences and into the forest undetected, others would then follow. They would seek refuge in
a hiding place prearranged by their Polish contact. They were also in
communication with "one of the Jewish camp leaders," who told them
of plans being made with the partisans to liberate the camp.[17]

This reference to "one of the Jewish camp leaders" may well have
been to a Jewish policeman, for another group planning resistance apparently included a number of disaffected Jewish policemen at its core.
The much-hated Szaja Langleben had emerged as the chief enforcer
on behalf of the Germans for a stricter control of the camp, but other
policemen were now ready not only to join but even to lead an escape

attempt.[18] Some witnesses mentioned Moshe Herblum as a leader.[19] Others mentioned Abraham Wilczek.[20] According to the postwar testimony of Abraham's future wife, the group was convinced of the need to procure weapons. Abraham argued that the Ukrainians were the best source for this, as they would "sell their souls" for money. Because he was good at "schmoozing" with them, he volunteered to make the attempt. The first gun was purchased at a very high price, through accessing valuables that had been hidden in Wierzbnik. While the group was collecting for the purchase of a second gun, however, the Ukrainian was caught and interrogated, and he confessed to selling a gun to a Jewish policeman. When the Germans then held a lineup of the Jewish police, he identified Abraham Wilczek.

Abraham was stripped naked except for a sack over his head, held down over a bench by two men, and given 100 lashes. He was supposed to count them all out, but apparently he passed out at around twenty. He was then sentenced to death by Baumgarten, and a grave was dug. Meanwhile, the camp council and Abraham's father feverishly collected watches, rings, and other valuables and then approached Baumgarten. He demanded one kilo of gold to reopen the investigation. When he apparently was satisfied with his haul, Abraham was released.[21]

Several other accounts also mention the attempt to procure arms. In one account, prisoners tried to make grenades, but one young prisoner was caught and killed and others associated with him were beaten.[22] Another prisoner claimed to have successfully traded a good pair of shoes to a Pole for a pistol.[23] In the most implausible account, prisoners managed to procure two machine guns through money they had received from a "Zionist organization" but never managed to obtain any ammunition.[24] In any case, obtaining weapons was extremely difficult, and the attempt was never sufficiently successful to provide any basis for armed revolt within the camp. Moreover, the pace of events soon overtook those planning some form of organized uprising and escape, and ultimately prisoners were left to react spontaneously and desperately to the imminent evacuation of the Starachowice camps.

The next concrete step the Germans took to close the Starachowice camps came with the evacuation of the Tartak sawmill and lumberyard. The manager of this camp, Fiedler, had previously assured the prisoners that nothing would happen to them as long as he was there. According to Josef Kohs's detailed testimony in 1948, he had added, "If he were to leave, we could do as we wanted. In this regard he always referred to the lack of any guard." Then one day he left camp abruptly. A half hour later, a truck with Ukrainian guards was seen approaching the camp. Some prisoners, particularly young ones who knew the city, tried to jump the stream running behind the camp, cross the main Skarżysko-Ostrowiec highway, and escape. Some managed to get away, but others were shot down. The sawmill and lumberyard were quickly surrounded, and the Jews were ordered to assemble for evacuation to the main camp on the factory grounds. To the astonishment of Josef Kohs, some Jews had already armed themselves with axes and knives and, fearing transport to an extermination camp, were prepared to fight to the death. Josef Kohs advised against resistance, arguing that in the main camp they would know better what was going on. And resistance there with greater numbers was possible, while in the sawmill it was hopeless. Most of the prisoners agreed with him and mounted two canopy-covered trucks. Some still tried to escape, but only a few made it.[25]

After the Jews from the lumberyard were unloaded at the main camp that evening, a dramatic event occurred that was described by no fewer than twelve witnesses. To illustrate the challenges and opportunities in using such evidence, I would like to examine in detail the testimony concerning this incident. The earliest testimony of the entire collection, by Meir Lewental, was given in Łódź on May 26, 1945. He stated that when the Tartak prisoners arrived at the factory camp, the silence convinced one woman among them that all the prisoners there had already been killed. She then attacked the head of the *Werkschutz*, who managed to pull out his pistol and shoot twice but missed. She was able to hide but came out when ordered. However, thanks to the intervention of a higher-ranking officer, she was left alone.[26]

Mendel Kac provided a long, detailed account, recorded in Cracow and dated August 21, 1945. According to him, when the male and female prisoners from Tartak were separated, a twenty-year-old girl attacked the head of the camp guard and pushed him to the ground. He freed himself from her grasp, drew his revolver, and shot her in the forehead. In fact, the bullet just grazed her, but she faked being dead. After the guards left, she crawled under the barracks to hide. The next morning, the commander of the guards returned and, not finding the body, searched for her. She then gave herself up.[27] This account does not tell us anything further about the fate of the girl.

Nearly a year later, on July 31, 1946, in France, eighteen-year-old Kalman Eisenberg gave an interview to the American psychologist David Boder—a pioneer in the early collection of survivor testimony—that was audiorecorded and subsequently transcribed.[28] Kalman Eisenberg testified that when the Jews from the small camps were brought into the main camp, a young girl originally from Łódź called out: "Jews, time now counts in minutes. Perhaps we will be able to escape. And whoever dies will die a hero's death." She then threw herself on the German commander of the Ukrainian guard, seized his revolver, and fired into the air. The guards ran up and fired on the Jewish prisoners. Because it was very dark, no one was killed. The girl was only slightly wounded and able to hide in the barracks. In the morning, she was dragged out of the barracks and taken to interrogation, where she defended herself.

Kalman Eisenberg then stated that, "with great difficulty, with much labor and struggle, we succeeded in saving the girl from death." When the incredulous Boder asked how this had been accomplished, Eisenberg explained: "It has cost us very much money. The Jews gave up their last possessions." He went on to explain how Jews from Starachowice had left possessions with Poles, and some of this property was later transferred into the camp when Polish and Jewish workers met at the factories. Because the camp commandant "was a big glutton for money" and "loved money and gold very much," the Jews handed over their possessions and the girl was saved.[29] In short, the Jewish prisoners had negotiated with the commandant and ransomed her at a high price.

The final early testimony was given two years later, on August 19, 1948, by Josef Kohs in Germany. He stated that it was dark when the Jews from Tartak arrived at the main camp. From the *Appellplatz* or roll-call grounds, they were taken away in groups of ten by Ukrainian guards. They feared that they were about to be shot. In one group of ten, a young woman named Blasowna threw herself on the commander of the Ukrainians, Willi Schroth (whom Kohs called "Schrutt"), and began to strangle him in desperation, while calling upon the other Jews to attack the Ukrainian guards. "But no one moved. We were as if paralyzed," Kohs recalled. Then suddenly the air-raid alarm sounded and the lights went out. Schroth threw the woman off, pulled his revolver, and shot her twice. Everyone assumed she was dead. When the German police chief Walther Becker ("Beck" in his version) arrived the next morning, the girl had disappeared and no one would betray her. But fearful that others would suffer, the "brave girl" gave herself up. When asked why she had done it, she answered that she feared being shot and in her fear had fallen on Schroth, which he had mistakenly thought was an attack. At this moment, Josef Kohs surmised, Becker was more concerned about a general uprising of the prisoners and knew the Jews were all going to Auschwitz anyway. He proclaimed that if two bullets had not killed her, she would not be killed on his orders, and the girl survived.[30]

In four early accounts given in three different countries, we see the same incident recounted—about a young female prisoner attacking the head of the Ukrainian camp guards at the moment the Jews of Tartak were brought into the main camp. However, the accounts lack unanimity in important ways. Only three note that the attacker was spared, and only two provide differing explanations for the very unusual behavior of the Germans in this regard. These accounts also differ on the identification of the man who made the decision to spare the woman. Meir Lewental refers only to a higher-ranking officer. Kalman Eisenberg's description refers to the insatiably greedy camp commandant, presumably Baumgarten, while Josef Kohs names Becker, the head of the German police in Starachowice. Only the fourth account identified the attacker, Blasowna, and the commander of the camp guards, Schroth, by name.

Three additional testimonies taken in 1966 and 1967 by German judicial investigators also describe the incident. All three were female friends of the attacker, whom they identified as Guta Blass. Otherwise their accounts differ. According to the first account, after the Tartak prisoners had been moved to the main camp, Guta argued with Schroth. He pulled his pistol and shot her. She fell. He kicked her and then drove the other prisoners into the barracks. They all thought she was dead, but she crawled into the barracks and was hidden and saved. In

short, in this version Guta confronted Schroth verbally but there was
no physical attack, and she was saved by fellow prisoners who hid her,
not by the decision of any German.[31] In the second account, Guta tried
to strangle not Schroth but Becker, who shot her and left her for dead.
Only wounded, she crawled to the barracks and survived.[32] In the third
account, the witness and four others had been taken out from the group
and were about to be shot by Schroth. He was running back and forth in
front of them with pistol drawn, when Guta leaped on his back. In the
ensuing struggle, he shot her in the leg and left her for dead. But when
he returned in the morning, the body was gone, and he demanded that
she be turned over. Her life was saved when another man in uniform
intervened and declared that she was "too brave" to be shot.[33]

Four late testimonies also mention the incident. One witness, in an
audiotaped interview in 1986, recalled that the night the lumberyard prisoners had been taken to the main camp by truck, one woman attacked
Schroth, who shot her. She pretended to be dead and then crawled under
the barracks. The next day, when the Germans could not find the body,
the prisoners bribed Schroth to spare her.[34] A second witness account of
1988 related how, after the lumberyard prisoners had been taken to the
main camp, the Germans got pleasure and enjoyment from scaring them.
They separated the men and the women and took people off into the
dark. One strong woman then jumped on a small German soldier and
almost choked him. After that, the Germans did not play games anymore but took the prisoners to their barracks. The woman was shot but
amazingly not killed, and by an unexplained "miracle," the commandant
let the woman live.[35] In a personal interview in 2001, another witness
confirmed that Guta, a beautiful young woman, had jumped on Schroth
on the evening the Tartak prisoners were being unloaded at the main
camp. Schroth shot her, but she survived and hid. It was Baumgarten
who arrived the next day and spared her.[36] The fourth late witness gave
two accounts in 2001 and 2004. Guta Blass told this witness that she had
attacked the guard because she had wanted the satisfaction of killing a
German before being killed. The Jewish camp leader had been able to
bribe the "commandant" for her release since the Jews were being sent to
Auschwitz anyway and he still wanted bribes.[37]

The twelfth witness was Guta Blass herself, who has provided at least seven accounts over the past forty years. She was interviewed by German investigators in 1967 in preparation for the trial of Willi Schroth in Düsseldorf and then gave sworn testimony for the court in 1971. In this account, the Jews of Tartak were brought before two large graves and told they were going to be shot. The prisoners pleaded for their lives, and a guard beat Guta to the ground and urged Schroth to shoot her. He replied that "the beast must first dance," but she successfully feigned unconsciousness. Schroth then shot her but only grazed her. Left for dead, she crawled under a barracks after dark, and other prisoners subsequently found and hid her. They also informed her at this point that it was Schroth—whom she did not know—who had shot her. The next day, Schroth returned, locked her in a small room, and threatened to kill her. But another German came and sent her to the sick barracks for bandaging. In the account to German investigators, therefore, she made no mention of having attacked Schroth or even knowing who he was before this encounter.[38]

In an interview given to an American reporter at the time of the Schroth trial in 1971, she again stated that when Schroth lined up the prisoners before two long graves (each 100 feet long and six feet wide), she pleaded with him. "Evidently he thought I was attacking him. He grabbed his rifle and with the back of it, hit me in the back of the head and knocked me down. At that moment, I knew that I had to do something more than just plead. I ran and grabbed his arms from behind and held on, trying to reason with him." They both fell, and one of the guards pulled them apart. Schroth wanted to torment her for amusement before killing her, but she feigned unconsciousness. He then shot and grazed her forehead, which left her covered with blood. Schroth, who had been acting on his own in threatening to kill all the prisoners, then let them go to the barracks. She crawled away in the dark, and other prisoners hid her until Schroth returned in the morning, demanding, "Where is the beast?" When he threatened to kill others, she gave herself up. She was not killed, however, because her fiancé gave a diamond to the man in charge.[39]

Subsequently, Guta gave an audiotaped interview in 1984 that is in the Museum of Jewish Heritage and a videotaped interview for the U.S. Holocaust Memorial Museum in 1990.[40] She described the incident in question in both accounts, admitting now that she had indeed attacked Schroth and not merely attempted to plead with him. In her first account, upon entering the main camp, the prisoners from Tartak were made to line up in front of two long graves, and Schroth told them they had one minute to pray, then they would be shot. Thinking especially of her mother who had turned pale, Guta ran out and jumped on Schroth's back, wrapped her legs around him, and dug her fingernails into his throat. Fearful of hitting him, the other guards did not shoot but eventually pulled them apart. Schroth did not shoot her immediately but wanted to make her dance first. She remained limp, and Schroth then shot her, grazing her forehead. At that point, Russian planes approached to bomb nearby targets, and the Germans ran for cover. The searchlights went out, and Guta crawled under the barracks and was subsequently hidden by her parents. When Schroth could not find her body the following morning, he threatened to shoot everyone, so she gave herself up. She was locked in a room and interrogated by the (unnamed) camp commandant, who demanded to know why she had attacked a German officer. She told him that she had only approached Schroth to beg for their lives but could remember nothing thereafter because of her head injuries. She was then released when her boyfriend and future husband gave the commandant a diamond that he had successfully kept hidden.

In her second videotaped interview, she repeated the story that they were lined up by a long grave and told they would be shot in one minute. She added that several weeks earlier a drunken Schroth had made sexual advances toward her, which she had barely evaded. She also noted that after receiving the diamond, Baumgarten (whom she now identified as "the man in charge") took her first to the camp infirmary for bandaging and then returned her to the barracks.

In an interview given in the late 1990s, Guta told of being lined up at the edge of a mass grave following evacuation from Tartak to the main camp (identified as Majówka rather than the new camp on the factory grounds) and being told by Schroth that they had one minute to pray before they would be shot. She jumped on Schroth's back and tried to choke him before they were pulled apart. After she was shot in the head with a grazing shot, Schroth tried to find her pulse and then left her for dead. In this account, she was reunited with her family for a number of days before Schroth discovered that she was still alive and locked her in a storeroom. Thereafter, she was beaten by another German, who none-theless sent her to be bandaged and allowed her to rejoin her family.[41]

In my interview with Guta in 2004, she immediately explained why her 1967 and 1971 testimony for the Düsseldorf trial concerning her attack on Schroth had not been accurate. She had been afraid to say that she jumped on him for fear that this would adversely affect the trial or even her. "When you have gone through what I have, when you have been scared, you don't get over it in one day." The attack had not been premeditated. "On the spur of the moment, something just exploded in me." She also described her two previous encounters with Schroth, first when he had escorted her and the doctor to Majówka to help deal with the typhus epidemic (presumably in the summer of 1943) and then when he visited Tartak to pursue her.[42]

Given the number of concurring accounts, I think that we can con-clude beyond any reasonable doubt that Guta Blass attacked the head of the Ukrainian camp guard, Willi Schroth, shortly after the Tartak prisoners arrived at the main camp, was shot in the head at point-blank range, and remarkably survived both this shooting and the expected Ger-man retribution. The preponderance of evidence suggests that Baum-garten was the man who made the decision to spare her life. Among the competing explanations—a "miracle," German respect for her heroism, hiding, and bribery—once again the preponderance of evidence suggests bribery as Baumgarten's key motive. Baumgarten was notorious for his corruption, and this was his final chance to extort one last payoff from his Jewish prisoners.[43]

The points at which Guta Blass's own testimony differs from that of other witnesses are more problematic. Her undoubted heroism at the age of eighteen is no guarantee of an infallible memory some two to six decades later. I think that she incorporated into her own memory the now-archetypal Holocaust image of Jews lined up at the edge of a mass grave about to be shot. No other witness mentions two mass graves or threatened mass executions inside the camp at this time, and the Germans as a rule did not carry out those kinds of executions within camp boundaries. The accounts of two other witnesses—saying that the guards were tormenting and scaring the prisoners rather than preparing an actual execution—are more probable than Guta's version.

The motive she gives for attacking Schroth in this setting was to save her parents from imminent execution, which in fact did not take place. According to Kalman Eisenberg's account, Guta called upon her fellow prisoners to attempt to escape. According to Josef Kohs, she urged them to attack the guards, but the other Jews remained paralyzed as she struggled with Schroth. Again, within the context of the failure of most of the Tartak prisoners to escape when Fiedler departed, an attempt by Guta to make up for this lost opportunity and instigate a mass escape upon arrival at the main camp has a contextual plausibility. In this case, her heroic attack on Schroth was not a miraculous success that saved the lives of her parents, as she remembered it, but rather a suicidal risk that failed to inspire any commensurate action among her fellow prisoners.

Finally, Guta remembers her rescue as the result of the singlehanded action of her boyfriend and future husband, who purchased her life with a diamond. The other witnesses who account for her rescue through bribery remember a collective action. There is no reason to doubt that her fiancé contributed a diamond to the ransom, but once again a larger ransom collected from numerous prisoners and negotiated through those who had experience in dealing with Baumgarten seems more plausible.

If my reconstruction is correct, then this episode has a twofold significance. First, it was a singular act of resistance, in which an unarmed eighteen-year-old woman risked a virtually suicidal attack on the head of the camp guard in order to give her fellow prisoners a last chance to escape but nonetheless survived. Second, on the eve of the evacuation of the camp, every prisoner must have been sorely tempted to husband his or her hidden valuables to increase the chances of survival in the face of a tremendously uncertain future. Instead, in an act of solidarity and collective endeavor, a number of prisoners pooled their resources to purchase the life of a fellow prisoner. The camp system was of course designed not only to divide prisoners but also to pit one against the other in a Darwinian struggle to survive. Numerous survivor accounts confirm the seemingly inexorable logic of the zero-sum game, in which one prisoner's gain could come only at the price of another prisoner's loss. But the cruel logic of the zero-sum game did not always prevail. In this case, Guta Blass attempted to sacrifice herself to save her fellow prisoners. In the end, it was they who sacrificed to save her.

23

The Final Days

I n trying to reconstruct not only the correct sequence but also the actual dates of events during the last week of the camp, the historian is faced with two difficulties. First, most survivors made no attempt to fit their memories into a precise chronological narrative much less provide precise dating. Second, those who did so invariably offer somewhat conflicting sequences. As a result, my attempt to place events in a particular sequence and to space and date them precisely is a hazardous venture at best. The beginning point must be the one date that seems to be reliably fixed. The numbers with which the Starachowice survivors were tattooed upon arrival in Birkenau were assigned to prisoners on a transport "with Polish Jews from the work camps in the Radom district," which arrived on Sunday, July 30, 1944.[1] This is according to the surviving camp records published in the Auschwitz *Kalendarium*. But even this date is not uncontested. The *Kalendarium* is not without dating errors, and one survivor distinctly remembers arriving in Birkenau on his birthday, July 31.[2]

Working backward, it is my best estimate that the Tartak prisoners had been brought into the main camp on the evening of Monday, July 24, and Guta Blass's life was ransomed from Baumgarten the next day, Tuesday, July 25. On Wednesday, July 26, the many rumors of impending evacuation were confirmed. A train arrived at the factory, and loading began. Then, mysteriously, the action was stopped. Those who had already been loaded were unloaded, and the prisoners were herded back into the factory camp.[3] The initial reaction of the prisoners was jubilation. Prisoners hugged and kissed as if they had been liberated.[4] No explanation was given, though some speculated that either there were not enough train cars for all the prisoners or the tracks had been bombed.[5]

After the initial jubilation, panic began to set in as prisoners realized that evacuation was still imminent. Some prisoners went to the kitchen and grabbed all the remaining food supplies.[6] Others who had been determined to attempt an escape resolved to make their bid that night. Not everyone was even aware of the impending attempt, as news had to be spread by word of mouth. Some were not informed or invited. For instance, Esther Kirschenblatt's brother came to her, gave her his bread, and said goodnight without mentioning a word about his impending escape attempt.[7] Others knew but decided against taking part. Many were dissuaded by pleas of family members.[8] Others could not conceive of leaving family members behind.[9] In yet other families, members argued, reached different decisions, and went their different ways.[10]

Some calculated the risk as too high or just became frightened. Josef Zolno from Płock decided against an attempt because he did not know the territory.[11] Josef Tauber feared that if he tried to hide in town, he would be turned over to the Germans, and if he went to the forest, he would be killed by partisans. After all, he noted, if there had been any place to go, he could have escaped from the factory at any time.[12] Josef Friedenson wanted to join the escape but could not muster the nerve.[13] Motel Feldstein also wanted to join but was held back by a premonition he could not explain.[14] Ironically, those with the best knowledge of local terrain were most likely to be impeded by fears of deserting their families, while those in camp without any family ties were the outsiders and latecomers least likely to feel confident about escaping into unknown terrain.

Survivors had varying estimates of how many prisoners tried to join the escape attempt, ranging from 150 to 400.[15] Of the 292 surviving witnesses whose accounts form the basis of this study, only twenty-five testified about their attempt to take part in the escape.[16] It should be kept in mind, however, that some of those interviewed by German judicial investigators may well have participated, but this part of their testimony on the escape attempt may have been deemed irrelevant to judicial purposes and therefore was not recorded.[17] In short, participation may have been underrecorded in my overall collection of testimonies.

The plan was simple. An initial group, armed with wire cutters and axes, was to make an opening in the fence. Second and third groups were ready to rush through, while many others hid under barracks and watched for their chance to join. According to no fewer than eleven witnesses—all based on hearsay and not direct participation in the event—contact was made with Polish partisans who were to facilitate the escape by shooting out the searchlights in some versions or neutralizing the watchtowers in others. In one such hearsay account, a half-million złoty had been paid in advance for this service, with another half-million promised afterward.[18] Against the many hearsay accounts of expected Polish help, one member of the Płock group that had been plotting escape testified that he had learned much earlier that Polish help was no longer to be expected. When the Polish partisans had learned how many elderly people and children were in the camp, they had changed their plans about liberating it.[19] In three accounts, the Ukrainian guards were alleged to have been bribed.[20]

In the version of events in which Polish help was expected, the Jews waited through the night for the partisans to shoot out the searchlights or neutralize the watchtowers. But they never came—a fact that is remembered bitterly by a number of the survivors as an act of Polish betrayal or deception. Suddenly the lights went off anyway, perhaps due to a nearby air raid. The first group ran for the first fence, cut through the wire, and then began pulling away boards from the second fence, which made a great deal of noise.[21] Overcrowding at the fence led to panic, and some of the more agile Jews tried to climb the fence instead of waiting for an opening to be made.[22] The Ukrainian guards were alerted by the commotion, turned on the searchlights, and opened fire. Chuna Grynbaum, who was with his sister and the policeman Moshe Herblum, was apparently one of the first to be hit. He suffered a head wound and briefly lost consciousness, but he remembers a "stampede" of people virtually running over him as he lay there. He then fled back to the women's barracks, where a cousin bandaged the three-inch gash in his head.[23] The initial fire from the towers did not halt the escape attempt. However, the head of the Ukrainian guards, Willi Schroth, arrived on the scene and tossed a hand grenade into the opening in the fence, with devastating effect. Schroth then moved a machine gun into position and opened fire, and the ensuing massacre of the first group was virtually complete.[24] Those who were already through the first wire and were now caught between the two fences tried desperately to get back into the camp and hide.[25] Many others who had been awaiting their chance to join the breakout gave up any attempt in the face of the hand-grenade explosion and the machine-gun fire.[26]

According to two witnesses, sixty-four prisoners were killed in the escape attempt.[27] While trying to account for the missing, Schroth approached Ida Gutman and asked where her brother-in-law Mayer was. She did not know, and he told her that her brother-in-law was not among the dead. By her account, he was among the seven who escaped that night, four of whom were captured and killed almost immediately.[28] In a classic example of the difficulty in using oral testimony for dating, while both Adam Gutman and his wife, Ida, told the same story concerning Mayer Gutman's escape in the nighttime breakout attempt in late July, Mayer himself dated the breakout attempt and his escape to April or May of 1944.[29] In fact, Ida Gutman's estimate of three successful escapees was somewhat low. There were at least five successful escapees who can be identified, and there were probably a few more about whom we will never know. One successful escapee, Jacob Szapszewicz, credited his prewar military training for enabling him to slip under the barbed wire without getting entangled and thus avoid the deadly bottleneck where the wire was being cut.[30] Esther Kirschenblatt's brother—who had given her his bread the night before—was not among the dead, and she presumed he initially got away, though he was killed later.[31] Yaacov Shafshevitz also made it through "the hail of bullets" and got away.[32] And according to Shlomo Einesman's daughter, Rozia, her father—who had arranged for a hiding place for the entire family on the outside— was the only one of the family to make it out of the camp (though he did not survive until liberation), while her brother and sister were both killed and her mother was injured in the attempt.[33]

The following morning (Thursday, July 27), around 10 a.m., the pris-

oners were assembled and counted to establish how many were missing. They were marched past the wire, where a number of prisoners (in
one estimate, twenty to thirty) lay badly wounded and were begging to
be either helped or shot. But Schroth prohibited any help from being
given; the wounded and dead were to be left for the dogs to eat, he
proclaimed.[34] Sesha Bromberger recognized her sister on a pile of bodies.[35] Chuna Grynbaum saw that his sister, the last surviving member
of his family in addition to himself, had died just several feet beyond
the last fence—"in freedom," as he put it. Next to her sat the policeman
Moshe Herblum, groaning with a terrible stomach wound.[36] In several
accounts, he was calling, "Kill me, kill me."[37] But the Germans were
obviously putting on this grisly display and prolonging the suffering of
Herblum and the others intentionally for the deterrent effect.

According to most accounts, Baumgarten, very possibly accompanied by the police chief Becker, then arrived at the camp. Though some
accounts named Becker, most witnesses stated that it was Baumgarten
who assembled prisoners and attempted to give them a reassuring and
calming, even "friendly" speech. In one account, he stood on a chair,
while Jeremiah Wilczek translated his speech from German into Yiddish. He was "disappointed" with them for the escape attempt, since he
had been so good to them. They were indeed going to be sent to another
but better camp in the Sudetenland, with hot and cold running water.
They had nothing to fear, for they were the best workers and much
needed. He could not understand how they had gotten such an idea that
they had to flee, but he blamed the camp police for instigating panic.
He then had Moshe Herblum shot by a Ukrainian guard as a warning
and deterrent.[38] In one account, Baumgarten displayed "a certain degree
of humanity." Although he had the order to shoot many more, he had
shot only a few of the wounded, specifically those who would not have
survived in any case.[39]

Even as Baumgarten spoke and continuing afterward, a number of
prisoners made further escape attempts in broad daylight.[40] Rather than
attempting a mass breakout by making an opening in the fence, small
groups as well as individuals rushed the fence at different points and
either scaled it or slithered under it. Others tried but could not make it.[41]
Sixteen-year-old Abramek Naiman, who had been wounded in the leg

in the breakout attempt the night before, discovered he was too short to get over the fence.[42] Several others got through at least the first fence but ran back into the camp when they encountered approaching guards or were fired upon.[43] But at least four groups, if not more, reached the forest and made good their escape.[44] Once again, among those participating in the escape were prominent members of the camp elite. The policemen Abraham Wilczek and Szmul Szczesliwy, and Mendel Mincberg, the son of the former head of the Jewish council, were among those who got away.[45] Willi Schroth set off after the largest group of escapees on his motorcycle and returned to camp claiming that he had caught and shot Abraham Wilczek before he could reach the forest, which turned out to be a false boast.[46]

Several narratives explicitly accused the Poles of aiding the recapture of escapees, who were dragged back to camp and killed. In one account, the church bells rang and the priest told Poles it was their obligation to bring back escaped Jews.[47] In another, Poles were offered a reward for using their dogs to track down and bring back Jews.[48] In a third, contrasting account, however, Schroth refused to pay the Pole who had brought back an escaped prisoner in clear expectation of a reward.[49] Whatever the disputed role of the Poles—whether in the absence of partisan help or in the tracking down of escapees—one thing seems clear. In terms of the ratio of escapees to casualties, the breakout attempts can hardly be termed a success. As one man who had hoped to escape but was knocked down by the fence and made his way back into camp stated, his life was probably saved because he did not get out.[50] Another man who did not join the attempt concluded that many more people survived who did not try to escape than who did.[51]

The Germans reacted to this flurry of breakout attempts in two ways. First, they increased the guard. Among the reinforcements were military police (*Feldgendarmerie*), whom the prisoners referred to as "canary birds" because of the yellow stripes on their uniforms.[52] Second, they collected all the prisoners' shoes and outer clothing, in the hope that the Jews would not attempt to escape barefoot and half naked.[53] Among at least a few of the Jewish prisoners, there was a reaction of a different sort. Mistrustful of the camp council and fearing that the camp elite was about to bribe its way out at the last moment, leaving the other prisoners behind to face German reprisal, they put the remaining camp leaders under watch.[54] There were in fact no further large-scale breakout attempts, though several women apparently still managed to slip out of the camp that night and join other escapees in the forest.[55]

On Friday, July 28,[56] the Starachowice prisoners were allowed to reclaim their shoes and clothes.[57] Rachel Piuti recalls the devastating effect on her father's morale when someone took the opportunity to steal his treasured pair before he could find them, leaving him with wooden clogs. Unable to walk in them, he felt stripped of his dignity and manhood.[58] In the now heavily guarded camp, machine guns had been set up between the two fences.[59] They were trained on the prisoners, who were assembled and left standing for hours in the hot July sun.[60] Some prisoners had dug burrows under barracks in a desperate attempt to hide and evade the evacuation of the camp. When such underground hiding places were discovered, the guards threw hand grenades or shot into the bunkers.[61] At least one prisoner who had been wounded in one of the breakout attempts and made it back into camp was now unable to join the assembled Jews and was shot.[62]

Josef Kohs approached one of the newly arrived guards (whom he identified as SS) and asked him outright if they were going to be gassed. At first the guard said that talk of gassing was "*quatsch*" (nonsense), that all the Jews were still alive. When Kohs pursued the conversation further, the guard finally assured him that while the older ones had to fear death, those capable of work would surely be left alive.[63]

A train then arrived on the track that led directly into the factory grounds, and loading began. Most witnesses remember Becker as the man in charge of the loading, though as in almost every such case, at least some named Baumgarten, Schroth, or even the long-departed Kolditz[64] instead. Such conflicting memory in multiple testimonies may be accepted by the historian as inevitable, but it was especially frustrating to the German judicial investigators who were thereby precluded later from including the lethal consequences of the overloading from becoming a point of indictment against Becker. There is no doubt that most of the train's closed freight cars were terribly overloaded. The women were loaded in different cars from the men. While most were filled so tightly that no one could sit or move about, at least the last women's car had only seventy-five people in it.[65] But the men's cars were packed with 100 to 150 people each.[66] When it proved physically impossible to pack the men any tighter, several open cars were brought in and added to the end of the train to take the remaining male prisoners.[67] The factory slave-labor camps in Starachowice were now all closed. The journey from Staracho-wice to Auschwitz-Birkenau was about to begin.

24

From Starachowice to Birkenau

The distance from Starachowice to Auschwitz is less than 140 miles by rail. Stopping in Częstochowa[1] as well as for priority trains along the way, the transport apparently took about thirty-six hours, leaving around sunset on Friday night and arriving in the dark early Sunday morning. While waiting in Częstochowa, one man learned from a Polish train worker that their destination was Auschwitz.[2] Not surprisingly, survivors offered widely varying estimates of how long the trip lasted, and virtually every survivor remembers it as having taken much longer than it actually did, most often estimating between three and five days. As one survivor observed, whatever the actual time, it "seemed like an eternity."[3] But if their memories of the length of the journey vary, their memories of the horrific conditions are virtually uniform. They traveled without food or water, or at best with one bucket of water and an additional bucket for human waste. In any case, the cars were packed too tightly for anyone to get to the latter. These late July days were sunny, and the heat within the closed cars was stifling. With just two tiny windows in each car, the prisoners gasped for air in the suffocating stench and heat.

In several of the women's cars, there was panic and hysteria.[4] In one case at least, fighting broke out between girls.[5] There were also some deaths, especially among the children and older people.[6] Only one woman survivor remembers Poles bringing water to her car at one stop.[7] Two other women remember receiving some help from Germans. One woman was singing a German song at night when the train had stopped, and a "Wehrmacht" soldier passing by asked who was singing. He returned with two halves of a cabbage, which he pushed through the small window, and she then shared with others.[8] Chanka Laks, who had worked in the camp office before the evacuation, had been approached by one of the military policemen or "canary birds" who was searching for an envelope. Chanka, from a relatively well-to-do family, had been the only Jewish girl from Starachowice to be admitted to a private high school in Radom, where she had studied French. Since the military policeman spoke with a French accent, Chanka conversed with him in French. Subsequently, during a stop on the trip, he searched the women's cars, asking for the girl who spoke French. Finding her, he allowed Chanka and several others to make several trips with a bucket to fetch water from a well. Before the last trip, Chanka recalled: "He said, 'Listen to what I'm going to tell you, the three of you, just run away. I'm going to pretend I don't see you, I'll shoot later. Just go.'" Chanka continued, "I didn't trust him, and we came back. Lots of times the Germans played games, I thought he'd shoot us. Then he appeared again, bringing us food, and then he told me, said 'I'm sorry, I gave you a chance to run away, I'm sorry that you didn't take a chance, because where you are going, you're not coming back.' He had a bottle of liquor he gave to me, with name (Leo Bernard) and address (on the French border), 'if you ever run away I'll help you.'" Years later, she wrote to Bernard but the letter came back as undeliverable.[9]

In the open men's cars at the end of the train, the trip was made without food or water but also without fatalities. Though the open cars had boards laid over the top, on which a guard stood, and the prisoners had to sit during the entire trip to prevent escape attempts, they were very aware of how "lucky" they were in comparison with the men in the closed cars.[10] In those cars, the heat and suffocating lack of air dominated a struggle to survive. Nineteen-year-old Ruben Zachronovitsky was "very lucky" to find a place beside the small window for fresh air at the beginning of the trip. He received several beatings from people who were desperate to get near the window, and he was finally pushed away and lost his place. He became so dizzy and weak that he could not remember what happened thereafter, other than that fifteen people had died in his car by the time they reached Birkenau.[11] Arren Arbeiter estimated that 150 prisoners had been packed into his car, and that three passed out and were dead when they arrived.[12] Abram Jakubowicz noted that, with the terrible heat and no food or drink, the older people in particular could not take it, and eight to ten people perished in his car.[13] Maurice Weinberger remembers protesting to Becker as he was being driven into a car overfilled with 120 to 150 men. Becker kicked him and threatened to shoot him for his "impudence." In his car, twenty-seven men suffocated during the trip.[14] Josef Kohs estimated that 120 men were loaded into his car. In the unbelievable heat, without food or water, men struggled to get near the window. "To me it seemed like a madhouse. Everything seemed to get wild. Bitter fights broke out over nothing. Were we in hell? Here the dying, there the unconscious, the screamers, those flailing wildly about.... It was a huge relief for us, when we finally arrived in Birkenau, the gassing camp of Auschwitz. Better already dead than to perish in such a death house. In our car out of 120 men 30 were dead."[15]

Neither Maurice Weinberger nor Josef Kohs, who reported, respectively, twenty-seven and thirty dead in their train car, said enough to identify whether they were in the same ill-fated car. But the likelihood is very great, since seven other witnesses also noted a high fatality rate of between twenty and thirty in one of the men's train cars in particular. One of these witnesses was the nephew of the head of the kitchen, who said that his uncle Rubenstein perished in that particular car. Two were members of the Lublin contingent, who said that twenty-five or twenty-seven dead were taken from their car. Yet another identified that particular one as the "first car" in the train, into which the camp leadership had been loaded and did not survive.[16]

Indeed, among the dead when the train arrived in Birkenau were the head of the camp police, Jeremiah Wilczek, and his younger son, seventeen-year-old Chil, as well as Jankiel Rubenstein, the man whom Wilczek had appointed head of the camp kitchen, and a number of other *Prominenten* of the Wilczek clique. Had they, like so many others, perished from dehydration, heat prostration, and suffocation? Or did the especially high fatality rate among the camp leadership traveling in the first car signify something more sinister? In the very earliest testimony of August 1945, Mendel Kac, when complaining that the camp elite had enriched itself at the prisoners' expense, noted cryptically, "Later they were punished with the death they deserved." He promised to return to the matter, but his account ended abruptly with the daylight breakout attempts on the day before the evacuation, and a fuller explanation was never given.[17] None of the other early testimonies even mentioned Wilczek's death, much less the circumstances surrounding it.

In the mid-1960s, when German investigators began interviewing survivors to assemble evidence against Becker, several witnesses explained Wilczek's death as yet another matter for which Becker should be held legally responsible. Matys Finkelstein told the investigators that Becker had conducted the loading of the train and especially sought out the "prominent Jews" and put them in a closed car packed with 120 prisoners. Matys Finkelstein's own car was not nearly as crowded, and there also had been open cars in which no one suffocated. Thus, the eighteen *Prominenten* who died on the way to Auschwitz had been, in effect, killed by Becker.[18] Hersz Tenenbaum likewise accused Becker of crowding twice as many men into the closed cars as opposed to the open ones—"above all the camp elders, camp leader, and camp police"— in which many (allegedly 90 percent—a vast exaggeration) died from the heat.[19]

At the same time, the investigators also heard a different version of events. Dina Rabinowicz, a daughter of the Wierzbnik rabbi, remembered that a man named Rubenstein as well as the head of the camp police, Wilczek, had been "killed" in a train car en route to Auschwitz, though she did not say how or by whom.[20] And another of the rabbi's daughters, Raca Rabinowicz, noting the large number of dead in the train cars upon their arrival in Auschwitz, added that, "in the men's cars, in any case, some prisoners were said to have killed others; for example, especially members of the camp administration were said to have been killed."[21] And Mayer Gutman, who had escaped in the nighttime breakout, confirmed that he had heard after the war that a policeman and his son had been killed by other prisoners.[22]

In subsequent interviews, survivors were obviously reluctant to confirm in front of German investigators a story that would shift blame for

at least some Jewish deaths from the Germans to fellow Jews and therefore acquit Becker of responsibility. Only one further witness stated outright that Wilczek and Rubenstein had been "strangled" by other Jewish
prisoners in the train car on the way to Auschwitz.[23] Another specifically
singled out Becker for blame: "At the loading for Auschwitz Becker
sought out people whom he knew particularly well, for example, people
who had given him gifts, members of the Jewish council or people who
had had special functions in the camp. He had them locked in a closed
car pressed together as tightly as possible. On the trip to Auschwitz many
died. Among them were the camp policeman Jarmia [sic] Wilczek and
his son."[24] But most were vague. Some merely confirmed that Wilczek
and Rubenstein had died on the trip, without specifying how.[25] Others
referred to altercations and trampling in the overcrowded car carrying
the camp *Prominenten* and remarked that many did not arrive alive in
Auschwitz.[26] Two witnesses conceded that the camp leaders had all been
crowded into one car, in which prisoners had killed one another.[27] But
all of these testimonies were hearsay. The German investigators stopped
pursuing the issue entirely when in 1967 they heard from one witness,
Ben Lant, who had actually ridden in the first car: "We were between
104 and 120 men locked in a sealed cattle car and received neither food
nor water during the journey. Because it was the height of the summer
of 1944, it was very hot, and the air holes in the car were too small to
supply enough air for so many people. . . . In our car there were 20 dead
upon arrival in Auschwitz. But it is not true, and this I want to declare
emphatically, that the men had killed one another. I would say that most
died from lack of air."[28]

Ben Lant's emphatic denial notwithstanding, in 1991 two survivors
independently gave accounts that lifted the veil on the fate of Wilczek
and other camp leaders on the train to Auschwitz. In a barely audible and
technically flawed videotaped testimony, one survivor was explaining the
tensions and conflict that arose between the camp council controlled by
Wilczek and the Starachowice old-timers and the newly arrived young
men from Majdanek, the "Lubliners" or "Klneks." In conclusion, she
noted, almost as an aside, that the "Lubliners" killed twenty of the camp
elite on the train to Auschwitz. Perhaps taken aback by the realization
that she had said something she had not intended, she paused and then

said with resignation that that too was also a part of history. In a retaping of her interview eighteen months later, she did not repeat the story.[29]

In the same year, 1991, Goldie Szachter Kalib published her memoir, *The Last Selection: A Child's Journey Through the Holocaust*. Her father, through contact with his boyhood friend Shlomo Einesman, of the Wierzbnik *Judenrat* and later of the camp council, had been able to obtain work papers for his family before the ghetto liquidation. The immediate family had survived Strelnica and Majówka intact. She related how, immediately upon arrival in Auschwitz, she learned of the death of her father and brother, who had ridden in the ill-fated first car. A male friend of her sister

> explained that when the Judenrat stepped into the train at Stara-
> chowice, the K-L Sonderkommando who had arrived in Staracho-
> wice from the Majdanek Concentration Camp aggressively forced
> its way into the same car. . . . The heat and lack of circulation sadly
> in the closely packed car brought people close to suffocation. As
> some of the former Judenrat members were attempting to maneu-
> ver themselves into a less awkward standing position, individuals
> of the K-L Sonderkommando began taunting: "Who do you think
> you're pushing around? What makes you think you're better than
> anyone else?" Tempers began to flare on both sides until the K-L
> Sonderkommando thundered, "All you pigs refused to share your
> privileges with anyone except those who were willing and able to
> make you rich. We'll show you what big shots you are now." And
> fighting broke out. Father desperately attempted to calm the vio-
> lence, only to incur the wrath of the K-L Sonderkommando, who
> now turned on him.

As her brother moved to defend her father, the "ruffians" began assaulting him too. The fight resulted in a number of fatalities, including her forty-four-year-old father and sixteen-year-old brother.[30]

Subsequently, three Starachowice survivors giving videotaped testimony and one writing his memoir chose to mention the unusual number of deaths in the first train car but attributed the fatalities to suffocation from lack of air.[31] Five testified that there was fighting and Jews killed "one another" or "each other."[32] And two specifically identified Wilczek as among those "killed" on the train. One of them described how Wilczek died. "They just stepped on him," she said.[33]

Six testimonies, however, were quite specific that a revenge killing had occurred as punishment for the misbehavior of the Jewish camp leadership but were moot about the identity of the killers. The camp elite had been killed because they had been "very bad" in terms of beating and robbing other prisoners.[34] They had incurred "strong animosity" because they had sold out their brothers.[35] They had been "so bad" to other prisoners that the latter "took vengeance" and "choked them to death."[36] One such witness raised the issue of the killers but said that no one told who did it.[37]

Two testimonies made clear that the revenge killings had not been perpetrated by Wierzbnikers. Rather, the killings were carried out by men from "another town"[38] or a "different camp."[39] Finally, three of the videotaped testimonies confirmed Goldie Kalib's identification of the killers as the "Klneks" from Majdanek,[40] and another identified the killers as concentration-camp prisoners but wrongly identified them as having come from Płaszów.[41]

The fate of the Wilczek coterie and others at the hands of the "Lubliners" was also confirmed in nine personal interviews.[42] Almost all of these survivors related what they had learned from others immediately upon arrival in Auschwitz. The bodies of the dead were in plain sight as the Starachowice Jews disembarked and marched past the first car. And the sensational news of how the deaths had occurred traveled very fast. Several of these witnesses were distressed that many "innocent" people had been killed alongside those who had most abused their power, and one was emphatic that "people from our town would never do it."[43] Only one among all the witnesses admitted to being in the first car and could confirm the events as a direct eyewitness. As the Jews were being loaded onto the train in Starachowice, Chuna Grynbaum spotted the "Lubliners." "I looked at these guys who had just arrived to our camp. They were pretty strong yet. They came from another place, another camp. I said why don't I run with these guys, they look toughened up. . . . Maybe they'll escape, I'll run with them. They stuck us in that wagon and sealed us up. Strong guys, pretty good sized boys." Wilczek, Rubenstein, and others of the camp elite were also in the car. "They stuck us in there like sardines. That's when the commotion started, fighting during the day, everybody tried to get a little bit of fresh air through that little window, they were pushing one another, getting angry." And then the killing began. Chuna Grynbaum arrived in Birkenau sitting on the pile of corpses.[44]

As a general rule, historians tend to prefer testimony that is given closer to the event to that given much later. But what is valid as a general rule is certainly not valid in the case of the fate of Jeremiah Wilczek and other camp leaders. Some events require a passage of time and the appropriate setting before witnesses are willing to speak. Clearly, the German investigation of Becker in the 1960s was not the propitious occasion, and the German judicial investigators were not the suitable interviewers for Holocaust survivors to discuss this painful episode of internecine strife and revenge killing of Jews by Jews. By the 1990s, some fifty years after the fateful train ride to Birkenau, many of the Starachowice survivors were willing to speak of these events not only among themselves as a communal memory but now also to others as a public memory. In doing so, they have disproved yet another disparaging cliché about Holocaust survivor testimony: that as time passes it becomes more simplified and sanitized and divorced from the perplexing ambiguities and terrifying complexities of an increasingly distant time and place. Some speak with anger and others with resignation, but many have spoken. The only voice that has not been heard is that of the "Lubliners" themselves, for whom this event still remains a communal rather than a public memory.

If survivors have struggled with how and even whether to include the revenge killings of Wilczek and other *Prominenten* in their accounts, and a clear preponderance of evidence concerning Wilczek's fate did not emerge until rather recently, the ways in which survivors described their first impressions upon arrival in Birkenau are stunningly similar. The train arrived in the dark, and light penetrated the morning mist only gradually. As the new arrivals first caught glimpses of scarecrow people with shaved heads running around in striped pajamas and wrapped in blankets, one common image sprang to mind. In the identical words of no fewer than ten survivors, they thought they had arrived in a "crazy house."[45] In the same spirit, three others pronounced it an "insane asylum,"[46] two others a "mad house,"[47] and yet two others that it was filled with "crazy people."[48]

This unity of initial reaction aside, what happened thereafter on this first day in Birkenau is recounted in significantly different ways. So far I have argued that, overall, the core of shared memory of the Starachowice survivors has proved relatively stable and reliable, despite the fact that the testimonies were given in a time span stretching over six decades. And as we have seen in the case of Wilczek and his fate on the train, there has been a growing tendency to speak more openly than before about sensitive or hitherto taboo topics. A chronological treatment of the history of the Starachowice factory slave laborers, however, requires me to end with precisely that episode—the arrival in Birkenau—about which survivor memory has proved increasingly problematic with the passage of time. In this case, however, another extremely important and complicating factor is at work.

The factory slave-labor camp is one of the most understudied and least well-known phenomena of the Holocaust; among such camps, Starachowice was both small and obscure. Except for those who were enslaved there, it is virtually unknown. For the historian, this has the significant advantage that survivor memories of Starachowice are relatively pristine, uncontaminated by the later incorporation into individual memories of archetypal images broadly disseminated in popular consciousness. The arrival in Birkenau, on the other hand, is an extraordinarily dramatic, archetypal Holocaust memory, graphically described in some of the most widely read memoirs, such as Elie Wiesel's *Night* and Primo Levi's *Survival in Auschwitz*, and visually portrayed in numerous documentaries and movies, most famously *Schindler's List*. How have the Starachowice survivors withstood the tendency to incorporate into their own memories the powerful and pervasive images about the arrival in Birkenau to which they have been exposed continuously in subsequent years?

On one important count, the preponderance of testimony is quite convincing that the entry of the Starachowice transport into Birkenau was atypical. Because the transport came from a work camp that had already undergone numerous selections, the Starachowice prisoners were brought into Auschwitz as a group without being subjected to the notorious selection on the ramp.[49] Particularly those who were children, or still had children in their family at the time, were emphatic on this point. The unusual admission into Birkenau without selection was perhaps the single most crucial stroke of luck or act of fate in a long chain of fortuitous and unlikely events that enabled them to survive.[50] In the words of one survivor, they were "the luckiest transport."[51] Two survivors surmised that the Germans did not work at the crematoria on Sunday, so they had been fortuitously spared because of the day of the week on which they arrived.[52] Others conjectured that the Germans were temporarily out of Zyklon B,[53] or that the crematoria were full.[54] Another survivor simply concluded that the Germans were not going to fire up the crematoria for a few kids.[55]

But for many, a less mundane, more miraculous explanation was needed; hence the story spread about "the letter." According to this explanation, which several witnesses cautiously qualified as just a "rumor," Baumgarten had intervened on behalf of his former prisoners and sent a letter with the transport assuring the authorities in Birkenau that the Starachowice Jews were all good workers.[56] This explanation took its most extreme form in the testimonies of two survivors, one of whom claimed that Baumgarten turned out after the war to have been a British secret agent and the other that he was really a Jew who had successfully concealed his identity.[57]

More common than the elaboration of an explanation as to why no selection had taken place was the memory that the transport had indeed undergone selection. Thirty-three survivors testified to this effect. All but one of these testimonies date from 1980 and later.[58] Perhaps not surprisingly, sixteen survivors remember encountering the notorious Dr. Josef Mengele on the ramp the morning of their arrival as part of the selection process.[59] In one survivor testimony, a selection occurred not on the ramp but after the showers, and it was conducted not by Mengele but rather by the equally infamous Adolf Eichmann.[60]

In my judgment, at least three factors are at work here. First, even among the witnesses who said there was no regular or systematic selection are some who attested to certain selectionlike occurrences that would have facilitated confusion of memory in this regard. Those who were too weak even to walk after disembarking from the train were taken aside.[61]

Women and younger children were separated from the men and older boys before being shaved, showered, and tattooed. And some women and children were designated not to receive a tattoo immediately and were only tattooed several weeks later.[62] Second, as mentioned above, the selection on the ramp by Dr. Mengele has become one of the most broadly recognized archetypal episodes of the Holocaust, widely disseminated in both books and films. Third, all of the Starachowice prisoners who arrived in Birkenau were later subjected to the routine selections of the camp conducted by SS doctors, and Mengele not infrequently took part in those. Thus, the actual memory of the separation of the women and children from the men, the ex post facto incorporation of widely disseminated images, and the telescoping of the subsequent experience of selection by SS doctors, including the notorious and feared Dr. Mengele, with the arrival in Birkenau, experienced in a state of utter exhaustion and trauma, could all contribute to creating a vivid memory of something that actually had not occurred. In contrast, there is no convincing explanation, in my opinion, as to how a preponderance of witnesses could have arrived at the common memory of an atypical entry into Birkenau without the standard selection, if this memory were false. Nor could such an assumption account for the empirical fact that so many of the women and children who would not have survived such a selection actually lived to testify to the contrary.

The Starachowice prisoners were taken from the ramp through the standard processing, where they were shaved, showered, tattooed, and given new camp clothing in place of the personal clothing they had worn before. According to the registration lists at Birkenau, 1,298 men and 409 women from the July 30 transport carrying "Polish Jews" from unnamed "work camps" in the Radom district received tattoo numbers.[63] It is not certain if all of these 1,707 prisoners receiving numbers at that time were from Starachowice; according to one source, additional train cars had been added to the transport in Częstochowa.[64]

As with the pattern of testimony of other Auschwitz survivors, the men made little comment about being shaved and given new clothes, but women were embarrassed by being forced to stand naked in front of male overseers and then upset by their transformed appearance in ill-fitting clothing with shaved heads.[65] The men had a different experience. While they were in the shower, old inmates came and asked whether there were any Jewish policemen among them and whether they had behaved badly. At first, the new arrivals did not understand the purpose of the question, but then they realized that the old inmates had come to "settle scores." Szaja Langleben, who apparently had not traveled in the ill-fated first train car, was identified and badly beaten. But, unlike Wilczek and other *Prominenten*, he survived. Apparently seeing the feared and hated Langleben being beaten was not a source of gratification but rather a demonstration of the newcomers' utter powerlessness in their new surroundings. Pinchas Hochmic commented that the episode "brought our morale even lower."[66]

Another aspect of the entry into camp, in addition to the selection on the ramp by Mengele, demonstrates the powerful capacity of popular media, especially film, to implant images and shape the way in which stories are retold. Before 1990, only one testimony—that of Josef Kohs from 1948—told how upon arrival in Birkenau the Starachowice prisoners did not dare to have hope until water rather than gas came from the showerheads.[67] This must have been a not-uncommon experience, yet it does not again appear in the testimonies for nearly fifty years. Then, after the remarkable shower scene in *Schindler's List* had become an iconic image of the Holocaust, no fewer than twenty survivors include in their narratives a reference to their surprise or relief when the showers proved to be real, and water rather than gas came from the showerheads.

Following the entry processing, the Starachowice prisoners were moved to one part of the so-called Gypsy camp or *Zigeunerlager* (which contained Roma and Sinti, who had been deported from Germany to Birkenau in 1943) and placed under quarantine. After the trauma of the train trip and entry, they were exhausted and hungry. But one aspect of their new setting struck many of them immediately. In comparison with Starachowice, Birkenau was "very clean" and there were "no lice."[68] As one survivor put it, "This was the good thing," but quickly added, "only in that way."[69]

The last common experience of the Starachowice prisoners—before they were dispersed to various camps, barracks, and work commandos of the vast Auschwitz-Birkenau complex following quarantine—came several days later, on the night of August 2, 1944. They had briefly observed the Gypsy family camp as their neighbors, and some had talked through the fence that separated their quarantine barracks from the Gypsies.[70] But that night they heard trucks rolling in and out of the Gypsy camp as well as screaming and crying.[71] The Gypsies, well aware of their impending fate, did not go quietly. The next morning, the Gypsy camp was entirely empty, and the Starachowice newcomers could see the smoke belching from the crematoria and smell the stench of burning flesh and hair that filled the air.[72] They had been temporarily spared, but they had now seen how Birkenau could devour nearly 3,000 people in a single night.[73]

25

The Starachowice Women and Children in Birkenau

In 1944, Auschwitz-Birkenau surpassed Treblinka as the Holocaust's most lethal killing center. It was in fact a complex of camps serving multiple functions: imprisonment, exploitation of labor, and mass killing. Auschwitz I—the base camp or *Stammlager*—was founded in 1940 on the site of former military barracks built of brick. Initially, it was intended for Polish political prisoners. In the spring of 1941, it was expanded to a maximum capacity of 30,000 inmates, after Himmler reached agreement with German industries, especially I. G. Farben, on the use of concentration-camp prisoners for labor in factories to be built in the region. In late 1941 and 1942, much vaster expansion was undertaken with the construction of two adjacent camps: Auschwitz II in the nearby village of Birkenau for more than 100,000 prisoners, and Auschwitz III on the site of the I. G. Farben plant at Monowitz. Some thirty-nine more subcamps were gradually added, making Auschwitz by far the largest complex of SS camps within the Nazi empire.[1]

The first gas chamber at Auschwitz had been improvised in the morgue of the crematory in Auschwitz I. In the spring of 1942, two peasant huts at the edge of the Birkenau camp were converted into gas chambers in which most of the Jews in the incoming transports from various European countries were killed upon arrival. Then, in the summer of 1942, Himmler visited Auschwitz and ordered the construction of four gas chamber–crematory structures in Birkenau. They were completed and put into service in the spring of 1943, providing Auschwitz-Birkenau with a killing and body-disposal capacity far exceeding the first generation of death camps, such as Treblinka. In the spring of 1944, the railway spur line was extended directly into the Birkenau camp, and a ramp was constructed for unloading and selection virtually at the doors of the gas chambers. It was on this ramp that the transport from the Radom district was unloaded on July 30, 1944, and from which some 1,200 to 1,400 Starachowice Jews entered Birkenau as prisoners of the SS without the usual selection.[2]

Following quarantine in the Gypsy camp, the Starachowice prisoners, particularly the men, were assigned to various work projects and dispersed as individuals or small groups throughout the vast complex of Auschwitz camps, including many to Monowitz or Buna. For all the Starachowice prisoners who entered Birkenau, two generalizations can be made. First, they were less starved and in better physical condition than the newcomers from the Łódź ghetto, who also arrived in the summer of 1944. Second, they were veterans of twenty-one months of camp experience, as opposed to the newly arrived Hungarian Jews, who had to learn from scratch how to cope with camp life. Aside from these two important factors, there is no common narrative of the men from Starachowice after their dispersal to various work assignments, as they blended into the larger Auschwitz prisoner community. Two questions concerning the fate of the Starachowice prisoners still beg to be answered, however, even if those answers remain somewhat speculative. First, how can one account for the seemingly disproportionate number of women survivors giving testimony after the war? Second, how can one account for the continuing survival of the Starachowice children after their unusual entry into Birkenau without selection?

In the fall of 1942, women made up approximately one-quarter of the initial prisoner population in the Starachowice camps. Women seem, moreover, to have been disproportionately targeted in the two largest selections and mass killings during the next twenty-one months—namely, the Bugaj Forest in March and Firlej in November 1943. Among the lists of newly arrived prisoners from Wolanów, Tomaszów-Mazowiecki, Mokoszyn, Radom, and Cracow in the summer and fall of 1943, men were again in the distinct majority.[3] And the Lublin contingent of April 1944 was overwhelmingly male. Thus, the gender imbalance would not have been redressed by newcomers. The proportion of men would probably have been diminished by their overrepresentation among those who escaped from the camp prior to evacuation, those who were killed trying to escape, and those who perished on the train. Indeed, according to Auschwitz registration figures, 1,298 men and 409 women from the July 30 transport from the Radom district work camps received tattoo numbers that day.[4] Some women and children did not receive tattoos the first day, so both the total number and the proportion of women would have been slightly higher. Thus, the rough estimation that approximately one-quarter of the Starachowice slave laborers were women at the beginning seems to have been restored at the end. Yet 44 percent of the postwar survivors whose testimonies I have seen (128 of 292) are women. That may be explained in part by a greater willingness of women to give postwar testimony,[5] but it also seems very likely that the fatality rate among women prisoners in Birkenau and afterward was lower than that among the men.[6]

On the basis of admittedly impressionistic rather than firm statistical evidence, I would argue that three important factors could have contributed to a lower fatality rate for women. First, while the men were widely dispersed, clusters of Starachowice women remained intact in their subsequent barracks and work assignments. According to one witness, for instance, Barracks 25 was filled entirely with prisoners from Starachowice.[7] The support networks of family and small groups that had sustained them in Starachowice did not have to be rebuilt from scratch.[8]

Second, the regime of terror within the Birkenau women's camp seems to have been somewhat less draconic and lethal—relatively speaking, of course—than in the various men's camps of the Auschwitz complex, especially in terms of the rigor of selection and the possibility of surviving hospitalization. For example, Basia Grynspan arrived in Birkenau on crutches with a broken leg. She was sent to the hospital barracks and survived two selections because she could get up and stand by her bunk and was allowed several months to heal.[9] Ruth Ehrlich was hospitalized for an infected knee, had surgery, and survived three subsequent selections—the first through the special pleading of a doctor and a nurse in attendance.[10] Mirjam Glatt was placed in the hospital barracks but could be visited by her sisters, and she survived selection when hidden by a friendly nurse.[11] By the time Goldie Szachter and her mother were taken in a selection in November 1944, the gas chambers had just been closed down, and they were sent to a "recuperation" barracks (*Schonungsblock*) instead.[12] While virtually all survivors' stories relate a series of "miracles" by virtue of which they improbably survived, there seem to be proportionally fewer such stories among the men than among the women in connection with selection and hospitalization in the Birkenau period.

Third, at least four transports with groups of Starachowice women left Birkenau for other camps or work sites before the end of 1944, thus sparing them from the horrific decimation of the death marches that began with the evacuation of Auschwitz-Birkenau in January 1945. Two were sent to sites in the Sudetenland. One was the Langenbielau camp.[13] Another was a textile factory in Zillertal.[14] Other transports went to Ravensbrück and Bergen-Belsen.[15] According to one of the women prisoners transferred to Bergen-Belsen before the end of 1944, conditions there at that point were still "bearable" in comparison with the catastrophic situation the following year, when it was not only flooded with evacuated prisoners but also assigned especially vicious personnel transferred from Auschwitz.[16]

Fifteen Starachowice prisoners who survived Birkenau to tell their stories were born after 1929 and thus entered and survived that camp when they were fourteen years old or younger. The youngest were two girls—Rutga Grynszpan, born in 1937, and Tola Grossman, born in 1938[17]—and one boy—Abraham Malach, born in 1935.[18] Goldie Szachter spoke for them all when she subsequently wrote, "It had been a miracle when the routine selection had been dispensed with on the day we arrived at Auschwitz. As a child of twelve, I most certainly would have been sent directly to the gas chambers."[19] But surviving that first day does not explain their continuing survival over the next six to ten months of captivity (depending upon whether they were liberated in Auschwitz in January 1945 or in Germany later in the spring). There is, of course, no comprehensive explanation for the children's unlikely survival under such conditions, but several themes recur in their stories.

Contrary to the common fate of women and children arriving at

Auschwitz, who usually were selected for immediate death, children who remained with their mothers, and in this case went into the women's camp, stood a better chance of survival than boys who went with their fathers into the men's camp. Nine-year-old Abraham Malach's parents made the conscious decision that he would remain with his mother, while his brother, older by two and a half years, would go with his father. Abraham survived in the women's camp, but his older, taller, and stronger brother fell victim to the more rigorous selection in the men's camp and perished.[20] Again, improbable as it sounds, the women's camp was equipped with a children's barracks. The youngest children were eventually sent there and spared both labor and further selection. Some remained there until liberation of the camp in January 1945, thus also being saved from the lethal winter death march out of Auschwitz.[21]

Boys in the men's camps survived the rigor of selection in two ways. First, their long experience with camp life equipped them to maximize their chances to evade selection. Michulek Baranek, born in 1930, noted that after various men had been picked for work commandos, mostly teenagers were left behind and given menial jobs, such as sorting clothing. This gave him the opportunity to steal but also left him exposed to selection as a dispensable unskilled worker. He was in fact picked twice but managed to escape each time. On the first occasion, those selected were held in a barracks where he hid in the oven until the others had been taken away. On the second occasion, while Hungarian Jews awaited their fate, he and a companion tried to slip out the window. His companion made good the escape and alerted his uncle. The uncle in turn bribed a *kapo* (a privileged prisoner with supervisory responsibilities) to have Michulek's number removed from the list, and he was removed from the selected group before it was taken away.[22] Jacob Kaufman, born in 1931, likewise avoided death in one selection by hiding in the oven. On another occasion, he slipped into a group of workers being chosen for Buna and marched out of Birkenau to a somewhat safer camp.[23]

Second, the teenagers who survived often did so through a protector who held a position of influence in the camp. David Mangarten, born in 1930, was fortunate enough to encounter a Starachowice prisoner who had been sent to Auschwitz much earlier and by 1944 had become a "big shot" in the prisoner hierarchy with an office job. He took care of Mangarten by sending him away—to clean offices or feed rabbits—whenever a selection was held.[24] Sixteen-year-old Chaim Wajchendler served as a "Puppe" or personal servant for an Austrian *kapo* but also found a clique of other boys to run with for mutual protection.[25] Once Jacob Kaufman had made his way from Birkenau to Buna, he was helped by a German foreman who had just lost his children in an air raid. He somehow identified Jacob with them and gave him light work.[26]

Such crucial protectors were in a position to exploit their power, and at least two Starachowice prisoners either hinted or admitted that sexual favors were expected in return. In one part of his interview, a Starachowice survivor interjected rather abruptly that the "homosexual prisoners" were "the toughest, the worst." In a different part of the interview, he described how one *kapo*—a good-looking German political prisoner in this case— had saved him by taking his name off a list. Having admitted that the *kapo* "embraced" him as the "youngest" prisoner in the barracks, he then stopped abruptly, as if realizing that he was touching upon a subject he did not wish to discuss further.[27] Abraham Malach had learned enough about camp life to make himself useful and worked as a messenger in the women's camp. But he noted that a woman *kapo* "took a great liking to me . . . and she would call me to her barracks from time to time and feed me." One day she took him into her barracks during the day when everyone was away and "commandeered a young attractive woman to wash me up and talking nicely to me that it's important to be clean and that girl carefully washed me and fondled me and that kapo took me on her bunk and tried to arouse me and as a nine year old boy lying beside her, on top of her and in any kind of position, whatever she tried must have been futile, futile but that was the life in the camp for this poor woman." It was an incident, he said, that he could only comprehend years later.[28]

Thus, women seemed to have experienced less dispersal, leaving families and support networks intact, and a less rigorous regime of selection. Many also were sent out of Auschwitz to new work sites in the fall of 1944 before the lethal death marches. Even very young children who entered the women's camp had some chance of survival. Young boys needed both the accumulated experience of many months of camp life and influential protectors to survive the more rigorous selections of the men's camps.

Finally, no discussion of the Starachowice women's experience in Birkenau would be complete without mention of one recurring but very bizarre story—the rumored encounter there with Willi Althoff's mother. The story comes in two distinct versions. In the first version, she was a "Gypsy" whom they encountered when they were first lodged next to the Gypsy camp.[29] In the second version, someone recognized the boots an older woman prisoner was wearing as the product of the *Konsum* shoemakers in Majówka. When questioned, the woman identified herself as the mother of Willi Althoff, though she had no idea about the position her son had held in Poland. She was in Birkenau because she had been caught trying to hide her Jewish son-in-law.[30] The tragic irony of either version—that the mother of the major killer of Starachowice Jews either perished as a "Gypsy" in Birkenau or was incarcerated there for hiding a Jewish son-in-law—gives the story a certain plausibility.

26

Escapees

W hile the vast majority of Jewish slave laborers still alive in the Starachowice camps in late July 1944 were shipped to Birkenau, and most of those who tried to escape in the last week did not survive the desperate breakout attempts, some prisoners did reach the forest. They, like the few other prisoners who had successfully risked escape earlier, then faced the daunting ordeal of surviving on the outside until the Soviet army—which had seemed so close but then unexpectedly stopped its offensive on the Vistula River, less than forty miles to the east—finally arrived in Starachowice nearly six months later, on January 18, 1945. It is to the experiences of a few of the surviving escapees—both those who had left earlier as well as those of July 1944—that we now turn.[1]

There are three patterns of survival among those who escaped at some point before July 1944: entering another labor camp, passing as Polish workers in Germany, or being hidden by courageous Poles. When the Ostrowiec ghetto was being liquidated in October 1942, 110 Jewish workers had been selected and taken to Starachowice to work on the construction of the labor camps there before liquidation of the Wierzbnik ghetto. Irving Weinberg subsequently learned that members of his family were still alive in the "small ghetto" in Ostrowiec, and he made plans to escape and rejoin them. He eluded the Ukrainian guards and caught a night train to Ostrowiec. Seeing Germans at the station there, he waited to jump off the moving train as it departed. He joined a column of Jews marching to work and was then reunited with his family in the ghetto.[2] Barek Blumenstock was in the same Ostrowiec contingent. Unable to sleep at night due to the huge lice all over his body, and assigned to bathing shell casings in acid, he felt he would never survive Strelnica, so he resolved to escape. At a change of shift, he slipped among the Polish workers leaving the factory. Spotting Germans at the train station, he set out on foot and eventually received a wagon ride. A Pole who joined the ride near Ostrowiec recognized him and took him home for a meal before advising him how to get into the ghetto. There he joined four cousins and a "wealthy uncle," so he did not go hungry.[3] Eventually, both Weinberg and Blumenstock lost all of their families in Ostrowiec and ended up, by different routes, in Auschwitz and then Germany.

In Opatów, Josef Czernikowski's family had consciously decided to separate in the hope that at least someone in the family would survive. He opted for Starachowice and bought a seat in one of Leopold Schwertner's trucks. In the spring of 1943, when he learned that his sister was still alive in a camp for agricultural laborers near Sandomierz, he resolved to join her. A Pole he had befriended at work offered to help. Josef jumped the camp fence and joined his friend, who bought train tickets, accompanied him to Sandomierz, and helped him locate his sister's camp. A Jewish policeman let him in, and after some negotiations, he was entered on the camp list and became "legal." When that camp was closed, he transferred to a labor camp at Pionki, from where he was loaded on a train for Auschwitz in July 1944. He jumped from the train after it had crossed into the "incorporated territories" that had been annexed to the Third Reich. Once again provided crucial help by several Poles, he eventually made his way across southern Poland to the Russian lines, where he encountered two other Starachowice escapees—the Eisenberg brothers.[4]

Mania Isser—who had long been preparing to escape and hence had her clothing and money ready—had slipped out of Wierzbnik in the early hours of October 27, 1942, and heard the screams of the ghetto liquidation while hiding in a woodshed. With the payment of money, she persuaded her very reluctant Polish host to let her stay for five days.

She traveled to Lwów in vain pursuit of a cousin, then to Warsaw in vain pursuit of a safe hiding place. Finally she returned to Wierzbnik and contacted her family in Tartak, but they advised her not to enter the camp. Taken off the train on her way back to Warsaw, she was sent to Germany as a Polish forced laborer.[5]

A native of Lwów, Lucyna Berkowicz had been transferred with her husband, Daniel, from Wolanów to Starachowice in the summer of 1943, where she survived an abortion and the Firlej selection. Fearing her supervisor, a Polish nationalist who had already denounced one of his Jewish female workers, but offered help by her Polish foreman, Ignaz Gura, she decided to attempt an escape. She was blonde and could hope to pass, while her husband was typically Jewish in appearance and could not hope to join her. To pay for her escape, he smuggled and sold a revolver from the blacksmith's shop where he worked. She was transferred to a team assigned to outside work digging potatoes. Ignaz Gura met her in the potato field, but the Jewish policeman Abraham Wilczek appeared and threatened to take her back to camp unless she took his girlfriend with her. Lucyna refused, Abraham relented, and Gura took her to a family friend for hiding. The next day, two other Poles took her by train to Warsaw. The Pole who was to hide her there lost his nerve, so after paying for an identification card, she reported to the Labor Office and volunteered for work in Germany.[6]

Of the early escapees, only one is known to have survived in hiding in Poland until the end of the war, and even then just barely. Tema Lichtenstein was among the expellees from Płock. In the fall of 1943, her Polish foreman offered to help her escape. A fellow Jew from Płock gave her the signal when she could safely peel off from the march to work without being seen. She was then taken to the village of Bronkowice, where she was hidden by Teofil Novak, but her presence raised suspicion. A villager who had spotted two Jews emerging from the forest asked her to detain them in conversation while he fetched his gun. She instead warned them to run back into the forest. Fearing that she would denounce him to the Russians when they arrived, the villager preemptively reported her to the Germans. She and her guardian Novak were arrested and imprisoned in Starachowice. In the truck on the way to Starachowice, Novak warned her not to believe the interrogators if they said he had already confessed that she was a Jew. He would die before he gave her away, he promised. Both were subjected to lengthy interrogation and finally released on January 12, 1945. They were afraid to return to Bronkowice until the Russians had arrived, after which they were received in the village with a big party.[7]

In July 1944, the arrival of the Soviet army seemed imminent, so the Germans moved to evacuate the camps. For those who risked trying to escape at this time, it was not an unreasonable calculation that they would have to survive on the outside for only a few days or weeks at most. Instead, the Soviet army halted on the Vistula River for six months. Thus, Starachowice and the surrounding area were not liberated until mid-January 1945. For those who had escaped in the final days before evacuation of the factory camp, there were again three patterns of survival: flight eastward to the Soviet lines, hiding, and joining the partisans. Most fortunate in this regard were the Eisenberg brothers, Yechiel and Mielach, who came from Iwaniska, just west of the Vistula. They were among those who participated in the nighttime breakout from Starachowice and reached the fence but retreated back into the camp when the guards opened fire. However, they successfully got through the fence and into the forest during the daylight breakout the following day. They walked to the southeast in order to return to Iwaniska. Mielach knew the territory, since he had worked the region as a horse trader before the war. Thus, when they reached the outskirts of Iwaniska, they were allowed to stay in the stables of a farm where he had traded horses before the war. By good fortune, an advance party of Soviet cavalry reached Iwaniska, and they were liberated. Finding the town very depressing and hearing rumors that the Germans were about to reoccupy the region, they wisely resumed their trip eastward and reached the safety of the Soviet lines just weeks after their escape.[8]

Leib Feintuch and his brother also failed to escape during the nighttime breakout but managed to get through the fence the following day, immediately following Baumgarten's speech. They went to various villages, where Poles would give them food out of fear of the Soviets, who were expected to arrive soon, but they would not let the Jews hide, out of fear of the Germans who were still nearby. By then part of a small group of fugitives, they contacted a partisan band that said it would take Jews.

Instead, the Jews were forced to surrender all of their valuables, and one Jew who was found to have kept one bill sewn into his clothing was shot. The rest were told to scatter and run. Leib and his brother continued eastward, receiving help along the way until they reached Russian lines on August 15.[9]

For those who did not move eastward and reach the Russian lines but sought instead to hide locally, the wait for liberation was longer and more precarious. In Tartak, when Naftula Korenwasser looked out a window near the machine at which he was working, he saw the trucks approaching. He ran to pick up his wife, and together they escaped across the creek behind the lumberyard before the camp was surrounded. A Polish policeman was on the Ostrowiec-Skarżysko highway, which they had to cross before they could reach the forest. Naftula asked him if he wanted them on his conscience, and he did not shoot. They proceeded to the village from which his wife had come. One farm couple let them stay in the hayloft for a few nights, but then they had to leave before the couple's son—an anti-Semite and a member of the Home Army (*Armia Krajowa* or AK)—returned. Naftula then was helped by several Poles with whom he had served in the army, one of whom provided a pick and shovel to dig an underground bunker in the forest. Speaking the local dialect, his wife—now joined by her sister—did tailoring for farmers in the area, and eventually Naftula began to do skilled carpentry work as well. When a less skilled carpenter threatened to denounce Naftula, the locals "dealt" with him, since they did not want to lose Naftula's valuable services. Hence they survived until the first Soviet troops arrived on January 17.[10]

Yaacov Shafshevitz was one of the very few Starachowice prisoners who made good his escape in the nighttime breakout. He made his way back to his hometown of Szydłowiec, where, during the still-warm summer months, he slept under the open sky and encountered various former schoolmates who exclaimed, "Yaacov, you're alive?" But none dared to hide him, as, "truth to tell, the danger for them was really great." He was joined by another fugitive Jew, and together they paid "a poor peasant" to hide them in his barn. They gave him "all the money we possessed," as well as a wristwatch, but after two weeks he demanded more. Unable to pay, the two Jews were given the ultimatum "to go and steal" from a wealthy neighbor for whom the peasant had worked. In the end, by virtue of carrying out two robberies on behalf of their host, Yaacov and his companion retained their hiding place until the Soviets arrived.[11]

Also during the night breakout, Jacob Szapszewicz used his prewar experience in the Polish army to slip under the barbed wire without getting entangled and made his way back to the family home in Śmiłów near Radom, from which the Germans had evicted his family much earlier. There he found that the Germans were still in his house and that his neighbors were all too afraid to hide him. He returned to Starachowice, rummaged through the now-empty barracks for food and clothing, and then went to the "old janitor" from the factory, who let him stay in his barn until the Soviets arrived.[12]

Mendel Mincberg, son of the former head of the *Judenrat* in Wierzbnik, was at the factory when the Jewish foreman of his department warned him that the camp was surrounded and he should not return to the barracks. Without a chance to plan, he and several other Jews slipped out of the factory and over the fence. Ukrainian guards spotted them as they crossed the road and opened fire, but in the growing darkness they made good their escape. Since two of the escapees were from Bodzentyn, they crossed the Kamienna River and headed for that town, where they found shelter in the cowshed of a Polish woman who was promised payment after liberation. After three weeks, when the hoped-for liberation had not come, the increasingly frightened Polish woman insisted that the hidden Jews shift to an underground hiding place much farther from her house. Out of money for food, Mendel returned to Wierzbnik one night to seek help from a friend. When he returned to the hiding place, he discovered that it had been raided by "partisans," and two of his companions had been killed. His friend in Wierzbnik procured identification papers for him, and he worked as a Polish agricultural laborer near Iłża. On several occasions, his employer was obligated to provide a horse and wagon to transport Germans from Starachowice and Wierzbnik. Mincberg was sent as the coachman to pick them up. Gentile acquaintances recognized Mincberg, but no one gave him away, so he survived.[13]

Like Leib Feintuch, whose brief encounter with a partisan band cost him all his money but not his life, other escapees who tried to survive by joining a partisan group ran the grave and probable risk of encountering the wrong group. While a few partisan groups in the forests—usually those associated with the AL (*Armia Ludowa*, the Communist-oriented underground)—would accept Jews, those associated with the AK (the conservative nationalist underground Home Army) usually rejected them. More dangerously, some AK units and especially extremist units associated with the notorious National Armed Forces (NSZ) would either rob Jews or simply kill them outright. Jakob Binstock and Chaim Salzberg were among a group of prisoners who planned a successful escape directly from the factory into the forest, with the goal of joining the partisans. The leader of the first group they encountered told them it was a big mistake to come to the forest without guns, and further-more he did not take Jews. "At least he was honest," Chaim noted. But the partisan leader did give them directions to another partisan who he thought was Jewish. They encountered a group of Soviet parachut-ists led by the Yiddish-speaking "Bolek." He had no guns to spare but before he moved on, he gave them valuable advice on how to survive in the forest. After various close calls, Jakob and Chaim finally were taken into a large AL unit of Mieczysław Moczar (a prominent leader in the Polish Communist Party and in its postwar security apparatus), and they fought in the area until that unit was ordered to cross over to the Soviet side in December, before the imminent Red Army offensive.[14]

David Sali was among those who escaped from Tartak before the prisoners there were taken to the factory camp. His group swelled in numbers, which caused the local peasants from whom they were asking for food to complain to a nearby AK unit that they were being harassed by Jewish partisans. The AK unit surrounded the Jewish escapees and threatened to kill them if they continued to demand food from the vil-lagers. Six of the escapees asked to join the AK group and ostensibly were welcomed. Four days later, the bodies of all six were found near the village. The Jews then tried to join a partisan group associated with the Communists. The advanced party that they encountered simply took all their possessions. The commander of the unit eventually restored their stolen items but still would not let them join. They finally encountered a third group that would permit them to join, if they acquired weapons. When they captured five weapons from a careless German requisition party, the group of thirty-seven Jewish men and three Jewish girls were allowed to become members. This turned out, once again, to be the large Communist unit of Mieczysław Moczar, made up of Poles, Jews, and escaped Soviet POWs of different nationalities. Even in this mixed unit, on one mission several Polish members took the opportunity to murder a Jewish comrade. When this was uncovered, however, two Poles were executed.[15]

Abraham Shiner had slipped through the fence unnoticed shortly before Baumgarten's speech, watched the daylight breakout attempts from the forest, and then fled north to the Iłża region with two other escapees. Most villagers they approached would neither give nor sell them food and instead informed the Germans, but a small number provided enough help to stay alive. Hoping to join the partisans to fight a "common enemy," Shiner instead found himself "at risk of being murdered by the partisans themselves." First, his group was caught by AK partisans, whose commander warned them that villagers had complained of being robbed and he would kill them if they did it again. A few days later, they fell into the hands of an NSZ unit, but Shiner bluffed that there was a Vlassov unit of German collaborators nearby who would come if they heard shots, and the NSZ partisans quickly fled. A third time, they narrowly escaped death at the hands of "common murderous bandits" who also shared the forest. Finally, he and his companion, Arie Lustgarten, decided to head for the Russian lines. When Abraham fell ill with a high fever and was no longer able to walk, the two were taken in by the Yezierski family. While Abraham recovered, Arie worked in the fields for the family. As neighbors became suspicious, the Yezierskis decided they could not hide more than one Jew. They helped Abraham find his way to a group of Soviet partisans.[16]

Abraham Rosenwald likewise encountered a bewildering array of different groups in the forest after he escaped from Tartak. First, he encountered Bolek, who would not take his group of Jews since they had no weapons. A second partisan group robbed them of their few possessions. To live, "we went to the fields and gathered potatoes. The peasants ambushed us and beat us up." A third group of partisans murdered one of Abraham's companions, Israel Rosenberg, because they coveted his clothes. In one village they encountered a fourth group of partisans, whose commander would not let them join but nonetheless gave them some grenades for self-defense. Members of a fifth group of partisans robbed them once again, but this time the commander returned the stolen goods. A sixth partisan group agreed to take any Jews with prior military experience but subsequently murdered them. Abraham was finally allowed to join a seventh group, from whom he received rifle training, but he became separated in escaping a German encirclement. An eighth group, led by "Piotor," allowed Jews to join but only to perform menial work, not fight. And the Jews were not allowed to stay with Piotor when he crossed over to the Russian lines. At this point, Abraham encountered Shlomo Einesman, who had left his hiding place. Einesman suggested the others return to that hiding place with him, since he had sufficient money. Instead, Abraham persisted in going east and this time made it across to the Soviets.[17]

Several escapees were able to take an active role with partisans in fighting the Germans. Abraham Wilczek—the elder son of Jeremiah Wilczek—was among a group of ten young men who made it through the fence and into the forest during the daylight breakout (and thereby probably saved himself from sharing the same fate as his father and younger brother on the train to Auschwitz). When they tried to join a partisan group, it would take only two of them, including Abraham. He became an expert in the dangerous job of placing explosives on bridges and rail lines. When he became seriously ill, he was left behind by his group, which was fleeing an anti-partisan sweep by columns of Central Asian auxiliaries of the German army. However, Poles took him in for ten days until his fever broke. When he tried to rejoin his band, he discovered that they all had been denounced and killed. He alone of the group survived until Soviet troops arrived in January.[18]

The very last successful escapee before the Starachowice Jews reached Birkenau was Szmul Chaim Wolfowicz, a native of eastern Poland (near Baranowicz) who had arrived in Starachowice as part of the Lublin contingent in the spring of 1944. He was in one of the very crowded and hot cattle cars that departed Starachowice on July 28 and decided to risk jumping. Others lifted him up to the small window, from which he leaped and rolled down the embankment. Making his way back toward Starachowice, he begged for food in villages, speaking Russian to appear as an escaped Soviet POW rather than a Jew, or stole potatoes from the fields. In the forest he helped a surrounded partisan unit find a way out of its encirclement. At first, the unit tried to chase him away but eventually it let him join, and finally he inherited a rifle from a very sick comrade. Thereafter, he fought and rose to command his own group before finally being ordered to go over to the Soviet lines.[19]

Among the 2,200 Jews who passed through the Starachowice factory slave-labor camps, very few tried to escape. After all, many had purchased work permits just to get into one of these camps, where working for the Germans in the munitions industry that was key to the war effort was judged to offer the best chance for survival. It was not particularly difficult to get out of these camps—many Jews left and reentered repeatedly—but surviving on the outside for any length of time was extremely difficult and dangerous. Long-term hiding faced almost insuperable odds, so most of those who survived an early escape did so by virtue of working either in Germany or in another labor camp in Poland. Even the late escapees, who had to survive just under six months on the outside, faced great odds. Ultimately, not only did few prisoners attempt escape, but among those who did, few survived until liberation.

One factor in the steep odds against survival on the outside brings the historian again to the complex issue of Jewish-Polish relations. Fear of denunciation by hostile Poles was one of the great deterrents to escape. Indeed, among those who escaped, many experienced not only denunciation but robbery and even murder. Others, however, encountered Poles who not only did not denounce them but even provided short-term help. Even these nonhostile and supportive Poles, however, would not provide long-term shelter, primarily out of tremendous fear of the dangers to which the long-term hiding of Jews would expose them and their families. Even so, virtually every escapee who did survive received—and often more than once—crucial help from Poles, without whom they would not have survived. And the Poles who did so usually received no benefit commensurate to the risk they incurred. Escaped Jews may have experienced much hostility and danger from Poles, but those who survived were also the recipients of many acts of courage and altruism.

PART VI

AFTERMATH

27

Return to and Flight from
Wierzbnik

T he former prisoners of the factory slave-labor camps in Starachowice had arrived in Birkenau as a result of the first wave of
mass camp evacuations that the Nazis undertook in the summer of 1944 in response to the rapid advance of the Red Army into
Poland. The Starachowice prisoners were then dispersed among various work sites at Auschwitz-Birkenau and its subsidiary camps. They
were further scattered in the maelstrom of two additional waves of mass
evacuations—effectively "death marches"—in 1945. The first took place
from Auschwitz in January 1945, when all but a few thousand prisoners were force-marched to railheads and then shipped to various camps
throughout Germany. These camps were horrifically overcrowded, shelter and food were lacking, and hygiene conditions were frightful. The
death rate among prisoners, both on the exhausting marches and in the
new camps, skyrocketed. Worse was still to come. As the Allied armies
penetrated into the Third Reich in March and April 1945, camp com-
manders sent off their starved and exhausted prisoners on yet another
wave of even more lethal death marches—often with no destination or
purpose other than to keep their dying prisoners one step ahead of the
Allied armies—until the final collapse of the Third Reich.[1] Starachowice prisoners blended into the mass of Nazi prisoners who suffered
extraordinary loss of life during these last five months of the war. Of
the approximately 1,200 to 1,400 Starachowice Jews who arrived in

Auschwitz-Birkenau at the end of July 1944, I would estimate that about one-half of them—some 600 to 700—were still alive at the end of the war.

After the war, most of the surviving Starachowice Jews gathered in various DP (displaced persons) camps established by the Allied occupation government in Germany, seeking to recover physically and to locate and reunite with any surviving family members. Gradually they left the DP camps and Europe behind and emigrated overseas. For the Starachowice Jews, three destinations in particular became their new homelands: Israel, the United States, and Canada. This was a common pattern for most Holocaust survivors. What distinguished the Wierzbnik-Starachowice Jews from other waves of immigration out of the DP camps was that their largest single community of survivors clustered in Toronto, Canada, where they continue to preserve their community ties to this day and annually meet with other Starachowice survivors in North America as well.

Precisely because the Starachowice prisoners were dispersed and followed different paths after their evacuation to Auschwitz-Birkenau, it is not possible to write a common narrative of their fate after July 1944. However, adequate closure of the history of the Jewish prisoners of the Starachowice factory slave-labor camps requires more detailed comment on two particular postwar developments: what happened when small numbers of Wierzbnik survivors trickled back into their hometown, and what happened to the German personnel of these camps when subjected to German judicial investigation.

In the already controversial subject of Polish-Jewish relations, one especially sensitive topic is the tragic fate of Polish Jews who—having survived the horrors of the Holocaust against all odds—were killed by Poles when they returned home after the war. Historian David Engel offers the conservative estimate of 500 to 600 Jews killed in Poland after the Germans had been driven out.[2] Princeton University scholar Jan Gross lauds Engel's impeccable scholarship in the existing documentation but is more comfortable with the higher traditional estimate of 1,500, since he thinks many such killings went unreported.[3] Gross focuses on the notorious Kielce pogrom of July 1946, the culminating massacre of a second wave of such killings. In contrast, the killing of returning survivors in Wierzbnik-Starachowice occurred earlier—in June 1945—in the midst of a first wave of such killings that stretched from March to August of that year. The region encompassing both Kielce and Starachowice was a stronghold not only of AK (*Armia Krajowa* or Home Army) activity but an area in which the extremist NSZ (National Armed Forces) was active. It was the region with the highest incidence of postwar killing of Jews even before the Kielce pogrom.[4]

In the wider historical context, Poland at this time was in the midst of what historian Daniel Blatman has called a "miniature civil war."[5] Large portions of the population supported the unequal struggle against an unpopular Communist takeover that was made possible only by the presence of the occupying Red Army and repressive Stalinist security apparatus—a struggle that resulted in some 10,000 Polish deaths on both sides and the arrest of an additional 150,000 to 200,000 Poles.[6] But why, in this wider context of civil war and widespread violence, were handfuls of desperate and skeletal Jewish survivors—emerging from hiding or coming from camps in Germany and returning to their hometowns in Poland primarily to see if any other family members were somehow still alive—targeted for murder?

At the heart of the anti-Communist resistance, and most frequently implicated in the killing of returning Jews, were conservative nationalist Polish forces in various underground groups. Their self-image of Polish identity (Catholic, culturally and linguistically Polish, patriotic, anti-Communist, victim) had been constructed in opposition to a diametrically contrasting "image of the enemy" (Jewish, cosmopolitan and Yiddish-speaking, traitor, Communist, perpetrator). This conglomeration of non-Polish traits was summed up in the fateful phrase and mythical concept of "Judeo-Communism" (*Żydokommuna*), which, like all myths, proved impervious to empirical refutation.[7] It was rather the lens through which they viewed political events and interpreted reality. The "overrepresentation" of Jews (in the form of some totally secularized Jews who had long abandoned any Jewish identity) in the Communist Party of the interwar period or in the Stalinist security apparatus after the war was taken as self-evident proof of the identity between "the Jews" and Communism. The fact that "the Jews" welcomed the entry of the Red Army into eastern Poland in 1939, saving them from Nazi occupation, and then welcomed the reentry into Poland of the Red Army in 1944 as "liberators" rescuing a surviving remnant, was confirmation that "the Jews" were traitors to Poland. In short, interpreting Polish history through the lens of "Judeo-Communism" transformed Polish violence against Jews into understandable acts of self-defense and justifiable acts of revenge.[8]

The lethal potential of "Judeo-Communism" to returning survivors was intensified by at least three additional factors. First, Jewish suffering in the Holocaust rivaled and threatened to obscure Poland's claim to double-victimization at the hands of both Hitler and Stalin. The traditional Christian accusation that proclaimed Jews as Christ-killers now neatly dovetailed with the new nationalist accusation that proclaimed Jews as the killers of Poland as the Christ among nations and conveniently transformed helpless Jewish victims into dangerous Jewish perpetrators.[9] Second, much Jewish property—now conveniently designated "formerly Jewish property"—came into Polish hands either during the war or after the German withdrawal. The return of survivors threatened the new owners, and resistance to restitution motivated by simple greed could now be legitimized as an act of patriotism and anti-Communist resistance.[10] Third, Jan Gross has argued that the intensity of hostility to returning Jews required more than political and material explanation. He therefore emphasizes an additional collective psychological factor— namely, the guilt that Poles felt in the presence of returning survivors over their behavior vis-à-vis the Jews during the Nazi persecution. In effect, to expunge any discomforting reminder, they now killed or drove out those whom they had already harmed.[11]

According to David Engel's research in Polish records, two Jewish women and two children were killed in Wierzbnik on June 8, 1945, two more victims perished on June 15, and a final victim was killed on June 17.[12] The community book lists a total of eleven Jews from Wierzbnik, Wąchock, and Bodzentyn who were killed when they returned to Poland after the war.[13] How do survivors remember these lethal events of June 1945, and what can this contribute to our understanding of the dynamics behind the murder of returning Polish Jewish survivors after the war?

The first Jews to return to Wierzbnik-Starachowice were those who had escaped from the camps and survived in hiding when the Soviet army liberated the region in January 1945. When Naftula Korenwasser, his wife, and other relatives returned from the village where they had hidden, people looked at them as if they were "crazy" and could not believe they were still alive. As other Jews returned, Naftula sensed that Poles with whom property had been left had "prayed" that their Jews would not come back, and the situation was becoming dangerous.[14] Abraham Rosenwald also emerged from hiding in the forest to join the group of survivors assembling in Wierzbnik-Starachowice. His first task was to join a grave-digging group that learned from Poles where Jews had been killed and left in shallow graves in order to give them a proper burial. It was he who disinterred the body of the beautiful Tobka Wajsblum, who had left camp with Walther Becker and never returned. She had been shot in the head.[15] He also traveled to Lublin on behalf of the assembling survivors to get money and clothing from the aid organization there.[16] Another forest survivor, Chaim Flancbaum from Wąchock, was warned by a Jewish officer in the Soviet army that Jews should stick to the large cities and not return to small towns. He came back anyway but fled in June 1945 when the killing began.[17]

Jakob Binstock from Szydłowiec had joined the partisan band of Mieczysław Moczar. He was in Łódź in June 1945 when he encountered Abraham Wilczek, who told Jakob that his aunt was still alive in Starachowice. As Abraham was going there, he asked Jakob if he had any message for his aunt. Jakob told him to tell his aunt to come immediately to Łódź, as he had lodging for her there. She departed for Łódź two days before the killing in Wierzbnik began.[18]

Perhaps the earliest returnee from camps to the west was Symcha Mincberg. Liberated at Fünf Teichen in January, he made his way on foot back to Wierzbnik, arriving on March 16, 1945. He first encountered Abraham Rosenwald and then was joined by his surviving son, Mendel. Returning to the camp grounds, he found the lists of Jewish slave laborers of Majówka that were subsequently reprinted in the community book. Initially, the returning survivors stayed together in the home of Leib Brodbekker on the marketplace, "since most of the Jewish homes in town were already taken over by Poles and even going out on the street alone was dangerous." When the Brodbekker house became too full, Mincberg and his son found shelter in another apartment.

Another early returnee from Germany was Mania Isser. Having survived posing as a Polish worker in Germany, she was liberated by the American army in Frankfurt and headed back to Poland even before the fall of Berlin and the end of hostilities. She too was warned in advance that it was dangerous to return to Starachowice. Nonetheless, she went from the train station directly to her house, where she encountered a Polish woman who asked her what she was doing there. When Mania replied that this was her house, she was told, "Shit is your house. I advise you quickly to go away." Since she came from one of the wealthier Jewish families in town, others warned her again that she was particularly in danger. This time she took the advice and left for Łódź one day before the killing began.[19] When Nathan Gelbard returned to Wierzbnik, he too received a "cold" welcome from Poles who warned him to leave. He took the warning seriously and departed for Łódź.[20]

By mid-May, the number of returning Jews in Wierzbnik had swelled to fifty-six, including ten children.[21] While infinitesimal in comparison to the prewar Jewish population, apparently it was enough to provoke the right-wing Polish underground into action in the form of a murderous assault on the Brodbekker house. A Polish family was living on the ground floor, and the returning Jews lived in two rooms on the second floor. The men lived in one room, and in the other were the widows and children of two former members of the *Judenrat* and the *Lagerrat*—Sarah Wolfowicz and her two children Fischl and Rifka, as well as Ruchele Einesman and her daughter Rozia. Rozia remembers the fine June day on which they were sitting at the entrance and enjoying the sun, when three men carrying rifles stopped and looked at them from a distance. In the middle of that night, they were awakened by shouts and knocking on the door. The man on the ground floor came up and told them all to flee to the roof before he would be forced to open the door. The men on the second floor reached the roof, jumped, and got away. Rozia and her mother made it to the roof as well, but the Wolfowicz family did not. The intruders called up, promising no harm, and the Einesmans returned to the apartment. Ruchele Einesman recognized one of the men and addressed him by name, but he did not answer her. Instead, the five Jews were lined up along the bed, after which the intruders turned off the lights and opened fire. Apparently they fired over Rozia, the shortest one in front, and she was initially not hit. But the other four were killed. Not wanting to be left alive alone, Rozia shouted. They shot again and she was hit in several places but was still alive. After the killers had left, she went downstairs, where the frightened neighbor eventually let her in. She was then rescued by her uncle Noah, who came and took her to the hospital.[22]

In addition to the men at Brodbekker house who got away over the rooftop, others also narrowly escaped the killing spree that night. When Sala and Channah Glatt had visited their old house, they found it inhabited by a school girlfriend who warned them to get out before her brother came back, for he would kill them if he found them there. The common greeting from Poles to returning Jews was: "The streets are yours but not the houses." One Polish family that had kept valuables for the Glatts returned a few silver spoons and cups, explaining that they had had to sell the rest to survive. The sisters found that believable and were glad at least for a few souvenirs. That evening, two men in trench coats (whom they identified as AK members) and a dog came to their room, asked some questions, and left. Next morning, the sisters learned that the two men with the dog had gone on to another room of Jewish refugees, where they had killed the Wolfowicz family and Ruchele Einesman, leaving only the badly wounded Rozia alive. The two sisters ran to the train station and left for Łódź the next day.[23]

Another pair of sisters, Rosalie and Chanka Laks, was staying with a Russian family, the Paleschewskis, who had been good friends of the Laks family before the war. They had saved the Passover silver and Passover wine cups that their mother, Pola Laks, had left with them. After the two men in trench coats—referred to as NSZ by Rosalie—had killed the two women and two children in the one room, they knocked on the door of the Paleschewski house and demanded to see the Jews staying there. The Paleschewskis refused, and the men left. The two girls remained in hiding all of the next day, but the Paleschewskis bought them tickets for the train the following day, took them to the train station in a covered wagon, and waited with them until the train had left for Łódź.[24]

Chava Faigenbaum was staying with one of the clusters of returning

Jews, but on the fatal day she and her aunt visited old family friends, the Wykrota family, who welcomed them. After consuming much vodka, the son warned them to "run away from here." They were then taken to the safety of another family member's house farther from the center of town. It was there that they heard the gunfire from the killing at the Brodbekker house. Chava and her aunt boarded the "first train" and fled.[25]

Also narrowly escaping were Perele Brodbekker and her sister. Returning from Theresienstadt (Terezin), they took up residence in the family house. Old Polish acquaintances greeted them with the astonished inquiry, "You're alive?" They, too, were warned that they were risking their lives by returning. On the day of the fatal attack, they visited the family graves in the Jewish cemetery. As it was getting dark when they were returning home, they accepted an invitation to stay overnight at a different apartment and thus did not return to the Brodbekker house on the marketplace. It was there that Leib Brodbekker later found them and told them about the slaughter in the family home. After giving the victims a Jewish burial, they left Wierzbnik "forever."[26]

When Jacob Kaufman arrived back in Starachowice on the morning of June 9, 1945, he was met at the station by a Jew who warned him that a number of Jews had been killed the night before, including the wife of a Jewish council member. He was told of three places where Jews were hiding, and he finally located a second cousin among the survivors who had returned. He left for Łódź the next night. Even the train trip was filled with uneasiness, for stories were spreading about Poles throwing Jews off trains.[27]

Channah Glatt was not content with having escaped Wierzbnik with a few silver spoons and cups. She knew that her father had hidden fabrics from the family store in the double wall of a warehouse that the Germans had confiscated. It was a good place to hide things, since a German warehouse was one place the Poles could not loot after the Jews had been deported. She suspected that the fabrics would still be there, but the problem of getting at, much less removing, half a store's worth of fabric was perplexing under the circumstances. She then encountered an old boyfriend who had fled to the Soviet zone in 1939 and had now returned as an officer in the Soviet army. Channah offered a deal. If he would provide two trucks and protection, she would split the recovered fabrics half and half. Channah, the Jewish officer, and eight Soviet soldiers drove to the warehouse. Some soldiers set up a perimeter guard, while others broke down the wall and filled the two trucks with fabrics. Some of the fabrics were water-damaged, but most were still in good condition. The soldiers then drove back to Łódź and split the take, as agreed.[28]

A subsequent attempt to recover Jewish property in Wierzbnik ended far more tragically. Abram Kadyszewicz heard of Channah Glatt's exploit and talked to her about it.[29] He decided to return to Wierzbnik to sell his father's buildings. His friend Moszek Szpagat warned him of the danger. Moszek traveled with Abram to Wierzbnik but parted company with him there and traveled immediately on to Ostrowiec. Abram negotiated the sale of his father's properties, but no sooner had he finished signing the papers than he was killed.[30] His killers chopped off his head and, by one account, placed it on a stick in the marketplace.[31] It would seem that in this case the killers were local Poles with whom Abram had negotiated the sale and who, once in possession of the ownership papers, killed rather than pay the seller.

As a fearful warning to any other Jew who might try to remain in Wierzbnik, much less dare to reclaim property, the beheading of Abram Kadyszewicz had the predictable effect. Icek Guterman had returned to Poland to fetch his father, but his father stubbornly refused to leave, since he did not feel he had enough money to start a new life elsewhere. The AK placed a death sentence on the father. When Icek went to the marketplace, a woman made the sign of the cross over him and warned him that a female mill owner had been shot the night before and a young man had been beheaded. Now "really afraid," Icek was able to get his father to the train station and aboard the next train, regardless of the direction in which it was going.[32]

Rozia Einesman languished in the hospital and never again saw her uncle Noah, who had taken her there, for he too was subsequently killed. The Polish doctor, Borkowski, who was treating her, reportedly received threatening letters, which he courageously ignored.[33] After two months, Rozia was taken to a farm in the countryside to recover further. In the fall of 1945, a relative fetched her and put her in an orphanage in Łódź.[34] Jewish life in Wierzbnik-Starachowice was at a complete end, and the last Jew to die there was murdered not by the Nazis but rather by Poles.[35]

Much of the discussion over the postwar killing of Polish Jewish survivors revolves around motive. At least in the case of Wierzbnik-Starachowice, the determination to preserve the benefits that Poles accrued from the Nazi murder of the Jews—in terms of both property transfer and homogenization of the Polish population—are most prominent, at least in the postwar testimonies of the survivors. The men who committed the first killing on June 8 were members of some Polish underground nationalist movement—whether AK or NSZ, the survivors naturally could not be expected to know for certain. What is clear is that these men surveyed the situation and, with calculation and premeditation, decided upon a murderous assault on the Jews in the Brodbekker house. In the end, they knew they were shooting only women and children. They were aiming not at active agents in league with the Communists but rather the most defenseless and helpless targets they could find, whose murders would have the most frightening effect in persuading other Jews to flee. Poland having been cleansed of Jews by the Nazis, these self-proclaimed guardians of Polish national purity were not about to sit by passively while handfuls of returning survivors posed the danger of a rebirth of Jewish life in Poland. In this regard, they were quite successful. In June 1945, the survivors who had returned to Wierzbnik fled to Łódź. In general, returning Jews found greater safety in larger cities and especially in the western regions that had been newly acquired by shifting the German-Polish boundary westward. The following year, those who had gathered in Łódź fled back to Germany in the wake of the Kielce pogrom. The June 1945 killings in Wierzbnik thus constituted just the first stage in a two-stage process of chasing these survivors out of Poland entirely.

Among the local Polish population in Wierzbnik-Starachowice, the issue of property was most salient. During the war, most Poles with whom Jews had left property had honored these arrangements, and Jews survived in the camps there in no small degree due to the access they had to their hidden property. But when they were deported from Starachowice in July 1944, it was as if a switch had been flicked. Those who had been keeping Jewish property or lived in Jewish houses now seemed to have felt that they had rightfully inherited the "formerly Jewish" properties whose previous owners were presumed dead. The trickle of survivors back to Wierzbnik-Starachowice in 1945 raised the unexpected prospect to all such Polish inheritors that their ownership of "formerly Jewish" property might be challenged—if they had the colossal "bad luck" that one of "their" Jews had survived. Those Jews who did return were greeted with numerous warnings from the new owners to make no claim to their property. When the Polish underground's deterrent killings on June 8 did not ward off all such claims, locals took matters into their own hands with the murder and beheading of Abram Kadyszewicz later that month. The complementary goals of the Polish underground on the one hand and local Poles on the other—no rebirth of Jewish life and no restitution of Jewish property—were achieved.

28

Postwar Investigations and Trials in Germany

I n the immediate postwar period, the victorious Allies conducted a number of trials. Most famous, of course, was the International Military Tribunal in Nürnberg in 1945–46, which tried the highest-ranking and most notorious Nazi leaders who had been captured alive (such as Hermann Göring). This was followed by twelve trials of the American Military Tribunal, in the same courtroom, that focused on groups from the next echelon of perpetrators: the officers of the mobile firing squads known as the *Einsatzgruppen*, the High Command of the armed forces, leading officials of the ministries, generals from the Balkan and southeast European theater, the doctors involved in "euthanasia" and medical experiments, key industrialists, and so forth. In addition, many suspected Nazi criminals were extradited to other countries in Europe, to be tried for crimes they were accused of committing there. For example, Rudolf Höss, the commandant of Auschwitz, was returned to Poland for trial, conviction, and execution. At this time, local authorities in occupied Germany were restricted to carrying out "denazification" hearings and trying crimes that German perpetrators had committed against German victims. The obscure, low-ranking German perpetrators from Starachowice were not among those extradited to Poland, so none of them faced trial in the immediate postwar period.

Once it was clear—after 1948—that the Allied occupiers were going to initiate no further trials in those occupation zones that were destined to become the Federal Republic of Germany ("West Germany"), local judicial authorities there were empowered to undertake the investigation and trial of those suspected of committing crimes against non-German victims as well. For the next decade, the prosecuting attorneys of the individual states (*Länder*) of the Federal Republic did undertake some investigations and trials, but these were limited in both number and scope. Local prosecutors were not trained, organized, or directed systematically to seek out the Nazi criminals who might be in their midst. They responded when the presence of such suspects was brought to their attention, often by former victims.

This passive or reactive stance began to change in 1958. When faced with the case of a former member of the Tilsit *Kommando*, the prosecuting attorney in Ulm, Erwin Schüle, chose to do the maximum instead of the minimum. Following his investigative leads, he uncovered and indicted ten members of the *Kommando* and obtained the convictions of all of them. At that time, the German criminal code contained a fifteen-year statute of limitations for murder. With 1945 taken as the point at which prosecutions could first have begun, the statute of limitations that would have foreclosed further prosecution of even the most heinous acts of Nazi mass murder was fast approaching. Schüle and others thus took the initiative to create the Central Agency for the Investigation of National Socialist Crimes. Following the Ulm model, it created teams to investigate proactively entire crime complexes to determine what crimes had been committed and who might still be brought to trial for them. Before the statute of limitations deadline was postponed at the last minute by the German *Bundestag*, the Central Agency also issued an appeal for international cooperation, so that it could begin as many investigations as possible, for anyone already under investigation would not enjoy immunity from prosecution when the statute of limitations ran out.

In response to this appeal, the World Jewish Congress informed the Central Agency in the spring of 1961 of the potentially incriminating testimony by two survivors against Walther Becker and Willi Althoff.[1] In 1962, German investigators conducted a preliminary round of interviews with two survivors in the United States and six in Israel. A handful of German witnesses who had been stationed in Starachowice or elsewhere in the Radom district during the war were interrogated in

1963. The Central Agency also discovered that an earlier investigation of Walther Becker had been undertaken by the Office of the State Prosecutor (*Staatsanwaltschaft*) in Hamburg in 1951, and this in turn had led to a brief investigation of Kurt Otto Baumgarten by the *Staatsanwaltschaft* in Hechingen. The investigations had been halted for lack of evidence in 1952.[2] Since Walther Becker still resided in Hamburg when the Central Agency reopened the case, it assigned further investigation of the case to the *Staatsanwaltschaft* in Hamburg in August 1963.[3]

Between 1966 and 1968, the Hamburg *Staatsanwaltschaft* carried out numerous interviews and interrogations of individuals who included Schwertner, Baumgarten, Schroth, Becker, and finally Kaschmieder. The potential cases against Baumgarten, Schroth, and Kaschmieder were separated from the Becker investigation and sent on to the state prosecutors in Stuttgart, Dortmund, and Traunstein, respectively, in 1968.[4] At the same time, the *Staatsanwaltschaft* in Hamburg decided that it had sufficient evidence to proceed to trial against Walther Becker.[5] An arrest order was issued for Becker, but it was quickly lifted on the condition that he report to the authorities three times per week and not leave the Hamburg area.[6]

While Becker, Baumgarten, Schroth, and Kaschmieder now faced potential judicial consequences of their actions in Poland some twenty-five years earlier, two Germans prominent in the memories of Starachowice survivors escaped judicial scrutiny entirely. Willi Althoff, living under the assumed name of Ralf Matthias Bracke, was never located before his death in 1964.[7] Walter Kolditz's name came up repeatedly in the early interviews concerning Starachowice, but he died in 1966 without ever being interrogated.[8] Fräulein Lutz, the feared secretary at Tartak, had also evaded judicial scrutiny. Morris (Moshe) Zucker, the father of one of the four typhus victims shot there after she had reported the cases, tracked down Fiedler in Germany after the war. Learning that Fiedler frequently visited Bad Tölz, Zucker followed him there, which led him to Fräulein Lutz and their two-to-three-year-old son. Zucker denounced her to the American authorities, who held and interrogated her for several days but then let her go. Both she and Fiedler thereupon disappeared for good.[9]

In addition to the lapse of time, which had allowed two prime suspects to die a natural death before they could be tried, the prosecutors in the now four separate Starachowice cases faced additional burdens or obstacles to obtaining convictions. One of these was the nature of the German law with which they had to work.[10] This involved both the German criminal code itself and a key precedent-setting interpretation. The Federal Republic refused to employ the legal concepts that had governed Allied trials, especially the notion of "crimes against humanity," which the Germans had bitterly criticized as an unfair application of *ex post facto* law. Thus, when the Federal Republic was once again a sovereign country in charge of all further prosecutions, it employed the German criminal code that had been in effect in 1940. By this statute, murder was the taking of a human life that was characterized by certain specific criteria. One of these involved acting out of a "base motive," such as race hatred. Several others involved the manner of the killing, such as the taking of a human life with "cruelty" or "maliciousness."

Prosecutors also faced an important distinction in German law between the perpetrator (*Täter*), who fully willed and identified with the deed committed, and the accomplice, who facilitated the deed but did not will the act as his own. In a key precedent, the so-called bathtub case, this legal distinction between perpetrator and accessory was given a crucial and counterintuitive twist. In this case, a woman had drowned the unwanted, illegitimate baby of her sister in the bathtub. The birth mother was found guilty of murder, but the sister who physically had committed the deed was declared guilty only of "accessory" (*Beihilfe*), because she had killed the baby on behalf of her sister and had not acted of her own will. This 1940 precedent was confirmed in 1962 through the Stachinski case, in which a KGB agent who killed two Ukrainian exiles in Munich was deemed a mere accomplice. This distinction was subsequently applied to those accused of Nazi crimes.[11]

As a result of this combination of statute and precedent, German judges ruled time and again in cases involving the Nazi mass murder of Jews that the true perpetrators who willed the deeds were a small number of notorious leaders—Hitler, Himmler, and Heydrich. All middle-echelon managers and organizers of the mass murder were mere accessories unless the prosecution could prove beyond a reasonable doubt not just what they did but also key elements of their state of mind—namely, that they willed the killing as their own act or that they acted out of race hatred. Since defendants were coached by their attorneys emphatically to deny either, and the contrary could seldom be proved beyond reasonable doubt, convictions for murder, as opposed to accessory, were rarely obtained. This legal distinction between "perpetrator" and "accessory" became especially vital after 1969, when an obscure and seemingly technical amendment to German law concerning the sentencing range for accessory to murder had the effect of placing most accessory cases beyond the statute of limitations.[12]

Concerning the perpetrators who physically committed the killings, as long as they acted according to orders and within prescribed routine, they too were mere accessories. Once again, only those who were noted for the cruelty and maliciousness with which they killed were exposed to conviction for actual murder. Convincing evidence concerning the manner in which a killing had been carried out was easier to gather than evidence concerning state of mind, so the low-level killers were legally at greater peril than their superiors in the middle management of the mass murder.

Given the greater ease with which the prosecution could deal with low-level killers, it is not surprising that the first Starachowice case to reach the courtroom was that of Willi Schroth. He had been captured by the advancing Soviet army in January 1945 and sentenced to twenty-five years of hard labor by a military court in Moscow in 1950. After ten years in captivity, he returned to Germany in October 1955 and lived with his sister in Düsseldorf. Thus, when his case was separated, it was sent to the branch of the *Staatsanwaltschaft* in nearby Dortmund that specialized in the investigation of Nazi crimes. The trial itself took place in the Düsseldorf state court (*Landgericht*) and ran from August 31, 1970, to March 29, 1971. It took testimony from forty-eight Jewish survivors as well as several German witnesses. Schroth was accused of murder in a number of individual cases and of being an accessory to murder in the November 1943 selection that sent at least 140 Jews to their deaths at Firlej. Some of the murder charges were dismissed for contradictory evidence (different witnesses at some point had named different killers) or insufficient evidence (no corroborating witness). A number of charges rested on convincing and consistent testimony by multiple witnesses (as well as Schroth's own earlier admissions in his initial interrogation, for which he had apparently not availed himself of skilled legal advice) as to his actually carrying out the killings. The court's legal analysis of these undisputed killings therefore was crucial; did they meet the high threshold of murder as defined by German law and interpreted in German court?

The first step was to establish whether Schroth killed out of a "base motive"—that is, race hatred—as the indictment charged. The court ruled to the contrary, portraying Schroth not as an anti-Semite but rather as a "primitive" and obsequious person holding a position far beyond his limited abilities and desperately trying to please his superiors. The court noted in effect that not all witnesses testified that he mistreated Jews all the time, and that, compared with some of the other Germans in the Starachowice camps, he was deemed "not so bad." The German witnesses, his former colleagues, testified that he was "decent" and "correct." As for the unfortunate incident in which Schroth urinated on Jewish corpses in an open grave while remarking that the dead Jews should "drink up"—an incident witnessed by three survivors—the court noted that other witnesses had described such an incident with a different German at a different time and place. Rather than concluding that this was a common ritual among the German personnel, the court started from the unexamined premise that such an act had happened only once. Since there was conflicting testimony, the possibility of mistaken identity had to be resolved to the benefit of the defendant.[13]

Having dealt with the crucial issue of "base motive," the court then had to analyze the charges accordingly. The court accepted that Schroth had shot Jadwiga Feldman and Mala Szuch on May 15, 1944, when the two women had not gone to work, and it accepted multiple witness testimonies that he had dragged Mala Szuch by the hair as she resisted being taken away. But it accepted Schroth's claim that he had killed the two women on Becker's order, neither on his own initiative nor out of race hatred. Thus, legally his act was one of accessory and as of 1969 beyond the statute of limitations.[14]

Concerning Schroth's first killing, that of the injured worker, the court again accepted Schroth's claim that he had done this on orders from above and to spare further suffering by the individual. As he had not willed the deed, or done it out of race hatred, or carried it out cruelly and maliciously, he was a mere accessory, and the statute of limitations had run out on that crime.[15] Concerning his role in the November 1943 selection, Schroth admitted that he had taken part and accompanied the victims to Firlej, but he claimed that he did not know they would be killed until he arrived there. The court concluded that it was "not impossible" that he did not know the selected Jews were going to be killed. Thus he was in practice an accessory, but this may not have been "intended" or "knowing" on his part and therefore was not punishable.[16]

Schroth's shooting of Szmul Wajsblum, after he had forced the old man to dig his own grave just outside the fence of the Majówka camp, had been perhaps the most widely witnessed individual killing there and one about which there was no conflicting testimony. When initially asked why he had forced Wajsblum to dig his own grave, Schroth had answered, "At that time I thought little about all that."[17] Though the court accepted Schroth's claim that he had shot Wajsblum on orders from above, it could not escape the conclusion that forcing Wajsblum to dig his own grave meant that the killing had been done "cruelly." Schroth's act of killing Wajsblum was categorized as accessory, but since he had done it "cruelly," it was one of the few cases of accessory not beyond the statute of limitations. On this count alone, he was convicted.[18] For this he was sentenced to six years in prison.[19]

Three months after Schroth's conviction, the *Staatsanwaltschaft* in Stuttgart moved to have all charges against Kurt Otto Baumgarten dropped and the case dismissed. Baumgarten had admitted that one Jewish worker in his division, Brenner, had been repeatedly reported for inadequate inspection of corrosion in 88 mm. shell casings. Brenner, he said, had been repeatedly warned, but in vain. Thus he had had no choice but to inform the Security Police in Radom, which then sent someone to execute Brenner. Those survivors who witnessed Brenner's execution had conflicting accounts about whether Baumgarten killed Brenner, ordered his killing, or was just present. In any case, the prosecutor concluded that, whatever Baumgarten's role, the shooting was occasioned by the goal of deterring sabotage, not "base motives." As such, it was manslaughter, not murder, and thus beyond the statute of limitations. Witnesses offered conflicting accounts of who killed the wounded prisoners after the breakout attempt. And one witness who had named Baumgarten as the killer had also stated that he displayed "a certain amount of humanity" in killing only the severely wounded who had no chance of survival and not all the wounded as ordered. On this count, the prosecutor also saw no chance of a conviction. As these were the two strongest charges, the recommendation to drop the case was promptly accepted.[20]

Walther Becker had escaped from Poland in January 1945, briefly taken up police duties in Regensburg until the capitulation, and then returned to Hamburg. He rejoined the police there, was temporarily suspended at the insistence of the British occupation authority, but was then reinstated in 1947. He was suspended once again in March 1951, while his case was being investigated for the first time. When that case was dismissed in August 1952, he resumed his police work until his retirement in 1957. He was placed under arrest briefly from March 1 to 3, 1968, conditionally released, and officially indicted on April 8, 1970.[21] Becker's trial finally opened in the Hamburg *Landgericht* in August 1971, just months after Willi Schroth's conviction.

Becker was on trial solely for crimes that he was accused of committing on October 27, 1942, not for any other acts committed during his nearly five years in the Security Police branch office in Starachowice. Most important, he was charged with participating in and giving orders during the ghetto-clearing, during which more than 3,000 Jews were sent to their deaths at Treblinka and many others were killed in the process. Additionally, he was charged with personally killing twelve Jews in nine distinct incidents. In all cases, he was accused of killing out of base motives and cruelly. The 1970 indictment listed fifty-nine Jewish witnesses and nine German witnesses whose testimony was the basis of the indictment.[22]

In contrast to Schroth, who had admitted to numerous killings but had pleaded superior orders, Becker had followed a defense strategy of total denial. His police office had not had jurisdiction over Jewish affairs in Starachowice, and he had not known of the impending deportation action. He had gone to the marketplace and briefly observed what was happening without reporting to anyone or giving anyone orders, and then had left. The prosecutor deemed his testimony "unbelievable" and "contradicted by the testimony of numerous witnesses."[23] After fifty-five court sessions stretching over seven months, during which the witness list had grown to 100 and an additional fifty-one depositions were read, the verdict was delivered on February 8, 1972, by the *Schwurgericht* or "jury court," comprising the presiding judge, *Senatspräsident* Wolf-Dietrich Ehrhardt, two associate judges, and six laymen.

The *Schwurgericht* combined elements of the jury trial and the bench trial in the American court system. The presiding judge conducted the proceedings. Every member of the panel of nine judges could intervene and ask questions of the witnesses. The panel then weighed the evidence and reached its verdict. A brief verdict was then read in court. The judicial reasoning behind the verdict subsequently was issued in a much more extensive written opinion. In this system, neither the particular roles of individual judges nor the actual authorship of the written verdict is revealed. Presumably, the presiding judge, who conducted the proceedings in court, also exercised considerable influence over the weighing of evidence. And presumably the written verdict that came out over his name was not issued without his input and approval.

The verdict in Becker's trial began by accepting his account in virtually every regard. In particular, "lacking any finding to the contrary," the court accepted that Becker, as a member of the Criminal Police rather than the Gestapo, had not been responsible for Jewish affairs in Starachowice, and that he had not been informed of the impending deportation, had not participated in the ghetto roundup and selections on the marketplace, much less commanded them, and did not know that the deported Jews would be killed. The verdict challenged his account on only two minor points. First, Becker's claim to have observed the ghetto liquidation for only a total of forty-five minutes before departing—first on the marketplace briefly and then for ten minutes at the loading of the train—defied the reconstruction of any possible timeline. By his own admission, and by the testimony of several German witnesses, Becker must have been on the marketplace by 8 a.m. The loading of the train could not possibly have begun before 10 a.m. Therefore, he must have been present for at least two hours. Second, the court accepted Leopold Schwertner's testimony that while on the marketplace Becker had not just observed but had spoken to members of the *Werkschutz*. However, the nature of that conversation remained unknown and thus not evidence of a command role. Otherwise, the crux of Becker's account—that he had no jurisdiction over Jewish affairs in Starachowice and was an uninformed and nonparticipatory observer on the day of the deportation—remained intact for the court. His account was "conceivable and could not be disproven," and thus he was acquitted on all counts.[24]

The court then turned to the eyewitness testimony of numerous Jewish survivors that contradicted the Becker account. The total dismissal of all Jewish testimony was achieved in three stages. The first was a statement of principle concerning the value of eyewitness testimony, which the court proclaimed to be "the most unreliable kind of evidence" available to the judicial process. In this particular case, it was even more unreliable because of the twenty-nine years that had elapsed. For the court, the "ideal witness" was an "indifferent, attentive, intelligent observer" who had watched the events in question in a "disinterested" and "detached" way. This the Jewish witnesses from Starachowice "certainly" were not. Given their situation, in fact, they had to be "bad witnesses."[25]

Second, the court turned to the individual instances in which Walther Becker was charged with personally having killed a total of twelve Jews in nine different instances. The prosecution was ill-advised to have brought at least three of these charges, which were easily dismissed for problematic evidence. To make its prophecy about the unreliability of Jewish survivor testimony self-fulfilling and to leave Becker's account intact, "without any finding to the contrary," the court required somewhat greater effort on the other counts.

On one count, three witnesses had testified that Becker had been by the steps of the alleyway leading up from the main street known as the Kolejowa to the marketplace, where he had personally beaten and shot Jews. The key witness had described in detail how Becker had shot two men, one of them quite elderly. But in one account he said that Becker knocked down the elderly man and shot him on the ground. In a different interview, he said Becker shot him while the man was still standing. His evidence was therefore dismissed as "discrepant." The testimony of a second witness was dismissed as too unspecific as to which and how many people Becker had shot in the alleyway, and the witness was accused of being untrustworthy in any event for an allegedly false claim he had made in an earlier restitution case. The third witness was dismissed out of hand for calling Becker a "bloody pig" and behaving in a threatening manner toward the defendant. Becker was therefore acquitted on this charge.[26]

Becker was charged with shooting an elderly couple (identified as the Biedermans by many witnesses but not identified by name in court). One witness admitted hearing the shots and then turning and seeing Becker standing over the couple with smoking pistol in hand. But the witness admitted that there were other Germans standing by Becker, and an expert witness testified that the ammunition in question was smokeless. Thus, the court could not exclude the possibility that another German had fired the fatal shots. A second witness had provided pretrial testimony but did not appear in court. The German judicial interviewer vouched in his professional opinion for the credibility of her testimony, but it was dismissed because the court had no possibility of making its own assessment in this regard or to establish whether the witness knew Becker well enough to identify him.[27]

Concerning the shooting of the teacher, Shlomo "Szkop" Zagdanski, three key witnesses differed on the exact location: in Krotka Street, at the corner of Krotka and Niska Streets, or coming from the direction of the synagogue (on Niska Street). They offered different times in the morning: 7 a.m., 8 to 8:30 a.m., or shortly before departure from the marketplace. They differed on whether Becker was alone or with a group of two or three Germans. Furthermore, the court doubted that two of these witnesses knew Becker well enough to be able to identify him with certainty. And the third had offered only one testimony in court, so his credibility could not be checked for consistency over time against earlier testimonies. The less detailed accounts of other witnesses only confused the situation further.[28]

Becker was accused of shooting the tailor Kirschenblatt. One witness gave two detailed and consistent testimonies in 1971 but had not mentioned this incident in his earliest testimony in 1968. Moreover, he displayed a tendency to "embellish" and "exaggerate." The court thus questioned his credibility. A second witness offered only hearsay evidence, since on seeing Kirschenblatt's body, she learned immediately from his wife how he had died, but she did not see the shooting itself. A third saw Becker shoot "the tailor" but then provided the name of a different tailor in Wierzbnik.[29]

It was obviously German policy during the ghetto-clearing to shoot all physically handicapped people, who were deemed likely to impede the speed with which the *Aktion* would be carried out. Unfortunately, the prosecution merged accounts of what most likely were the killings of two different handicapped people into one incident, which predictably led to irreconcilable contradiction between otherwise compelling testimonies. Mendel Mincberg, the son of the head of the *Judenrat*, testified that he saw Becker summon a man from Bodzentyn with a bandaged leg and foot to the open door of the courtyard off the square and shoot him. The court conceded that Mincberg's testimony and demeanor in court were "clear, calm, and objective." However, he claimed to see Becker's pistol smoking, had not mentioned this particular shooting in his earliest testimony in 1962, and then over time had added details to his account, such as the town from which the man came. Moreover, the court noted, when Mincberg was directly accusing Becker, his voice became slightly "strained" and "nervous." The court could not exclude that this was possibly an indication of inner "uncertainty and doubt" on his part.

The second witness, Rachmil Zynger, the historian of the Wierzbnik community memory book, was praised by the court for his demeanor and unusual memory for detail. However, Zynger testified that Becker and another man took a one-legged man on crutches behind the half-closed doorway of the courtyard, after which he heard a shot fired. He too had omitted describing this incident in detail in his early 1962 testimony, merely stating that he had seen Becker shoot people. Noting the differences in the two testimonies—summoned versus taken, bandaged foot versus one-legged man on crutches, open door versus half-closed door, Becker alone versus Becker and another German, saw the killing versus heard the shot—the court concluded that these seemingly believable accounts were "irreconcilable," hence neither could be used to convict the defendant. That others mentioned the killing of or seeing the dead bodies of handicapped persons in different places and circumstances was not taken to confirm an overall policy of killing all the handicapped, thus enhancing the credibility of testimony concerning the killing of both a one-legged man on crutches and a man with a bandaged leg and foot. Instead, such accounts were treated as divergent and conflicting testimony concerning the killing of one handicapped person, rendering them even more contradictory and thus even less compelling for the court.[30]

It was also clear that the Germans killed elderly people in the Wierzbnik ghetto liquidation. Two such elderly victims were Abram Rubenstein and Henoch Kaufman. One "calm" and "composed" witness testified that he saw Becker alone take these two men through the courtyard doorway, after which he heard shots and later saw the bodies. Becker was the only German seen in the area at that time. The verdict noted that someone else could have remained unseen in the courtyard and done the shooting. Furthermore, a second witness—Abram Rubenstein's daughter-in-law—testified that just as her column was marching away from the marketplace, she saw her father-in-law emerge from a doorway. He was alone when a man she identified as Becker came up and shot him. The court doubted whether she could identify Becker with certainty but had no doubt she could identify her father-in-law. Thus, once again it had two irreconcilable accounts that canceled one another. There were also differing accounts of Henoch Kaufman's death.[31] As on all other charges of individual killings, Becker was acquitted.

Some testimonies about Walther Becker were clearly dubious and raised the suspicion that Becker had been named by the witnesses for specific acts committed by others who could never be identified. And clearly, given the passage of time and the traumatic circumstances in which the events were experienced, accounts of the same incidents by different witnesses inevitably differed from one another in minor, and in some cases major, ways. But the problematic nature of eyewitness testimony so many years after the crime did not prevent every court in Germany from working its way through such evidence with a somewhat less dismissive attitude. Although every court had to begin with the presumption of innocence on the part of the defendant, not every court began with the presumption that the Jewish survivors who came to give testimony were "bad witnesses" before even examining their evidence.

Whatever the discrepancies among the accounts of different witnesses, or among different accounts by the same witness, upon which the court primarily based its acquittal for each charge of individual killing on Becker's part, it still faced the consensus testimony of numerous witnesses concerning Becker's active role during the *Aktion* that conflicted with the brief, nonparticipatory role that he claimed and about which the court had declared it could make "no finding to the contrary." To justify acquittal on this basic charge, the court categorically had to dismiss from consideration the testimony of whole groups of witnesses. And that is precisely what it did. It created whole categories of evidentiary flaws, whereby the least suspicion about the reliability of a witness's testimony in one regard led to its dismissal in all regards. Category by category, entire blocks of witnesses were removed from further consideration concerning their testimony on the crucial issue as to whether Becker had played an active role in the *Aktion*.

A large number of witnesses were dismissed because the accounts they gave over a series of interviews were inconsistent and contained discrepancies. In particular, the court noted the tendency of witnesses to become more detailed and specific and hence more damaging in accusations about Becker from one testimony to another. As the opposite of "natural memory loss" over time had occurred, the court concluded that these witnesses were "consciously or unconsciously inclined" to "project" onto the defendant their "understandable" hatred of the Nazi regime. Seeing Becker as the representative of the Nazi regime in Starachowice, they blamed him personally for the suffering caused by other unknown perpetrators who were not in court and could not be brought to justice. Therefore, the court would not use evidence to convict Becker that had been provided by witnesses whose various testimonies exhibited inconsistency and especially a pattern over time of intensifying accusation.[32]

What the court did not say is that a pattern for increasing specificity in witness testimony in such cases was *systemically inherent* in the way that the prosecution collected evidence. Initially unfamiliar even with the basic facts, the judicial investigators conducted general interviews.

As they became increasingly knowledgeable about the case and began to focus on those events, suspects, and witness accounts that held the greatest promise for an effective prosecution, they reinterviewed witnesses. By then, the investigators were far more informed about the case and conducted the interviews with the specific purpose of collecting more detailed information on particular points. The pattern among Jewish survivor testimonies in this case, which the "jury court" in Hamburg found so suspicious and attributed to Jewish "hatred" and "projection," was perfectly evident in other investigations of Nazi crimes based almost entirely on the testimony of Germans.[33] In short, the court cited a pattern in the evidence, a pattern that was systemic in the way that German prosecutors built their cases, to dismiss categorically the evidence thereby collected in this case, and blamed the witnesses' alleged "hatred" and "projection" as its justification.

Another category of witnesses whose testimony was dismissed entirely were those who, in the view of the court, did not know Becker "face to face." Those who used general formulations—such as saying that Becker was known to everyone in the ghetto, or those who said that Becker had merely been identified or pointed out to them by others— were deemed too susceptible to mistaken identity. This was justified on two grounds. First, there would have been many German officers on the marketplace that day, all wearing similar uniforms as well as caps with brims that partially shielded their faces. To the Jews, they all would have looked alike. Second, given the situation on the marketplace, the Jews were "in no way critical and disinterested observers." Thus, unless each individual witness provided the explicit grounds by which the court could be convinced that he or she knew Becker "face to face," the danger of mistaken identity was too great for that testimony to be used to convict him.[34]

The court dismissed testimonies categorically for a number of other reasons as well. Those testimonies that alleged Becker was seen shooting and beating in the marketplace but did not provide more detail were deemed too general and lacked sufficient specificity.[35] Witnesses who manifested or admitted to any visible memory problem or confusion were discounted.[36] If the court regarded a witness as too young at the time—in one case, fifteen years old—then that testimony was questionable as well.[37] In short, if the witness either had been too young in 1942 or seemed too old in 1971, the testimony was rejected. If a witness testified in court for the first time and had provided no earlier accounts, the courtroom testimony was dismissed because it could not be judged for consistency over time.[38] If the witness had given one or more pretrial depositions but could not appear in court, the testimony was dismissed because the court could make no assessment about demeanor and trustworthiness.[39] If the witness displayed emotion or animosity toward the defendant, the evidence was dismissed.[40]

And finally, there was what amounted to a "perfection test." Testimonies that were demonstrably in error in one regard could not have evidentiary value toward convicting Becker in any other regard. This included not only the already noted discrepancy between testimonies over time but also hyperbolic exaggeration ("hundreds were shot"), mistaken details (such as the color of German uniforms), mistaken sequence (Becker collecting valuables on the marketplace rather than upon entry to Strelnica), and other assertions the court deemed demonstrably false (Becker shooting Esther Manela or Szmul Isser on the marketplace, Becker holding a smoking pistol or wearing white gloves, Becker with pistol and dog rather than pistol and club).[41]

Since virtually all Jewish witnesses could be placed in one or more of the above categories, their testimonies concerning Becker's active role in the deportation were dismissed from consideration. There were, however, three Jewish witnesses and two German witnesses who had offered specific and damaging testimonies that were not yet disqualified.

Nathan Gelbard had testified that he had heard two shots and turned to see the elderly couple lying on the ground and Becker and another German standing at the corner of the marketplace. But Gelbard had "not testified to an exact observation" (*eine exakte Warhnehmungen nicht bekundet*), in that he stated only that he thought Becker was holding a pistol. The court could not exclude that Gelbard had seen some other kind of object in Becker's hand, and his testimony simply concerning Becker's presence on the marketplace was deemed "irrelevant."[42]

Mendel Mincberg had testified not only that he had seen Becker shoot the man with the bandaged leg and foot but also that Becker had personally struck Mincberg as well as others as they made their way to the marketplace. Aside from Mincberg's slightly strained voice when giving parts of his testimony, however, the court claimed "inconsistency" (*Inkonstanz*) between Mincberg's early testimonies in Israel (1962 and 1968) and his subsequent court testimony.[43] The court then turned to invoke the scores of witnesses it had hitherto dismissed. As the son of the head of the *Judenrat*, Mincberg was well known. Surely if Becker had struck him, at least one other witness would have mentioned this fact. Thus, the court "could not exclude with total certainty" that Mincberg had accused Becker "unjustly."[44]

Rachmil Zynger had testified not only about Becker and the physically handicapped man but also that Becker had stood at the corner of Krotka Street and given orders to others. But for the court, such testimony was too vague to exclude the possibility that Zynger saw Becker merely talking with the *Werkschutz*, as Leopold Schwertner had testified, and the content of that conversation was unknown.[45]

The court still faced two more hurdles. Dr. Kurt Puzicha, the German engineer who had been in charge of the mines that supplied ore to the Braunschweig Steel Works in Starachowice, had claimed during the 1951–52 investigation that he had neither witnessed the Wierzbnik deportation nor knew who directed it. Now he came before the court in Hamburg and testified that he had been at the train station on the day of the deportation. He saw the Jews being marched to the loading ramp, with Becker at the head of the column. Among the Jews was an elderly couple. When the old man tripped, an SS man struck him, and the wife pleaded that her husband was blind. Upon hearing this, Becker pulled the couple out of line and shot them both. Puzicha had not testified in 1952, he said, because he did not want to have anything to do with the entire business, but now he wanted to tell the truth.

The court thought otherwise. In 1933, Puzicha had been taken into "protective custody" and later had been held back in his career because of his "political unreliability." After the war, it was too late professionally to recover and make the career to which he felt he was entitled. In short, Dr. Puzicha was bitter. Furthermore, Puzicha had suffered under the Nazi regime, and Becker was "the representative" of that Nazi regime in Starachowice. Left unsaid but clearly implied, in the court's view Puzicha too had "projected" his resentment of mistreatment at the hands of the Nazi regime onto Becker and thus his evidence likewise had to be discounted. Not just Jews but anti-Nazis also were considered "bad witnesses" in this courtroom.

One last German witness, Wilhelm Swoboda, testified that on the night after the *Aktion*, he had found Becker in a drunken stupor, stammering incoherently that it was only bearable when drunk.[46] The court argued that no conclusions about Becker's guilt could be drawn from this evidence. It was "possible," as the defendant maintained, that he was merely shaken by the terrible events he had just witnessed.[47] Becker walked out of court not only a free man but also financially compensated for the three days he had been placed under arrest.

Almost immediately upon hearing of the Hamburg verdict against Becker, the *Landgericht* Traunstein, where the last Starachowice defendant, Gerhard Kaschmieder, was awaiting trial, issued a decision bringing the proceedings to a halt. Explicitly referring to the Hamburg verdict, the court noted that despite a far greater number of witnesses and far more damaging testimony, Becker had been acquitted. There was little chance, the court concluded, that Kaschmieder could be convicted.[48] The Traunstein *Staatsanwaltschaft* successfully appealed this decision.[49] Kaschmieder went to trial for the reprisal shooting of ten Jewish prisoners in the spring of 1944, but the testimony was contradictory. Some witnesses said they saw Kaschmieder lead the victims out of camp and out of sight below the cliff before they heard the shots. Others said they witnessed the shooting directly outside the fence above the cliff. One witness had testified in 1951 that the shooting had been carried out by Becker. He now included Kaschmieder among the perpetrators but said that the Germans had led the prisoners into the woods, from which he heard but did not see the actual shooting. Since Kaschmieder's role could not be ascertained with the necessary certainty, he was acquitted.[50]

I cannot conclude this chapter without more personal reflections on the Becker verdict. I have worked in the German court records of trials of accused Nazi criminals for more than thirty-five years. They are an invaluable source to the historian, and the numerous survivor testimonies collected by conscientious investigators for the Starachowice trials are no exception. I must say that in those thirty-five years I have read scores of trial verdicts, and many I found disheartening. But never have

I studied a case in detail and encountered a verdict that represented such a miscarriage of justice and disgrace to the German judicial system as that in the trial of Walther Becker.

Numerous studies of German postwar trials have noted the difficulties posed by the nature of German law that stood in the way of obtaining satisfactory verdicts. A 1940 criminal code to deal with individual offenses against society was an inadequate legal tool to deal with state-designed and state-sanctioned crimes against individuals. However, the problems posed by German law were not, ultimately, the primary cause of the verdict in the Becker case. In this case, the trial turned not on any controversial interpretation of German law but rather on the court's assessment of witness credibility. The former could provide grounds for review but not the latter, which was entirely within the court's discretion. Thus, the prosecution's appeal was summarily rejected as "obviously unfounded."[51]

More recently, several scholars of the postwar trials have shifted their focus away from the problems posed by German law to the problem posed by German judges. The legal profession in the Third Reich was among the most Nazified, and lawyers seemed to have been disproportionately attracted to the party's elite organization, the SS.[52] After the war, it was simply impossible to staff the German court system without readmitting to the bench many who had served as judges under the Third Reich. And, so the critics suggest, it is inconceivable that this did not affect how they shaped the interpretation of German law and reached verdicts in the trials of accused Nazi criminals.[53]

What then can be said about the presiding judge, Wolf-Dietrich Ehrhardt, in the Becker trial? A review of the Nazi Party files of the Berlin Document Center microfilms in the U.S. National Archives produced no surviving party card for Ehrhardt. His obituary in a professional publication in Hamburg provided a useful outline of his life.[54] Ehrhardt was born in Münster in 1913 and raised in Berlin. His father was killed in World War I, but despite family financial hardship, Ehrhardt passed his *Abitur* in 1932 and his first and second state law exams in 1935 and 1938, respectively. Drafted into the Luftwaffe, Ehrhardt was transferred to the artillery, where he reached the rank of *Oberleutnant* (first lieutenant) by the end of the war.

Ehrhardt entered the Hamburg justice system in February 1946, an early entry date that could scarcely have occurred if he had had conspicuous involvement with the Nazi Party. He rose steadily. According to the obituary, he won special recognition among Hamburg jurists for his role as presiding judge over "jury trials" (comprising three judges and six laymen) through his strict leadership and natural authority. He was, so the obituary claimed, especially moved by the large trials involving National Socialist crimes, whose particular demands always exhausted his "last personal reserves." In July 1972, just months after the Becker trial, he was promoted from *Senatspräsident* of the regional criminal court to president of the entire Hamburg *Landgericht*. He retired in 1980 and died in 2002.

In contrast to the portrayal of his professional accomplishments in his obituary, however, Ehrhardt had earned minor notoriety in a critical article in *Der Spiegel* for his conduct in court in several cases in 1964. On two occasions, when exercising his prerogative to question German female witnesses, Ehrhardt had posed irrelevant inquiries about their sexual relations with non-German men and then openly expressed his dismay and disapproval.[55]

I could not put together the Becker verdict and the *Spiegel* article on the one hand and the highly regarded and professionally successful judge portrayed in the obituary on the other. Who was this man who, entering the legal profession in the mid-1930s, had not even joined the Nazi Party, while his cohort of aspiring young lawyers had flocked to the SS? Who was this man who could express in open court his disapproval of German women who had relations with Turkish men and write the Becker verdict so dismissive of the Jewish witnesses in his courtroom, and do this with total professional impunity and then be named president of the Hamburg *Landgericht*? I revisited the microfilmed documents of the Berlin Document Center at the National Archives to check again, and this time I looked at the index of SS officers who had files from the Race and Settlement Main Office (RuSHA) of the SS, which examined the membership and marriage applications of SS officers for racial suitability. Wolf-Dietrich Ehrhardt's name appeared in the index, but on the roll of microfilm was the briefest such file I had ever seen. It contained precisely three documents of interest. The first document, one sentence on an otherwise-empty page, explained why the file was so slim. Ehrhardt's documents were no longer in the file but rather in the "secret safe" of the chief of staff. The second noted that the now-missing Ehrhardt documentation had been returned to RuSHA by the chief of the *Sippenamt*, the office of ancestral research consulted by the SS for proof of the five generations of racial purity required of each SS member. The third explained, again in one sentence, that Ehrhardt's name had been "stricken from the list of SS applicants, because he had non-aryan ancestors."[56]

29

Conclusion

O ne of the most fruitful trends in recent Holocaust research has been the plethora of regional and local histories that have allowed in-depth studies of the variegated, complex, multi-ethnic environment in which the Holocaust occurred in different places in Eastern Europe. It is increasingly clear that the history of the Holocaust cannot be written solely as either perpetrator history or history from above. It is also increasingly clear that the Holocaust in Eastern Europe cannot be framed simply as a German assault upon Jews, with the rest of the population considered to be bystanders. The microhistorical approach offers one way to explore the history of the Holocaust from below, as experienced by the victims and involving multiple actors.

This microhistory of the Starachowice factory slave-labor camps is, of course, based primarily on one kind of source—namely, survivor testimonies. Such a source base does not permit equal treatment of all participants and perspectives. It reveals events primarily through the experiences and memories of the victims, but the richness and number of testimonies do permit the historian to pierce through broad generalizations and examine relations between Jews and other ethnic groups and the kaleidoscope of differences within ethnic groups.

Most broadly, Jewish survivors portrayed themselves as a relatively homogeneous victim group faced by three implacable enemies who carried out their persecution of the Jews through a convenient division of labor. Ukrainians guarded the labor camps and mercilessly beat the Jewish workers at every opportunity, especially during the daily march from the camps to the factories and back. The Germans exploited the prisoners and, having murdered most of their families and neighbors already, stood poised to murder them as well. And the Poles despised and reviled the Jews before the war, took their property and informed on them during the war, and threatened to kill those few who survived and dared to return to their homes after the war. There is certainly more than a kernel of truth in each of these stereotypical perceptions and accusations, and there is no shortage of evidence to support each of them. But there is also evidence for a kaleidoscope of nuances and differences that lies beneath these stereotypes and presents a far more complex picture of multiethnic relations in Nazi-occupied Central and Eastern Europe that can be uncovered through the microhistorical study of a single town and its complex of camps.

The Jewish slave-labor society was not homogeneous but rather composed of many layers. The original Wierzbnik Jewish community comprised mostly orthodox, Yiddish-speaking provincial Jews who lived modestly as craftsmen and tradesmen, but there was also a small, more secular, assimilated, and affluent Jewish upper class. They were joined by a wave of more urban and sophisticated Jewish expellees from Łódź and Płock in 1940–41 and a second wave of refugees from nearby towns who fled to Starachowice in 1942 in search of lifesaving work cards and factory jobs. Finally, a third wave of "outside" Jews came in the form of transferees from other camps, including the resentful and angry Lubliners.

All of these Jews were targeted by the same anti-Jewish policies of the Nazi regime. They faced a common fate. But the differences among them significantly impacted the internal dynamics of the prisoner community and affected their chances for survival. First, women were clearly disadvantaged in comparison to men in obtaining work cards for factory labor as well as in surviving subsequent selections within the Starachowice camps. Second, well-off Jews were better able to buy work cards for themselves and often for many of their family members as well, while Jews without means could not. The very old and very young were uniformly excluded from obtaining factory work cards. Thus, wealth, gender, and age clearly shaped the initial makeup of the prisoner community that survived the liquidation of the ghetto and entered the camps.

Within the camps, key political and economic divisions emerged. As throughout the Nazi camp system, the Germans created an insidious mechanism of manipulation through divide-and-rule by empowering a small group of privileged prisoners to control the internal affairs of the camp community. This coterie of privileged prisoners exercised its dominance through the camp council, camp police, barracks supervisors, kitchen staff, and assignment of jobs. They also set the tone for a camp culture of inequality and corruption, in which everything from extra food to job assignments had a price. This culture of inequality based on political privilege was intensified even further by the systemic economic inequality that resulted from the extra advantage local Jews had in being able to access property that they had left with Poles they knew. In short, inequality in camp society was linked to reinforcing differences in geographical origin, date of arrival, class, gender, and age, as well as structures of political privilege and systemic economic advantage.

Despite the generalized picture of sadistic Ukrainian guards who mercilessly beat their Jewish prisoners, individual stories also tell of a few "nice" Ukrainian guards who did not report sick Jews or became fond of illegal children in the camp. More important, Ukrainian guards routinely made arrangements concerning smuggling into the camp, and some either turned their backs when prisoners left camp to conduct business or on occasion accompanied them into town for safety in return for a cut. The Ukrainians formed an extremely porous perimeter guard riddled by laxness and corruption, and this was an essential condition for the viability of the underground camp economy.

Given the centrality of the Germans to the history of the Holocaust, it is somewhat surprising how little they appear in survivor testimonies, many of which do not mention a single German by name and focus instead on the fate of family and loved ones. It was my good fortune as a historian that 125 of my Starachowice testimonies originated as German judicial interviews undertaken in preparation for postwar trials. Because German law stipulated very specific criteria for first-degree murder—such as a base motive (racial hatred), maliciousness, or cruelty—and all lesser crimes such as manslaughter were beyond the statute of limitations, investigators had to seek very specific evidence about what *motivated* German perpetrators, not just what they *did*. Under such targeted questioning, survivors provided much detailed information about individual Germans in Starachowice that they rarely included when they constructed their own accounts.

The Germans in general were the oppressive rulers threatening Polish Jews with total extinction. Within the confines of the Wierzbnik ghetto and the Starachowice camps, however, survival depended in part upon knowing the differences among the local Germans with whom Jews had to deal. The very language that survivors frequently employed in describing individual Germans suggests that, for the practical purposes of navigating survival, they had roughly divided the Germans into three categories: the "feared" and "dangerous," the "corruptible," and the "decent."

The "feared" and "dangerous" Germans killed often and enthusiastically. The most notorious example, of course, was Willi Althoff. The most prominent "corruptible" Germans were Leopold Rudolf Schwertner during the ghetto period and Kurt Otto Baumgarten during the camp period. The small number of Germans in Starachowice categorized as "decent" Germans included Willi Frania and Bruno Pappe, but especially Fiedler and Piatek at Tartak. These categories were not fixed, and several key Germans behaved unpredictably. Willi Schroth received bribes but also exhibited outbursts of lethal violence. And the Jews who had initially categorized Walther Becker among the corrupt were dismayed by his zeal and violence on the marketplace during the *Aktion* that liquidated the Wierzbnik ghetto.

Even more complex and contested than survivor perceptions and memories of Ukrainians and Germans are their perceptions and memories of Poles and Polish-Jewish relations. While survivors differed on the intensity of Polish anti-Semitism in Wierzbnik before the war, a negative portrayal of Polish-Jewish relations after 1939 is a matter of consensus. Four specific accusations of misbehavior occur frequently in the postwar testimony. The first is that Poles openly displayed their joy at the suffering and humiliation of the Jews. The second is that Poles made no attempt to help Jews, even when such help could have been provided at no risk and little costs. The third frequent accusation is that in the beginning Poles identified and pointed out Jews to the Germans—who otherwise would not have been able to distinguish between Poles and Jews—and later informed on or turned in Jews attempting to escape or hide. Many Jews would have been far more willing to risk fleeing to the forest, going into hiding, or trying to live on false papers if that did not mean living under the constant threat of denunciation from Polish informers. And finally, a handful of survivors—having endured all the horrors of the Holocaust and returned to Wierzbnik in search of other family members—were grotesquely murdered by Poles.

Even as many survivors made sweeping accusations of Polish misbehavior, however, they could not tell their stories without at the same time including the mention of individual benefactors. Most important in these accounts were the Polish friends, neighbors, and business associates with whom the families of survivors had left property for safekeeping. And in most accounts, Poles with whom property had been left proved "decent" and "honorable" in this regard. Access to hidden property was one key to survival.

Polish friends and acquaintances were individuals and could be identified as such. In contrast, the Polish population at large was anonymous and faceless, and beleaguered Jews could not distinguish who among them was a potential informer or predator. As a composite, they represented a grave and unknown danger to any Jew risking hiding, escape, or even brief business transactions outside the camp. Thus, Jews who could speak of individual Polish friends and acquaintances with whom they left property and from whom they received help could simultaneously speak of "the Poles" or even "the Polacks" as anti-Semites and collaborators in German persecution. Individual Polish friends and helpers on the one hand and "the Poles" as a source of hostility and danger on the other were simply experienced, remembered, and spoken about in a compartmentalized manner.

For the historian to have testimonies, some multiple, from 292 Jewish survivors from a single, relatively small complex of Nazi camps is highly unusual. Many such camps had only a handful of survivors at most. Given that Wierzbnik at its peak, just before ghetto liquidation, had at least 5,400 Jews, the survival of perhaps 600 to 700—of whom nearly half gave testimonies—can be no cause for celebration. But it does call for explanation. In my opinion, a conjuncture of factors must be taken into account. First, Jewish leadership made a conscious decision to use bribery to maximize the number of Jewish workers in the Stara-chowice factories, and individual Jewish families consciously invested in the purchase of work cards to fill these positions. Thus, more than 25 percent of the Jews in the Wierzbnik ghetto were spared deportation and immediate death in Treblinka. The average rate of Jews in this region initially exempted for labor was a mere 5 to 10 percent. Second, a large percentage of the Starachowice prisoners were incarcerated in their hometown. Unlike outsiders, they could avail themselves of property left with friends, which enabled them to create an underground camp economy of great complexity, supplement their inadequate nutrition, and bribe susceptible Germans and Ukrainians. Third, unlike in regions farther east, where Himmler's maniacal campaign to liquidate Jewish slave labor in 1943 was horrifyingly successful, the Radom district factory camps lay just beyond this destructive swath and were spared. By the fall of 1943, the munitions production of the Radom factories was too vital to the German war effort for even the ideological fervor of Himmler to overcome. Fourth, unlike the other labor camps spared destruction, such as those in Silesia, the Radom camps were not incorporated into the SS concentration-camp system but remained under the control of pragmatic and corruptible factory managers. Fifth, though Majówka and Tartak were family camps in some aspects, the Staracho-wice evacuation transport entered Birkenau as a transfer of workers without a systematic selection on the ramp. Precisely those who were most vulnerable—namely, women and young children—were sent to the women's camp, where, in contrast to the men's camp, the regimen was relatively lax and most survived. Finally, the Starachowice prisoners who arrived in Birkenau were not as malnourished as the newly arriving Łódź Jews and were far more experienced in camp life than the uninitiated Hungarian Jews. They were, in short, better positioned to survive Birkenau than others among their fellow incoming prisoners.

Many of these factors can be attributed at least in part to coincidence, fate, or "luck," which is what most survivors invoke to account for their survival. But clearly Jewish agency played a significant role. In the first decades after the Holocaust, too much discussion concerning Jewish response revolved around the false dichotomy of resistance and passivity. In the debate over resistance or the lack thereof, the term was subsequently expanded beyond its initial understanding as "armed resistance" to encompass many forms of Jewish agency, self-assertion, and opposition, which were characterized by the Hebrew term *amidah* or "standing up against."[1] In the words of Yehuda Bauer, *amidah* included "trying to preserve their dignity as long as possible, trying to obtain food, trying to preserve health, protect the children and the infirm, support cultural activities and other morale-building projects. . . ."[2] Much of this occurred within the Wierzbnik ghetto and the Starachowice factory slave-labor camps, but the main strategies for survival involved putting money in German pockets and bullets in German rifles. In order to survive, Starachowice Jews bought their way into slavery, produced for the German war effort, and enriched their oppressors. In doing so, some of them thereby ultimately thwarted the intention of the Nazi regime that none of them should survive. This certainly was not a course of passivity but neither can it usefully be termed resistance or *amidah*. We need a different vocabulary to describe their struggle for survival, and I would suggest words such as *ingenuity*, *resourcefulness*, *adaptability*, *perseverance*, and *endurance* as the most appropriate and accurate.

In analyzing the struggle for survival of Jewish individuals, families, and communities during the Holocaust, we should avoid false heroics and sanitizing censorship. One of the saddest "lessons" of the Holocaust is confirmation that terrible persecution does not ennoble victims. A few magnificent exceptions notwithstanding, persecution, enslavement, starvation, and mass murder do not turn ordinary people into saints and martyrs. The suffering of the victims—both those who survived and those who did not—is the overwhelming reality. We must be grateful for the testimonies of those who survived and are willing to speak, but we have no right to expect from them tales of edification and redemption. As one survivor put it, the story of Jeremiah Wilczek and his fate is also a part of history.

We also have no right to make facile moral judgments. In the camps, the normal moral world was totally inverted, in that the basic axiom "Do no harm" was often rendered meaningless. Nazi power placed Jews in a "less than zero-sum game" in which they had some agency or choice, but all choices caused harm to many and no choice guaranteed saving the life of anyone. As one Starachowice survivor put it succinctly, if you helped one person, it was usually at the expense of another.[3] Lawrence Langer coined the classic phrase "choiceless choices" to capture this impossible situation. One possible reaction to such an impossible situation was to adopt what Primo Levi called "the law of the Lager," to live by the Social Darwinian laws of struggle for survival and survival of the fittest through uninhibited assertion of self-interest.

In my study of the factory slave-labor camps of Starachowice, I do not find that unrestrained self-assertion was the typical response of the prisoners, however. Rather than entirely abandoning any notion of moral obligation, the prisoners in effect created a moral system more appropriate to their situation of agency combined with powerlessness. This system was based on a hierarchy of moral obligation rather than either an impossible universality or a total annulment of moral obligation. What they expected and accepted of one another was first of all loyalty to one's own remaining family members. Second, one had obligations to one's friends and neighbors, third to one's townspeople, and fourth to Jews vis-à-vis other non-Jewish prisoners. I remember my initial discomfort when interviewing a Starachowice survivor who was telling me how his little sister had been taken away in a selection. To this day, he would not forgive another survivor, a Jewish camp policeman who had lived on the same street and had been his childhood playmate. The camp policeman, he said, could and should have saved his sister because "there was [sic] plenty of people from out of town there that he could have sent."[4] Only gradually did I realize that this unguarded statement reflected precisely the hierarchy of moral obligation within the prisoner community, in which a camp policeman with limited agency was expected to rescue the little sister of a neighborhood playmate, even at the expense of someone else in a more distant circle of moral obligation.

In the unusual circumstance in which much of the prisoner community was composed of partial families, almost every prisoner had suffered grievous loss but still had loved ones alive. The searing experience of family loss did not lead to the total rupture of all bonds but rather to a total commitment to those family members who were still there. Family ties became the key associational and bonding factor of prisoner society in Starachowice and in the end also helped to account for the unusually high survival rate. It is no mere coincidence that I know of no fewer than twelve families in which three or more siblings survived Starachowice and the subsequent camps and marches together. The "choiceless choices" they had made turned out in this rare instance to be not so "choiceless" after all, and the camp morality they created helped to alleviate camp mortality and save remaining family members as well. And, like the story of Wilczek, this too should be a part of history.

NOTES

Introduction

1 Landgericht Hamburg (50) 35/70, Judgment in the Case of Walther Becker, February 8, 1972 (copies in Yad Vashem Archives, TR-10/776, and Zentrale Stelle der Landesjustiz-verwaltungen 206 AR-Z 39/62).

2 *Wierzbnik-Starachowitz: A Memorial Book* (Tel Aviv, 1973), ed. by Mark Schutzman. This *yizkor*, or community memorial book, has a few chapters written in English, but most were written in Yiddish, portions of which were kindly translated for me by Andrew Kos. It is cited hereafter as: *Wierzbnik-Starachowitz*. An English translation of the entire book was made available in May 2008 on CD by the Wierzbniker Society of Toronto, Canada, for its members. This English-language version will be cited hereafter as: *Wierzbnik-Starachowice Memorial Book* (CD version). I am grateful to Howard Chandler and Stanley Zukerman for providing me with a copy.

3 Goldie Szachter Kalib, *The Last Selection: A Child's Journey Through the Holocaust* (Amherst: University of Massachusetts Press, 1991). A second memoir—Roman Fris-ter, *The Cap: The Price of Life* (New York: Grove Press, 1999)—was first published in Hebrew in 1993. By the time I read it, I was well advanced in my research. I encountered so many assertions and small details in the parts pertaining to Starachowice that were at odds with the narrative as I had already constructed it from other testimonies that I decided not to cite or rely upon Frister's account. There are reportedly two memoirs in Hebrew—by Yerachmiel Tenenbaum and Yehiel Scharfer—that I have not been able to access.

4 Tobcia Lustman (Tova Pagi), *"The way it was . . .": The Diary of a 12 year old Jewish girl who survived Auschwitz (1939–1945)* (written in late 1945, published privately in Israel in 2000).

5 Henry Krystal, "Psychological Approaches to Trauma: A Forty-Year Retrospective," *Mapping Trauma and Its Wake: Autobiographic Essays by Pioneer Trauma Scholars*, ed. by Charles R. Figley (New York: Routledge, 2006).

6 Shlomo Moskowicz, *My Little Town Glinojeck: Souvenirs* (France, 1976). I am grateful to Silvio Gryc for the translation of this chapter.

7   *Leo Bach's Memoir: Coming of Age during the Holocaust* (www.cheme.cornell.edu/cheme/people/profile/moreinfo/dlk15-leobach.cfm).

8   Mark Raphael Baker, *The Fiftieth Gate: A Journey Through Memory* (Sydney: Harper-Collins, 1997).

9   *The Diary of Rubinowicz* (Edmonds, WA: Creative Options, 1982) relates to his family's stay in nearbyBodzentyn from March through May 1942.

10 The best-known such camp—portrayed in the movie *Schindler's List*—is, of course, the Jewish slave-labor camp attached to the enamelware factory of Oskar Schindler, outside Cracow.

11 Amsterdam: Harwood Academic Publishers.

12 Paderborn, Germany: Schöningh.

13 Darmstadt, Germany: Wissenschaftliche Buchgesellschaft.

14 The David Boder collection of more than 100 interviews can be consulted either in hard copy at the United States Holocaust Memorial Museum or through the Illinois Institute of Technology Website "Voices of the Holocaust," at: http://voices.lit.edu. The testimony of Starachowice survivor Kalman Eisenberg has been excerpted and published in: *Fresh Wounds: Early Narratives of Holocaust Survival*, ed. by Donald Niewyk (Chapel Hill: University of North Carolina Press, 1998), pp. 87–93.

15 In addition to the testimony of Kalman Eisenberg taken by David Boder and published in excerpted form in Donald Niewyk's *Fresh Wounds*, the testimonies of four other Starachowice survivors have been published in various anthologies. For Howard Chandler: Martin Gilbert, *The Boys: The Untold Story of 732 Young Concentration Camp Survivors* (New York: Henry Holt, 1997). For Guta Blass Weintraub: Joy Erlichman Miller, *Love Carried Me Home: Women Surviving Auschwitz* (Deerfield Beach, FL: Simcha Press, 2000). For Regina Laks Gelb: Tadeusz Piotrowski, *Poland's Holocaust: Ethnic Strife, Collaboration with Occupying Forces and Genocide in the Second Republic, 1918–1947* (Jefferson, NC: McFarland & Co., 1998). For Martin Baranek: Emily Taitz, *Holocaust Survivors: A Biographical Dictionary* (Westport, CT: Greenwood Press, 2007).

16 For the most recent studies of survivor testimony, see: Zoë Vania Waxman, *Writing the Holocaust: Identity, Testimony, Representation* (New York: Oxford University Press, 2006), and Annette Wievorka, *The Era of the Witness* (Ithaca, NY: Cornell University Press, 2006).

17 Jan Gross, *Neighbors: The Destruction of the Jewish Community in Jedwabne, Poland* (Princeton, NJ: Princeton University Press, 2001). Omer Bartov is preparing a history of "communal genocide" in Buczacz in Eastern Galicia, which would likewise be impossible without the use of survivor testimony as the primary source.

18 Peter Black, "A Response to Some New Approaches to the History of the Holocaust," *The New England Journal of History* 59/1 (fall 2000), pp. 47–48.

19 Benjamin Wilkomirski, *Fragments: Memoirs of a Wartime Childhood* (New York: Schocken, 1996); and Stefan Mächler, *The Wilkomirski Affair: A Study in Biographical Truth* (New York: Schocken, 2001). More recently, Herman Rosenblat's purported memoir, *Angel at the Fence*, was similarly exposed as invention.

20 Henry Greenspan, "The Awakening of Memory: Survivor Testimony in the First Years after the Holocaust and Today," Monna and Otto Weinmann Annual Lecture, May 2000, printed as an occasional paper by the U.S. Holocaust Memorial Museum (Washington, DC, 2001), p. 20.

21 Tyler Thompson, *Freedom in Internment: Under Japanese Rule in Singapore 1941–1945* (Singapore: Kefford Press, n.d.).

1: The Prewar Jewish Community of Wierzbnik-Starachowice

1 Moshe Sali, "Sketches of the Town," *Wierzbnik-Starachowice Memorial Book* (CD version), p. 18.

2 Visual History Archive, USC Shoah Foundation Institute for Visual History and Education, University of Southern California (hereafter VHA) interviews: 5410 (Charles Kleinman, 1995).

3 Today the blast-furnace complex, designated as an industrial heritage preservation site, is an open-air museum of "the history of material culture," exemplifying the earliest stages of Polish industrialization. No mention is made of the Jewish identity of the founding family or of the Jewish slave laborers who worked there during World War II. For information on early industrialization in Wierzbnik-Starachowice, see: Symcha Mincberg, "Before the Flood," and Jerahmiel Singer, "Chronicles of the Town and its Jews," *Wierzbnik-Starachowice Memorial Book* (CD version), pp. 52–54, 68–73.

4 After World War II, the former munitions factory was converted and enlarged for the production of tractors and trucks, now known as Manstar.

5 VHA 1833 (Isidore Guterman, 1995), 2643 (Howard Kleinberg, 1995), 5096 (Malka Pola, 1995), 51793 (Sally Recht, 2001), 40372 (Harry Spicer, 1998). Author's interview (Sally Recht, 2004).

6 Singer, "Chronicles of the Town and its Jews," and "Rabbis of the Community," *Wierzbnik-Starachowice Memorial Book* (CD version), pp. 73–74, 96–97.

7 Of the 117 testimonies with birth dates that I have from the VHA, eighteen were born before 1920, forty-seven between 1920 and 1924, forty between 1925 and 1929, and twelve in 1930 or after. In short, only 15 percent were already twenty years old and 45 percent were not yet fifteen when the war broke out.

8 VHA 9136 (Lola Sussman, 1995).

9 VHA 13613 (Alex Herblum, 1996).

10 United States Holocaust Memorial Museum Archives (hereafter USHMM), RG-50.030*0396 (Chris Lerman, 1998); VHA 2651 (Toby Steiman, 1995).

11 VHA 25175 (Elizabeth Styk, 1997).

12 VHA 7366 (Naftula Korenwasser, 1995).

13 For example, Yitzhak Zuckerman, *A Surplus of Memory: Chronicle of the Warsaw Ghetto Uprising* (Berkeley: University of California Press, 1993).

14 VHA: 943 (Harold Rubenstein, 1995), 4334 (Miriam Miklin, 1995), 13515 (Saul Miller, 1996), 16492 (Eva Herling, 1996).

15 Goldie Szachter Kalib, *The Last Selection: A Child's Journey Through the Holocaust* (Amherst: University of Massachusetts Press, 1991), p. 9.

16 Zehava Zitelna, "Beit Yaakov School for Girls," *Wierzbnik-Starachowice Memorial Book* (CD version), p. 144.

17 Yitzhak Kerbel, "The Youth Movements in Wierzbnik," *Wierzbnik-Starachowice Memorial Book* (CD version), p. 121.

18 Moshe Sali, "Wierzbnik, a Proud Example of Zionism," *Wierzbnik-Starachowice Memorial Book* (CD version), p. 136.

19 Mincberg, "Before the Flood," and Singer, "Chronicles of the Town and its Jews," *Wierzbnik-Starachowice Memorial Book* (CD version), pp. 55, 75–76.

20 Singer, "Chronicles of the Town and its Jews"; Reuven Lis Shuali, "The Gordonia Movement and the National Labor Committee for Palestinian Youth League" and "The Maccabi Society"; Rivka Greenberg and Rachel Laor, "The Zionist Youth Movement"; Sali, "Wierzbnik, a Proud Example of Zionism"; Shmuel Nudelman, "The Gviazda

Sports Society"; Yaakov Snir, "The Beitar Movement"; Gershon Rosenwald, "The Revisionist Movement in Wierzbnik"; and Uri Shtramer, "A Bundle of Memories": all in *Wierzbnik-Starachowice Memorial Book* (CD version), pp. 76–78, 128–29, 131, 137, 149–50, 154–55, 156–57, 158–59, 175.

21   Singer, "Chronicles of the Town and its Jews," *Wierzbnik-Starachowice Memorial Book* (CD version), p. 76.

22   USHMM, RG-50.030*0411 (Anna Wilson, 2001).

23   Singer, "Chronicles of the Town and its Jews," and Kerbel, "The Youth Movements in Wierzbnik," *Wierzbnik-Starachowice Memorial Book* (CD version), pp. 81, 121.

24   Singer, "Chronicles of the Town and its Jews," *Wierzbnik-Starachowice Memorial Book* (CD version), p. 78.

25   Mincberg, "Before the Flood," and Singer, "Chronicles of the Town and its Jews," *Wierzbnik-Starachowice Memorial Book* (CD version), pp. 56–57, 80.

26   Shtramer, "A Bundle of Memories," and Singer, "Chronicles of the Town and its Jews," *Wierzbnik-Starachowice Memorial Book* (CD version), pp. 174–76, 80–81.

27   Fortunoff Archive (hereafter FA), T-955 (Gutta T., 1987). The Fortunoff Archive requires preservation of confidentiality of the interviewees in their collection. Thus, interviewees of the Fortunoff Archive collection will be identified by first name and first initial of last name.

28   VHA: 7366 (Naftula Korenwasser, 1995, who described Polish-Jewish relations in Wierzbnik as "very good"), 11583 (Zachary Greenbaum, 1996).

29   Author's interview (Henry Greenbaum, 2000). VHA 16876 (Henry Greenbaum, 1996). For two other accounts that claimed no personal experience of anti-Semitism in Wierzbnik: VHA: 25175 (Elizabeth Styk, 1997), 43845 (Morris Spagat, 1998).

30   Yad Vashem Archives (hereafter YVA): O-3/8231 (Jakov Heyblum, 1995), O-3/8476 (Meir Ginosar, 1995). VHA 13613 (Alex Herblum, 1996).

31   Singer, "Chronicles of the Town and its Jews," *Wierzbnik-Starachowice Memorial Book* (CD version), pp. 82–83.

32   VHA 33807 (Gloria Borenstein, 1997, who characterized the Poles as "uneducated," "drunk," and "disgusting" and Poland as an "ugly, ugly country").

33   VHA 45673 (Sam Isenberg, 1998).

34   VHA: 9584 (Henia Burman, 1995), 23533 (Jacob Kaufman, 1996), 5096 (Malka Isser Perla, 1995). Several survivors explicitly noted that Jewish craftsmen and retailers made "a nice living" from their predominantly Polish working-class customers. VHA: 7366 (Naftula Korenwasser, 1995), 13613 (Alex Herblum, 1996).

35   USHMM, RG-50.030*0396 (Chris Lerman, 1998). VHA: 5096 (Malka Isser Perla, 1995), 8656 (Paul Cymerman, 1995).

36   VHA: 3948 (Irene Szachter Horn, 1995), 31380 (Jack Spicer, 1997), 44270 (Shalom Lindenbaum, 1998).

37   VHA 40372 (Harry Spicer, 1998).

38   VHA 10154 (Alan Newman, 1995).

39   According to Mark Raphael Baker, *The Fiftieth Gate: A Journey Through Memory* (Sydney: HarperCollins, 1997), p. 64, "a local parish priest" spearheaded the anti-Jewish efforts of the National Party in Wierzbnik.

40   VHA: 2643 (Howard Kleinberg, 1995), 5410 (Charles Kleinman, 1995). When Yitzhak Kerbel knocked down a bully who tried to stuff pork into his mouth, he was punished by the school principal but thereafter left alone. Yitzhak Kerbel, "The Carousel," *Wierzbnik-Starachowice Memorial Book* (CD version), p. 200.

41 VHA 1833 (Isidore Guterman, 1995). On leaving early: Pinchas Hochmitz, "Maccabi's Youths," *Wierzbnik-Starachowice Memorial Book* (CD version), p. 153. VHA 45673 (Sam Isenberg, 1998, also referred less specifically to the existence of places Jews could not go without risk of beating).

42 VHA: 2139 (Sarah Welbel, 1995), 3241 (Leah Finkel, 1995). Another Starachowice survivor, Henry Krystal, also lost two paternal grandparents to a murderous pogrom in a small village outside Kielce in 1938. Holocaust Survivor Oral Testimonies, University of Michigan–Dearborn (hereafter UMD) (Henry Krystal, 1996).

2: The Outbreak of War

1   YVA, O-3/8476 (Meir Ginosar, 1995).

2   Jerahmiel Singer, "Dark Days of Horror and Ruin," *Wierzbnik-Starachowitz*, ed. by M. Shutzman et al. (Tel Aviv, 1973), pp. 20–22.

3   For typical brief accounts, see: VHA: 943 (Harold Rubenstein, 1995), 2643 (Howard Kleinberg, 1995), 2651 (Toby Steiman, 1995), 23533 (Jacob Kaufman, 1996), 40372 (Harry Spicer, 1998). Museum of Jewish Heritage (hereafter MJH), RG-1383 (Pola Funk, 1986). FA, T-955 (Gutta T., 1987).

4   VHA 5096 (Malka Isser Perla, 1995).

5   Author's interview (Faye Gold, 2002).

6   VHA: 5410 (Charles Kleinman, 1995), 7313 (Hyman Reichzeig, 1995), 12634 (Fay Sendyk Rosebruch, 1996). USHMM, RG-50.030*0396 (Chris Lerman, 1998). Niewyk, *Fresh Wounds*, p. 86 (Kalman Eisenberg, 1946). Rivka Greenberg (Mincberg), "My Journey Through the Valley of the Shadow of Death," *Wierzbnik-Starachowice Memorial Book* (CD version), p. 298.

7   VHA 9135 (Lola Sussman, 1995).

8   Malka Cohen, "Wierzbnik, Auschwitz, Bergen-Belsen," *Wierzbnik-Starachowice Memorial Book* (CD version), p. 279.

9   VHA 9113 (Hyman Flancbaum, 1995).

10 Kalib, *The Last Selection*, pp. 3, 28, 80–89. VHA: 3916 (Rachell Szachter Eisenberg, 1995), 3948 (Irene Szachter Horn, 1995).

11 VHA: 15188 (Annie Glass, 1996), 51793 (Sally Recht, 2001). Author's interviews (Annie Glass and Sally Recht, 2004). According to Robert Seidel, *Deutsche Besatzungspolitik in Polen: Der Distrikt Radom 1939–1945*, p. 177, in the first ten days of the German occupation in the Radom district, German forces killed 1,049 civilians, including 129 Jews.

12 VHA: 451 (Helen Starkman, 1994), 3189 (Pola Schlenger, 1995).

13 VHA 13514 (Saul Miller, 1996).

14 UMD (Henry Krystal, 1996).

15 USHMM, RG-50.030*250 (Guta Blass Weintraub, 1990). MJH, RG-1165 (Guta Blass Weintraub, 1984).

16 Zentrale Stelle der Landesjustizverwaltungen, Ludwigsburg (hereafter ZStL), 206 AR-Z 39/62 (Hamburg StA 147 Js 1312/63, Investigation of Walther Becker) [hereafter cited as Becker], p. 1141 (Sam Lang, 1968).

17 According to Seidel, *Deutsche Besatzungspolitik in Polen*, p. 233, German officials in the Radom district were told to encourage "voluntary" Jewish emigration to the Soviet zone in the fall of 1939. Indeed, none of the following Wierzbnik accounts indicate any difficulty in leaving town, just in crossing the Lublin district and the demarcation line.

18 Rachel Laor (Dreksler), "To the Wilderness of the Taiga," *Wierzbnik-Starachowice Memorial Book* (CD version), pp. 314–18.

19 Pinchas Nudelman, "In the 'Camps for the Correction of Man'," *Wierzbnik-Starachowice Memorial Book* (CD version), p. 262.

20 Abe Zukerman, "Where No Birds Fly," *Wierzbnik-Starachowice Memorial Book* (CD version), p. 340.

21 Moshe Samet, "In the Ranks of the Polish Army," and Yitzhak Kerbel, "The Town Elder Lied Deliberately," *Wierzbnik-Starachowice Memorial Book* (CD version), pp. 493–94, 567–68.

22 Yaacov Snir, "Fighting the Nazi Conquerors," *Wierzbnik-Starachowice Memorial Book* (CD version), pp. 477–82.

23 Gershon Rosenwald, "In the Shade of the Thick Forest," *Wierzbnik-Starachowice Memorial Book* (CD version), pp. 504–6.

24 VHA 30134 (Joseph Chernikowski, 1997).

25 VHA 42666 (Morris Pinczewski, 1998).

26 VHA 5874 (Anita Tuchmayer, 1995).

27 Kalib, *The Last Selection*, pp. 99–100.

28 VHA 18046 (David Mangarten, 1996).

29 Author's interview (Sally Recht, 2004).

3: The Early Months of German Occupation

1 VHA 1833 (Isidore Guterman, 1995).

2 Rivka Greenberg (Mincberg), "My Journey Through the Valley of the Shadow of Death," *Wierzbnik-Starachowice Memorial Book* (CD version), p. 299.

3 Kalib, *The Last Selection*, pp. 93, 97.

4 USHMM, RG-50.030*0396 (Chris Lerman, 1998). VHA 51793 (Sally Recht, 2001).

5 Kalib, *The Last Selection*, p. 90. VHA: 3916 (Rachell Eisenberg, 1995), 18046 (David Mangarten, 1996). Becker, p. 513 (Ruth Wagner, 1966), p. 913 (Zvi Hersz Faigenbaum, 1968).

6 Kalib, *The Last Selection*, p. 96. VHA: 1833 (Isidore Guterman, 1995), 1983 (Martin Baranek, 1995).

7 Jerahmiel Singer, "Dark Days of Horror and Ruins," *Wierzbnik-Starachowitz*, pp. 24, 26. VHA 1213 (Rose Weitzen, 1995). USHMM, RG-50.030*0396 (Chris Lerman, 1998).

8 VHA: 1983 (Martin Baranek, 1993), 12634 (Fay Rosebruch, 1996), 23533 (Jacob Kaufman, 1996).

9 USHMM, RG-50.030*0396 (Chris Lerman, 1998).

10 Seidel, *Deutsche Besatzungspolitik in Polen*, p. 33.

11 VHA: 1213 (Rose Weitzen, 1995), 1833 (Isidore Guterman, 1995), 5410 (Charles Kleinman, 1995), 18406 (David Mangarten, 1996). Becker: p. 513 (Ruth Wagner, 1966), p. 885 (Frymeta Maslowicz, 1967), p. 958 (Sara Postawski, 1968).

12 VHA 51793 (Sally Recht, 2001).

13 Singer, "Dark Days," *Wierzbnik-Starachowitz*, p. 24.

14 VHA 43845 (Morris Spagat, 1998).

15 According to Singer, "Dark Days," *Wierzbnik-Starachowitz*, p. 23, it was the night after Yom Kippur. YV, O-3/6773 (Chaim Hilf, 1992, who placed the arson two days before Yom Kippur). USHMM, RG-50.030*0396 (Chris Lerman, 1998, who dated the arson

to the "eve" of Yom Kippur). Symcha Mincberg, "The Beginning of the Downfall," *Wierzbnik-Starachowice Memorial Book* (CD version), p. 396, placed it on the "first evening" of Yom Kippur. VHA 5096 (Malka Isser Perla, 1995, who dated it to "around" Yom Kippur). Zvi Faigenbaum, "The Synagogue is Burning," *Wierzbnik-Starachowice Memorial Book* (CD version), p. 269, placed the arson on Yom Kippur.

16 Faigenbaum, "The Synagogue is Burning," and Mincberg, "The Beginning of the Downfall," *Wierzbnik-Starachowice Memorial Book* (CD version), pp. 268–69, 369.

17 Becker, p. 514 (Ruth Wagner, 1966).

18 VHA: 943 (Harold Rubenstein, 1995), 18046 (David Mangarten, 1996), 40372 (Harry Spicer, 1998), 51793 (Sally Recht, 2001). USHMM, RG-50.030*0396 (Chris Lerman, 1998). Becker, p. 758 (Mina Binsztok, 1966, gave the age of workers subject to forced labor as thirteen to sixty years old. Singer, "Dark Days," *Wierzbnik-Starachowitz*, p. 26, gave fourteen to sixty-five.

19 Becker, p. 62 (Rywka Grinberg, 1962).

20 VHA 9584 (Henia Burman, 1995).

21 Becker, p. 1171 (Rose Herling, 1968).

22 VHA 5190 (Ceil Saltzman, 1995).

23 USHMM, RG-50.030*0396 (Chris Lerman, 1998).

24 VHA: 2643 (Howard Kleinberg, 1995), 9135 (Lola Sussman, 1995), 12634 (Fay Rosebruch, 1996), 40372 (Harry Spicer, 1998). Author's interview (Sally Recht, 2004). Becker: p. 62 (Rywka Grinberg, 1962), p. 76 (Pinchas Hochmic, 1962), p. 81 (Mendel Mincberg, 1962). Kalib, *The Last Selection*, p. 95.

25 VHA 1983 (Martin Baranek, 1995).

4: The *Judenrat*

1 Nürnberg Document 3363-PS: Heydrich Schnellbrief, September 21, 1939.

2 *Faschismus, Getto, Massenmord: Dokumentation über Ausrottung und Widerstand der Juden in Polen während des zweiten Weltkrieges*, ed. by Tatiana Berenstein, Artur Eisenbach, Bernard Mark, and Adam Rutkowski (Berlin [East]: Rütten und Loening, 1960), p. 71.

3 *The Warsaw Diary of Adam Czerniakow*, ed. by Raul Hilberg, Stanislaw Staron, and Josef Kermisz (New York: Stein and Day, 1969), p. 402 (appended document: Auerswald to Medeazza, November 24, 1941).

4 The standard work in the topic is still: Isaiah Trunk, *Judenrat: The Jewish Councils in Eastern Europe under Nazi Occupation* (New York: Stein and Day, 1972). See also the contrasting assessments: Raul Hilberg, "The Ghetto as a Form of Government: An Analysis of Isaiah Trunk's *Judenrat*," and Yehuda Bauer, "Jewish Leadership Reactions to Nazi Policies," in *The Holocaust as Historical Experience*, ed. by Yehuda Bauer and Nathan Rotenstreich (New York: Holmes & Meier, 1981), pp. 155–92. For the negative change in *Judenrat* composition over time, see: Aharon Weiss, "Jewish Leadership in Occupied Poland—Postures and Attitudes," *Yad Vashem Studies* XII (1977), pp. 335–65.

5 Philip Friedman, "Pseudo-Saviors in the Polish Ghettos: Mordechai Chaim Rumkowski of Lodz," and "The Messianic Complex of a Nazi Collaborator in a Ghetto: Moses Merin of Sosnowiec," in *Roads to Extinction: Essays on the Holocaust* (Philadelphia: The Jewish Publication Society of America, 1980), pp. 333–64. Leni Yahil titled her subchapter on Merin and Rumkowski "Coercive Leadership," in: *The Holocaust: The Fate of European Jewry* (New York: Oxford University Press, 1990), pp. 206–14.

6 Zvi Faigenbaum, "The Synagogue is Burning," *Wierzbnik-Starachowice Memorial Book* (CD version), p. 271.

7 Author's interview (Howard Chandler, 2001).

8 The list of September 17, 1940, contains twenty-two names (as spelled in the original document): Symcha Mincberg, Moszek Birencweig, Josef Tencer, Rachmil Wolfowicz, Szmul Kahan, Szmul Isser, Lejb Lipsztein, Izrael Klajnberg, Szlama Ejnesman, Rachmil Zynger, Szaja Szarfarc, Janiel Kopf, Josek Rozenberg, Moszek Baranek, Jakub Kramarz, Lejzor Kurta, Mojzesz Adler, Wolf Jankielewicz, Piotr Lwenton, Josek Klajner, Izaak Laks, and Mordka Lis. The first seventeen were classified as "members" and the last five as "staff." Archivum Pánstwowe w Kielcach, oddzial w Starachowicach, zespol akt. miaste Starachowic (hereafter APK), sygn. arch. 46, nr. 256 and 260.

9 Becker: p. 934 (Zvi Faigenbaum, 1968), pp. 994, 996 (Nathan Gelbard, 1968), p. 1312 (Guta Blass Weintraub, 1968).

10 Author's interview (Faye Gold, 2002).

11 Author's interview (Chris Lerman, 2001).

12 Becker, p. 1006 (Mendel Mincberg, 1968).

13 Author's interview (Chris Lerman, 2001). Becker: p. 405 (Fred Baum, 1966), p. 1291 (Annie Glass, 1968). VHA 2651 (Toby Steiman, 1995).

14 Becker, p. 1291 (Annie Glass, 1968).

15 APK, sygn. arch. 45, nr. 289 and 291 (Bürgermeister Starachowice to Kreishauptmann Iłża, November 16, 1940, and Kreishauptmann Iłża to Judenrat, November 21, 1940).

16 Jerahmiel Singer, "Dark Days of Horror and Ruin," *Wierzbnik-Starachowitz*, p. 28; MJH, RG-1383 (Pola Funk, 1986). Vaguer references to beatings of members of the *Judenrat*: Becker, p. 508 (Dina Tenenbaum, 1966), p. 1193 (Helen Weisbloom, 1968).

17 Symcha Mincberg, "The Beginning of the Downfall," *Wierzbnik-Starachowice Memorial Book* (CD version), p. 397. For the positive assessment of Mayor Sokol (alternatively spelled Sokul), see: Jerahmiel Singer, "Chronicles of the Town and Its Jews," and Faigenbaum, "The Synagogue is Burning," *Wierzbnik-Starachowice Memorial Book* (CD version), pp. 80, 267.

18 Author's interviews (Chris Lerman and Anna Wilson, 2001). USHMM, RG-50.030*0396 (Chris Lerman, 1998), RG-50.030*0411 (Anna Wilson, 2001). Becker, p. 866 (Anna Wilson, 1967). Singer, "Dark Days," *Wierzbnik-Starachowitz*, p. 26. YVA, O-3/6773 (Chaim Hilf, 1992).

19 APK, sygn. arch. 45, nr. 1 (Bürgermeister to Mincberg, January 2, 1940, and reply).

20 Mincberg, "The Beginning of the Downfall," *Wierzbnik-Starachowice Memorial Book* (CD version), p. 397.

21 USHMM, RG-50.030*0396 (Chris Lerman, 1998).

22 Singer, "Dark Days," *Wierzbnik-Starachowitz*, p. 26.

23 VHA 2643 (Howard Kleinberg, 1995).

24 VHA 5096 (Malka Isser Perla, 1995).

25 VHA 2643 (Howard Kleinberg, 1995).

26 VHA 25175 (Elizabeth Styk, 1997). She claimed that her cousin, Josef Dreksler, escaped to the Soviet side two days after his appointment in order to avoid serving on the *Judenrat*. She also claimed that the *Judenrat* gave false assurances to her brother, who was in hiding. When he came out of his hiding place, he was arrested and subsequently died in German custody. She thus held the *Judenrat* responsible for her brother's death.

27 MJH, RG-1383 (Pola Funk, 1986).
28 Author's interview (Chris Lerman, 2001).
29 Author's interviews (Chris Lerman, 2001; Sally Recht, 2004).
30 MJH, RG-1165 (Guta Blass Weintraub, 1984).
31 Author's interview (Faye Gold, 2002).
32 VHA 2643 (Howard Kleinberg, 1995).
33 VHA 1833 (Isidore Guterman, 1995).
34 VHA 7366 (Naftula Korenwasser, 1995).
35 Kalib, *The Last Selection*, pp. 102–3.
36 UMD (Henry Krystal, 1996).
37 Kalib, *The Last Selection*, pp. 107–9, 113–14.

5: The German Occupiers in Wierzbnik-Starachowice

 1 VHA 2651 (Toby Steiman, 1995).
 2 Becker, p. 748 (Leona Finkler, 1966).
 3 VHA 16680 (Emil Najman, 1996).
 4 Kalib, *The Last Selection*, p. 95.
 5 VHA 1833 (Isidore Guterman, 1995).
 6 Moshe Neiman, "Hunted to Extinction," *Wierbznik-Starachowice Memorial Book* (CD version), p. 570.
 7 Kalib, *The Last Selection*, pp. 106–14. VHA 3916 (Rachell Szachter Eisenberg, 1995).
 8 Becker, p. 780 (Rose Herling, 1967).
 9 Author's interview (Regina Naiman, 2001).
10 FA, T-955 (Gutta T., 1987).
11 Becker, pp. 903, 905 (Mordka Maslowicz, 1967).
12 Author's interview (Harold Rubenstein, 2002).
13 Becker, pp. 968–69 (Rachmiel Zynger, 1968).
14 Becker, p. 1384 (Pinchas Heldstein, 1968).
15 Becker, p. 969 (Rachmiel Zynger, 1968).
16 Becker, p. 1384 (Pinchas Heldstein, 1968). Because the Jews knew German names only orally, not through written documents, survivors often provided different spellings of German names.
17 Becker: p. 431 (Hersz Tenenbaum, 1966), p. 727 (Bella Winograd, 1967), p. 742 (Mendel Tenenbaum, 1966), p. 979 (Josef Unger, 1968), pp. 999–1000 (Mendel Mincberg, 1968), p. 1142 (Sam Lang, 1968).
18 Becker: p. 742 (Mendel Tenenbaum, 1966), p. 764 (Howard Chandler, 1966), p. 774 (Fay Gotlib, 1967), p. 785 (Max Naiman, 1967), pp. 876–77 (Adrian Wilson, 1967).
19 Becker, p. 796 (Abraham Gershon Rosenwald, 1967).
20 Becker: p. 789 (Leib Rabinowicz, 1967), p. 809 (Helen Weisbloom, 1967), p. 796 (Abraham Gershon Rosenwald, 1967), p. 861 (Eva Zuckier, 1967).
21 Becker, p. 431 (Hersz Tenenbaum, 1966, who testified that he was ordered to bury four of Ertel's victims). Sara Postawski-Steinhardt, "The First Murder," *Wierzbnik-Starachowice Memorial Book* (CD version), p. 277: "Neizel" shot four Jews, including a young boy and three newcomers from Iłża, during the establishment of the ghetto.
22 Becker, p. 814 (Alter Weisbloom, 1967).
23 Becker, p. 1384 (Pinchas Heldstein, 1968).
24 Becker, p. 727 (Bella Winograd, 1967).

25 Becker: p. 764 (Howard Chandler, 1966), p. 796 (Abraham Gershon Rosenwald, 1967), p. 809 (Helen Weisbloom, 1967), p. 814 (Alter Weisbloom, 1967), p. 1042 (Josef-Chaim Rubenstein, 1968).

26 Becker, pp. 1049–50 (Pinchas Heldstein, 1967). For a beating from Schmidt: Becker, p. 1042 (Josef-Chaim Rubenstein, 1968).

27 Becker, pp. 1049–50, 1384 (Pinchas Heldstein, 1967 and 1968). Another witness recounted the same story but in telling the story wrongly referred to Schmidt as "Näsel." Becker: p. 570 (Moshe Rubenstein, 1966), pp. 1044–45 (Moshe Rubenstein, 1968, in which he correctly identifies Näsel as Ertel but does not make clear which was the killer of Herblum).

28 Kalib, *The Last Selection*, pp. 95–96. VHA: 3916 (Rachell Eisenberg, 1995), 16492 (Eva Herling, 1996).

29 Becker: pp. 134–35 (Otto Mittmann, 1963), pp. 196–97 (Abschlussbericht, 1962), p. 389 (Heinrich Edel, 1966), p. 390 (Karl Fröhle, 1966), pp. 397–400 (Otto Mittmann, 1966). The Zentrale Stelle der Landesjustizverwaltungen's preliminary investigation of the Gendarmerie-Posten Iłża, Kreis Starachowice (205 AR-Z 27/85), likewise did not uncover any of these three names.

30 Becker, p. 876 (Adrian Wilson, 1967).

31 Becker, p. 822 (Ben Zukerman, 1967).

32 Becker: p. 822 (Ben Zukerman, 1967), p. 856 (Israel Chaiton, 1967), pp. 999–1000 (Mendel Mincberg, 1968).

33 Becker: p. 389 (Heinrich Edel), p. 398 (Otto Mittmann).

34 Becker, pp. 473, 1106–15 (Walther Becker, 1966). National Archives, Berlin Document Center microfilm: party card and RuSHA file.

35 Becker: p. 793 (Leah Rabinowicz, 1967), p. 978 (Zvi Unger, 1968).

36 Becker: p. 412 (Anna Arbeiter, 1966), pp. 494, 1156 (Ralph Chaiton, 1966 and 1968).

37 Becker: p. 960 (Sara Postawski, 1968), p. 1000 (Mendel Mincberg, 1968), p. 1017 (Rywka Grinberg, 1968).

38 Becker: p. 26 (Israel Arbeiter, 1962), p. 412 (Anna Arbeiter, 1966), pp. 923–28 (Walther Becker, 1968), p. 1123 (Israel Arbeiter, 1968), p. 1130 (Anna Arbeiter, 1968).

39 Becker: pp. 99, 969 (Rachmiel Zynger, 1966 and 1968), p. 960 (Sara Postawski, 1968), p. 988 (Pinchas Hochmic, 1968), p. 1000 (Mendel Mincberg, 1968), p. 1028 (Zahava Prowizor, 1968).

40 Becker: pp. 99, 978 (Zvi Unger, 1966 and 1968), pp. 808, 1193 (Helen Weisbloom, 1967 and 1968), p. 1265 (Morris Zucker, 1968), p. 1409 (Abe Freeman).

41 Becker: p. 938 (Zvi Faigenbaum, 1968), p. 1006 (Mendel Mincberg, 1968), pp. 1021–22 (Rywka Grinberg, 1968). Faigenbaum based his account on information he received directly from a member of the *Judenrat*, Szmul Kahan; Mendel and Rywka were the son and daughter of Symcha Mincberg. Thus, all of these are "inside" sources in this regard.

42 Becker: pp. 434–35 (Toby Steiman, 1966), p. 1068 (Rachel Langer, 1968), p. 1132 (Anna Arbeiter, 1968).

43 Becker: p. 764 (Howard Chandler, 1966), p. 1343 (Meyer Herblum, 1968).

44 Becker: p. 796 (Abraham Gershon Rosenwald, 1967, according to whom Becker struck his mother with a riding whip when he caught her buying butter from a Pole), p. 780 (Rose Herling, 1967, according to whom Becker beat her husband when he presumed to ask Becker to be patient), p. 978 (Zvi Unger, 1968, whose father was beaten by Becker and Hayduk when the latter were falsely informed that his father was hiding supplies of fabric).

45 Becker, p. 1425 (Naftula Korenwasser, 1968, according to whom Becker shot a sixty-year-old man from Bodzentyn when the latter was unable to produce proper papers).

46 There was in fact a third alternative, that of being sent to trial and prison. When one Jew was arrested for picking up a piece of coal along the railway track, Becker screamed that he should confess to sabotage, and someone else beat him. He was sent to a court in Radom and convicted, and he then spent many months in the Polish prison in Staracho-wice. Becker, p. 1166 (Israel Chaiton, 1968).

47 Becker, pp. 26–27, 1123–24 (Israel Arbeiter, 1962 and 1968).

48 Becker, p. 1124 (Israel Arbeiter, 1968).

49 Becker, p. 1156 (Ralph Chaiton, 1968).

50 Becker, p. 991 (Nathan Gelbard, 1968).

51 VHA 8656 (Paul Cymerman, 1995).

52 Becker, pp. 460, 1291–92 (Annie Glass, 1966 and 1968).

53 Becker, p. 368 (Chaim Rubenstein, 1966).

54 VHA 8656 (Paul Cymerman, 1995).

55 FA, T-955 (Gutta T., 1987).

56 FA, T-1884 (Regina N., 1991 and 1992). Becker, p. 875 (Adrian Wilson, 1967). VHA: 15188 (Annie Glass, 1996), 18046 (David Mangarten, 1996).

57 VHA 8656 (Paul Cymerman, 1995).

6: Coping with Adversity in Wierzbnik, 1940–1942

1 APK, sygn. arch. 46, nr. 94 (Bürgermeister of Starachowice to the Jewish council, April 1, 1940).

2 Becker: p. 418 (Celia Nower, 1966), pp. 1122, 1129 (Anna Arbeiter, 1968). Celia Nower gives the date of January 1940, while Anna Arbeiter incorrectly places it in mid- or late 1940, after the Łódź ghetto was sealed and Jews were no longer being expelled from there.

3 For the German expulsion plans from western Poland, see: Götz Aly, *'Final Solution': Nazi Population Policy and the Murder of the European Jews* (London: Arnold, 1999), pp. 33–87; Christopher R. Browning, *The Origins of the Final Solution: The Evolution of Nazi Jewish Policy, September 1939–March 1942* (Lincoln: University of Nebraska Press, 2004), pp. 36–110.

4 VHA: 3654 (Joseph Zolno, 1995, who estimated 15,000), 4272 (Tema Lichtenstein, 1995, who estimated 12,000), 18588 (Israel Arbeiter, 1996, who estimated 10,000 Jews).

5 VHA: 3654 (Joseph Zolno, 1995, for the Bund); 4272 (Tema Lichtenstein, 1995) and 18588 (Israel Arbeiter, 1996) for the Maccabi and Zionist organizations.

6 MJH, RG-1984 (Regina Najman, 1988).

7 VHA: 3645 (Joseph Zolno, 1995), 18588 (Israel Arbeiter, 1996).

8 VHA 5190 (Ceil Saltzman, 1995).

9 Becker, p. 1359 (Chaim Asch, 1967). FA, T-1884 (Regina N., 1991 and 1992).

10 VHA 4272 (Tema Lichtenstein, 1995).

11 VHA 26120 (Mirjam Zylberberg, 1997).

12 VHA 18588 (Israel Arbeiter, 1996).

13 FA, T-1884 (Regina N., 1991 and 1992). MJH, RG-1984 (Regina Najman, 1988).

14 MJH, RG-1984 (Regina Najman, 1988).

15 Excerpt from the Płock community memorial book, available at: http://www.zchor.org/plock/sefer5.htm. Survivor testimonies differ on the exact dates of the two deporta-

tions. VHA 3654 (Joseph Zolno, 1995), who was in the second group, claims that the first deportation occurred on the night of February 25–26 and the second deportation occurred one week later, as does MJH, RG-1984 (Regina Najman, 1988). VHA 18588 (Israel Arbeiter, 1996), who was in the first group, claims the second deportation took place just two days later, on February 28, 1941.

16   VHA: 3654 (Joseph Zolno, 1995), 5190 (Ceil Saltzman, 1995), 9917 (Halina Zeleznik, 1995), 12073 (Helene Fellenbaum, 1996), 17629 (Sonia Ash, 1996), 2543 (Irving Leib-gott, 1997), 26120 (Mirjam Zylberberg, 1997). The community book likewise relates that deportation from Płock to Soldau was by truck.

17   VHA 18588 (Israel Arbeiter, 1996).

18   VHA 4272 (Tema Lichtenstein, 1995).

19   FA, T-1884 (Regina N., 1991 and 1992).

20   Browning, *The Origins of the Final Solution*, p. 34; Christopher R. Browning, *Fateful Months: Essay on the Emergence of the Final Solution* (New York: Holmes & Meier, 1985), p. 59.

21   Nürnberg Documents NO-1073 (affidavit of Otto Rasch, June 16, 1943) and NO-1774 (affidavit of Friedrich Schlegel, June 3, 1943, and Kaltenbrunner to SS judge, February 11, 1943).

22   Becker, p. 829 (Ben Lant, 1967).

23   VHA: 5190 (Ceil Saltzman, 1995), 18588 (Israel Arbeiter, 1996).

24   VHA 9917 (Halina Zeleznik, 1995).

25   For two to three days: VHA: 3645 (Joseph Zolno, 1995), 4272 (Tema Lichtenstein, 1995), 26120 (Mirjam Zylberberg, 1997); and FA, T-1884 (Regina N., 1991 and 1992). For two weeks: VHA: 5190 (Ceil Saltzman, 1995), 18588 (Israel Arbeiter, 1996).

26   FA, T-1884 (Regina N., 1991 and 1992, whose boyfriend was sent to Warsaw).

27   According to the Płock community memorial book, 1,500 Jews were sent to Bodzen-tyn, 800 to Chmielnik, 700 to Suchedniów, and 300 each to Wierzbnik and three other towns. According to Kalib, *The Last Selection*, p. 103, 200 Płock Jews were sent to Bodzentyn.

28   Kalib, *The Last Selection*, pp. 103–5, 113, 120. VHA 3916 (Rachell Eisenberg, 1995).

29   VHA: 3654 (Joseph Zolno, 1995), 18588 (Israel Arbeiter, 1996).

30   Author's interview (Regina Naiman, 2001). FA, T-1884 (Regina N., 1991 and 1992).

31   VHA 5190 (Ceil Saltzman, 1995).

32   VHA 4272 (Tema Lichtenstein, 1995).

33   VHA 25434 (Irving Leibgott, 1997).

34   The date is provided in Baker, *The Fiftieth Gate: A Journey Through Memory*, p. 76. Three days' notice is from Jerahmiel Singer, "Dark Days of Horror and Ruin," *Wierzbnik-Starachowitz*, p. 27.

35   VHA: 451 (Helen Starkman, 1994), 1213 (Rose Weitzen, 1995), 5096 (Malka Isser Perla, 1995), 23533 (Jacob Kaufman, 1996).

36   Singer, "Dark Days," *Wierzbnik-Starachowitz*, p. 27.

37   VHA 7739 (Howard Chandler, 1995). Author's interview (Chris Lerman, 2001).

38   VHA 7739 (Howard Chandler, 1995).

39   VHA: 2643 (Howard Kleinman, 1995), 10154 (Alan Newman, 1995), 12634 (Fay Rose-bruch, 1996), 15188 (Annie Glass, 1996), 18046 (David Mangarten, 1996), 26394 (Chana Sandovsky, 1997), 51793 (Sally Recht, 2001). FA, T-955 (Gutta T., 1987). USHMM, RG-50.030*0396 (Chris Lerman, 1998). Author's interviews (Henry Greenbaum, 2000; Faye Gold, 2002; Annie Glass, 2004).

40   VHA: 3645 (Joseph Zolno, 1995), 7739 (Howard Chandler, 1995), 15188 (Annie Glass, 1996), 18588 (Israel Arbeiter, 1996), 40372 (Harry Spicer, 1998).

41   VHA: 3268 (Nancy Kleinberg, 1995), 27533 (Jacob Kaufman, 1996).

42   VHA 1833 (Isidore Guterman, 1995).

43   VHA 16680 (Emil Najman, 1996).

44   VHA 5410 (Charles Kleinman, 1995).

45   VHA: 943 (Harold Rubenstein, 1995), 2643 (Howard Kleinman, 1995), 3189 (Pola Schlenger, 1995), 5410 (David Mangarten, 1996), 7739 (Howard Chandler, 1995), 12834 (Fay Rosebruch, 1996), 37728 (Tovi Pagi, 1998).

46   Becker, p. 1167 (Israel Chaiton, 1968).

47   VHA 7366 (Naftula Korenwasser, 1995).

48   VHA 45673 (Sam Isenberg, 1998).

49   APK, sygn. arch. 46, nr. 115: Bürgermeister Starachowice to Kreishauptmann Iłża, May 5, 1940.

50   APK, sygn. arch. 46, nr. 116: Bürgermeister Starachowice to Jewish council Wierzbnik, May 6, 1940. Singer, "Dark Days," *Wierzbnik-Starachowitz*, p. 28.

51   APK, sygn. arch. 46, nr. 126, 132, 134, 137, 138, 151.

52   APK, sygn. arch. 46, nr. 178 (file note of June 15, 1940).

53   On this conflict over jurisdiction of Jewish labor in the Lublin district, see: Browning, *The Origins of the Final Solution*, pp. 145–49.

54   For the date: Singer, "Dark Days," *Wierzbnik-Starachowitz*, p. 28.

55   For the lower number: Symcha Mincberg, "The Beginning of the Downfall," *Wierzbnik-Starachowice Memorial Book* (CD version), p. 400. For the number of 300 to 500: MJH, R-1383 (Pola Funk, 1986).

56   VHA: 13514 (Saul Miller, 1996), 27852 (Ann Zworth, 1997). Becker, p. 1274 (Irene Lipschultz, 1968).

57   Natan-Neta Gelbart, "We Ate Grass and Coal," and Mincberg, "The Beginning of the Downfall," *Wierzbnik-Starachowice Memorial Book* (CD version), pp. 332, 400. Becker, pp. 878, 1269 (Morris Zucker, 1967).

58   Singer, "Dark Days," *Wierzbnik-Starachowitz*, p. 28. VHA 1314 (Saul Miller, 1996). Another survivor testified that he was arrested in early 1940 and sent to the camp at Lipowa Strasse 17 in Lublin. After several months, his father and Mincberg obtained his release by delivering gold to Becker. Given both the different date and different camp, this may have been an entirely separate episode. Becker, pp. 878, 1269 (Morris Zucker, 1967).

59   Mincberg, "The Beginning of the Downfall," *Wierzbnik-Starachowice Memorial Book* (CD version), p. 401.

60   MJH, RG-1383 (Pola Singer Funk, 1986). Interestingly, neither Gutta T. herself [FA, T-955 (1987)] nor her brother, Jerahmiel Singer, mentions this episode.

61   Becker, p. 1274 (Irene Lipschultz, 1968). VHA: 17852 (Ann Zworth, 1997), 43845 (Morris Spagat, 1998). Moshe Neiman, "Hunted to Extinction," *Wierzbnik-Starachowice Memorial Book* (CD version), p. 571.

62   VHA 13613 (Alex Herblum, 1996).

63   YVA, M-1.E/1742 (Solomon Binsztok, 1948), O-3/8231 (Yakov Heyblum, 1995). For other survivors who were part of the contingent of workers sent to the Lublin district but did not discuss this episode in any detail: FA, T-1883 (Meyer K., 1988, who returned with the married men); YVA, O-3/6773 (Chaim Hilf, 1992).

64   Seidel, *Deutsche Besatzungspolitik in Polen*, pp. 264–67. According to Jacek Andrzej

Młynarczyk, *Judenmord in Zentralpolen* (Darmstadt, Germany: Wissenschaftliche Buch-gesellschaft, 2007), pp. 145–46, 270 Jewish workers departed Starachowice for Lublin on August 28, 1940, and on September 2, Zettelmeyer complained that more than 100 of them were married men, taken contrary to prior agreement.

65 Becker, p. 775 (Fay Gotlib, 1967), p. 1197 (Helen Weisbloom, 1968). VHA: 9584 (Henia Burman, 1995), 13613 (Alex Herblum, 1996).

66 Baker, *The Fiftieth Gate*, pp. 88–106, 112, 118. Kalib, *The Last Selection*, pp. 108–9, 112–14. VHA: 943 (Harold Rubenstein, 1995), 25175 (Elizabeth Styk, 1997). Author's interview (Harold Rubenstein, 2002).

67 VHA 25175 (Elizabeth Styk, 1997).

68 Singer, "Dark Days," *Wierzbnik-Starachowitz*, pp. 26–27. YVA, O-3/2860 (Chava Faigen-baum, 1965). Becker, pp. 821–22 (Ben Zukerman, 1967, who, in contrast to the other two accounts, said the group was held for three or four months).

69 USHMM, RG-50.030*0396 (Chris Lerman, 1998). VHA: 943 (Harold Rubenstein, 1995), 3189 (Pola Schlenger, 1995), 7739 (Howard Chandler, 1995), 18588 (Israel Arbeiter, 1996), 23533 (Jacob Kaufman, 1996), 25434 (Irving Leibgott, 1997), 40372 (Harry Spicer, 1998). Author's interviews (Howard Chandler, 2001; Harold Rubenstein, 2002).

70 VHA: 7739 (Howard Chandler), 2643 (Howard Kleinberg, 1995). USHMM, RG-50.030*0396 (Chris Lerman, 1998).

71 VHA: 1833 (Isidore Guterman, 1995), 13514 (Saul Miller, 1996), 25175 (Elizabeth Styk, 1997). YVA, O-3/6773 (Chaim Hilf, 1992). Quite untypically (since testimonies by the same survivor at different times are usually relatively consistent), one survivor testified to being paid on one occasion and not being paid on another. VHA 943 (Harold Ruben-stein, 1995), and author's interview (Harold Rubenstein, 2002).

72 VHA 8658 (Paul Cymerman, 1995).

73 Kalib, *The Last Selection*, p. 105; USHMM, RG-50.030*0411 (Anna Wilson, 2001). MJH, RG-1165 (Guta Blass Weintraub, 1984). Author's interview (Alan Newman, 2001).

74 MJH: RG-1165 (Guta Blass Weintraub, 1984), RG-1984 (Regina Najman, 1988). USHMM, RG-50.030*250 (Guta Blass Weintraub, 1990). FA, T-1884 (Regina N., 1991 and 1992). VHA 15188 (Annie Glass, 1996).

75 VHA: 943 (Harold Rubenstein, 1995), 1833 (Isidore Guterman, 1995), 1983 (Martin Baranek, 1995). Mincberg, "The Beginning of the Downfall," *Wierzbnik-Starachowice Memorial Book* (CD version), p. 398.

76 Singer, "Dark Days," *Wierzbnik-Starachowitz*, p. 25.

77 VHA 5190 (Ceil Saltzman, 1995).

78 This stands in contrast to Bodzentyn, where the influx of Płock Jews overwhelmed the local community, and, according to the Płock community memorial book—citing letters sent to Warsaw and preserved in the Ringelblum archives—the newcomers complained about the lack of help from the local Jews. (The Ringelblum Archives contained docu-ments collected and buried in the Warsaw ghetto and recovered after the war.)

7: Wierzbnik on the Eve of Destruction

1 For a fuller discussion of these crucial developments in the summer and fall of 1941, see: Browning, *The Origins of the Final Solution*.

2 YVA, O-53/134/1816 (weekly report of March 28, 1942, of the Hauptabteilung Propa-ganda of the General Government).

3   *Die Tagebücher von Joseph Goebbels*, Series II, volume 3, p. 561 (entry of March 27, 1942).

4   Christopher R. Browning, "Beyond Warsaw and Łódź: The Holocaust in Poland," in *Perspectives on the Holocaust: Essays in Honor of Raul Hilberg*, ed. by James S. Pacy and Alan P. Wertheimer (Boulder, CO: Westview Press, 1995), p. 77.

5   For the history of the three death camps in the General Government, see: Adalbert Rückerl, *NS-Vernichtungslager im Spiegel deutscher Strafprozesse: Belzec, Sobibor, Treblinka, Chelmno* (Munich: DTV, 1977); Yitzhak Arad, *Belzec, Sobibor, Treblinka: The Operation Reinhard Death Camps* (Bloomington: Indiana University Press, 1987).

6   ZStL, II 206 AR-Z 16/65 (Staatsanwaltschaft Hamburg, indictment of Weinrich, Fuchs, Kapke, et al.), pp. 69–85. Seidel, *Deutsche Besatzungspolitik in Polen*, pp. 310–13.

7   ZStL, 206 AR-Z 157/60, vol. 9 (Staatsanwaltschaft Darmstadt, indictment of Wollschläger, pp. 78–87); YVA, TR-10/673 (Innsbruck Indictment of Gerulf Mayer, Karl Macher, et al.), pp. 38–42. Seidel, *Deutsche Besatzungspolitik in Polen*, pp. 313–14.

8   ZStL, II 206 AR-Z 16/65, pp. 62–64, 77. YVA, TR-10/673: Innsbruck Indictment 12/67, of Mayer, Macher, et al., p. 28. Seidel, *Deutsche Besatzungspolitik in Polen*, pp. 303–5. Młynarczyk, *Judenmord in Zentralpolen*, pp. 254–56, 259.

9   Gitta Sereny, *Into That Darkness: From Mercy Killing to Mass Murder* (London: Andre Deutsch, 1974), pp. 154–64. Arad, *Belzec, Sobibor, Treblinka*, pp. 89–96, 119–23.

10 Arad, *Belzec, Sobibor, Treblinka*, pp. 393–94. YVA, TR-10/673 (Indictment of Mayer, Macher, et al.), pp. 54–57. Seidel, *Deutsche Besatzungspolitik in Polen*, pp. 317–23.

11 YVA, TR-10/585 (Landgericht Lüneberg 2 a Ks 2/65, Judgment of Degenhardt), pp. 9–27. *Justiz und NS-Verbrechen: Sammlung deutscher Strafurteile wegen national-sozialistischer Tötungsverbrechen, 1945–1966*, ed. by Fritz Bauer et al. (Amsterdam: University Press of Amsterdam, 1968) [hereafter JNSV], XXII, Nr. 600a (Landgericht Schweinfurt Ks 1/64), pp. 326–31. Seidel, *Deutsche Besatzungspolitik in Polen*, pp. 315–17.

12 Seidel, *Deutsche Besatzungspolitik in Polen*, pp. 323–29. Arad, *Belzec, Sobibor, Treblinka*, pp. 393–95.

13 For tables listing the shifting Jewish populations of all towns in the Radom district during the Nazi occupation, prepared by the Jewish Historical Institute in Warsaw, see: Adam Rutkowski, "Martyrologia, walka i zagłada ludności żydowskiej w dystrykcie radomskim podczas okupacji hitlerowskiej," *Biuletyn Żydowskiego Instytutu Historycznego*, vols. 15–16 (1955), pp. 138–65. For the history of the Jews of Bodzentyn and the Holocaust, there is now a Website: www.bodzentyn.net.

14 Jerahmiel Singer, "Dark Days of Horror and Ruin," *Wierzbnik-Starachowitz*, p. 30.

15 Becker, p. 1124 (Israel Arbeiter, 1968).

16 USHMM, RG-50.030*0396 (Chris Lerman, 1998); Author's interview (Chris Lerman, 2001).

17 Becker, p. 970 (Rachmiel Zynger, 1968).

18 Zvi Faigenbaum, "Led like Lambs to the Slaughter," *Wierzbnik-Starachowice Memorial Book* (CD version), p. 432.

19 UMD (Henry Krystal, 1996).

20 VHA 42666 (Morris Pinczewski, 1998). In two other testimonies, given three decades earlier, Pinczewski was considerably more restrained, noting only that the Polish underground had confirmed rumors about mass killing and camps like Treblinka, and thus

"some" Jews knew they were being sent to their deaths. Becker, pp. 604, 1331 (Morris Pinczewski, 1966 and 1968).

21 Becker, p. 1060 (Pesia Gruda, 1968).

22 Kalib, *The Last Selection*, p. 122.

23 VHA 40372 (Harry Spicer, 1998).

24 VHA: 2643 (Howard Kleinberg, 1996), 18588 (Israel Arbeiter, 1996). USHMM, RG-50.030*0411 (Anna Wilson, 2001).

25 Becker, p. 680 (Dora Kaminer, 1966).

26 Becker, p. 943 (Avraham Scheiner, 1968). In the community book, he gave a somewhat different version. He had fled to Stanislawów in Eastern Galicia, but when the killing had begun there, he managed to get back to Wierzbnik. In light of what he had already experienced in Stanislawów, he believed what gentile friends told him about Treblinka. Avraham Shiner, "The Policeman Shot and Missed," *Wierzbnik-Starachowice Memorial Book* (CD version), p. 449.

27 Becker, p. 1216 (Ben Zukerman, 1968).

28 FA, T-1884 (Regina N., 1991 and 1992).

29 Becker: p. 796 (Abraham Gershon Rosenwald, 1967), p. 1018 (Rywka Grinberg, 1968), p. 1240 (Eva Zuckier, 1968), p. 1274 (Irene Lipschultz, 1968). VHA 37728 (Tovi Pagi, 1998).

30 Becker: pp. 952–53 (Schmuel Erlichson, 1968), p. 964 (Sara Postawski, 1968), p. 1045 (Moshe Rubenstein, 1968), p. 1124 (Israel Arbeiter, 1968), p. 1311 (Guta Blass Weintraub, 1968). VHA 2643 (Howard Kleinberg, 1995). FA, T-1682 (Mania K., 1988). USHMM, RG-50.030*0411 (Anna Wilson, 2001).

31 Becker, p. 1325 (Alan Newman, 1968).

32 Becker: pp. 952–53 (Schmuel Erlichson, 1968), p. 1124 (Israel Arbeiter, 1968). VHA 3916 (Rachell Eisenberg, 1995).

33 VHA: 1983 (Martin Baranek, 1995), 2643 (Howard Kleinberg, 1995), 5096 (Malka Perla, 1995).

34 Gershon Rosenwald, "Deep in the Forest," *Wierzbnik-Starachowice Memorial Book* (CD version), p. 521.

35 VHA 3261 (Nancy Kleinberg, 1995). Becker, p. 1010 (Rywka Schabeton, 1968).

36 Author's interview (Martin Baranek, 2001). Młynarczyk, *Judenmord in Zentralpolen*, pp. 286–93, also emphasizes repression, denial, and wishful thinking as the dominant Jewish responses to the looming threat.

37 VHA 40881 (Salek Benedikt, 1998). See also: VHA 16114 (Jacob Szapszewicz, 1996, who was grabbed off the street by Jewish police as early as 1941and sent to work in the Starachowice factories).

38 Becker, p. 847 (Ruth Rosengarten, 1967).

39 VHA: 5874 (Anita Tuchmayer, 1995), 29327 (Ray Langer, 1997). Becker, p. 842 (Anita Tuchmayer, 1967).

40 Becker, p. 1089 (Leopold Rudolf Schwertner, 1968).

41 Yaacov Shafshevitz, "Starcavitz," *Shidlovtser Yizkor Bukh* (Shidlovtsa Benevolent Society of New York, 1974), p. 219. Translation from Yiddish in: USHMM, RG-02.025.

42 VHA 33025 (Joseph Tauber, 1997).

43 VHA 8889 (Jack Pomeranz, 1995).

44 VHA 15716 (Joseph Friedenson, 1996). Author's interview (Joseph Friedenson, 2002).

45 VHA 20030 (Anna Freilich, 1996).

46 FA, T-442 (Sarah W., 1983). Becker, pp. 835, 1305 (Zelda Waiman, 1966 and 1968).

47 VHA 16116 (Maria Szapszewicz, 1996).

48 Becker, pp. 769, 773 (Arnold Finkler, 1966).

49 VHA 5030 (Jakob Binstock, 1995).

50 VHA 20030 (Anna Freilich, 1996).

51 VHA 466 (Berel Blum, 1995).

52 Becker, p. 1331 (Morris Pinczewski, 1968).

53 Becker: pp. 423, 1244 (Jack Steiman, 1966 and 1968), p. 504 (Max Steiman), p. 1377 (Toby Steiman). See also: Becker, p. 1317 (Emil Milbert, 1968).

54 VHA 30134 (Joseph Chernikowski, 1997).

55 Becker, p. 736 (Toby Weisfeld, 1966). VHA 6061 (Toby Weisfeld, 1995).

56 VHA: 40866 (Helen Sonshine, 1998), 43397 (Louis Feintuch, 1998).

57 Rutkowski, "Martyrologia, walka i zagłada ludności żydowskiej w dystrykcie radomskim," pp. 149–50. Kalib, *The Last Selection*, p. 145, gives the date for the clearing of Bodzentyn as October 3, 1942.

58 Kalib, *The Last Selection*, pp. 123–33. VHA: 3916 (Rachell Eisenberg, 1995), 3948 (Irene Horn, 1995).

59 VHA 44259 (Ruth Turek, 1998).

60 UMD (Henry Krystal, 1996).

61 VHA 16492 (Eva Herling, 1996).

62 VHA 4334 (Miriam Miklin, 1995).

63 VHA 8028 (Abraham Bleeman, 1995).

64 Becker, p. 1024 (Natan Wajchendler, 1968). VHA 9113 (Hyman Flancbaum, 1995).

65 Symcha Mincberg, "The Beginning of the Downfall," *Wierzbnik-Starachowice Memorial Book* (CD version), p. 402.

66 Private account of Henry (Yechiel) Eisenberg, taken in 2003, and generously shared with me by the family.

67 MJH, RG-1165 (Guta Blass Weintraub, 1984).

68 VHA 7366 (Naftula Korenwasser, 1995).

69 Becker, p. 935 (Zvi Faigenbaum, 1968). FA, T-955 (Gutta T., 1987). Becker, p. 1274 (Irene Lipschultz, 1968).

70 VHA 5096 (Malka Isser Perla, 1995).

71 Singer, "Dark Days," *Wierzbnik-Starachowitz*, p. 30.

72 Ibid.

73 YVA, M-49E/155 (Symcha Mincberg, 1945).

74 Becker, p. 956 (Schmuel Erlichson, 1968).

75 Becker, p. 1053 (Pinchas Heldstein, 1968).

76 Nürnberg Document NO-1611: Himmler Order, October 9, 1942.

77 Christopher R. Browning, *Nazi Policy, Jewish Workers, German Killers* (New York: Cambridge University Press, 2000), pp. 76–80.

78 Singer, "Dark Days," *Wierzbnik-Starachowitz*, p. 30.

79 Becker: p. 938 (Zvi Faigenbaum, 1968), p. 961 (Sara Postawski, 1988), p. 1053 (Pinchas Heldstein, 1968).

80 Becker, p. 970 (Rachmiel Zynger, 1968).

81 Becker, p. 1290 (Annie Glass, 1968). VHA 15188 (Annie Glass, 1996). Author's interview (Annie Glass, 2004).

82 VHA 1833 (Isidore Guterman, 1995).

83 Author's interview (Faye Gold, 2002).

84 MJH, RG-1383 (Pola Funk, 1986). According to the same source, missionaries also came to town and were given children for conversion.

85 Becker, p. 905 (Mordka Maslowicz, 1967). VHA 5410 (Charles Kleinman, 1995).

86 Kalib, *The Last Selection*, pp. 133–39. VHA 3916 (Rachell Eisenberg, 1995).

87 Pagi, *"The way it was . . .": The Diary of a 12 year old Jewish girl who survived Auschwitz (1939–1945)*, pp. 8–9. VHA 37728 (Tovi Pagi, 1998). Two-year-old Necha Baranek was also successfully placed in hiding. Necha Baranek, "It was a Great Shock," *Wierzbnik-Starachowitz*, pp. 51. Author's interview (Martin Baranek, 2001).

88 MJH, RG-1383 (Pola Singer Funk, 1986). The mother continued to believe her infant had lived but that the woman would not give it up. FA, T-955 (Gutta T., 1987).

89 VHA 20030 (Anna Freilich, 1996).

90 Author's interview (Howard Chandler, 2001). On another occasion, Howard Chandler did not express uncertainty, stating, "I knew that the people who were to hide him had betrayed him." Gilbert, *The Boys*, p. 124.

91 VHA 15188 (Annie Glass, 1996). For her sister's slightly different version: VHA 51793 (Sally Recht, 2001).

92 Becker, p. 781 (Rose Herling, 1967). VHA 8424 (Regina Levenstadt, 1995).

93 FA, T-1884 (Regina N., 1991 and 1992). Author's interview (Regina Naiman, 2001).

94 FA, T-955 (Gutta T., 1987).

95 Singer, "Dark Days," *Wierzbnik-Starachowitz*, pp. 31, 33. Kalib, *The Last Selection*, p. 149. Author's interview (Faye Gold, 2002). VHA: 403 (Ruth Charney, 1994, who stayed in the electricity works at night), 5190 (Ceil Saltzman, 1995, who as a sixteen-year-old girl was taken to the factory the night before the deportation), 33807 (Gloria Borenstein, 1997, whose father insisted that she and her sister remain at the factory day and night).

96 Singer, "Dark Days," *Wierzbnik-Starachowitz*, p. 31. Author's interview (Howard Chandler, 2001).

97 VHA 45673 (Sam Isenberg, 1998).

98 Becker, pp. 935–36 (Zvi Faigenbaum, 1968). FA, T-1884 (Regina N., 1991 and 1992). Author's interview (Regina Naiman, 2001). USHMM, RG-50.030*0411 (Anna Wilson, 2001). Author's interview (Anna Wilson, 2001).

99 Becker, p. 1158 (Ralph Chaiton, 1968).

100 Becker, p. 748 (Leonia Finkler, 1966).

101 Becker, p. 1092 (Leopold Rudolf Schwertner, 1968, who mentioned Birenzweig specifically in this regard). Author's interview (Shoshana Fiedelman, 2008).

102 Becker, p. 1018 (Rywka Grinberg, 1968).

103 Becker, p. 993 (Nathan Gelbard, 1968).

104 Zvi Magen (Hershel Pancer), "From Slavery to Freedom," *Wierbznik-Starachowice Memorial Book* (CD version), p. 574.

105 Becker: p. 1010 (Riwka Schabeton, 1968, who gave the source of the information as the *Judenrat*), p. 1024 (Natan Weichendler, 1968).

106 VHA 5190 (Ceil Saltzman, 1995). MJH: RG-1383 (Pola Funk, 1986), RG-1165 (Guta Blass Weintraub, 1984). USHMM, RG-50.030*250 (Guta Blass Weintraub, 1990).

107 Becker: p. 945 (Avraham Scheiner, 1968), p. 964 (Sara Postawski, 1968), p. 1045 (Moshe Rubenstein, 1968), p. 1145 (Sam Lang, 1968), p. 1274 (Irene Lipschultz, 1968), pp. 1324–25 (Alan Newman, 1968). USHMM, RG-50.030*0411 (Anna Wilson, 2001). Author's interview (Anna Wilson, 2001).

108 Niewyk, *Fresh Wounds*, p. 88 (Kalman Eisenberg, 1946). Becker, p. 1014 (Lea Greiwer, 1968).

109 Becker, p. 1381 (Adam Kogut, 1968).

8: The *Aktion*, October 27, 1942

1 Becker: p. 961 (Sara Postawski, 1968), p. 1124 (Israel Arbeiter, 1968). Author's interview (Martin Baranek, 2001).

2 Becker: p. 497 (Helen Starkman, 1966), pp. 731, 1324 (Alan Newman, 1967 and 1968), pp. 861, 1239 (Eva Zuckier, 1967 and 1968), p. 886 (Frymeta Maslowicz, 1967), pp. 1037–38, 1381 (Adam Kogut, 1968), p. 1059 (Pesia Gruda, 1968), p. 1224 (Howard Chandler, 1968), p. 1286 (Fred Baum, 1968). VHA 2561 (Toby Steiman, 1995). Gilbert, *The Boys*, p. 123 (Howard Chandler).

3 Becker, p. 943 (Avraham Scheiner, 1968).

4 Becker, pp. 1051, 1385 (Pinchas Heldstein, 1968). In his first account, Heldstein placed this episode in the early morning after the ghetto was surrounded. In a subsequent account, this occurred the night before the ghetto was surrounded, and Heldstein encountered the ghetto cordon only on his way back.

5 VHA 28993 (Chaim Wolgroch, 1997).

6 VHA 5096 (Malka Isser Perla, 1995).

7 Becker, p. 993 (Nathan Gelbard, 1968).

8 Becker: pp. 424, 1244 (Jack Steiman, 1966 and 1968), p. 604 (Moshe Pinczewski, 1966), p. 936 (Zvi Faigenbaum, 1968), p. 943 (Avraham Scheiner, 1968), p. 953 (Schmuel Erlichson, 1968), p. 971 (Rachmiel Zynger, 1968), p. 1028 (Zahava Prowizor, 1968), p. 1068 (Rachel Langer, 1968), p. 1143 (Sam Lang, 1968), p. 1151 (Leib Rabinowicz, 1968), p. 1216 (Ben Zukerman, 1968), p. 1239 (Eva Zuckier, 1968). Jerahmiel Singer, "Dark Days of Horror and Ruin," *Wierzbnik-Starachowitz*, p. 33.

9 Becker, p. 1211 (Sylvia Russak, 1968).

10 Becker, p. 1019 (Rywka Grinberg, 1968).

11 Becker, p. 1019 (Rywka Grinberg, 1968). Rivka Greenberg, "My Journey Through the Valley of the Shadow of Death," *Wierzbnik-Starachowice Memorial Book* (CD version), p. 301. See also Becker, p. 1001 (Mendel Mincberg, 1968).

12 Becker: p. 1059 (Pesia Gruda, 1968), p. 797 (Abraham Gershon Rosenwald, 1968, a neighbor of the Kumecs).

13 Becker: pp. 371, 1046 (Moshe Rubenstein, 1966 and 1968), p. 972 (Rachmiel Zynger, 1968), p. 1372 (Jankiel Chaiton, 1968). VHA: 9917 (Halina Zeleznik, 1995), 23533 (Jacob Kaufman, 1996), 33807 (Gloria Borenstein, 1997), 51793 (Sally Recht, 2001).

14 Becker, p. 1029 (Zahava Prowizor, 1968).

15 Becker, p. 719 (Rywka Slomowicz, 1967).

16 Becker, p. 1067 (Rachel Langer, 1968).

17 Becker, p. 901 (Sonia Posner, 1967).

18 VHA 16680 (Emil Najman, 1996).

19 VHA 16876 (Henry Greenbaum, 1996).

20 These are the descriptive verbs that appear most frequently in the testimonies. According to Eva Zuckier, her father was bitten by a dog when he did not run fast enough. Becker, p. 1240 (Eva Zuckier, 1968).

21 Becker: pp. 22, 1137 (Mack Arbeiter, 1962 and 1968), pp. 27–28, 1125 (Israel Arbeiter, 1962 and 1968), p. 1292 (Annie Glass, 1968), p. 1289 (Fred Baum, 1968), p. 1298 (Arthur Armont, 1968).

22 Becker: pp. 424, 1245 (Jack Steiman, 1966 and 1968), pp. 504–5 (Max Steiman, 1966), p. 775 (Fay Gotlib, 1967), p. 944 (Avraham Scheiner, 1968), p. 954 (Schmuel Erlichson, 1968), p. 960 (Sara Postawski, 1968), p. 1020 (Rywka Grinberg, 1968), p. 1137 (Mack

Arbeiter, 1968), p. 1043 (Josef-Chaim Rubenstein, 1968), pp. 1046–47 (Moshe Rubenstein, 1968), pp. 1143–44 (Sam Lang, 1968), p. 1151 (Leib Rabinowicz, 1968), p. 1172 (Rose Herling, 1968), p. 1184 (Naftula Korenwasser, 1968), p. 1190 (Abe Freeman, 1968), pp. 1194–95 (Helen Weisbloom, 1968), p. 1283 (Mania Kaufman, 1968). Gershon Rosenwald, "A Mountain of Corpses in the Kornwassers' Yard," *Wierzbnik-Starachowice Memorial Book* (CD version), p. 330. [Two witnesses that babies had heads smashed here: Rose Herling in Becker, pp. 779, 1172; and Rywka Grinberg, in Becker, pp. 62, 1018.]

23 VHA 16680 (Emil Najman, 1996).

24 Becker, pp. 1039, 1381 (Adam Kogut, 1968).

25 Becker, p. 1292 (Annie Glass, 1968).

26 Becker, p. 1324 (Alan Newman, 1968).

27 Becker: p. 972 (Rachmiel Zynger, 1968), p. 1318 (Emil Milbert, 1968).

28 Becker: p. 1144 (Sam Lang, 1968), p. 1151 (Leib Rabinowicz, 1968), p. 1246 (Jack Steiman, 1968), p. 1283 (Mania Kaufman, 1968).

29 Becker, p. 1002 (Mendel Mincberg, 1968). VHA 7366 (Naftula Korenwasser, 1995).

30 Becker: pp. 434, 1205 (Toby Wolfowicz, 1966 and 1968), p. 1179 (Max Naiman, 1968), p. 1185 (Naftula Korenwasser, 1968), p. 1190 (Abe Freeman, 1968), p. 1343 (Meyer Herblum, 1968). Howard Chandler first testified that he *saw* the killing and then later that he had only *heard* about it. Becker, pp. 764, 1226.

31 Becker: p. 428 (Hersz Tenenbaum, 1966), p. 679 (Dora Kaminer, 1966), p. 823 (Ben Zukerman, 1967), p. 963 (Sara Postawski, 1968), pp. 992–93 (Nathan Gelbard, 1968), p. 1011 (Riwka Schabeton, 1968), p. 1195 (Helen Weisbloom, 1968), p. 1274 (Irene Lipschultz, 1968). Several testified only to the old couple being beaten. Becker: p. 797 (Abraham Gershon Rosenwald, 1967), p. 1172 (Rose Herling, 1968). VHA 25175 (Elizabeth Styk, 1997).

32 Becker, p. 1015 (Lea Greiwer, 1968).

33 Becker: pp. 823, 1217 (Ben Zukerman, 1967 and 1968), p. 862 (Eva Zuckier, 1967), p. 943 (Avraham Scheiner, 1968), p. 1311 (Guta Blass Weintraub, 1968).

34 Becker, p. 1212 (Sylvia Russak, 1968).

35 Becker, p. 1283 (Mania Kaufman, 1968). See also Becker, p. 1220 (Ben Zukerman, 1968, who also claimed to have seen Manela shot on the marketplace), and p. 1276 (Irene Lipschultz, 1968, who claimed to have seen Manela on the marketplace struggling against being marched to the trains and to have heard that Manela was then subsequently shot).

36 Malka Weissbloom, "The Heroism of Esther Manela," *Wierbznik-Starachowice Memorial Book* (CD version), p. 517.

37 Becker, p. 680 (Dora Kaminer, 1966).

38 Becker: p. 604 (Morris Pinczewski, 1966), p. 943 (Avraham Scheiner, 1968), p. 971 (Rachmiel Zynger, 1968), p. 1167 (Irving Chaiton, 1968), p. 1190 (Abe Freeman, 1968), p. 1278 (Rywka Slomowicz, 1968), p. 1292 (Annie Glass, 1968), p. 1299 (Henry Armont, 1968), p. 1306 (Zelda Waiman, 1968), p. 1343 (Meyer Herblum, 1968).

39 Yaakov Katz, "The Sixteenth Day of Cheshvan: The Liquidation of our Town," *Wierzbnik-Starachowitz*, p. 49.

40 Singer, "Dark Days," *Wierzbnik-Starachowitz*, p. 34.

41 Becker, p. 1043 (Josef-Chaim Rubenstein, 1968).

42 Becker: p. 27 (Rywka Grinberg, 1962), p. 797 (Abraham Gershon Rosenwald, 1967), p. 937 (Zvi Faigenbaum, 1968), p. 955 (Schmuel Erlichson, 1968). YVA, M-49E/155 (Symcha Mincberg, 1945).

43 Becker: p. 22 (Israel Arbeiter, 1962, offered an estimate of 200), p. 1298 (Fred Baum, 1968, offered 150), p. 719 (Rywka Slomowicz, 1967, offered "hundreds").

44 Becker, p. 993 (Nathan Gelbard, 1968).

45 Becker: p. 62 (Rywka Grinberg, 1962), p. 98 (Rachmiel Zynger, 1962), pp. 406, 1207 (Fred Baum, 1966 and 1968), p. 1053 (Pinchas Heldstein, 1968), p. 1158 (Ralph Chaiton, 1968), p. 1274 (Irene Lipschultz, 1968), p. 1293 (Annie Glass, 1968), p. 1333 (Morris Pinczewski, 1968).

46 Becker: pp. 764–65 (Howard Chandler, 1966), p. 1125 (Israel Arbeiter, 1968).

47 Becker: p. 944 (Avraham Scheiner, 1968), p. 1324 (Alan Newman 1968).

48 One survivor estimated the number of German "Gestapo officials" present that day at ten to fifteen. Becker, p. 995 (Nathan Gelbard, 1968).

49 Becker, p. 1207 (Fred Baum, 1968).

50 Becker, p. 843 (Anita Tuchmayer, 1967). One survivor estimated the number of "Latvians" brought into Wierzbnik that day as eight to ten, which seems a very low estimate. Becker, p. 956 (Schmuel Erlichson, 1968).

51 Becker, p. 764 (Howard Chandler, 1966).

52 Becker, p. 944 (Avraham Scheiner, 1968). No survivors specifically mentioned the presence of green-uniformed German Order Police, but Seidel, *Deutsche Besatzungspolitik in Polen*, p. 327, and Młynarczyk, *Judenmord in Zentralpolen*, pp. 145–46, agree that a handful (ten according to Seidel, a platoon according to Młynarczyk) of Order Police from Reserve Police Company "Munich" were also present at the ghetto-clearing that day.

53 Becker: p. 797 (Abraham Gershon Rosenwald, 1967), p. 823 (Ben Zukerman, 1967). Gershon Rosenwald, "Deep in the Forest," *Wierzbnik-Starachowice Memorial Book* (CD version), p. 522. On the drunkenness of the *Hiwis* during killing operations, see also: Christopher R. Browning, *Ordinary Men: Reserve Police Battalion 101 and the Final Solution in Poland* (New York: HarperCollins, 1992), pp. 78–87.

54 ZStL, II AR 643/71, especially vol. 1 (Staatsanwaltschaft Hamburg 147 Js 43/69, Indictment of Karl Streibel), pp. 33–38, 65–66.

55 For "*fremdvölkischen Hiwis*" (Ukrainian, Latvian, or Lithuanian), see: YVA, TR-10/745 (Staatsanwaltschaft Hamburg 147 Js 34/65, Indictment of Hellmut Lange and Ernst Hugo Thomas), p. 25. For "Baltic auxiliaries," see: JNSV, XIV, nr. 463, p. 746. For Latvians, see: JNSV, XIII, nr. 433, p. 694. For Ukrainians: JNSV, XXII, nr. 600b, p. 346, and ZStL, II 206 AR-Z 16/65 (Hamburg 147 Js 38/65, indictment of Hermann Weinrich, Paul Fuchs, Erich Kapke, and Paul Nell), p. 53. For Ukrainians or Latvians, JNSV, XII, nr. 600a, 329.

56 Becker, p. 1106 (Erich Kapke, 1968).

57 ZStL, II 206 AR-Z 16/65, pp. 62–64, 77. YVA, TR-10/673: Innsbruck Indictment 12/67, of Gerulf Mayer, Karl Macher, et al., p. 28.

58 During one phase of the interviews, potential witnesses were shown a sequence of photo lineups with Becker's photo displayed only in the last of three batches. Generally they recognized his photo correctly and without hesitation.

59 No fewer than twenty-four witnesses made this point.

60 Becker, p. 1221 (Ben Zukerman, 1968). One witness acknowledged that there were other unknown German officers, presumably from Radom, "haughtily" observing the *Aktion*. She opined that Becker was so frantic, precisely because of his need to impress his superiors. Becker, p. 1022 (Rywka Grinberg, 1968). Another witness identified one of the German officers from Radom as a man named Schippers, who was in fact the man in

charge of Jewish labor on SS and police leader Böttcher's staff. Becker, p. 1159 (Ralph Chaiton, 1968).

61 Becker, pp. 1022–23 (Rywka Grinberg, 1968). See also: Becker, p. 1006 (Mendel Mincberg, 1968).

62 Becker, p. 1205 (Toby Wolfowicz, 1968).

63 Becker, p. 980 (Zvi Unger, 1968), p. 1192 (Helen Weisbloom, 1968). For similar expressions, see also: p. 1131 (Anna Arbeiter, 1968), p. 1173 (Rose Herling, 1968).

64 Becker: p. 1002 (Mendel Mincberg, 1968), p. 1205 (Toby Wolfowicz, 1968).

65 Becker: p. 963 (Sara Postawski, 1968), p. 990 (Pinchas Hochmic, 1968), p. 411 (Anna Arbeiter, 1966), p. 1179 (Max Naiman, 1968).

66 Becker, p. 1002 (Mendel Mincberg, 1968).

67 Becker, pp. 944–45 (Avraham Scheiner, 1968).

68 Becker: p. 427 (Hersz Tenenbaum, 1966), pp. 961–62 (Sara Postawski, 1968), p. 993 (Nathan Gelbard, 1968), p. 1011 (Riwka Schabeton, 1968), p. 1195 (Helen Weisbloom, 1968).

69 Becker: pp. 433, 1205 (Toby Wolfowicz, 1966 and 1968), p. 764 (Howard Chandler, 1967), p. 1393 (Meyer Herblum, 1968). Subsequently, one of the three changed his testimony from direct eyewitness to hearsay. Becker, p. 1226 (Howard Chandler, 1968).

70 Becker: pp. 22, 1137 (Mack Arbeiter, 1962 and 1968), pp. 28, 1125 (Israel Arbeiter, 1962 and 1968), p. 1298 (Henry Armont, 1968).

71 Becker: p. 428 (Hersz Tenenbaum, 1966), p. 954 (Schmuel Erlichson).

72 Becker, pp. 63, 1021 (Rywka Grinberg, 1962 and 1968). The same kind of killing, though not attributed to Becker, was also described by one other witness. Becker, pp. 779, 1172 (Rose Herling, 1967 and 1968).

73 According to the diary of a German, the number 3748 was written on the deportation train. Landgericht Hamburg, Urteil (50) 35/70 in der Strafsache gegen Walther Becker, p. 17. For a corroborating estimate of 3,000 to 4,000 Jews sent from Wierzbnik to Treblinka: Becker: p. 63 (Rywka Grinburg, 1962), p. 68 (Zvi Faigenbaum, 1962), p. 99 (Rachmiel Zynger, 1962). For the work-camp figure of 1,200 men and 400 women sent to the camps: YVA, M-49E/155 (Symcha Mincberg, 1945), and Becker, p. 732 (Alan Newman, 1967). For a lower estimate of 1,000 men and 200 women: VHA 44259 (Ruth Turek, 1998). For a higher estimate of 1,800: Becker: p. 63 (Rywka Grinberg, 1962), p. 68 (Zvi Faigenbaum, 1962). For the highest estimate of 2,000: Becker: p. 86 (Kalman Czernikowski, 1962), p. 93 (Zvi Unger, 1962), p. 837 (Zelda Waiman, 1967); and VHA 18046 (David Mangarten, 1996).

74 According to the calculations of Seidel, *Deutsche Besatzungspolitik in Polen*, pp. 329–30, during the ghetto-clearing operations of August–November 1942 in the Radom district, some 330,000 Jews were deported to Treblinka, between 8,800 and 11,000 were shot on the spot, and between 20,300 and 22,400 were exempted from deportation. Those exempted for labor were therefore less than 7 percent of the total.

75 Kalib, *The Last Selection*, pp. 152–53.

76 Lawrence L. Langer, *Versions of Survival: The Holocaust and the Human Spirit* (Albany: State University of New York Press, 1982), p. 72.

77 Becker, p. 1283 (Mania Kaufman, 1968).

78 MJH, RG-1383 (Pola Funk, 1986). Mirjam Zylberberg and her middle sister had work cards, but their mother and little sister did not. Mirjam told her little sister to come over anyway and found someone with a work card who was willing to give it up in order

to stay with her family. Only later did she discover that her middle sister had in the meantime given up her work card to remain with their mother. VHA 26120 (Mirjam Zylberberg, 1997).

79   Becker, p. 1046 (Moshe Rubenstein, 1968).
80   Becker, p. 1298 (Henry Armont, 1968).
81   Becker, p. 854 (Israel Chaiton, 1967).
82   VHA 12643 (Fay Rosebruch, 1996).
83   VHA 2643 (Howard Kleinman, 1995).
84   Becker, p. 962 (Sara Postawski, 1968).
85   Becker, p. 1005 (Mendel Mincberg, 1968).
86   Singer, "Dark Days," *Wierzbnik-Starachowitz*, p. 33.
87   Becker, p. 797 (Abraham Gershon Rosenwald, 1967).
88   Becker, p. 804 (Sylvia Russak, 1967).
89   Becker, pp. 809, 1195 (Helen Weisbloom, 1967 and 1968).
90   Becker, p. 953 (Schmuel Erlichson, 1968).
91   Becker, p. 1025 (Natan Weichendler, 1968).
92   Becker, p. 1190 (Abe Freeman, 1968).
93   Becker, p. 1218 (Ben Zukerman, 1968).
94   Becker, p. 1059 (Pesia Gruda, 1968).
95   VHA 8656 (Paul Cymerman, 1995).
96   VHA 3261 (Nancy Kleinberg, 1995).
97   VHA 25434 (Irving Leibgott, 1997).
98   VHA 1213 (Rose Weitzen, 1995).
99   Becker, pp. 435, 1207 (Toby Wolfe, 1966 and 1968).
100 VHA 2651 (Toby Steiman, 1995).
101 VHA 7313 (Hyman Reichzeig, 1995).
102 Dvora Rubenstein-Erlichson, "It Began on an Autumn Day," *Wierzbnik-Starachowice Memorial Book* (CD version), p. 546.
103 VHA 1833 (Isidore Guterman, 1995).
104 For example: Zvi Unger, "From Wierzbnik to Mauthausen," *Wierzbnik-Starachowitz*, pp. 218–20; VHA: 7739 (Howard Chandler, 1995), 10154 (Alan Newman, 1995).
105 Becker, p. 1143 (Sam Lang, 1968, who was separated from his wife and three children).
106 Becker, pp. 836–37 (Zelda Waiman, 1967). VHA 4272 (Tema Lichtenstein, 1995).
107 The degree to which the fate of a Jew depended upon the discretionary power of different Germans is exemplified by the story of Helen Sonshine. Though she had no work card, she was selected for work by one German and taken to the other side of the marketplace. There a second German rejected her because she had no work card and sent her back. The first German then selected her again and took her once more to the workers' side. Not surprisingly, she attributed her survival to "only luck." VHA 40866 (Helen Sonshine, 1998). Nechama Tec has pointed out to me that the Germans preferred to keep mothers and children together, because that enabled the deportation and killing procedures to go more quietly and smoothly.
108 Becker, p. 1267 (Morris Zucker, 1968).
109 Becker, pp. 490, 1158 (Ralph Chaiton, 1966 and 1968).
110 Author's interview (Henry Greenbaum, 2000).
111 Becker, p. 1325 (Alan Newman, 1968).
112 VHA 3916 (Rachell Eisenberg, 1995).

113   Kalib, *The Last Selection*, p. 156.
114   Becker, pp. 765, 1225 (Howard Chandler, 1967 and 1968). VHA 7739 (Howard Chandler, 1995). Gilbert, *The Boys*, p. 123.
115   VHA 1983 (Martin Baranek, 1995). Author's interview (Martin Baranek, 2001). At least one other boy made a similar escape. Becker, p. 810 (Helen Weisbloom, 1967).
116   Becker, p. 510 (Dina Tenenbaum, 1966). Author's interview (Faye Gold, 2002).
117   Becker, pp. 823, 1218 (Ben Zukerman, 1967 and 1968).
118   Becker, p. 797 (Abraham Gershon Rosenwald, 1967).
119   Becker, pp. 732, 1327 (Alan Newman, 1967 and 1968). VHA 10154 (Alan Newman, 1995).
120   Becker: p. 1173 (Rose Herling, 1968), p. 1195 (Helen Weisbloom, 1968). VHA: 8424 (Regina Levenstadt, 1995), 18046 (David Mangarten, 1996).
121   Becker: p. 639 (Henry Armand, 1966), p. 775 (Fay Gotlib, 1967), p. 797 (Abraham Gershon Rosenwald, 1967). Singer, "Dark Days," *Wierzbnik-Starachowitz*, p. 33. Donald Niewyk, *Fresh Wounds*, p. 89 (Kalman Eisenberg).
122   Arad, *Belzec, Sobibor, Treblinka*. Rutkowski, "Martyrologia, walka i zagłada ludności żydowskiej w dystrykcie radomskim podczas okupacji hitlerowskiej," pp. 138–65.

9: Into the Camps

 1   Becker, p. 946 (Avraham Scheiner, 1968). For Piatek's role in the selection, see also: Becker: p. 847 (Ruth Rosengarten, 1967), pp. 809, 1195 (Helen Weisbloom, 1967 and 1968). VHA 7366 (Naftula Korenwasser, 1995).
 2   Becker: p. 995 (Avraham Scheiner, 1968), p. 1283 (Mania Kaufman, 1968).
 3   Becker: p. 1283 (Mania Kaufman, 1968), pp. 1426–27 (Naftula Korenwasser, 1968). In neither of these accounts was Becker present, and the killing was done by the two German policemen. In two other accounts, Becker was there and either shot or ordered the shooting. Becker: p. 848 (Ruth Rosengarten, 1967, who said only one young man was shot for concealing money), p. 1195 (Helen Weisbloom, 1968). VHA 17629 (Sonia Ash, 1996, spoke of only one victim from Płock but did not identify the shooters).
 4   Becker, p. 1426 (Naftula Korenwasser, 1968).
 5   Becker: p. 887 (Frymeta Maslowicz, 1967), p. 1196 (Helen Weisbloom, 1968). The story was also related as hearsay from a survivor who knew Tenenbaum's sister. According to this version, Schmidt mendaciously promised that nothing would happen to the mother if she came forward. Becker, p. 1050 (Pinchas Heldstein, 1968).
 6   VHA 1983 (Martin Baranek, 1995). Author's interview (Martin Baranek, 2001).
 7   Becker, pp. 810, 1197 (Helen Weisbloom, 1967 and 1968).
 8   Becker, p. 1039 (Adam Kogut, 1968).
 9   Becker, p. 824 (Ben Zukerman, 1967).
10   Becker: p. 862 (Eva Zuckier, 1967), p. 895 (Anna Brzoza, 1967), p. 1032 (Zahava Prowizor, 1968), pp. 1055–56 (Chaim Hilf, 1968). VHA: 16876 (Henry Greenbaum, 1996), 30134 (Joseph Chernikowski, 1997).
11   VHA: 2643 (Howard Kleinberg, 1995), 28793 (Chaim Wolgroch, 1997). Hana Tenzer, "At the Edge of the Abyss," *Wierzbnik-Starachowitz*, p. 191.
12   Becker: p. 956 (Schmuel Erlichson, 1968), p. 974 (Rachmiel Zynger, 1968), p. 1326 (Alan Newman, 1968).
13   Becker, p. 510 (Dina Tenenbaum, 1966).
14   Becker, p. 780 (Rose Herling, 1967).

15 VHA 43845 (Morris Spagat, 1998).

16 Becker, p. 1054 (Pinchas Heldstein, 1968).

17 VHA 9393 (Irving Weinberg, 1995).

18 Becker, p. 651 (Mayer Gutman, 1966). VHA 466 (Berel Blum, 1995). Jerahmiel Singer, "Dark Days of Horror and Ruin," *Wierzbnik-Starachowitz*, p. 31. This applies to the second camp, Majówka, as well.

19 See chapter 7, notes 99–102. See also: VHA 3916 (Rachell Eisenberg, 1995, who identified the family of the "bootmaker" as among this group).

20 Becker: p. 1127 (Israel Arbeiter, 1968), p. 1145 (Sam Lang, 1968), p. 1294 (Annie Glass, 1968).

21 Becker: p. 417 (Fred Baum, 1966, who identifies the man as Mikulki), pp. 22, 1138 (Mack Arbeiter, 1962 and 1968), pp. 28, 1127 (Israel Arbeiter, 1962 and 1968), p. 798 (Abraham Gershon Rosenwald, 1967). VHA 5410 (Charles Kleinman, 1995).

22 Becker: pp. 425, 1247 (Jack Steiman, 1966 and 1968), p. 786 (Max Naiman, 1967), pp. 790, 1183 (Leib Rabinowicz, 1967 and 1968), p. 1386 (Pinchas Heldstein, 1968), p. 1420 (Mayer Frenkel, 1968). Rabinowicz, Heldstein, and Frenkel identify the young man as Kumec. VHA 4272 (Tema Lichtenstein, 1995).

23 Becker, p. 83 (Mendel Mincberg, 1962).

24 Becker, p. 1146 (Sam Lang, 1968). For other references to this killing: Becker: pp. 425, 1247 (Jack Steiman, 1966 and 1968), p. 895 (Anna Brzoza, 1967), p. 1127 (Israel Arbeiter, 1968), p. 1208 (Toby Wolfe, 1968), p. 1320 (Emil Milbert, 1968), p. 1409 (Abe Freeman, 1968). VHA 33025 (Joseph Tauber, 1997). Singer, "Dark Days," *Wierzbnik-Starachowitz*, p. 34.

25 Jerahmiel Singer, "Aba Kumetz Dared to Swear," *Wierzbnik-Starachowice Memorial Book* (CD version), p. 461.

26 Singer, "Dark Days," *Wierzbnik-Starachowitz*, p. 34. Becker: p. 371 (Moshe Rubenstein, 1966), p. 765 (Howard Chandler, 1967), p. 791 (Leib Rabinowicz, 1967). Author's interview (Howard Chandler, 2001). VHA 13613 (Alex Herblum, 1996).

27 MJH, RG-1383 (Pola Funk, 1986, whose father and brother threw away the hats into which she had sewn coins). USHMM, RG-50.030*0396 (Chris Lerman, 1998). VHA 466 (Berel Blum, 1995).

28 VHA: 2651 (Toby Steiman, 1995), 17629 (Sonia Ash, 1996), 40881 (Salek Benedikt, 1998).

29 VHA 3916 (Rachell Eisenberg, 1995).

30 VHA 10154 (Alan Newman, 1995). Author's interview (Alan Newman, 2001).

31 Martin Gilbert, *The Boys* (New York: Henry Holt, 1997), p. 154. VHA 7739 (Howard Chandler, 1995).

32 Becker: p. 100 (Rachmiel Zynger, 1962), p. 428 (Hersz Tenenbaum, 1966), p. 605 (Morris Pinczewski, 1966), p. 744 (Mendel Tenenbaum, 1966), p. 765 (Howard Chandler, 1967), p. 824 (Ben Zukerman, 1967), pp. 1039, 1382 (Adam Kogut, 1968), pp. 1191, 1409 (Abe Freeman, 1968), p. 1279 (SS, 1968), p. 1294 (Annie Glass, 1968), p. 1320 (Emil Milbert, 1968).

33 Becker: pp. 76–77, 989–90 (Pinchas Hochmic, 1962 and 1968), pp. 630–31 (Mania Blicher, 1966), pp. 758–59 (Mina Binsztok, 1967), pp. 1055–56, 1389–90 (Chaim Hilf, 1968), p. 1414 (Akiva Rutmanowicz, 1968). VHA 3948 (Irene Horn, 1995). USHMM, RG-50.030*0396 (Chris Lerman, 1998).

34 VHA 1833 (Isidore Guterman, 1995). Zvi Magen (Hershel Pancer), "From Slavery to Freedom," *Wierzbnik-Starachowice Memorial Book* (CD version), p. 574.

35   Becker: pp. 77, 989–90 (Pinchas Hochmic, 1962 and 1968, who was permitted to watch the loading for ten to fifteen minutes from a rise on the factory grounds), p. 759 (Mina Binsztok, 1967), pp. 1056, 1389–90 (Chaim Hilf, 1968), p. 1414 (Akiva Rutmanowicz, 1968). USHMM, RG-50.030*0396 (Chris Lerman, 1998, who was taken to an upper floor of the brick factory by a "gentile school friend" to be able to see what was happening).

36   Becker: p. 723 (Bella Winograd, 1967), p. 759 (Mina Binsztok, 1967), p. 1395 (Salamon Binsztok, 1968).

37   Becker: p. 78 (Pinchas Hochmic, 1962), p. 1390 (Chaim Hilf, 1968). VHA 3948 (Irene Horn, 1995). Author's interview (Joseph Friedenson, 2002). Magen, "From Slavery to Freedom," *Wierzbnik-Starachowice Memorial Book* (CD version), p. 574.

38   Becker: pp. 994, 996 (Nathan Gelbard, 1968, who was joined by his father), p. 1275 (Irene Lipschultz, 1968, who testified that her husband, Chaim Kogut, a policeman, was also chosen). VHA 403 (Ruth Charney, 1994, said she was among the group of boys and girls who, along with the Jewish policemen, were chosen to clean up).

39   Yaakov Katz (Leibush Herblum), "The Sixteenth Day of Cheshvan: The Liquidation of Our Town," *Wierzbnik-Starachowitz*, p. 48.

40   Private family account (2003) of Yechiel Eisenberg, shared with author.

41   USHMM, RG-50.030*250 (Guta Blass Weintraub, 1990). Author's interview (Guta Blass Weintraub, 2004).

42   Becker, pp. 838, 1307–8 (Zelda Waiman, 1967 and 1968, who claims six to eight girls). VHA 5874 (Anita Tuchmayer, 1995, who claims nine girls). In contrast, Yechiel Eisenberg says that twenty girls worked in the cleanup commando. Private family account (2003) of Yechiel Eisenberg, shared with author.

43   For cemetery duty, see: Katz, "The Sixteenth Day of Cheshvan," *Wierzbnik-Starachowitz*, p. 49. For body collection: Becker: p. 996 (Nathan Gelbard, 1968), and private family account (2003) of Yechiel Eisenberg, shared with author.

44   Becker: p. 996 (Nathan Gelbard, 1968), p. 1308 (Zelda Waiman, 1968).

45   Private family account (2003) of Yechiel Eisenberg, shared with author.

46   Becker: p. 838 (Zelda Waiman, 1967), p. 996 (Nathan Gelbard, 1968). Private family account (2003) of Yechiel Eisenberg, shared with author.

10: Personalities and Structures

1   Richard Overy, "The Reichswerke 'Hermann Göring'," in *War and Economy in the Third Reich* (Oxford: Clarendon Press, 2002), pp. 144–74.

2   Becker: p. 695 (Fritz Hofmann, 1966), and p. 619 (Franz Köhler, 1966).

3   For Meyer's SS rank: ZStL II 206 AR 513/68 (hereafter Kaschmieder Investigation), p. 23 (Kurt Otto Baumgarten, 1968). In the various testimonies, Meyer's name—known only phonetically to the prisoners—was also spelled Mayer, Maier, and Meier.

4   Kaschmieder Investigation, p. 10; Landgericht Düsseldorf 8 Ks 2/70 (Judgment against Willi Schroth), p. 29.

5   YVA, O-2/319 (Moses Weinberg, no date).

6   VHA 22640 (Lucyna Berkowicz, 1996).

7   Becker, p. 1433 (Else Althoff, 1968, who was Willi Althoff's sister-in-law).

8   National Archives, Berlin Document Center microfilm: Ortskartei, number 239346.

9   Becker: p. 391 (Helmuth Hackeney, 1966, who was a German *Unterwachführer* in the *Werkschutz*), p. 625 (Franz Köhler, 1968).

10   Becker, p. 64 (Rywka Grinberg, 1962). Author's interview (Anna Wilson, 2001).

11 Becker, p. 406 (Fred Baum, 1966).
12 Becker, p. 435 (Toby Wolfe, 1966).
13 VHA 40866 (Helen Sonshine, 1998).
14 Becker, p. 1373 (Jankiel Chaiton, 1968).
15 Author's interview (Anna Wilson, 2001).
16 Becker: p. 743 (Mendel Tenenbaum, 1966), p. 836 (Zelda Waiman, 1967).
17 Becker, p. 896 (Anna Brzoza, 1967).
18 VHA 2643 (Howard Kleinberg, 1995).
19 Becker, p. 515 (Ruth Wagner, 1966).
20 Becker, p. 759 (Mina Binsztok, 1966).
21 Becker: p. 824 (Ben Zukerman, 1967), p. 867 (Anna Wilson, 1967), p. 874 (Adrian Wilson, 1967). VHA 40866 (Helen Sonshine, 1998).
22 VHA 5190 (Ceil Saltzman, 1995).
23 Becker, p. 843 (Anita Tuchmayer, 1967). FA, T-955 (Gutta T., 1987). VHA 5874 (Anita Tuchmayer, 1995).
24 Becker: p. 641 (Henry Armand, 1966), p. 724 (Bella Winograd, 1967), p. 759 (Mina Binsztok, 1867), p. 775 (Fay Gotlib, 1967). VHA: 28993 (Chaim Wolgroch, 1997), 4334 (Miriam Miklin, 1995). Author's interview (Joseph Friedenson, 2002).
25 Becker: p. 509 (Dina Tenenbaum, 1966), p. 860 (Eva Zuckier, 1967). VHA: 943 (Harold Rubenstein, 1995), 40866 (Helen Sonshine, 1998). MJH, RG-1383 (Pola Funk, 1986). Author's interview (Faye Gold, 2002).
26 Becker: p. 70 (Zvi Hersz Faigenbaum, 1962), p. 595 (Maurice Weinberger, 1966), p. 775 (Fay Gotlib, 1967). USHMM, RG-50.030*0411 (Anna Wilson, 2001).
27 Becker, p. 867 (Anna Wilson, 1968). VHA 13514 (Saul Miller, 1996).
28 Becker, p. 1386 (Pinchas Heldstein, 1968).
29 Becker: p. 791 (Leib Rabinowicz, 1967), p. 831 (Ben Lant, 1967).
30 Becker: p. 675 (Meyer Herblum), p. 759 (Mina Binsztok, 1967).
31 Becker, p. 625 (Franz Köhler).
32 Becker, p. 445 (Kurt Otto Baumgarten, 1966).
33 Becker, p. 688 (Paul Fischer, 1966).
34 Becker, p. 701 (Fritz Hofmann, 1966).
35 USHMM, RG-50.030*0411 (Anna Wilson, 2001). Author's interview (Anna Wilson, 2001).
36 USHMM, RG-50.030*0411 (Anna Wilson, 2001). Becker, p. 767 (Howard Chandler, 1966).
37 Becker, p. 753 (Leonia Finkler, 1966), p. 494 (Ralph Chaiton, 1966). USHMM, RG-50.030*0411 (Anna Wilson, 2001).
38 Becker: p. 862 (Eva Zuckier, 1967), p. 1390 (Chaim Hilf, 1968). VHA (Irving Graifman, 14182, whose description probably confuses Waschek with Althoff).
39 USHMM, RG-50.030*0411 (Anna Wilson, 2001). Author's interview (Chris Lerman, 2001).
40 Kalib, *The Last Selection*, p. 170.
41 USHMM, RG-50.030*0411 (Anna Wilson, 2001). Author's interviews (Faye Gold, 2002; Annie Glass and Sally Recht, 2004).
42 Author's interviews (Faye Gold, 2002; Sally Recht, 2004).
43 Author's interview (Anna Wilson, 2001).
44 Author's interview (Joseph Friedenson, 2002).
45 YVA, M-49/1172 (Mendel Kac, 1945).

46   Author's interview (Sally Recht, 2004).

47   Becker, p. 1335 (Moshe Pinczewski, 1968). FA, T-1884 (Regina N., 1991 and 1992). VHA: 2651 (Toby Steiman, 1995), 3916 Rachell Eisenberg, 1995), 6061 (Toby Weisfeld, 1995), 37728 (Tovi Pagi, 1998), 40881 (Salek Benedikt, 1968). USHMM, RG-50.030*0396 (Chris Lerman, 1998). Kalib, *The Last Selection*, p. 174 . Author's interview (Shoshana Fiedelman, 2008).

48   Becker, p. 652 (Mayer Gutman, 1966). FA, T-955 (Gutta T., 1987). YVA, O-3/9394 (Ruben Zachronovitsky, 1996). Kalib, *The Last Selection*, p. 174.

49   Becker, p. 652 (Mayer Gutman, 1966). YVA: M-49/1112 (Mendel Kac, 1945), and O-3/9394 (Ruben Zachronovitsky, 1996). Author's interview (Anna Wilson, 2002).

50   Becker, p. 728 (Bella Winograd, 1967). VHA: 2651 (Toby Steiman, 1995), 28993 (Chaim Wolgroch, 1997), 37728 (Tovi Pagi, 1998). YVA, M-49/1112 (Mendel Kac, 1945). Author's interview (Anna Wilson, 2002).

51   Author's interviews (Howard Chandler, 2001; Faye Gold, 2002; Guta Blass Weintraub, 2004).

52   Becker, p. 1273 (Irene Lipschultz, 1968).

53   Becker, p. 370 (Moshe Rubenstein, 1966).

54   VHA: 3916 (Rachell Eisenberg, 1995).

55   Author's interview (Henry Krystal, 2002).

56   USHMM: David Boder interview collection (Kalman Eisenberg, 1946), pp. 2552–53.

57   USHMM: David Boder interview collection (Kalman Eisenberg, 1946), p. 2552.

58   Author's interview (Guta Blass Weintraub, 2004).

59   Becker, p. 855 (Israel Chaiton, 1967). VHA: 15941 (Ernst Abraham, 1996), 28993 (Chaim Wolgroch, 1997). Zvi Unger, "From Wierzbnik to Mauthausen," *Wierzbnik-Starachowitz*, pp. 218–20. Author's interview (Howard Chandler, 2001).

60   Author's interviews (Anna Wilson, 2001; Guta Blass Weintraub, 2004).

61   USHMM, David Boder interview collection (Kalman Eisenberg, 1946), p. 2553.

62   Author's interview (Howard Chandler, 2001).

63   Author's interview (Anna Wilson, 2001).

64   Becker, p. 868 (Anna Wilson, 1967).

65   Becker, p. 370 (Moshe Rubenstein, 1966).

66   Author's interview (Joseph Friedenson, 2002).

67   Becker, pp. 654–55 (Mayer Gutman, 1966). VHA 28993 (Chaim Wolgroch, 1997). USHMM, RG-15.084m (Golda Teichman, n.d., from the Jewish Historical Institute Archives). Author's interview (Gitta Friedenson, 2002, who simply called Wilczek a "murderer," without further specifics).

68   For the most articulate critical testimonies in this regard, see: YVA, M-49/1112 (Mendel Kac, 1945), and author's interview (Alan Newman, 2001).

69   The commandant, Kornblum, and Nathan Gelbard were sent to Majówka and Tartak, respectively, but neither seems to have remained a policeman. Becker, p. 996 (Nathan Gelbard, 1968).

70   VHA 1213 (Rose Weitzen, 1995).

71   VHA 16680 (Emil Najman, 1996). FA, T-1884 (Regina N., 1991 and 1992). Author's interview (Regina Naiman, 2001).

72   VHA: 25164 (Michael Feldstein, 1997), 36226 (Toby Kott, 1997).

73   VHA 5190 (Ceil Saltzman, 1995).

74   VHA 5030 (Jakob Binstock, 1995).

75   Kalib, *The Last Selection*, p. 175.

76 Ibid.

77 VHA 28993 (Chaim Wolgroch, 1997).

78 Becker, p. 428 (Jack Steiman, 1966). Author's interview (Sally Recht, 2004).

79 On Linzon: Becker, p. 804 (Sylvia Russak, 1967). On Hilf: Author's interviews (Henry Greenbaum, 2000; Faye Gold, 2002). On Moshe Herblum: VHA 25164 (Michael Feldstein, 1997). On Goldfarb: VHA 40881 (Salek Benedikt, 1998). On Turek: VHA36414 (Rachel Akierman, 1997).

80 Author's interview (Sally Recht, 2004).

81 YVA, M-49/1112 (Mendel Kac, 1945).

82 Author's interview (Alan Newman, 2001).

83 There were no mixed views about the younger son, who was described as "obnoxious" and "mean." Author's interviews (Alan Newman, 2001; Guta Blass Weintraub, 2004).

84 VHA 25175 (Elizabeth Styk, 1997).

85 Author's interview (Joseph Friedenson, 2002).

86 FA, T-1881 (Regina N., 1991 and 1992). Author's interviews (Henry Greenbaum, 2000; Regina Naiman, 2001).

87 Author's interview (Joseph Friedenson, 2002).

88 Becker, p. 716 (Ida Gutman, 1967).

89 Author's interview (Alan Newman, 2001). VHA 36414 (Rachel Akierman, 1997).

11: The Typhus Epidemic

1 VHA: 1707 (Edward Koslowski, 1995), 28993 (Chaim Wolgroch, 1997).

2 VHA: 12634 (Fay Rosebruch, 1996), 33025 (Joseph Tauber, 1997).

3 VHA: 51793 (Sally Recht, 2001), 18588 (Israel Arbeiter, 1996). Becker, p. 22 (Mack Arbeiter, 1962).

4 VHA 23715 (Barry Kaufman, 1996).

5 YVA, O-3/9394 (Ruben Zachronovitsky, 1996).

6 VHA: 2651 (Toby Steiman, 1995), 4334 (Miriam Miklin, 1995), 8889 (Jack Pomeranz, 1995), 10154 (Alan Newman, 1995), 20030 (Anna Freilich, 1996).

7 VHA 1883 (Isidore Guterman, 1995).

8 VHA: 1883 (Isidore Guterman, 1995), 4334 (Miriam Miklin, 1995), 9113 (Hyman Flancbaum, 1995), 16230 (Sol Lottman, 1996), 16680 (Emil Najman, 1996), 40881 (Salek Benedikt, 1998).

9 VHA 12728 (Ann Spicer, 1996).

10 VHA 8656 (Paul Cymerman, 1995).

11 Author's interviews (Howard Chandler, 2001; Chris Lerman, 2001). VHA 7739 (Howard Chandler, 1995).

12 Naomi Baumslag, *Murderous Science: Nazi Doctors, Human Experimentation, and Typhus* (Westport, CT: Praeger, 2005), pp. 2–5, 11–15.

13 For a history of the German encounter with typhus in Eastern Europe, see: Paul Julian Weindling, *Epidemics and Genocide in Eastern Europe, 1890–1945* (Oxford: Oxford University Press, 2000).

14 *Kampf den Seuchen! Deutscher Ärzte-Einsatz im Osten. Die Aufbauarbeit im Gesundheitswesen des Generalgouvernementes*, ed. by Jost Walbaum (Cracow: Buchverlag "Deutscher Osten," 1941), pp. 34, 145. This book is an anthology of articles written by Walbaum and his associates in 1940.

15 Ibid., pp. 84, 144.

16 Christopher R. Browning, "Genocide and Public Health: German Doctors and Polish Jews, 1939–1941," *Holocaust and Genocide Studies*, 3/1 (1988), pp. 21–36. Weindling, *Epidemics and Genocide in Eastern Europe*, pp. 271–77.

17 VHA: 1652 (David Meadow, 1995), 3948 (Irene Horn, 1995), 5190 (Ceil Saltzman, 1995), 8896 (Maury Adams, 1995), 12634 (Fay Rosebruch, 1996), 33025 (Joseph Tauber), 44259 (Ruth Turek, 1998). USHMM, RG-50.030*0396 (Chris Lerman, 1998). Author's interview (Sally Recht, 2004).

18 VHA: 3948 (Irene Horn, 1995), 7739 (Howard Chandler, 1995), 16114 (Jacob Szapszewicz, 1996), 26120 (Mirjam Zylberberg, 1997), 43397 (Louis Feintuch, 1998). MJH, RG-1383 (Pola Funk, 1986). USHMM, RG-50.030*0396 (Chris Lerman, 1998). Author's interviews (Howard Chandler, 2001; Gitta Friedenson, 2002; Guta Blass Weintraub, 2004).

19 Goldie Szachter Kalib, *The Last Selection* (Amherst: University of Massachusetts Press, 1991), p. 176.

20 VHA: 9135 (Lola Sussman, 1995), 12634 (Fay Rosebruch, 1996), 15941 (Ernest Abraham, 1996), 33807 (Gloria Borenstein, 1997).

21 VHA: 1213 (Rose Weitzen, 1995), 18046 (David Mangarten, 1996). Author's interview (Sally Recht, 2004). Kalib, *The Last Selection*, p. 176.

22 VHA: 1652 (David Meadow, 1995), 1883 (Isidore Guterman, 1995), 9113 (Hyman Flancbaum, 1995), 16116 (Maria Szapszewicz, 1996), 16230 (Sol Lottman, 1996).

12: The Althoff Massacres

1 YVA, M-49E/155 (Symcha Mincberg, 1945). Becker, pp. 93–94 (Zvi Unger, 1962).

2 Becker: p. 64 (Rywka Grinberg, 1962), pp. 406–7 (Fred Baum, 1966), p. 414 (Anna Arbeiter, 1966), p. 436 (Toby Wolfe, 1966), p. 792 (Leib Rabinowicz, 1967), p. 860 (Eva Zuckier, 1967), p. 1409 (Abe Freeman, 1968). VHA: 3261 (Nancy Kleinberg, 1995), 40866 (Helen Sonshine, 1998).

3 Becker: p. 87 (Kalman Czernikowski, 1962), p. 407 (Fred Baum, 1966), p. 423 (Jack Steiman, 1966), p. 493 (Ralph Chaiton, 1966), p. 497 (Helen Starkman, 1966), p. 755 (Leonia Finkler, 1966), p. 776 (Fay Gotlib, 1967), p. 860 (Eva Zuckier, 1967), p. 867 (Anna Wilson, 1967), p. 874 (Adrian Wilson, 1967), p. 896 (Anna Brzoza, 1967), p. 900 (Sonia Posner, 1967). VHA: 4272 (Tema Lichtenstein, 1995), 40881 (Salek Benedikt, 1998). No two testimonies on this event are alike. Most mention the selection and shooting of ten prisoners in response to an escape. Fred Baum, Eva Zuckier, Anna Wilson, and Adrian Wilson mention the blindfolds; Tema Lichtenstein and Salek Benedikt mention the truck headlights; and Eva Zuckier and Anna Brzoza mention Althoff's staging the occasion as target practice.

4 Symcha Mincberg, "The Beginning of the Downfall," *Wierzbnik-Starachowice Memorial Book* (CD version), p. 403.

5 Becker, p. 720 (Rywka Slomowicz, 1967). VHA 40866 (Helen Sonshine, 1998)

6 Becker: p. 435 (Toby Wolfe, 1966), p. 491 (Ralph Chaiton, 1966), p. 495 (Helen Starkman, 1966), p. 631 (Mania Blicher, 1966). VHA: 3934 (Irene Horn, 1995), 4334 (Miriam Miklin, 1995).

7 Becker, p. 495 (Helen Starkman, 1966). VHA 3934 (Irene Horn, 1995).

8 VHA: 5190 (Ceil Saltzman, 1995), 16876 (Henry Greenbaum, 1996).

9 Becker: p. 420 (Celia Nower, 1966), p. 429 (Hersz Tenenbaum, 1966), p. 732 (Alan New-

man, 1966), p. 743 (Mendel Tenenbaum, 1966), p. 778 (Fay Gotlib, 1967), p. 791 (Leib Rabinowicz, 1967). VHA: 943 (Harold Rubenstein, 1995), 33025 (Joseph Tauber, 1997).

10   For the three accounts of Israel Arbeiter: Becker, p. 29 (1962); FA, T-91 (1980); and VHA 18588 (1996).

11   Becker, p. 749 (Leonia Finkler, 1966). She gave the total number of victims that day as fifty-one. Others gave an estimate of fifty to seventy. Becker: p. 791 (Leib Rabinowicz, 1967, for fifty), p. 23 (Mack Arbeiter, 1962, for seventy).

12   MJH, RG-1383 (Pola Funk, 1986).

13   Becker, p. 839 (Zelda Waiman, 1967).

14   This phrase comes from Becker, p. 791 (Leib Rabinowicz, 1967).

15   Becker, p. 641 (Henry Armand, 1966).

16   Becker, p. 407 (Fred Baum, 1966).

17   Becker, p. 423 (Jack Steiman, 1966). Toby Weisfeld's first husband, Hersz Jadek, tried to follow but was caught and shot in the neck by Althoff. She dated the killing of her husband and her giving birth to a child the following day to three months after entry into the camp. Becker, p. 738 (Toby Weisfeld, 1966).

18   Becker, p. 831 (Ben Lant, 1967, who heard the story from the man who survived the attack, Shlomo Weiss).

19   VHA 9113 (Hyman Flancbaum, 1995).

20   VHA 28993 (Chaim Wolgroch, 1997).

21   Becker, p. 83 (Mendel Mincberg, 1962).

22   Becker, p. 29 (Israel Arbeiter, 1962). FA, T-91 (Israel A., 1980). VHA 18588 (Israel Arbeiter, 1996).

23   Zvi Unger, "From Wierzbnik to Mauthausen," *Wierzbnik-Starachowitz*, pp. 218–20. Becker, p. 94 (Zvi Hersh Unger, 1962, provides a slightly different version).

24   Author's interview (Alan Newman, 2001). Alan Newman dated his escape from the truck to December because he was reunited with his parents in Majówka in early 1943.

25   Becker, p. 806 (Sylvia Russak, 1967). VHA 16492 (Eva Herling, 1996).

26   This date is provided by one of the three surviving daughters of Rabbi Rabinowicz, who lost their mother that day. Becker, p. 818 (Faye Gold, 1967). Another sister affirmed March but offered no specific day. Becker, p. 509 (Dina Tenenbaum, 1966). Four others simply offered the date vaguely as the "spring" of 1943. Becker: p. 64 (Rywka Grinberg, 1962), p. 83 (Mendel Mincberg, 1962), p. 413 (Anna Arbeiter, 1966), p. 491 (Ralph Chaiton, 1966). A number of other witnesses seem to have conflated the December and March selections, with trucks taking the victims to the forest, into one event closely tied to the first liquidation of the sick barracks.

27   YVA, M49E/155 (Symcha Mincberg, 1945).

28   Becker, p. 792 (Leib Rabinowicz, 1967).

29   On the number of trucks: Becker, p. 425 (Jack Steiman, 1966).

30   Becker: p. 859 (Eva Zuckier, 1967), p. 865 (Anna Wilson, 1967), p. 897 (Anna Brzoza, 1968).

31   Becker: p. 64 (Rywka Grinberg, 1962), p. 1386 (Pinchas Heldstein, 1968). Both agreed on the presence of the Gendarmes; only the latter testified to the presence of Schmidt.

32   Seidel, *Deutsche Besatzungspolitik in Polen*, p. 341.

33   Becker: p. 498 (Helen Starkman, 1966), p. 859 (Eva Zuckier, 1967), p. 865 (Anna Wilson, 1967). VHA: 3916 (Rachell Eisenberg, 1995), 16492 (Eva Herling, 1996).

34   Becker, pp. 1414–15 (Akiva Rutmanowicz, 1968).

35 Becker, p. 498 (Helen Starkman, 1966).

36 Becker, p. 865 (Anna Wilson, 1967).

37 Ibid.

38 Becker: p. 498 (Helen Starkman, 1966), p. 509 (Dina Tenenbaum, 1966), p. 515 (Ruth Wagner, 1966), p. 725 (Bella Winograd, 1967), p. 818 (Faye Gold, 1967), p. 859 (Eva Zuckier, 1967), p. 987 (Anna Brzoza, 1967).

39 Becker, p. 515 (Ruth Wagner, 1966).

40 Kalib, *The Last Selection*, p. 179. VHA 3916 (Rachell Eisenberg, 1995).

41 Becker, p. 425 (Jack Steiman, 1966).

42 Becker: p. 64 (Rywka Grinberg, 1962), p. 83 (Mendel Mincberg, 1962), p. 100 (Rachmiel Zynger, 1962), p. 840 (Zelda Waiman, 1968), p. 859 (Eva Zuckier, 1968). YVA, M49E/155 (Symcha Mincberg, 1945).

43 Becker: p. 491 (Ralph Chaiton, 1966), p. 498 (Helen Starkman, 1966), p. 1388 (Pinchas Heldstein, 1968).

44 Becker: p. 509 (Dina Tenenbaum, 1966), p. 515 (Ruth Wagner, 1966), p. 681 (Dora Kaminer, 1966), p. 859 (Eva Zuckier, 1967). VHA 7739 (Howard Chandler, 1995). Author's interview (Faye Gold, 2002).

45 Landgericht Düsseldorf, 8 Ks/70 (Judgment against Willi Schroth), pp. 32, 56. The Jewish prisoners were quite aware that the cause of Meyer's death was typhus. Becker: p. 65 (Rywka Grinberg, 1962), p. 78 (Pinchas Hochmic, 1962), p. 501 (Helen Starkman, 1966), p. 516 (Ruth Wagner, 1966), p. 870 (Anna Wilson, 1967).

46 The director of the factory and the head of personnel gave transparently specious explanations for Althoff's dismissal in order to sustain their own claims to have known nothing about the killing of sick Jews at that time. The director conceded that there were "rumors" that Althoff had shot Jews, but he explained his departure more in terms of Althoff's abrasiveness and bad relations with Polish workers. Becker, pp. 697, 701 (Fritz Hofmann, 1966). The head of personnel attributed Althoff's dismissal to inappropriate sexual escapades (*Frauengeschichte*), especially with "Polish women." Becker, p. 625 (Franz Köhler, 1966).

47 Becker, p. 818 (Faye Gold, 1967).

48 Becker, p. 828 (Ben Zukerman, 1967).

49 Author's interview (Joseph Friedenson, 2002).

50 VHA 43397 (Louis Feintuch, 1998).

51 VHA 13514 (Saul Miller, 1996).

52 Becker, p. 415 (Matys Finkelstein, 1966).

53 VHA 1652 (David Meadow, 1995). The other two testimonies of Kielce transferees are: VHA: 12906 (Eli Oberman, 1996), 51710 (Morris Wilson, 2001).

54 Becker, p. 415 (Matys Finkelstein, 1966). VHA 1652 (David Meadow, 1995).

55 Becker, pp. 589–91 (Maurice Weinberger, 1966, who dates his arrival between January and March 1943). VHA 2847 (Gerald Rosenberg, 1995, who dates his arrival in March or April 1943). MJH, RG-1387 (Mina Brenman, n.d.). USHMM, RG-50.092*0030 (Ruth Webber, 1992).

56 Private family account shared with the author (Yechiel Eisenberg, 2003).

57 VHA: 16114 (Jacob Szapszewicz, 1996), 36797 (Esther Rothman, 1997). MJH, RG-1383 (Pola Funk, 1986). YVA, O-3/9394 (Ruben Zachronovitsky, 1996). Yosef Honigsberg, "Echoes from the Vale of Tears," *Wierzbnik-Starachowitz*, p. 240–44.

58 VHA: 1212 (Rose Weitzen, 1995), 3948 (Irene Horn, 1995). FA, T-91 (Israel A., 1980).

59   VHA: 1212 (Rose Weitzen, 1995), 5030 (Jakob Binstock, 1995), 16116 (Maria Szapsze-wicz, 1996), 12073 (Helene Fellenbaum, 1996), 51710 (Morris Wilson, 2001).

60   VHA 18046 (David Mangarten, 1996).

61   VHA 20030 (Anna Freilich, 1996).

62   USHMM, RG-50.030*0396 (Chris Lerman, 1998).

63   VHA 2643 (Howard Kleinberg, 1995).

13: Tartak

1   Becker, p. 801 (Abraham Gershon Rosenwald, 1967).

2   Becker, p. 1411 (Abe Freeman, 1968).

3   Zvi Faigenbaum, "Led Like Lambs to the Slaughter," *Wierzbnik-Starachowice Memorial Book* (CD version), p. 437.

4   Becker: p. 69 (Zvi Hersz Faigenbaum, 1962), p. 798 (Abraham Gershon Rosenwald, 1967). Faigenbaum, "Led Like Lambs to the Slaughter," and Gershon Rosenwald, "Deep in the Forest," *Wierzbnik-Starachowice Memorial Book* (CD version), pp. 436–38 and 521–22.

5   Becker: p. 939 (Zvi Hersz Faigenbaum, 1968). Chava Faigenbaum (Shraga), "Hell's Dungeon," and Zvi Faigenbaum, "We Jumped from the Railway Car of Death," *Wierzbnik-Starachowice Memorial Book* (CD version), pp. 445, 457–60. In the community-book account, Zvi Faigenbaum said they jumped from the first transport through a small, high window, not from an opening the prisoners had made. For other testimonies that confirm what prisoners learned from Faigenbaum upon his reentry into camp: Becker: p. 429 (Hersz Tenenbaum, 1966), p. 435 (Toby Wolfe, 1966), p. 510 (Dina Tenenbaum, 1966), p. 516 (Ruth Wagner, 1966). VHA 8656 (Paul Cymerman, 1995). Author's interviews (Annie Glass and Sally Recht, 2004, two sisters whose father—a worker at Zeork—had helped make the opening through which the Faigenbaums escaped but refused to abandon his sick brother-in-law in the train car and join them in the attempt).

6   Becker: p. 781 (Rose Herling, 1967), p. 805 (Sylvia Russak, 1967), p. 904 (Mordka Maslowicz, 1967). FA, T-1682 (Mania K., 1988).

7   Becker, p. 849 (Ruth Rosengarten, 1967).

8   VHA 25175 (Elizabeth Styk, 1997).

9   Becker, p. 887 (Frymeta Maslowicz, 1967).

10   Becker, p. 810 (Helen Weisbloom, 1967).

11   Becker: p. 800 (Abraham Gershon Rosenwald, 1967), p. 1271 (Morris Zucker, 1968). Rosenwald, "Deep in the Forest," *Wierzbnik-Starachowice Memorial Book* (CD version), p. 523.

12   Becker: p. 810 (Helen Weisbloom, 1967), p. 1186 (Naftula Korenwasser, 1968). MJH, RG-1165 (Guta Blass Weintraub, 1984). Author's interview (Martin Baranek, 2001).

13   Becker, p. 810 (Helen Weisbloom, 1967).

14   Rosenwald, "Deep in the Forest," *Wierzbnik-Starachowice Memorial Book* (CD version), p. 523, who accused Novak of sending him from the relative security of Tartak to Majówka and work in the munitions factory.

15   Becker, p. 781 (Rose Herling, 1967).

16   Becker, p. 847 (Ruth Rosengarten, 1967).

17   Becker: p. 805 (Sylvia Russak, 1967), p. 810 (Helen Weisbloom, 1967).

18   Becker, p. 904 (Mordka Maslowicz, 1967).

19   Becker: p. 799 (Abraham Gershon Rosenwald, 1967), p. 804 (Sylvia Russak, 1967).

20   Becker, p. 1266 (Morris Zucker, 1968).

21   Becker, p. 810 (Helen Weisbloom, 1967).

22   Becker: p. 800 (Abraham Gershon Rosenwald, 1967), p. 810 (Helen Weisbloom, 1967), p. 880 (Morris Zucker, 1967), p. 1361 (Chaim Asch, 1968). USHMM, RG-50.030*250 (Guta Blass Weintraub, 1990). Author's interview (Martin Baranek, 2001).

23   Becker, p. 804 (Sylvia Russak, 1967).

24   Becker, p. 810 (Helen Weisbloom, 1967). VHA: 8424 (Regina Levenstadt, 1995), 25434 (Irving Gottlieb, 1997). YVA, M-1/E.2469 (Josef Kohs, 1948).

25   Becker: p. 1393a (Hillel Kadyieswicz, 1968, for the event), p. 798 (Abraham Gershon Rosenwald, 1966, for the dating).

26   YVA, M-1/E.2469 (Josef Kohs, 1948). FA, T-1682 (Mania K., 1988).

27   Becker: p. 888 (Frymeta Maslowicz, 1967), p. 1427 (Naftula Korenwasser, 1968). Rosen-wald, "Deep in the Forest," *Wierzbnik-Starachowice Memorial Book* (CD version), p. 524. Three of the men were: Frymeta's first husband, Abraham Goldstein; Moshe Zucker's fourteen-year-old son Gershon, who had just been transferred from Strelnica through his father's successful bribes; and Jitzrak Asch. The first two were from Wierzbnik, the third from Płock. In one version, the last victim was a pharmacist from Szydłowiec named Frimerman. In another, it was a man named Lublinski.

28   Whatever other differences in their accounts, virtually every witness agreed on Lutz's fateful role in summoning the police. Becker: p. 708 (Lea Greiwer, 1966, whose sister worked for Lutz), p. 800 (Abraham Gershon Rosenwald, 1967), p. 810 (Helen Weis-bloom, 1967), pp. 881, 1270 (Morris Zucker, 1967 and 1968), p. 1360 (Chaim Asch, 1968), p. 1427 (Naftula Korenwasser, 1968). VHA: 7366 (Naftula Korenwasser, 1995), 25175 (Elizabeth Styk, 1997). FA, T-1682 (Mania K., 1988). Author's interview (Martin Baranek, 2001).

29   Becker: pp. 881, 1270 (Morris Zucker, 1967 and 1968), p. 888 (Frymeta Maslowicz, 1967), p. 1360 (Chaim Asch, 1968). VHA 25175 (Elizabeth Styk, 1997).

30   Testifying that Becker was personally in charge: Becker: p. 810 (Helen Weisbloom, 1967), pp. 881, 1270 (Morris Zucker, 1967 and 1968); MJH, RG-1165 (Guta Blass Wein-traub, 1984); and author's interview (Guta Blass Weintraub, 2004). Testifying that men from Becker's police station came: Becker: p. 800 (Abraham Gershon Rosenwald, 1967, who said the police squad was commanded by a fat, little man with glasses named Kreitschmann), p. 1360 (Chaim Asch, 1968), p. 1427 (Naftula Korenwasser, 1968); author's interview (Martin Baranek, 2001).

31   In her 1968 interview with German judicial investigators preparing for Becker's trial, Guta Blass Weintraub said she learned from others what had happened to the four men under Becker's orders. In subsequent accounts, she said she was one of the stretcher bearers and thus a direct eyewitness. Becker, p. 1314 (Guta Blass Weintraub, 1968). MJH, RG-1165 (Guta Blass Weintraub, 1984). Author's interview (Guta Blass Weintraub, 2004).

32   For the accounts of four surviving stretcher bearers, given with only slight variation, see Becker: p. 800 (Abraham Gershon Rosenwald, 1967), pp. 881, 1270 (Morris Zucker, 1967 and 1968), p. 1360 (Chaim Asch, 1968), p. 1427 (Naftula Korenwasser, 1968).

33   Becker, p. 800 (Abraham Gershon Rosenwald, 1967).

34   Becker, p. 1427 (Naftula Korenwasser, 1968).

35   Becker, p. 1360 (Chaim Asch, 1968).

36   Becker, p. 849 (Ruth Rosengarten, 1967).

37 VHA 25175 (Elizabeth Styk, 1997).
38 FA, T-1682 (Mania K., 1988).

14: The Kolditz Era: Summer–Fall 1943

1   Symcha Mincberg, "The Beginning of the Downfall," *Wierzbnik-Starachowice Memorial Book* (CD version), p. 404.
2   Investigation of Kaschmieder, p. 15 (Gerhard Kaschmieder, 1968).
3   ZStL II 206 AR 298/68 (hereafter Investigation of Schroth), p. 31 (Willi Schroth, 1968). Nothing is known about him other than that he was a man of large stature. Landgericht Düsseldorf 8 Ks 2/70, Judgment against Willi Schroth, p. 33.
4   ZStL 206 AR 125/68 (hereafter Investigation of Baumgarten), pp. 9–13 (Kurt Otto Baumgarten, 1966).
5   Becker: p. 436 (Toby Wolfe, 1966), p. 516 (Ruth Wagner, 1966), p. 753 (Leonia Finkler, 1966), p. 770 (Arnold Finkler, 1966), p. 832 (Ben Lant, 1967).
6   Becker, p. 406 (Fred Baum, 1966).
7   Becker, p. 422 (Jack Steiman, 1966).
8   Becker, p. 516 (Ruth Wagner, 1966).
9   Becker, p. 448 (Kurt Otto Baumgarten, 1966).
10 Investigation of Baumgarten, p. 14 (Kurt Otto Baumgarten, 1966).
11 Becker, p. 447 (Kurt Otto Baumgarten, 1966). Investigation of Kaschmieder, p. 24 (Kurt Otto Baumgarten, 1968).
12 Becker, p. 873 (Adrian Wilson, 1967).
13 Becker, p. 868 (Anna Wilson, 1967).
14 YVA, M-49/1172 (Mendel Kac, 1945). USHMM: David Boder interview collection (Kalman Eisenberg, 1946).
15 Becker, p. 874 (Adrian Wilson, 1967).
16 National Archives, Berlin Document Center microfilm: RuSHA file for Walter Kolditz.
17 Author's interview (Henry Greenbaum, 2000).
18 VHA: 2651 (Toby Steiman, 1995), 3916 (Rachell Eisenberg, 1995), 44259 (Ruth Turek, 1998). UMD (Henry Krystal, 1996). Kalib, *The Last Selection*, p. 180.
19 Author's interviews (Anna Wilson, 2001; Sally Recht, 2004). Kalib, *The Last Selection*, p. 180.
20 VHA 16876 (Henry Greenbaum, 1996). Author's interviews (Howard Chandler and Chris Lerman, 2001).
21 Becker, p. 766 (Howard Chandler, 1966). See also: Becker, p. 420 (Celia Nower, 1966).
22 Becker, p. 429 (Hersz Tenenbaum, 1966). Author's interview (Howard Chandler, 2001). Kalib, *The Last Selection*, pp. 199, 204–5.
23 These figures and dates come from lists found by Symcha Mincberg in Starachowice after the war and published in *Wierzbnik-Starachowitz: A Memorial Book*, pp. 77–83. The date of February 18, 1943, given for the arrival of the Płaszow group is clearly wrong. For the date of November 18, 1943, see: YVA, M-49E/1669 (Leon Wolf, n.d., but shortly after the war), and Judgment against Schroth, p. 126. The former head of the Wierzbnik *Judenrat*, Symcha Mincberg (YVA, M-49E/155), in testimony taken on June 10, 1945, estimated 260 from Wolanów, 150 from Cracow (Płaszow), 100 from Radom, and 36 from Tomaszów-Mazowiecki. Alan Newman estimated 150 each from Cracow, Radom, and Tomaszów-Mazowiecki, and 100 from other nearby sites (Becker, p. 732). One of those in

the transport from the Płaszow camp said it brought 200 Cracow Jews to Starachowice. *Leo Bach's Memoir: Coming of Age during the Holocaust*, p. 231 (this unpublished memoir is electronically posted at: www.cheme.cornell.edu/cheme/people/profile/moreinfo/dlk15-leobach.cfm).

24 VHA 555 (Hyman Salzberg, 1995). YVA, M-49/1172 (Mendel Kac, 1945).

25 VHA: 12165 (Abram Jakubowicz, 1996), 31592 (Regina Cymberg, 1997), 36226 (Toby Kott, 1997), 47647 (Tova Friedman, 1998).

26 VHA 29585 (Alter Szainwald, 1997).

27 Becker, p. 645 (Leo Bach, 1966). VHA: 8896 (Maury Adams, 1995), 12459 (Leon Miller, 1996), 15941 (Ernest Abraham, 1996), 29322 (Max Kozma, 1997), 16230 (Sol Lottman, 1996). YVA, M-49E/1669 (Leon Wolf, n.d.).

28 VHA: 1707 (Edward Koslowski, 1995), 9288 (Freda Landau, 1995), 16230 (Sol Lottman, 1996), 30309 (Irwin Gottfried, 1997), 42564 (Rachel Piuti, 1998). YVA, M-49/1172 (Mendel Kac, 1945).

29 VHA: 23715 (Barry Kaufman, 1996), 42564 (Rachel Piuti, 1998). YVA, M-49/1172 (Mendel Kac, 1945).

30 For Mokoszyn: VHA 29585 (Alter Szainwald, 1997); YVA, O-2/319 (Moses Weinberg, n.d.). For Płaszow: VHA: 8896 (Maury Adams, 1995), 12459 (Leon Miller, 1996), 29322 (Max Kozma, 1997), 16230 (Sol Lottman, 1996); *Leo Bach's Memoir*, pp. 238–41.

31 VHA: 12728 (Ann Spicer, 1996), 31592 (Regina Cymberg, 1997).

32 VHA 44607 (Rachmil Piker, 1998).

33 VHA 44270 (Shalom Lindenbaum, 1998).

34 YVA, M-49/1172 (Mendel Kac, 1945).

35 VHA 36226 (Toby Kott, 1997).

36 *Leo Bach's Memoir*, pp. 232, 235–36.

37 For Wilczek: VHA 15941 (Ernest Abraham, 1996). For Einesman: VHA 555 (Hyman Salzberg, 1995), 12165 (Abram Jakubowicz, 1996). For Rubenstein: VHA 1707 (Edward Koslowski, 1995).

38 VHA: 21326 (Abraham Malach, 1996), 47647 (Tova Friedman, 1998). USHMM, RG-50.030*0144 (Avraham Malach, 1990).

39 Nürnberg Document NO-1020 (Meeting of Heydrich, Meyer, Schlatterer, Leibbrandt, and Ehrlich, October 4, 1941).

40 Nürnberg Document NO-1611 (Himmler to Pohl, Krüger, Globocnik, RSHA, and Wolff, October 9, 1942).

41 For a more detailed study of Himmler's role in the Nazi exploitation and destruction of Jewish slave labor in Poland, see: Browning, *Nazi Policy, Jewish Workers, German Killers*, pp. 58–88.

42 Becker, p. 1364 (Rachel Piuti, 1968). In her later testimony of 1998 (VHA 42564), she gave the date of November 9.

43 Becker, p. 79 (Pinchas Hochmic, 1962).

44 Becker: p. 95 (Zvi Unger, 1962), p. 100 (Rachmiel Zynger, 1966), p. 372 (Moshe Rubenstein, 1966), p. 714 (Ida Gutman, 1967), p. 733 (Alan Newman, 1966), p. 1365 (Rachel Piuti).

45 Becker: p. 714 (Ida Gutman, 1967), p. 733 (Alan Newman, 1966).

46 For two trucks: Becker, p. 1364 (Rachel Piuti, 1968), and author's interview (Alan Newman, 2001). For three or four trucks: Becker, p. 859 (Eva Zuckier, 1967).

47 YVA, M-49/1172 (Mendel Kac, 1945).

48 Becker, p. 859 (Eva Zuckier, 1967).

49 Kalib, *The Last Selection*, p. 207. Becker, p. 759 (Mina Binsztok, 1966).

50 VHA 23091 (Ruth Korman, 1996).

51 YVA, M-49/1172 (Mendel Kac, 1945).

52 Becker: p. 732 (Alan Newman, 1966), p. 750 (Leonia Finkler, 1967). VHA: 555 (Hyman Salzberg, 1995), 42564 (Rachel Piuti, 1998).

53 VHA 555 (Hyman Salzberg, 1995).

54 Becker, p. 733 (Alan Newman, 1966).

55 Kalib, *The Last Selection*, p. 207.

56 USHMM, RG-15.084m (Meir Lewental, 1945).

57 VHA 5190 (Ceil Saltzman, 1995).

58 VHA 36414 (Rachel Akierman, 1997).

59 Becker, p. 859 (Eva Zuckier, 1967).

60 VHA 23091 (Ruth Korman, 1996).

61 Becker, p. 714 (Ida Gutman, 1967). VHA 3241 (Leah Finkel, 1995).

62 Author's interview (Alan Newman, 2001).

63 Becker: p. 760 (Mina Binsztok, 1966, who said someone was pulled off the trucks and shot), p. 844 (Anita Tuchmayer, 1967, who said Kolditz shot a girl found hiding), p. 2011 (Chaim Hilf, 1968, who said Kolditz shot a young man of Austrian origin who dared to argue with him).

64 Zvi Magen (Hershel Pancer), "From Slavery to Freedom," *Wierzbnik-Starachowice Memorial Book* (CD version), p. 575, had attended the wedding.

65 Becker, p. 770 (Abraham Finkler, 1966).

66 Becker: pp. 750–51 (Leonia Finkler, 1966), pp. 770–71 (Arnold Finkler, 1966).

67 Becker, p. 825 (Ben Zukerman, 1967).

68 Firlej had been used by the Radom SS as an execution site since 1940. Seidel, *Deutsche Besatzungspolitik in Polen*, p. 189.

69 Investigation of Schroth, pp. 40–42 (Willi Schroth, 1968).

70 Becker: p. 66 (Rywka Grinberg, 1962), p. 79 (Pinchas Hochmic, 1962), p. 100 (Rachmiel Zynger, 1962), p. 469 (Adam Gutman, 1966), p. 714 (Ida Gutman, 1967), p. 1369 (Max Richman, 1968). VHA: 5190 (Ceil Saltzman, 1995), 23091 (Ruth Korman, 1996).

71 Becker, p. 872 (Ben Lant, 1967). VHA 22640 (Lucyna Berkowicz, 1996).

72 Becker, p. 750 (Leonia Finkler, 1966).

73 Becker, p. 859 (Eva Zuckier, 1967).

74 Apparently 180 Jews from the nearby camp complex of Skarżysko-Kamienna were killed at the same time. Felicja Karay, *Death Comes in Yellow: Skarżysko-Kamienna Slave Labor Camp*, p. 198.

75 Becker: p. 469 (Adam Gutman, 1966), p. 714 (Ida Gutman, 1967).

76 Becker, p. 869 (Anna Wilson, 1967, who provides the primary description), p. 413 (Anna Arbeiter, 1966, who confirms that "through Kolditz and a Ukrainian guard two young brothers were shot" after an attempted escape). *Leo Bach's Memoir*, p. 243, dates the recapture and execution (by Schroth and two Ukrainian guards) of the "Meloch brothers" from Cracow to the spring of 1944, long after Kolditz had departed.

77 Becker: p. 456 (Willi Schroth, 1966), p. 629 (Franz Köhler, 1966), pp. 685, 692 (Ferdinand Fischer, 1966).

78 Investigation of Baumgarten, p. 23 (Kurt Otto Baumgarten, 1968).

79 Investigation of Schroth, p. 32 (Willi Schroth, 1968).

80   Schroth Judgment, p. 34.
81   Investigation of Baumgarten, pp. 23–24 (Kurt Otto Baumgarten, 1968).

15: Jewish Work

1   This phrase originates from Justice Minister Otto Thierack, who reached agreement with Heinrich Himmler on September 18, 1942, that "asocials"—Jews, Gypsies, Russians, Poles, and Ukrainians—serving more than three-year sentences in the prison system would be turned over to the SS for "destruction through work" (Nürnberg Document PS-654). In this context, therefore, the phrase did not designate a comprehensive Nazi policy toward Jewish labor. At the Wannsee Conference on January 20, 1942, Reinhard Heydrich did refer to the "natural diminution" (*natürliche Verminderung*) of European Jews deported to the East and subjected to hard labor.

2   Daniel Jonah Goldhagen, *Hitler's Willing Executioners: Ordinary Germans and the Holocaust* (New York: Knopf, 1996), Part IV (which narrowly focuses on two Lublin labor camps during the peak killing period of the Final Solution).

3   Götz Aly, "The Economics of the Final Solution: A Case Study from the General Government," *The Simon Wiesenthal Center Annual* V (1988), pp. 3–48; Götz Aly, *Hitler's Beneficiaries: Plunder, Racial War, and the Nazi Welfare State* (Boston: Henry Holt, 2007). Arno Mayer, *Why Did the Heavens Not Darken? The "Final Solution" in History* (New York: Knopf, 1989).

4   Wolf Gruner, *Jewish Forced Labor under the Nazis: Economic Needs and Racial Aims, 1939–1941* (New York: Cambridge University Press, 2006). Donald Bloxham, "A Survey of Jewish Slave Labour in the Nazi System," *The Journal of Holocaust Education* 10/3 (winter 2001), pp. 29–59, and " 'Extermination through Work': Jewish Slave Labor under the Third Reich," *Holocaust Educational Trust Research Papers* I/1 (1999–2000). On the conflict within the SS over work as punishment versus work as production, see: Michael Thad Allen, *The Business of Genocide: The SS, Slave Labor, and the Concentration Camps* (Chapel Hill: University of North Carolina Press, 2002). Also basic are the works of Ulrich Herbert: *Hitler's Foreign Workers: Enforced Foreign Labor in Germany Under the Third Reich* (New York: Cambridge University Press, 1997), and "Labour and Extermination, Economic Interest and the Primacy of 'Weltanschauung' in National Socialism," *Past and Present*, 138 (1993), pp. 144–95.

5   Karay, *Death Comes in Yellow*.

6   Karay, *Death Comes in Yellow*, p. 53. Seidel, *Deutsche Besatzungspolitik in Polen*, p. 360. Jacek Andrzej Młynarczyk, *Judenmord in Zentralpolen*, p. 342.

7   Karay, *Death Comes in Yellow*, p. 70.

8   VHA: 15716 (Joseph Friedenson, 1996), 23533 (Jacob Kaufman, 1996), 42666 (Morris Pinczewski, 1998). *Leo Bach's Memoir*, p. 233. Zvi Unger, "From Wierzbnik to Mauthausen," *Wierzbnik-Starachowice Memorial Book* (CD version), p. 348.

9   Becker, p. 768 (Howard Chandler, 1966). VHA: 9288 (Freda Landau, 1995), 9390 (Henry Ehrlich, 1995), 10154 (Alan Newman, 1995), 15941 (Ernest Abraham, 1996), 16230 (Sol Lottman, 1996), 28993 (Chaim Wolgroch, 1997), 51710 (Morris Wilson, 2001). USHMM: David Boder interview collection (Kalman Eisenberg).

10   VHA: 1652 (David Meadow, 1995), 1707 (Edward Koslowski, 1995), 16116 (Maria Szapszewicz, 1996), 40372 (Harry Spicer, 1998), 44607 (Rachmil Piker, 1998). Author's interview (Faye Gold, 2002). Family account shared with author (Yechiel Eisenberg, 2003). *Leo Bach's Memoir*, p. 233.

11 VHA 466 (Berel Blum, 1995). FA, T-1881 (Regina N., 1991 and 1992). UMD (Henry Krystal, 1996).

12 VHA 29585 (Alter Szainwald, 1997).

13 VHA 5410 (Charles Kleinman, 1995).

14 VHA: 3189 (Pola Schlegel, 1995), 9917 (Halina Zeleznik, 1995), 16116 (Maria Szapszewicz, 1996), 23091 (Ruth Korman, 1996).

15 Becker, p. 713 (Ida Gutman, 1967).

16 VHA: 3261 (Nancy Kleinberg, 1995), 16230 (Sol Lottman, 1996), 23091 (Ruth Korman, 1996), 42666 (Morris Pinczewski, 1998). FA, T-1884 (Regina N., 1991 and 1992). YVA, O-2/319 (Moses Weinberg, n.d.). USHMM: David Boder interview collection (Kalman Eisenberg).

17 USHMM: RG-50.030*0396 (Chris Lerman, 1998), *0411 (Anna Wilson, 2001). Author's interviews (Chris Lerman and Anna Wilson, 2001).

18 VHA 23533 (Jacob Kaufman, 1996). YVA, M-49/1172 (Mendel Kac, 1945).

19 VHA 25434 (Irving Leibgott, 1997).

20 VHA: 25164 (Michael Feldstein, 1997), 42564 (Rachel Piuti, 1998).

21 VHA 33807 (Gloria Borenstein, 1997).

22 VHA 9113 (Hyman Flancbaum, 1995). See also: YVA: M-49E/1669 (Leon Wolf, n.d.), M-49/1172 (Mendel Kac, 1945); VHA 3948 (Irene Horn, 1995).

23 *Leo Bach's Memoir*, pp. 234–35.

24 Becker, p. 768 (Howard Chandler, 1966).

25 Becker, p. 502 (Helen Starkman, 1966).

26 Becker: p. 492 (Ralph Chaiton, 1966), p. 773 (Arnold Finkler, 1966), p. 819 (Faye Gold, 1967).

27 VHA 15716 (Joseph Friedenson, 1996). Author's interviews (Joseph and Gitta Friedenson, 2002).

28 Becker, p. 492 (Ralph Chaiton, 1966).

29 Becker: p. 761 (Mina Binsztok, 1966), p. 777 (Fay Gotlib, 1967).

30 VHA: 31380 (Jack Spicer, 1997), 43397 (Louis Feintuch, 1998). MJH, RG-1383 (Pola Funk, 1986). Kalib, *The Last Selection*, p. 176.

31 VHA 9135 (Lola Sussman, 1995). Author's interview (Anna Wilson, 2001).

32 Becker, pp. 652–53 (Mayer Gutman, 1966).

33 YVA, M-49/1172 (Mendel Kac, 1945). Two people who obtained kitchen jobs were the daughter of the former head of the *Judenrat* and the nephew of Yankiel Rubenstein, the head of the kitchen. Becker: p. 64 (Rywka Grinberg, 1962). Author's interview (Harold Rubenstein, 2002).

34 VHA 3261 (Nancy Kleinberg, 1995).

35 Kalib, *The Last Selection*, pp. 171–72. VHA 3916 (Rachell Eisenberg, 1995).

36 VHA 16120 (Mirjam Zylberberg, 1997).

37 VHA 40881 (Salek Benedikt, 1998).

38 VHA 23091 (Ruth Korman, 1996). Author's interview (Regina Naiman, 2001).

16: Food, Property, and the Underground Economy

1 This dilemma had already manifested itself in 1940–42 when "productionist" ghetto managers had generally prevailed over "attritionists" in seeking to create self-maintaining ghetto economies, only to find it still nearly impossible to adequately feed the Jewish

workers on whose productivity their plans depended. Browning, *The Path to Genocide: Essays on Launching the Final Solution*, pp. 28–56.

2   VHA 943 (Harold Rubenstein, 1995).

3   VHA 43397 (Louis Feintuch, 1998). Zvi Unger, "From Wierzbnik to Mauthausen," *Wierzbnik-Starachowice Memorial Book* (CD version), p. 348.

4   Becker, p. 447 (Kurt Otto Baumgarten, 1966).

5   VHA 3189 (Pola Schlenger, 1995). FA, T-1881 (Regina N., 1991 and 1992).

6   *Leo Bach's Memoir*, pp. 232, 234.

7   VHA: 2643 (Howard Kleinberg, 1995), 9135 (Lola Sussman, 1995), 13514 (Saul Miller, 1996), 16116 (Maria Szapszewicz, 1996), 23533 (Jacob Kaufman, 1996). MJH, RG-1383 (Pola Funk, 1986).

8   VHA: 2667 (Jack Miller, 1995), 3916 (Rachell Eisenberg, 1995), 12073 (Helene Fellenbaum, 1996), 43397 (Louis Feintuch, 1998). Author's interviews (Henry Greenbaum, 2000; Faye Gold, 2002).

9   VHA 1707 (Edward Koslowski, 1995).

10   YVA, M-49/1172 (Mendel Kac, 1945).

11   VHA 4255 (Tola Pinkus, 1995).

12   VHA 7366 (Naftula Korenwasser, 1995).

13   VHA 12459 (Leon Miller, 1996).

14   VHA 17629 (Sonia Ash, 1996).

15   Kalib, *The Last Selection*, p. 174.

16   VHA 51793 (Sally Recht, 2001). Author's interview (Sally Recht, 2004).

17   Becker, p. 517 (Ruth Wagner, 1966).

18   *Leo Bach's Memoir*, p. 234.

19   VHA 12906 (Eli Oberman, 1996).

20   VHA: 23533 (Jacob Kaufman, 1996), 51710 (Morris Wilson, 2001).

21   VHA 23533 (Jacob Kaufman, 1996).

22   Kalib, *The Last Selection*, p. 172.

23   VHA 31592 (Regina Cymberg, 1997).

24   VHA 29327 (Ray Langer, 1997).

25   VHA 16116 (Maria Szapszewicz, 1996).

26   Kalib, *The Last Selection*, pp. 180–84.

27   VHA 7739 (Howard Chandler, 1995). FA, T-955 (Gutta T., 1987). Author's interviews (Martin Baranek and Chris Lerman, 2001; Annie Glass, 2004).

28   VHA 25434 (Irving Leibgott, 1997). On at least one occasion, however, a night trip from Tartak into town proved hazardous. Abraham Shiner left Tartak to visit an "old acquaintance," the Polish policeman Kocharzow, who was keeping valuables for him. Returning to Tartak, he was intercepted by another Polish policeman—the sadistic "informer" Wolczek—who had already killed three hidden Jewish children he had uncovered. Shiner ran for his life as Wolczek repeatedly shot at him. Only Wolczek's continual poor aim allowed Shiner to escape alive and return to camp. Abraham Shiner, "The Policeman Shot and Missed," *Wierzbnik-Starachowice Memorial Book* (CD version), pp. 451–54.

29   VHA 7739 (Howard Chandler, 1995). Author's interview (Howard Chandler, 2001).

30   VHA 1833 (Isidore Guterman, 1995).

31   VHA 3261 (Nancy Kleinberg, 1995).

32   VHA 1213 (Rose Weitzen, 1995).

33 VHA 33807 (Gloria Borenstein, 1997).
34 Author's interview (Alan Newman, 2001).
35 Author's interview (Sally Recht, 2004).
36 VHA 40881 (Salek Benedikt, 1998).
37 MJH, RG-1984 (Regina Najman, 1988). FA, T-1884 (Regina N., 1991 and 1992). Author's interview (Regina Naiman, 2001).
38 VHA 5410 (Charles Kleinman 1995).
39 VHA 12906 (Eli Oberman, 1996).
40 VHA 5030 (Jakob Binstock, 1995).
41 VHA 9917 (Halina Zeleznik, 1995).
42 VHA16114 (Jacob Szapszewicz, 1996).
43 YVA, M-49/1172 (Mendel Kac, 1945). Also confirming the disappearance of 2,000 to 3,000 pair of boots: author's interview (Alan Newman, 2001). On the denial of replacement shoes and clothing, especially to outsiders, and instead selling these items on the black market, see: *Leo Bach's Memoir*, pp. 236–38.
44 Author's interview (Alan Newman, 2001).
45 USHMM, RG-50.030*0396 (Chris Lerman, 1998).
46 *Leo Bach's Memoir*, p. 236.

17: The Ukrainian Guards

1 Becker, p. 652 (Mayer Gutman, 1966).
2 Becker: p. 595 (Maurice Weinberger, 1966), p. 777 (Fay Gotlib, 1967), p. 857 (Israel Chaiton, 1967), p. 870 (Anna Wilson, 1967), p. 877 (Adrian Wilson, 1967).
3 Becker: p. 870 (Anna Wilson, 1967), p. 877 (Adrian Wilson, 1967).
4 Becker, p. 877 (Adrian Wilson, 1967).
5 Becker, p. 870 (Anna Wilson, 1967). Author's interview (Alan Newman, 2001).
6 VHA 7739 (Howard Chandler, 1995). Author's interviews (Howard Chandler and Anna Wilson, 2001).
7 VHA: 1213 (Rose Weitzen, 1995), 3189 (Pola Schlenger, 1995).
8 Author's interview (Regina Naiman, 2001). MJH, RG-1984 (Regina Najman, 1988).
9 VHA: 2847 (Gerald Rosenberg, 1995), 37728 (Tovi Pagi, 1998).
10 VHA 22640 (Lucyna Berkowicz, 1996). Author's interview (Howard Chandler, 2001).
11 Author's interview (Howard Chandler, 2001).
12 USHMM, RG-50.030*0396 (Chris Lerman, 1998). Author's interview (Alan Newman, 2001).
13 VHA 44607 (Rachmil Piker, 1998). MJH, RG-1984 (Regina Najman, 1988). Author's interviews (Howard Chandler and Alan Newman, 2001; Faye Gold, 2002).
14 Author's interview (Alan Newman, 2001).
15 VHA 18046 (David Mangarten, 1996).
16 VHA 27852 (Ann Zworth, 1997). Author's interviews (Regina Naiman, 2001; Joseph Friedenson, 2002).
17 Author's interview (Howard Chandler, 2001).
18 VHA: 1213 (Rose Weitzen, 1995), 27852 (Ann Zworth, 1997), 33807 (Gloria Borenstein, 1997). Author's interview (Sally Recht, 2004).
19 Author's interview (Sally Recht, 2004).
20 Author's interview (Howard Chandler, 2001).

21   VHA: 9113 (Hyman Flancbaum, 1995), 9135 (Lola Sussman, 1995).

22   VHA: 451 (Helen Starkman, 1994), 25164 (Michael Feldstein, 1997), 29585 (Alter Szainwald, 1997), 30309 (Irwin Gottfried, 1997), 33807 (Gloria Borenstein, 1997).

18: Poles and Jews

1   VHA: 2643 (Howard Kleinberg, 1995), 28793 (Chaim Wolgroch, 1997). Hanna Tentzer, "At the Edge of the Abyss," *Wierzbnik-Starachowitz*, p. 191.

2   VHA 3261 (Nancy Kleinberg, 1995).

3   VHA: 2643 (Howard Kleinberg, 1995), 8889 (Jack Pomeranz, 1997), 30309 (Irwin Gottfried, 1997).

4   VHA: 403 (Ruth Charney, 1994), 4334 (Miriam Miklin, 1995).

5   VHA: 943 (Harold Rubenstein, 1995), 8656 (Paul Cymerman, 1995), 25164 (Michael Feldstein, 1997). Author's interviews (Henry Greenbaum, 2000; Harold Rubenstein, 2002).

6   Author's interview (Harold Rubenstein, 2002).

7   VHA: 5030 (Jakob Binstock, 1995), 5096 (Malka Perla, 1995), 9135 (Lola Sussman, 1995). FA, T-91 (Israel A., 1980). Josef Honigsberg, "Echoes from the Vale of Tears," *Wierzbnik-Starachowitz*, p. 244.

8   MJH, RG-1165 (Guta Blass Weintraub, 1984).

9   MJH, RG-1988 (Regina Najman, 1984).

10   VHA 30134 (Joseph Chernikowski, 1997).

11   Author's interview (Alan Newman, 2001).

12   VHA, 25175 (Elizabeth Styk, 1997).

13   VHA: 6061 (Toby Weisfeld, 1995), 9135 (Lola Sussman, 1995), 13514 (Saul Miller, 1996), 16116 (Maria Szapszewicz, 1996), 23533 (Jacob Kaufman, 1996). MJH, RG-1383 (Pola Funk, 1986).

14   VHA 2643 (Howard Kleinberg, 1995).

15   VHA: 451 (Helen Starkman, 1994), 466 (Berel Blum, 1995), 3189 (Pola Schlenger, 1995), 5410 (Charles Kleinman, 1995), 5874 (Anita Tuchmayer, 1995). YVA, M-1/E.2469 (Josef Kohs, 1948).

16   Four survivors noted that at least one of the Poles with whom their families had left property refused to return anything. VHA: 3261 (Nancy Kleinberg, 1995), 31380 (Jack Spicer, 1997), 7739 (Howard Chandler, 1995). Author's interviews (Howard Chandler and Alan Newman, 2001). It was not uncommon to leave property with more than one Pole, precisely to hedge against the expectation that some would not relinquish the property left behind. VHA 42666 (Morris Pinczewski, 1998).

17   For testimonies of those who were able to access at least some of the property they left with Poles, see: VHA: 1213 (Rose Weitzen, 1995), 1833 (Isidore Guterman, 1995), 7739 (Howard Chandler, 1995), 8082 (Abraham Bleeman, 1995), 29327 (Ruth Langer, 1997), 33807 (Gloria Borenstein, 1997), 40372 (Harry Spicer, 1998), 42666 (Morris Pinczewski, 1998). USHMM, RG-50.030*0396 (Chris Lerman, 1998). Author's interviews (Martin Baranek, Chris Lerman, and Alan Newman, 2001).

18   VHA: 1833 (Isidore Guterman, 1995), 7739 (Howard Chandler, 1995), 8028 (Abraham Bleeman, 1995), 42666 (Morris Pinczewski, 1998). USHMM, RG-50.030*0411 (Anna Wilson, 2001).

19   Author's interview (Chris Lerman, 2001).

20 VHA 1213 (Rose Weitzen, 1995).

21 VHA 29327 (Ruth Langer, 1997).

22 VHA: 16680 (Emil Najman, 1996), 40372 (Harry Spicer, 1998)

23 VHA 1833 (Isidore Guterman, 1995).

24 VHA 33807 (Gloria Borenstein, 1997).

25 Malka Cohen, "Wierzbnik, Auschwitz, Bergen-Belsen," *Wierzbnik-Starachowice Memorial Book* (CD version), p. 282.

26 USHMM, RG-50.030*0396 (Chris Lerman, 1998).

19: Children in the Camps

1 Author's interview (Joseph Friedenson, 2002).

2 Author's interview (Shoshana Fiedelman, 2008).

3 Author's interview (Howard Chandler, 2001).

4 Becker: p. 1092 (Leopold Rudolf Schwertner, 1968), p. 1334 (Morris Pinczewski, 1968). USHMM, RG-50.030*0411 (Anna Wilson, 2001).

5 Becker, pp. 1049–54, 1384–88 (Pinchas Heldstein, 1968). German interviewers were concerned only about what Heldstein could tell them about German crimes, not about life in the *Konsum*, so these interviews unfortunately reveal nothing about the latter.

6 Author's interviews (Howard Chandler and Regina Naiman, 2001).

7 VHA 31380 (Jack Spicer, 1997).

8 Author's interview (Shoshana Fiedelman, 2008).

9 Becker: pp. 859–62, 1239–40 (Eva Zuckier, 1967 and 1968).

10 Becker: pp. 93, 982 (Zvi Hersz Unger, 1962 and 1968). Zvi Unger, "From Wierzbnik to Mauthausen," *Wierzbnik-Starachowice Memorial Book* (CD version), p. 347.

11 VHA 18046 (David Mangarten, 1996).

12 VHA 1983 (Martin Baranek, 1995). Author's interview (Martin Baranek, 2001).

13 According to Abraham Gershon Rosenwald, the two children hidden in the double wall were the sons of Moshe Kopf. Gershon Rosenwald, "Deep in the Forest," *Wierzbnik-Starachowice Memorial Book* (CD version), p. 324. See also: VHA 25175 (Elizabeth Styk, 1997), and author's interview (Guta Blass Weintraub, 2004).

14 VHA 23533 (Jacob Kaufman, 1996).

15 Kalib, *The Last Selection*, pp. 138–42, 158–69, 182–213.

16 VHA 37728 (Tovi Pagi, 1998). Tova Pagi, *"The way it was . . .": The Diary of a 12 year old Jewish girl who survived Auschwitz (1939–1945)*. I am grateful to Tova Pagi for giving me a copy of her privately published account. She wrote this account as a twelve-year-old in the DP camp in Bergen-Belsen immediately after the war.

17 Author's interviews (Annie Glass and Sally Recht, 2004).

18 UMD (Ruth Muschkies Webber, 1987). USHMM, RG-50.042*0030 (Ruth Webber, 1992).

19 VHA 2847 (Gerald Rosenberg, 1995).

20 VHA 36414 (Rachel Akierman, 1997).

21 VHA 21326 (Abraham Malach, 1996). USHMM, RG-50.030*01445 (Avraham Malach, 1990).

22 VHA 6007 (Bronia Cyngiser, 1995).

23 VHA 31579 (Rachel Hymans, 1997).

24 VHA 31592 (Regina Cymberg, 1997).
25 VHA 47647 (Tova Friedman, 1998).
26 *Wierzbnik-Starachowitz*, pp. 78–83.
27 Becker, p. 447 (Kurt Otto Baumgarten, 1966).
28 Author's interview (anonymous).

20: Childbirth, Abortion, Sex, and Rape

1 Becker, pp. 1430–31 (Rozia Leper, 1968).
2 Becker, p. 799 (Abraham Gershon Rosenwald, 1967). Gershon Rosenwald, "Deep in the Forest," *Wierzbnik-Starachowice Memorial Book* (CD version), p. 523.
3 Becker, p. 811 (Helen Weisbloom, 1967).
4 Author's interview (Annie Glass, 2004). VHA: 15188 (Annie Glass, 1996), 51793 (Sally Recht, 2001).
5 Becker, p. 738 (Toby Weisfeld, 1966).
6 VHA 6061 (Toby Weisfeld, 1995).
7 Becker, p. 1378 (Toby Steiman, 1968).
8 VHA 2651 (Toby Steiman, 1995).
9 Becker, p. 749 (Leonia Finkler, 1966).
10 VHA 16680 (Emil Najman, 1996).
11 FA, T-1881 (Regina N., 1991 and 1992). Author's interview (Regina Naiman, 2001). In this last account, Regina severely compressed events. She placed the May 22, 1943, birth of her daughter after the move from Strelnica to Majówka and the arrival of Kolditz and just a week before the Firlej selection of mothers and children (on November 8).
12 VHA 40881 (Salek Benedikt, 1998).
13 VHA 22640 (Lucyna Berkowicz, 1996).
14 VHA 4272 (Tema Lichtenstein, 1995).
15 VHA: 9917 (Halina Zeleznik, 1995), 36797 (Esther Rothman, 1997). USHMM, RG-50.030*0411 (Anna Wilson, 2001).
16 USHMM, RG-50.030*0411 (Anna Wilson, 2001).
17 Author's interview (Annie Glass, 2004).
18 VHA 47647 (Tova Friedman, 1998).
19 Author's interview (Annie Glass, 2004).
20 Karay, *Death Comes in Yellow*, pp. 115–16, 125, 158, 209, 245. Karay notes the unique case of Fela Markowiczowa, a woman in charge of the internal Jewish administration of the camp for Werke C in Skarżysko-Kamienna, who also had no qualms about exploiting her position to surround herself with dependent male "courtiers" and lovers.
21 Kalib, *The Last Selection*, p. 208.
22 Shlomo Moskowicz, *My Little Town Glinojeck: Souvenirs*, p. 225.
23 Author's interview (Joseph Friedenson, 2002).
24 FA, T-1881 (Regina N., 1991 and 1992). Author's interview (Regina Naiman, 2001).
25 Karay, *Death Comes in Yellow*, pp. 80–81, 95–96, 147.
26 VHA: 3241 (Leah Finkel, 1995), 22640 (Lucyna Berkowicz, 1996).
27 VHA 4272 (Tema Lichtenstein, 1995).
28 USHMM, RG-50.030*250 (Guta Blass Weintraub, 1990). Author's interview (Guta Blass Weintraub, 2004).
29 Author's interviews (anonymous).

21: The Schroth Era: Winter–Spring 1944

1   Schroth Investigation, pp. 26–28 (Willi Schroth, 1968). Becker, pp. 452–53 (Willi Schroth, 1966). Staatsanwaltschaft Dortmund, Anklageschrift 45 Js 19/67 (hereafter Schroth Indictment), pp. 26–28. Landgericht Düsseldorf, Urteil 8 Ks 2/70 (hereafter Schroth Judgment), pp. 42–43.

2   Becker, p. 793 (Louis Rabinowicz, 1967). Schroth Judgment, pp. 112–13.

3   Schroth Judgment, p. 57.

4   Becker: p. 752 (Leonia Finkler, 1966, who accused Gerhard Kaschmieder), p. 873 (Adrian Wilson, 1967, who accused Alois Schleser).

5   Schroth Investigation, pp. 31, 40–42 (Willi Schroth, 1968).

6   Becker, p. 1397 (Salamon Binsztok, 1968). Schroth Indictment, p. 101. *Leo Bach's Memoir*, pp. 238–39, 243, places the execution of the "Meloch brothers" by Schroth in the spring of 1944, not during the Kolditz era.

7   Becker: p. 436 (Toby Wolfe, 1966), p. 760 (Mina Binsztok, 1967), pp. 770–71 (Arnold Finkler, 1966), p. 856 (Israel Chaiton, 1967), p. 862 (Eva Zuckier, 1967).

8   Becker, p. 873 (Adrian Wilson, 1967). Author's interview (Anna Wilson, 2001).

9   Schroth Investigation, p. 32 (Willi Schroth, 1968).

10 Becker, pp. 613–15 (Otto Reibel, 1966).

11 Becker, pp. 440, 445, 609 (Kurt Otto Baumgarten, 1966).

12 Becker, pp. 1090–91 (Leopold Rudolf Schwertner, 1968).

13 Becker, p. 1090 (Leopold Rudolf Schwertner, 1968).

14 Becker, p. 874 (Adrian Wilson, 1967).

15 Becker, p. 753 (Leonia Finkler, 1966).

16 Schroth Investigation, pp. 30–31 (Willi Schroth, 1968).

17 Author's interview (Chris Lerman, 2001).

18 VHA 15188 (Annie Glass, 1996). Becker, p. 646 (Leo Bach, 1966).

19 Becker: p. 423 (Jack Steiman, 1966), p. 505 (Max Steiman, 1966), p. 1369 (Max Richman, 1968), p. 1387 (Pinchas Heldstein, 1968).

20 Becker, p. 1391 (Chaim Hilf, 1968).

21 Becker, p. 1382 (Adam Kogut, 1968).

22 Becker, p. 856 (Israel Chaiton, 1967).

23 Becker: p. 754 (Leonia Finkler, 1966), p. 824 (Ben Zukerman, 1967).

24 Becker, p. 606 (Morris Pinczewski, 1966).

25 Becker: p. 606 (Morris Pinczewski, 1966), p. 640 (Arthur Armand, 1966).

26 Becker, pp. 864–65 (Anna Wilson, 1967).

27 Becker, p. 824 (Ben Zukerman, 1967).

28 Becker, pp. 864–65 (Anna Wilson, 1967).

29 Becker: p. 517 (Ruth Wagner, 1966), p. 801 (Abraham Gershon Rosenwald, 1966).

30 Becker, p. 815 (Alter Weisbloom, 1967).

31 Becker: p. 423 (Zvi Unger, 1966), p. 429 (Hersz Tenenbaum, 1966), p. 500 (Helen Starkman, 1966), pp. 593–94 (Maurice Weinberger, 1966), p. 1410 (Abe Freeman, 1968). According to the Schroth Judgment, p. 91, German judicial officials dated this killing to the end of March or early April 1944.

32 For the judicial summary and precise date of this killing: Schroth Indictment, pp. 94–96, and Schroth Judgment, pp. 64–68.

33 Becker: p. 101 (Rachmiel Zynger, 1966), p. 372 (Moshe Rubenstein, 1966), p. 406 (Fred

Baum, 1966), p. 646 (Leo Bach, 1966), p. 825 (Ben Zukerman, 1967), p. 871 (Anna Wilson, 1967). VHA 44270 (Shalom Lindenbaum, 1998).

34 Becker: p. 423 (Jack Steiman, 1966), p. 499 (Helen Starkman, 1966), p. 770 (Arnold Finkler, 1966), p. 814 (Alter Weisbloom, 1967), p. 825 (Ben Zukerman, 1967), p. 1421 (Meyer Frenkel, 1968). VHA 44270 (Shalom Lindenbaum, 1998). Author's interview (Howard Chandler, 2001).

35 VHA 16116 (Maria Szapszewicz, 1996). Becker: p. 462 (Annie Glass, 1966), p. 518 (Ruth Wagner, 1966).

36 VHA 16116 (Maria Szapszewicz, 1996).

37 Becker, p. 462 (Annie Glass, 1966).

38 Becker, p. 413 (Anna Arbeiter, 1966).

39 VHA 16116 (Maria Szapszewicz, 1996). Becker, p. 766 (Howard Chandler, 1966). Others identifying Schroth as the shooter but without the detail about the jammed pistol: Becker: p. 413 (Anna Arbeiter, 1966), p. 681 (Dora Kaminer, 1966).

40 Becker: p. 406 (Fred Baum, 1966), p. 720 (Rywka Slomowicz, 1967), p. 727 (Bella Winograd, 1967). Several other accounts state that the bodies were buried "near" the toilets. Becker: p. 413 (Anna Arbeiter, 1966), p. 518 (Ruth Wagner, 1966). In an entirely different version of the execution, the two sisters were thrown either off the cliff above the quarry or from the guard tower and shot in midair. USHMM, David Boder interview collection (Kalman Eisenberg, 1946), and author's interview (Regina Naiman, 2001).

41 Becker: p. 406 (Fred Baum, 1966), p. 770 (Arnold Finkler, 1967), p. 814 (Alter Weisbloom, 1967).

42 Becker: p. 516 (Ruth Wagner, 1966), p. 773 (Leonia Finkler, 1967).

43 Becker: p. 422 (Jack Steiman, 1966), p. 466 (Josef Mincberg, 1966), p. 832 (Ben Lant, 1967), p. 855 (Israel Chaiton, 1967).

44 Becker: p. 506 (Max Steiman, 1966), p. 590 (Maurice Weinberger, 1966).

45 Becker: p. 84 (Mendel Mincberg, 1962), p. 406 (Fred Baum, 1966), p. 733 (Alan Newman, 1967).

46 Becker, p. 448 (Kurt Otto Baumgarten, 1966). Baumgarten Investigation, pp. 17–20 (Kurt Otto Baumgarten, 1968).

47 Becker, pp. 590, 592–93 (Maurice Weinberger, 1966).

48 YVA, M-49/1172 (Mendel Kac, 1945).

49 The surviving testimony of the sixth Lubliner refers only to his time in Starachowice and Birkenau. YVA, O-3/2924 (Israel Spiegelstein, 1966), and Kaschmieder Investigation, pp. 51–53 (Israel Spiegelstein, 1968).

50 For the sequence of deportations from Międzyrzec conducted by Reserve Police Battalion 101, see: Browning, *Ordinary Men*.

51 VHA 9567 (Morris Burman, 1995).

52 VHA 9390 (Henry Ehrlich, 1995).

53 VHA 6071 (Harry Wolfe, 1995).

54 VHA 2589 (David Goldfarb, 1995).

55 VHA 37264 (Abram Goldman, 1997).

56 VHA: 3916 (Rachell Eisenberg, 1995), 40881 (Salek Benedikt, 1998). YVA, M-49/1172 (Mendel Kac, 1945). Becker, p. 23 (Mack Arbeiter, 1962). Author's interview (Howard Chandler, 2001).

57 VHA: 29322 (Max Kozma, 1997), 37264 (Abram Goldman, 1997).

58 YVA, M-49/1172 (Mendel Kac, 1945). VHA 37264 (Abram Goldman, 1997).

59 Kaschmieder Investigation, p. 90 (Heribert von Merfort, 1968).

60 Kaschmieder Investigation, p. 13. National Archives, Berlin Document Center microfilm: Ortskartei and RuSHA files.

61 Becker: p. 753 (Leonia Finkler, 1966), p. 761 (Mina Binsztok, 1966). Kaschmieder Investigation, p. 53 (Israel Spiegelstein, 1968).

62 Becker: pp. 646, 650 (Leo Bach, 1966), p. 832 (Ben Lant, 1967). Kaschmieder Investigation: p. 50 (Edward Schick, 1968), pp. 64–65 (Schmul Leib Lenczycki, 1968), pp. 68–69 (Leonia Finkler, 1968), pp. 72–76c (Arnold Finkler, 1968). According to Edward Schick and Arnold Finkler, the shootings took place out of sight of the camp in the quarry but were heard and immediately reported on by the accompanying Jewish police. According to Schmul Lenczycki, Leonia Finkler, and Leo Bach, the shooting and burial took place on the flat ground behind the camp above the quarry and in sight of the camp. Several of the witnesses (Schmul Leib Lenczycki and Leo Bach) described the leader of the execution as an SS man but did not identify Kaschmieder by name. Unfortunately, during an earlier interrogation, one Starachowice survivor attributed this killing to Becker rather than Kaschmieder (Kaschmieder Investigation, pp. 52–53, 149). According to his later testimony in *Leo Bach's Memoir*, p. 246, the escapees as well as the assembled prisoners (including Bach himself) from whom the reprisal victims were selected included men from Cracow as well as Lublin, and the executions took place below the cliff. The ten shots were heard, and the bodies were later seen from a vantage point by the fence from which prisoners could look down.

63 Becker, p. 752 (Leonia Finkler, 1966).

64 Symcha Mincberg, "The Beginning of the Downfall," *Wierzbnik-Starachowice Memorial Book* (CD version), pp. 405–6.

65 VHA 37264 (Abram Goldman, 1997).

66 VHA 9390 (Henry Ehrlich, 1995).

67 VHA 4255 (Tola Pinkus, 1995).

68 YVA, M-49/1172 (Mendel Kac, 1945).

69 YVA, M-49/1172 (Mendel Kac, 1945). Author's interview (Howard Chandler, 2001).

70 Author's interview (Sally Recht, 2004).

71 Author's interview (Anna Wilson, 2001).

72 VHA 3916 (Rachell Eisenberg, 1995).

73 Author's interview (Joseph Friedenson, 2002).

74 UMD (Henry Krystal, 1996), p. 23.

22: Closing Majówka and Tartak

1 *Leo Bach's Memoir*, p. 247. Becker, p. 772 (Arnold Finkler, 1966). USHMM, RG-50.030*0411 (Anna Wilson, 2001). Leo Bach wrote that the move occurred "by the beginning of July." Both Arnold Finkler and Anna Wilson placed the move just weeks before the evacuation—in early July. Other prisoners suggest earlier dates. Alan Newman dated it to April or May 1944. Becker, p. 735 (Alan Newman, 1967). Rachmiel Zynger placed it in May. Becker, p. 101 (Rachmiel Zynger, 1962). Zvi Hersz Unger placed it in the spring. Becker, p. 95 (Zvi Hersz Unger, 1962). Pinchas Hochmic placed it in June. Becker, p. 79 (Pinchas Hochmic, 1962). Tobcia Lustman—a ten-year-old girl smuggled into camp the previous fall—remembered that she was allowed to go a little way outside the front gate to pick raspberries, which would also suggest early July. Tova Pagi, *"The way it was . . .": The Diary of a 12 year old Jewish girl who survived Auschwitz (1939–1945)*, p. 14.

2 Shlomo Moskowicz, *My Little Town Glinojeck: Souvenirs*, p. 224. *Leo Bach's Memoir*, p. 242, places the attack at the smelter guardhouse.

3 Ester Zukerman-Zilberberg, "Sad Hiding Places," *Wierzbnik-Starachowitz*, p. 224.

4 VHA 3948 (Irene Horn, 1995).

5 VHA: 7739 (Howard Chandler, 1995), 16114 (Jacob Szapszewicz, 1996). Author's interview (Howard Chandler, 2001).

6 VHA: 2643 (Howard Kleinberg, 1995), 7739 (Howard Chandler, 1995), 29585 (Alter Szainwald, 1997), 44259 (Ruth Turek, 1998).

7 VHA: 33807 (Gloria Borenstein, 1997), 40372 (Harry Spicer, 1998). Yaacov Shafshevitz, "Starcavitz," *Shidlovtser Yizkor Bukh* (Shidlortsa Benevolent Society of New York, 1974), p. 652 [USHMM, RG-02.025], excerpts translated from Yiddish by Frieda Stone.

8 Moskowicz, *My Little Town Glinojeck: Souvenirs*, p. 225. According to *Leo Bach's Memoir*, p. 251, he was also convinced that there was a secret radio in camp, since some prisoners learned quickly of the July 20 assassination attempt on Hitler.

9 USHMM, RG-50.030*0396 (Chris Lerman, 1998).

10 YVA, M-49/1172 (Mendel Kac, 1945).

11 VHA: 5190 (Ceil Saltzman, 1995), 43397 (Louis Feintuch, 1998), 44270 (Shalom Lindenbaum, 1998). Becker, p. 23 (Mack Arbeiter, 1962). *Leo Bach's Memoir*, p. 248.

12 VHA 15941 (Ernest Abraham, 1996).

13 VHA 2643 (Howard Kleinberg, 1995). USHMM, RG-15.084 (Meir Lewental, 1945, from the Jewish Historical Institute Archives, 301/358).

14 VHA: 9390 (Henry Ehrlich, 1995), 15188 (Annie Glass, 1996).

15 USHMM, RG-50.030*0411 (Anna Wilson, 2001). Presumably fear of further reprisal shootings led some to block escape attempts. For instance, when yet another group of Lubliners working at the blast furnace planned to escape, a Jewish policeman found out. To block their attempt, he took their clothes and prevented them from going to work for several days. VHA 6071 (Harry Wolfe, 1995).

16 VHA 16876 (Henry Greenbaum, 1996).

17 Moskowicz, *My Little Town Glinojeck: Souvenirs*, pp. 225–27.

18 YVA, M-49/1172 (Mendel Kac, 1945).

19 Becker: p. 372 (Moshe Rubenstein, 1966), p. 414 (Anna Arbeiter, 1966).

20 FA, T-91 (Israel Arbeiter, 1980). USHMM, RG-50.030*0411 (Anna Wilson, 2001). Author's interview (Anna Wilson, 2001).

21 USHMM, RG-50.030*0411 (Anna Wilson, 2001). Author's interview (Anna Wilson, 2001). The videotaped interview varies slightly from my interview in two details— namely, that Abraham was not caught until purchasing the second gun and that Becker as well as Baumgarten had to be paid off.

22 VHA 44270 (Shalom Lindenbaum, 1998).

23 VHA 8656 (Paul Cymerman, 1995).

24 YVA, O-2/319 (Moses Weinberg, n.d.).

25 YVA, M-1/E.2469 (Josef Kohs, 1948). FA, T-1682 (Mania K., 1988). MJH, RG-1165 (Guta Blass Weintraub, 1984). Author's interview (Martin Baranek, 2001). For successful escapes at this time, see also: Becker, p. 800 (Abraham Gershon Rosenwald, 1967); VHA 7366 (Naftula Korenwasser, 1995, with his wife); David Sali, "In the Woods of Wierzbnik," *Wierzbnik-Starachowitz*, p. 35; Malka Weisbloom, "Saved by Finkelstein's Sacrifice," and Gershon Rosenwald, "Deep in the Forest," *Wierzbnik-Starachowice Memorial Book* (CD version), pp. 516, 524.

26 USHMM, RG-15.084m (Meir Lewental, 1945).

27 YVA, M-49/1172 (Mendel Kac, 1945).

28 Donald Niewyk, who worked through all of the David Boder testimonies and published edited versions of some of them, concluded that Kalman Eisenberg "sought to dramatize his story to the hilt" and that "parts may strain credulity." Niewyk, *Fresh Wounds*, p. 87.

29 USHMM, David Boder interview collection (Kalman Eisenberg, 1946), portions printed in Niewyk, *Fresh Wounds*, pp. 87–93.

30 YVA, M-1/E.2469 (Josef Kohs, 1948).

31 Becker, p. 709 (Lea Greiwer, 1966).

32 Becker, p. 850 (Ruth Rosengarten, 1967).

33 Becker, p. 782 (Rose Herling, 1967).

34 MJH, RG-1383 (Pola Funk, 1986).

35 FA, T-1682 (Mania K., 1988).

36 Author's interview (Martin Baranek, 2001).

37 VHA 51793 (Sally Recht, 2001). Author's interview (Sally Recht, 2004).

38 Schroth Judgment, pp. 59–61.

39 Wendy Tucker, "German Trial Stirs Memory of Horror Camp," *Wierzbnik-Starachowitz*, pp. 45–47.

40 MJH, RG-1165 (Guta Blass Weintraub, 1984); USHMM, RG-50.030*250 (Guta Blass Weintraub, 1990).

41 Joy Erlichman Miller, *Love Carried Me Home: Women Surviving Auschwitz*, pp. 95–96.

42 Author's interview (Guta Blass Weintraub, 2004).

43 Though not a direct witness, Goldie Szachter Kalib related a somewhat different version of the incident, based on what she must have heard later. In her memoirs, she wrote that when the trucks were about to leave the lumberyard, a young Jewish girl slapped a German officer in the face twice, and he merely walked away. *The Last Selection*, pp. 211–12. Another secondhand rather than eyewitness account, included in the community book, is also at odds with the other twelve accounts in significant ways. In this version, Guta charged Schroth and snatched the pistol from his holster. The Germans were "stunned" by this "daring act," which allowed Guta to slip away in the confusion and darkness. Schroth was embarrassed by the loss of his gun but also had "some appreciation" for Guta's courage. He thus promised that she would not be harmed if the gun was returned. Some who were "eager to earn his favor" persuaded Guta to return the gun, and the otherwise "unscrupulous murderer" Schroth actually kept his word not to harm her. Yerahmiel Singer, "Guta Blass Weintraub Snatched the Gun," *Wierzbnik-Starachowice Memorial Book* (CD version), pp. 502–3.

23: The Final Days

1 Danuta Czech, *Kalendarium der Ereignisse im Konzentrationslager Auschwitz-Birkenau 1939–1945* (Reinbek bei Hamburg: Rowohlt, 1989), p. 832. This is also the precise date given by Kalib, *The Last Selection*, p. 218.

2 VHA 12459 (Leon Miller, 1996).

3 For testimony that explicitly placed the loading and unloading before the ensuing breakout: Becker, pp. 79–80 (Pinchas Hochmic, 1962), p. 95 (Zvi Unger, 1962); VHA 29322 (Max Kozma, 1997); MJH, RG-1383 (Pola Funk, 1986). For those who explicitly placed the first breakout attempt before the loading and unloading: author's interview (Alan Newman, 2001); YVA, O 2/319 (Moses Weinberg, n.d.); and Hana Tenzer, "At the Edge

of the Abyss," *Wierzbnik-Starachowitz*, pp. 190–96; and, in contrast to his 1962 testimony, Pinchas Hochmitz, "A Hole in the Floor of the Railway Car," *Wierzbnik-Starachowice Memorial Book* (CD version), pp. 455–56. In this second Hochmitz account, as well as one other, the train was loaded, unloaded, then reloaded in the same day: YVA, M-1/E.2469 (Josef Kohs, 1948). Other accounts of the loading and unloading: Becker, p. 518 (Ruth Wagner, 1966), p. 787 (Max Naiman, 1967), p. 805 (Sylvia Russak, 1967), p. 816 (Alter Weisbloom, 1967), p. 819 (Faye Gold, 1967), p. 826 (Ben Zukerman, 1967), p. 1380 (Toby Steiman, 1968), p. 1416 (Akiva Rutmanowicz, 1968); VHA: 403 (Ruth Charney, 1994), 1213 (Rose Weitzen, 1995), 8896 (Maury Adams, 1995), 33025 (Joseph Tauber, 1997), 34749 (Barbara Burton, 1997), 51793 (Sally Recht, 2001); author's interviews (Martin Baranek and Howard Chandler, 2001; Joseph Friedenson, 2002; Sally Recht and Guta Blass Weintraub, 2004).

4   VHA: 403 (Ruth Charney, 1994), 29322 (Max Kozma, 1997), 51793 (Sally Recht, 2001).

5   For the first hypothesis: VHA: 403 (Ruth Charney, 1994), 34749 (Barbara Burton, 1997). For the second: USHMM, RG-50.030*250 (Guta Blass Weintraub, 1990). Author's interview (Guta Blass Weintraub, 2004).

6   VHA 29322 (Max Kozma, 1997).

7   VHA 31601 (Esther Kirschenblatt, 1997).

8   Becker: p. 826 (Ben Zukerman, 1967), p. 856 (Israel Chaiton, 1967). VHA 3948 (Irene Horn, 1995).

9   VHA: 1833 (Isidore Guterman, 1995), 44270 (Shalom Lindenbaum, 1998), 15188 (Annie Glass, 1996). Author's interview (Sally Recht, 2004).

10   VHA 9390 (Henry Ehrlich, 1995). USHMM, RG-02.025 (Yaacov Shafshevitz, excerpt from *Shidlovtser Yizkor Bukh*).

11   VHA 3645 (Joseph Zolno, 1995).

12   VHA 33025 (Joseph Tauber, 1997).

13   Author's interview (Joseph Friedenson, 2002).

14   VHA 25164 (Michael Feldstein, 1997).

15   VHA: 1833 (Isidore Guterman, 1995, estimated 150), 16114 (Jacob Szapszewicz, 1996, estimated 400), 18046 (David Mangarten, 1996, estimated 300), 40866 (Helen Sonshine, 1998, estimated 180). Both Rivka Greenberg, "My Journey Through the Valley of the Shadow of Death," and Avraham Shiner, "Hunted and Murdered by Polish Partisans," *Wierzbnik-Starachowice Memorial Book* (CD version), pp. 302 and 528, estimated 200. Decidedly on the low side was the estimate of thirty to forty in *Leo Bach's Memoir*.

16   The twenty-five who testified were: Israel Arbeiter, Toby Wolfowicz, Ralph Chaiton, Toby Weisfeld, Alan Newman, Jankiel Chaiton, Regina Naiman, Lena Waldman, Pola Funk, Henry Greenbaum, Emil Naiman, Mendel Kac, Leonia Finkler, Kalman Eisenberg, Henry Ehrlich, Louis Feintuch, Ceil Saltzman, Howard Kleinberg, Irwin Gottfried, Helen Sonshine, Jacob Szapszewicz, Meir Lowenthal, Yechiel Eisenberg, Yaakov Shafshevitz, and Abraham Shiner. Four others testified about other family members having taken part. VHA: 1213 (Rose Weitzen, 1995), 5874 (Anita Tuchmayer, 1995), 34749 (Barbara Burton, 1997); author's interview (Shoshana Fiedelman, 2008).

17   For example, Abraham Schiner escaped from either Tartak or the factory camp in late July 1944, and those who helped him were later designated "Righteous Gentiles" by Yad Vashem. However, his testimony to German investigators makes no mention of either his escape or his subsequent survival. Becker, pp. 941–48 (Avraham Scheiner, 1968).

18   For the payment: MJH, RG-1984 (Regina Najman, 1988); FA, T-1884 (Regina N., 1991 and 1992); author's interview (Regina Naiman, 2001). The other seven: author's inter-

views (Henry Greenbaum, 2000; Alan Newman, 2001; Harold Rubenstein, 2002); VHA: 1213 (Rose Weitzen, 1995), 1652 (David Mangarten, 1995), 10154 (Alan Newman, 1995), 16680 (Emil Najman, 1996), 16871 (Henry Greenbaum, 1996), 37728 (Tovi Pagi, 1998), 42666 (Morris Pinczewski, 1998), 43397 (Louis Feintuch, 1998); FA, T-955 (Gutta T., 1987).

19   Moskowicz, *My Little Town Glinojeck: Souvenirs*, p. 226.

20   FA, T-955 (Gutta T., 1987). MJH, RG-1383 (Pola Funk, 1986). VHA 1833 (Isidore Guterman, 1995).

21   YVA, M-49/1172 (Mendel Kac, 1945).

22   YVA, M-49E/1742 (Lena Waldman, 1946).

23   Author's interview (Henry Greenbaum, 2000). VHA 16876 (Henry Greenbaum, 1996). In the cousin's account, he and others pulled Chuna Grynbaum back to the safety of the barracks. VHA 943 (Harold Rubenstein, 1995).

24   In addition to Lena Waldman and Mendel Kac, cited above: Becker, p. 648 (Leo Bach, 1966), p. 826 (Ben Zukerman, 1967), p. 861 (Eva Zuckier, 1967), p. 1329 (Alan Newman, 1968). VHA: 15188 (Annie Glass, 19960, 16114 (Jacob Szapszewicz, 1996), 30309 (Irwin Gottfried, 1997), 40372 (Harry Spicer, 1998). USHMM, RG-02.025 (Yaacov Shafshevitz, excerpt from *Shidlovtser Yizkor Bukh*). Author's interview (Alan Newman, 2001). As usual, at least one witness remembers a different person and names Schleser rather than Schroth as the one responsible for throwing the hand grenade. Becker, p. 640 (Henry Armand, 1966).

25   Becker: p. 437 (Toby Wolfowicz, 1966), p. 755 (Leonia Finkler, 1966). VHA: 10154 (Alan Newman, 1995), 40866 (Helen Sonshine, 1998). Yechiel Eisenberg (family account, 2003).

26   YVA, M-49/1172 (Mendel Kac, 1945). Niewyk, *Fresh Wounds*, p. 93 (Kalman Eisenberg, 1946). Becker: p. 738 (Toby Weisfeld, 1966), p. 775 (Leonia Finkler, 1966), p. 1375 (Jankiel Chaiton, 1968). FA, T-1884 (Regina N., 1992). VHA: 2643 (Howard Kleinberg, 1995), 5190 (Ceil Saltzman, 1995), 9390 (Henry Ehrlich, 1995), 43397 (Louis Feintuch, 1998).

27   Becker, p. 470 (Adam Gutman, 1966). FA, T-1884 (Regina N., 1991).

28   Becker, p. 715 (Ida Gutman, 1967).

29   Becker, p. 654 (Mayer Gutman, 1966).

30   VHA 16114 (Jacob Szapszewicz, 1996).

31   VHA 31601 (Esther Kirschenblatt, 1997).

32   USHMM, RG-02.025 (excerpts from *Shidlovtser Yizkor Bukh*).

33   Author's interview (Shoshana Fiedelman, 2008). According to other witnesses, however, Einesman and his son were killed at the fence trying to escape the following day. Becker, p. 635 (Mania Blicher, 1966). Author's interview (Regina Naiman, 2001). VHA 3948 (Irene Horn, 1995). Kalib, *The Last Selection*, p. 212. Confirming Einesman's escape, Abraham Gershon Rosenwald—a successful escapee from Tartak—testified that he encountered Einesman later in the woods. Gershon Rosenwald, "Deep in the Forest," *Wierzbnik-Starachowice Memorial Book* (CD version), p. 527.

34   On Schroth's proclamation: Becker: pp. 733, 1329 (Alan Newman, 1967 and 1968). On the 10 a.m. roll call and being prevented from helping the wounded, who were left to suffer: VHA: 1833 (Isidore Guterman, 1995), 37728 (Tovi Pagi, 1998), 43397 (Louis Feintuch, 1998); USHMM, RG-15.084m (Meir Lewental, 1945). Hana Tenzer, "At the Edge of the Abyss," *Wierzbnik-Starachowitz*, pp. 190–96; Tova Pagi, *"The way it was . . .": The Diary of a 12 year old Jewish girl who survived Auschwitz (1939–1945)*, p. 14.

35   VHA 5190 (Ceil Saltzman, 1995).

36   Author's interviews (Henry Greenbaum, 2000; Howard Chandler, 2001). Becker: p. 715 (Ida Gutman, 1967), p. 726 (Bella Winograd, 1967), p. 1365 (Rachel Piuti, 1968). VHA 16876 (Henry Greenbaum, 1996).

37   VHA: 25164 (Michael Feldstein, 1997), 25175 (Elizabeth Styk, 1997).

38   Becker: p. 23 (Mack Arbeiter, 1962), p. 30 (Israel Arbeiter, 1962), p. 80 (Pinchas Hochmic, 1962), p. 95 (Zvi Unger, 1962), p. 648 (Leo Bach, 1966), p. 715 (Ida Gutman, 1967), p. 742 (Mendel Tenenbaum, 1966), p. 1365 (Rachel Piuti, 1968), p. 1369 (Max Richman, 1968), p. 1416 (Akiva Rutmanowicz, 1968). YVA: O-2/319 (Moses Weinberg, n.d.), M-49/1172 (Mendel Kac, 1945), M-1/E.2469 (Josef Kohs, 1948). VHA 43397 (Louis Feintuch, 1998). MJH, RG-1984 (Regina Najman, 1988). *Leo Bach's Memoir*, p. 250. Moskowicz, *My Little Town Glinojeck*, p. 231. The brothers Israel and Mack Arbeiter, Mendel Tenenbaum, Josef Kohs, and Shlomo Moskowicz credited the speech to Becker, not Baumgarten. Three witnesses gave different versions of the death of Moshe Herblum. According to two, he was left to die a slow, painful death. Becker: p. 430 (Hersz Tenenbaum, 1966), p. 1375 (Jankiel Chaiton, 1968). According to another, he slit his wrists. Becker, p. 726 (Bella Winograd, 1967).

39   Becker, p. 462 (Annie Gold, 1966).

40   Becker, p. 95 (Zvi Unger, 1962). YVA: M-49/1172 (Mendel Kac, 1945), M-1/E.2469 (Josef Kohs, 1948), O-2/319 (Moses Weinberg, n.d.). VHA 16876 (Henry Greenbaum, 1996). USHMM, RG-15.084m (Meir Lewental, 1945). Niewyk, *Fresh Wounds*, p. 93 (Kalman Eisenberg, 1946).

41   VHA 2643 (Howard Kleinberg, 1995).

42   Becker, p. 1329 (Alan Newman, 1968); author's interview (Alan Newman, 2001).

43   Becker, p. 1397 (Salamon Binsztok, 1968); VHA 8656 (Paul Cymerman, 1995).

44   For a group of ten, including Abraham Wilczek: USHMM, RG-50.030*0411 (Anna Wilson, 2001); author's interview (Anna Wilson, 2001). For the other three smaller groups, see: VHA 43397 (Louis Feintuch, 1995, with his brother and others); Becker, p. 1382 (Adam Kogut, 1968), and VHA 1213 (Rose Weitzen, 1995, who said her brother Adam got out with two others); and Yechiel Eisenberg (family account, 2003), who escaped with his brother Meilech. Abraham Shiner sneaked through the fence alone and unobserved before the cluster of daylight breakout attempts, which he watched from the forest, drew fire from the guards. Avraham Shiner, "Hunted and Murdered by Polish Partisans," *Wierzbnik-Starachowice Memorial Book* (CD version), pp. 528–29.

45   Becker, p. 85 (Mendel Mincberg, 1962); author's interviews (Anna Wilson, Alan Newman, and Howard Chandler, 2001).

46   USHMM, RG-50.030*0411 (Anna Wilson, 2001); author's interview (Anna Wilson, 2001).

47   VHA 2643 (Howard Kleinberg, 1995).

48   VHA 40372 (Harry Spicer, 1998).

49   *Leo Bach's Memoir*, pp. 252–53.

50   VHA 30309 (Irwin Gottfried, 1997).

51   Author's interview (Joseph Friedenson, 2002).

52   Becker, p. 866 (Anna Wilson, 1967). *Leo Bach's Memoir*, p. 251, identified the reinforcements as 200 Wehrmacht soldiers but did not identify them explicitly as military police.

53   Becker: p. 80 (Pinchas Hochmic, 1962), p. 95 (Zvi Unger, 1962), p. 733 (Alan Newman, 1967). VHA: 3948 (Irene Horn, 1998), 42564 (Rachel Piuti, 1998), 44259 (Ruth Turek, 1998). YVA, O-3/8489 (Chaim Gil, 1995). Niewyk, *Fresh Wounds*, p. 93 (Kalman Eisenberg, 1946). *Leo Bach's Memoir*, p. 251. Zvi Unger, "From Wierzbnik to Mauthausen,"

and Pinchas Hochmitz, "A Hole in the Floor of the Railway Car," *Wierzbnik-Staracho-wice Memorial Book* (CD version), pp. 349, 455.

54 MJH, RG-1383 (Pola Funk, 1986). VHA 8656 (Paul Cymerman, 1995). YVA, M-49/1172 (Mendel Kac, 1945). These three accounts differ as to exactly when and for how long the *Lagerrat* members were under watch.

55 VHA 43397 (Louis Feintuch, 1998).

56 For Friday, July 28, 1944, as the date of the evacuation of the camp, see: Becker, p. 80 (Pinchas Hochmic, 1962). Author's interviews (Martin Baranek and Howard Chandler, 2001). Kalib, *The Last Selection*, p. 213.

57 Becker: p. 80 (Pinchas Hochmic, 1962), p. 95 (Zvi Unger, 1962).

58 VHA 42564 (Rachel Piuti, 1998).

59 Becker, p. 23 (Mack Arbeiter, 1962).

60 Becker: p. 1365 (Rachel Piuti, 1968), p. 1370 (Max Richman, 1968).

61 Becker: p. 767 (Howard Chandler, 1966), p. 839 (Zelda Waiman, 1967).

62 Moskowicz, *My Little Town Glinojeck*, pp. 231–32.

63 YVA, M-1/E.2469 (Josef Kohs, 1948).

64 For Kolditz: Becker, p. 409 (Fred Baum, 1966).

65 Author's interview (Anna Wilson, 2001); Becker, p. 870 (Anna Wilson, 1967).

66 Becker: p. 591 (Maurice Weinberger, 1966), p. 643 (Henry Armand, 1966), p. 1370 (Max Richman, 1968). VHA: 13514 (Saul Miller, 1996), 28993 (Chaim Wolgroch, 1997). Hoch-mitz, "A Hole in the Floor of the Railway Car," *Wierzbnik-Starachowice Memorial Book* (CD version), p. 456. Only one male survivor of the closed cars stated that his car was not overfilled and carried only eighty prisoners. Becker, p. 416 (Matys Finkelstein, 1966).

67 Becker, p. 649 (Leo Bach, 1966). *Leo Bach's Memoir*, p. 252.

24: From Starachowice to Birkenau

1 VHA: 8028 (Abraham Bleeman, 1995), 10154 (Alan Newman, 1995), 16680 (Emil Naj-man, 1996), 33807 (Gloria Borenstein). *Leo Bach's Memoir*, p. 253. According to Abraham Bleeman, additional cars were added to the train in Częstochowa.

2 Pinchas Hochmitz, "A Hole in the Floor of the Railway Car," *Wierzbnik-Starachowice Memorial Book* (CD version), p. 456.

3 Author's interview (Howard Chandler, 2001). Just two testimonies in fact gave estimates of thirty-six and forty hours, respectively. VHA: 16876 (Henry Greenbaum, 1996), 12728 (Anne Spicer, 1996).

4 Becker, p. 635 (Mania Blicher, 1966), p. 819 (Faye Gold, 1967).

5 Author's interview (Gitta Friedenson, 2002).

6 Becker, p. 511 (Dina Tenenbaum, 1966), p. 760 (Mina Binsztok, 1966). VHA 12073 (Helene Fellenbaum, 1996).

7 FA, T-955 (Gutta T., 1987).

8 VHA 12728 (Anne Spicer, 1996).

9 Author's interview (Anna Wilson, 2001).

10 Becker, p. 409 (Fred Baum, 1966), p. 494 (Ralph Chaiton, 1966), p. 506 (Max Steiman, 1966), p. 649 (Leo Bach, 1966), p. 787 (Max Naiman, 1967), pp. 827–28 (Ben Zuker-man, 1967). VHA: 943 (Harold Rubenstein, 1995), 5410 (Charles Kleinman, 1995), 15716 (Joseph Friedenson, 1996), 29322 (Max Kozma, 1997). *Leo Bach's Memoir*, pp. 253–54.

11 YVA, O-3/9394 (Ruben Zachronovitsky, 1996).

12 Becker, p. 643 (Henry Armand, 1966).

13   VHA 12165 (Abram Jakubowicz, 1996).

14   Becker, p. 591 (Maurice Weinberger, 1966).

15   YVA, M-1/E.2469 (Josef Kohs, 1948).

16   VHA: 943 (Harold Rubenstein, 1995, whose uncle perished in that car), 9567 (Morris Burman, 1995, a Lubliner who rode in that car), 13514 (Saul Miller, 1996), 16680 (Emil Najman, 1996, who identified that car as the "first car" containing most of the camp leadership), 20030 (Anna Freilich, 1996), 37264 (Abram Goldman, 1997, the other Lubliner who rode in that car). USHMM, RG-15.084m (Meir Lewental, 1945).

17   YVA, M-49/1172 (Mendel Kac, 1945).

18   Becker, p. 416 (Matys Finkelstein, 1966).

19   Becker, p. 430 (Hersz Tenenbaum, 1966).

20   Becker, p. 511 (Dina Tenenbaum, 1966).

21   Becker, p. 518 (Ruth Wagner, 1966).

22   Becker, pp. 655–56 (Mayer Gutman, 1966). Mayer Gutman, however, gave the name of Kogut instead of Wilczek.

23   Becker, p. 728 (Bella Winograd, 1967).

24   Becker, pp. 742–43 (Mendel Tenenbaum, 1966).

25   Becker, p. 648 (Leo Bach, 1966), p. 717 (Ida Gutman, 1967), p. 815 (Alter Weisbloom, 1967).

26   Becker, p. 827 (Ben Zukerman, 1967), p. 870 (Anna Wilson, 1967). Ben Zukerman stated explicitly that he had wanted to get into the first car, having heard the rumor that the camp council had arranged to be freed by the underground, but he then reconsidered for two reasons. He feared getting caught in a shootout and the car was so crowded that struggles had already broken out for places near the windows.

27   Becker, p. 787 (Max Naiman, 1967), p. 819 (Faye Gold, 1967).

28   Becker, p. 833 (Ben Lant, 1967).

29   FA, T-1884 (Regina N., 1991 and 1992).

30   Kalib, *The Last Selection*, p. 220.

31   VHA: 943 (Harold Rubenstein, 1995, whose uncle—the head of the kitchen—was among those who perished in the first train car), 8895 (Maury Adams, 1995), 9567 (Morris Burman, 1995, a Lubliner). *Leo Bach's Memoir*, p. 256, acknowledged that "many of the privileged" Jews did not survive the journey, but he attributed that to "the extremely hot air" inside the train car.

32   VHA: 3748 (Irene Horn, 1995), 5874 (Anita Tuchmayer, 1995), 13514 (Saul Miller, 1996), 20030 (Anna Freilich, 1996), 33807 (Gloria Borenstein, 1997),

33   VHA: 9135 (Lola Sussman, 1995), and for the quote, 12906 (Eli Oberman, 1996).

34   VHA 36414 (Rachel Akierman, 1997).

35   VHA 2643 (Howard Kleinberg, 1995).

36   VHA 12728 (Anne Spicer, 1996). For other testimonies that made clear these were revenge killings: UMD (Henry Krystal, 1996), VHA 27852 (Ann Zworth, 1997).

37   VHA 36226 (Toby Kott, 1997).

38   VHA 3261 (Nancy Kleinberg, 1995).

39   VHA 10154 (Alan Newman, 1995).

40   VHA: 3916 (Rachell Eisenberg, 1995), 4255 (Tola Pinkus, 1995), 5190 (Ceil Saltzman, 1995).

41   VHA 1873 (Isidore Guterman, 1995).

42   Author's interviews (Emil Naiman, 1997; Henry Greenbaum, 2000; Alan Newman, Howard Chandler, and Harry Chandler, 2001; Joseph Friedenson and Faye Gold, 2002; Sally Recht, 2004; Guta Blass Weintraub, 2005). My talks with Emil Naiman and Harry Chandler were brief conversations, not full interviews.

43   Author's interviews (Joseph Friedenson and Faye Gold, 2002).

44   Author's interview (Henry Greenbaum, 2000). *Leo Bach's Memoir*, p. 252, confirms that the privileged prisoners wanted to travel together in their own car but that others pushed their way into the same car despite the objections by the privileged prisoners.

45   VHA: 403 (Ruth Charney, 1994), 1833 (Isidore Guterman, 1995), 3261 (Nancy Kleinberg, 1995), 5190 (Ceil Saltzman, 1995), 6061 (Toby Weisfeld, 1995), 12728 (Anne Spicer, 1996), 16492 (Eva Herling, 1996), 40866 (Helen Sonshine, 1998), 51710 (Morris Wilson, 2001). Author's interview (Faye Gold, 2002).

46   VHA: 3948 (Irene Horn, 1995), 6007 (Bronia Cyngiser, 1995), 51793 (Sally Recht, 2001).

47   VHA 9971 (Halina Zeleznik, 1995). Author's interview (Joseph Friedenson, 2002).

48   VHA 36797 (Esther Rothman, 1997). Author's interview (Sally Recht, 2004).

49   I will not attempt to list the *forty-nine* different testimonies to this effect.

50   For testimony of the children and the weak coming into the camp, see: Kalib, *The Last Selection*, p. 220; VHA: 3948 (Irene Horn, 1995), 3916 (Rachell Eisenberg, 1995), 12459 (Leon Miller, 1996), 31601 (Esther Kirschenblatt, 1997), 36226 (Toby Kott, 1997), 36414 (Rachel Akierman, 1997); author's interview (Martin Baranek, 2001).

51   VHA 36226 (Toby Kott, 1997).

52   VHA: 9135 (Lola Sussman, 1995), 15716 (Joseph Friedenson, 1996).

53   VHA: 27852 (Ann Zworth, 1997), 31592 (Regina Cymberg, 1997).

54   VHA 8896 (Maury Adams, 1995).

55   Author's interview (Martin Baranek, 2001).

56   Becker, p. 373 (Chaim Rubenstein 1966), p. 462 (Annie Glass, 1966). FA, T-1884 (Regina N., 1992). VHA: 15188 (Annie Glass, 1996), 20030 (Anna Freilich, 1996, who credited the letter to the long-departed Schwertner), 23091 (Ruth Korman, 1996), 28993 (Chaim Wolgroch, 1997), 44259 (Ruth Turek, 1998). Qualified as "rumor": VHA: 3916 (Rachell Eisenberg, 1995), 15716 (Joseph Friedenson, 1996).

57   FA, T-955 (Gutta T., 1987); VHA 36414 (Rachel Akierman, 1997).

58   The one exception is the 1945 testimony of Meir Lewental, USHMM, RG-15.084m.

59   For selection with Mengele: FA, T-91 (Israel A., 1980). Author's interview (Henry Greenbaum, 2001). VHA: 451 (Helen Starkman, 1994), 1833 (Isidore Guterman, 1995), 3645 (Joseph Zolno, 1995), 5874 (Anita Tuchmayer, 1995), 8656 (Paul Cymerman, 1995), 3189 (Pola Schlenger, 1995), 3261 (Nancy Kleinberg, 1995), 16880 (Emil Najman, 1996), 37164 (Abe Goldman, 1997), 42564 (Rachel Piuti, 1998), 5410 (Charles Kleinman, 1995), 9390 (Henry Ehrlich, 1995). Zvi Unger, "From Wierzbnik to Mauthausen," *Wierzbnik-Starachowitz*, p. 220. For mention of seeing Mengele on the first day, but without the normal selection: FA, T-1884 (Regina N., 1992). VHA: 6007 (Bronia Cyngiser, 1995), 20030 (Anna Freilich, 1996), 34794 (Barbara Burton, 1997), 36414 (Rachel Akierman, 1997).

60   USHMM, RG-50.030*250 (Guta Blass Weintraub, 1990). Joy Erlichman Miller, *Love Carried Me Home: Women Surviving Auschwitz*, p. 97.

61   UMD (Henry Krystal, 1996). *Leo Bach's Memoir*, p. 255.

62   VHA: 3916 (Rachell Eisenberg, 1995), 21326 (Abraham Malach, 1996), 31597 (Rachel Hymans, 1997), 36414 (Rachel Akierman, 1997). Tova Pagi, *"The way it was..."*: *The Diary of a 12 year old Jewish girl who survived Auschwitz (1939–1945)*, p. 16.

63   Danuta Czech, *Kalendarium der Ereignisse im Konzentrationslager Auschwitz-Birkenau 1939–1945*, p. 832. Erroneously, this source states that those not receiving numbers were sent to the gas chambers, but, according to a number of testimonies, a few women and children received their tattooed numbers several weeks later.

64   VHA 8028 (Abraham Bleeman, 1995).

65 Nechama Tec, *Courage and Resilience: Women, Men, and the Holocaust* (New Haven, CT: Yale University Press, 2003), pp. 127–28, confirms the stronger emotional impact on women than on men of experiencing shaved heads and enforced nudity.

66 VHA 40881 (Salek Benedikt, 1998). Pinchas Hochmitz, "We Were Ten Brothers," *Wierzbnik-Starachowice Memorial Book* (CD version), pp. 368–69. *Leo Bach's Memoir*, p. 257, relates a similar event but places it later in the Gypsy camp and names Einesman, not Langleben, as the target.

67 YVA, M-1/E.2469 (Josef Kohs, 1948).

68 VHA: 4334 (Miram Miklin, 1995), 6061 (Toby Weisfeld, 1995), 16492 (Eva Herling, 1996), 16680 (Emil Najman, 1996), 18046 (David Mangarten, 1996), 25434 (Irving Leibgott, 1997), 28993 (Chaim Wolgroch, 1997). Author's interview (Faye Gold, 2002).

69 VHA 12906 (Eli Oberman, 1996).

70 VHA 2643 (Howard Kleinberg, 1995).

71 VHA: 5410 (Charles Kleinman, 1995), 12906 (Eli Oberman, 1996), 15716 (Joseph Friedenson, 1996), 15941 (Ernest Abraham, 1996), 16876 (Henry Greenbaum, 1996), 25434 (Irving Leibgott, 1997), 29322 (Max Kozma, 1997). UMD (Henry Krystal, 1996).

72 VHA: 1707 (Edward Koslowski, 1995), 7739 (Howard Chandler, 1995), 9390 (Henry Ehrlich, 1995), 12164 (Abram Jakubowicz, 1996).

73 Czech, *Kalendarium*, p. 838. This source provides the exact date, August 2, on which the Gypsy camp was liquidated, as well as the exact number, 2,897, of "Gypsies" killed. As four further transports evacuating prisoners from work camps in central Poland arrived in Birkenau on July 31 and August 1, and large numbers of workers from at least two of these transports entered the camp rather than being gassed upon arrival, the need to make space in Birkenau may well have been a factor in triggering the liquidation of the Gypsy camp on that particular date.

25: The Starachowice Women and Children in Birkenau

1 For general histories of Auschwitz: Deborah Dwork and Robert Jan Van Pelt, *Auschwitz, 1270–Present* (New York: Norton, 1996); Michael Berenbaum and Israel Gutman, ed., *Auschwitz: Anatomy of a Death Camp* (Bloomington: Indiana University Press, 1994); Sybille Steinbacher, *Auschwitz: A History* (London: Penguin, 2005).

2 I base this estimate on the following calculation. In German reports, the number of Jewish workers at the Braunschweig Steel Works was listed at 1,400 for July 1944. Karay, *Death Comes in Yellow*, p. 71. Seidel, *Deutsche Besatzungspolitik in Polen*, p. 367. I am guessing that the combination of subsequent escapes, deaths in the breakout attempts, and deaths on the train totaled about 200. What is not clear is whether the Tartak workers were included in the July 1944 figure of 1,400. If not, that could increase the estimate to approximately 1,600. The total number of Jews on the Radom transport receiving numbers upon arrival was 1,707, and some Starachowice Jews said that they were not given numbers until later. This would support the testimony of one survivor (VHA 8028, Abraham Bleeman, 1995) that train cars of additional Jewish workers had been added to the transport in Częstochowa.

3 *Wierzbnik-Starachowitz*, pp. 77–83.

4 Czech, *Kalendarium*, p. 832.

5 My colleague Nechama Tec, who has conducted extensive interviews among survivors, shares the impression that women have been more willing than men to give oral testimony about their experiences after the war.

6 According to the research of Nechama Tec, *Resilience and Courage: Women, Men, and the Holocaust*, pp. 130–38, women survivors had the distinct impression that they survived the concentration-camp experience in higher percentages than men.

7 VHA 3916 (Rachell Eisenberg, 1995). Several other witnesses also noted the continuation of a large group of Starachowice women prisoners living together. VHA 42564 (Rachel Piuti, 1998). MJH, RG-1165 (Guta Blass Weintraub, 1984).

8 Tec, *Resilience and Courage*, pp. 175–204, emphasizes the importance of "bonding" as a survival factor in the camps.

9 VHA 34749 (Barbara Burton, 1997).

10 VHA 44259 (Ruth Turek, 1998). Kalib, *The Last Selection*, pp. 233–34.

11 VHA 15188 (Annie Glass, 1996), 51793 (Sally Recht, 2001). Author's interview (Annie Glass, 2004).

12 VHA 3916 (Rachell Eisenberg, 1995). Kalib, *The Last Selection*, pp. 238–40.

13 VHA 5190 (Ceil Saltzman, 1995).

14 VHA: VHA 2139 (Sarah Welbel, 1995), 5874 (Anita Tuchmayer, 1995, who refers to a Silesian factory in Simienthal rather than Zillertal), 16492 (Eva Herling, 1996). The Langenbielau and Zillertal camps were part of the Gross Rosen camp system now studied in Bella Gutterman, *A Narrow Bridge to Life: Jewish Forced Labor and Survival in the Gross Rosen Camp System, 1940–1945* (New York: Berghahn, 2008).

15 Author's interview (Faye Gold, 2002). VHA 27852 (Ann Zworth, 1997).

16 MJH, RG-1383 (Pola Funk, 1986).

17 VHA: 32597 (Rachel Hymans, 1997), 47647 (Tova Friedman, 1998).

18 VHA 21326 (Abraham Malach, 1996). USHMM, RG-50.030*0144 (Avraham Malach, 1990).

19 Kalib, *The Last Selection*, p. 241.

20 VHA 21326 (Abraham Malach, 1996). USHMM, RG-50.030*0144 (Avraham Malach, 1990).

21 VHA: 32597 (Rachel Hymans, 1997). Tova Pagi, *"The way it was . . . ,"* pp. 18–19. USHMM, RG-50.030*0144 (Avraham Malach, 1990).

22 VHA 1983 (Martin Baranek, 1995). Author's interview (Martin Baranek, 2001).

23 VHA 23533 (Jacob Kaufman, 1996).

24 VHA 18046 (David Mangarten, 1996).

25 VHA 7739 (Howard Chandler, 1995).

26 VHA 23533 (Jacob Kaufman, 1996).

27 VHA 12459 (Leon Miller, 1996).

28 USHMM, RG-50.030*0144 (Avraham Malach, 1990).

29 FA, T-955 (Gutta T., 1987). USHMM, RG-50.030*0411 (Anna Wilson, 2001). Author's interview (Anna Wilson, 2001).

30 Becker, p. 499 (Helen Starkman, 1966). VHA 13514 (Saul Miller, 1996). Other testimonies that mentioned the encounter with Althoff's mother in Birkenau but without specifics: Becker, p. 493 (Ralph Chaiton, 1966), p. 724 (Bella Winograd, 1967).

26: Escapees

1 Unfortunately, one major source of this study—the German judicial interrogations of the 1960s—is of little help for this chapter. The accounts recorded by the German investigators always stopped abruptly at the moment of escape, for what followed was no longer of interest in terms of collecting evidence for use in court against suspected and accused

perpetrators. Thus, there are a number of survivors who are known to have escaped but whose subsequent stories cannot be told from their judicial testimony. This was one key area in which the interests of the judicial investigator and the historian diverged.

2   VHA 9393 (Irving Weinberg, 1995).

3   VHA 466 (Berel Blum, 1995).

4   VHA 30134 (Joseph Chernikowski, 1997).

5   VHA 5096 (Malka Isser Perla, 1995).

6   VHA 22640 (Lucyna Berkowicz, 1996).

7   VHA 4277 (Tema Lichtenstein, 1995).

8   Family account shared with author (Yechiel Eisenberg, 2003).

9   VHA43397 (Louis Feintuch, 1998).

10   VHA 7366 (Naftula Korenwasser, 1995).

11   USHMM, RG-02.025 (testimony of Yaacov Shafshevitz, excerpted from *The Shidlovtser Yizkor Bukh*).

12   VHA 16114 (Jacob Szapszewicz, 1996).

13   Menachem Mincberg, "Between the Teeth of Fate," *Wierzbnik-Starachowitz*, pp. 176–79.

14   VHA: 5030 (Jakob Binstock, 1995) and 555 (Hyman Salzberg, 1995). Jakob Binstock noted that Moczar's attitude toward Jews changed sharply after the war, when he was chief of police in Łódź and Stalinist policy became more blatantly anti-Semitic. According to historian Jan Gross, when Moczar was minister of the interior in 1968, he staged the "most outlandish episode of official anti-Semitism" that drove virtually all the remaining Jews out of Poland. Jan T. Gross, *Fear: Anti-Semitism in Poland after Auschwitz. An Essay in Historical Interpretation* (New York: Random House, 2006), pp. 229, 231, 238.

15   David Sali, "In the Woods of Wierzbnik," *Wierzbnik-Starachowitz*, pp. 35–40.

16   Avraham Shiner, "Hunted and Murdered by Polish Partisans," *Wierzbnik-Starachowice Memorial Book* (CD version), pp. 528–33.

17   Gershon Rosenwald, "Deep in the Forest," *Wierzbnik-Starachowice Memorial Book* (CD version), pp. 524–27.

18   Author's interview (Anna Wilson, 2001).

19   VHA 6071 (Harry Wolfe, 1995).

27: Return to and Flight from Wierzbnik

1   Yehuda Bauer, "The Death Marches, January–May 1945," *Modern Judaism* 3 (1983), pp. 1–21. Daniel Blatman, "The Death Marches, January–May 1945: Who Was Responsible for What?" *Yad Vashem Studies* 28 (2000), pp. 155–201. Daniel Jonah Goldhagen, *Hitler's Willing Executioners: Ordinary Germans and the Holocaust* (New York: Knopf, 1996), Part V, pp. 327–71.

2   David Engel, "Patterns of Anti-Jewish Violence in Poland, 1944–46," *Yad Vashem Studies* 26 (1998), pp. 43–85.

3   Gross, *Fear*, p. 35. Agnieszka Pufelska, *Die "Judäo-Kommune": Ein Feindbild in Polen. Das polnische Selbstverständnis im Schatten des Antisemitismus 1939–1948* (Paderborn, Germany: Schöningh, 2007), p. 198, and Joanna Michlic-Coren, "Anti-Jewish Violence in Poland, 1918–1939 and 1945–1947," *Polin: Studies in Polish Jewry* 13 (2000), p. 39, offer an even higher estimate of 2,000.

4   For both the geographical and the chronological patterns of anti-Jewish violence, see: Engel, "Patterns of Anti-Jewish Violence in Poland," pp. 49–60. For the first wave

of anti-Jewish violence in the neighboring Lublin region, see: Daniel Blatman, "The Encounter between Jews and Poles in the Lublin District after Liberation, 1944–1945," *East European Politics and Societies* 24/4 (2006), pp. 598–621.

5   Blatman, "The Encounter between Jews and Poles," p. 599.

6   Pufelska, *Die "Judäo-Kommune,"* p. 190.

7   The most sophisticated study of the historical development and evolution of this concept is: Pufelska, *Die "Judäo-Kommune."*

8   Joanna Michlic-Coren puts less emphasis specifically upon the myth of Judeo-Communism and instead emphasizes the more general concept of the Jew in Poland as "the Threatening Other." But she sees "the myth of the Jew as the Threatening Other" functioning in the same ways: "firstly, to mandate and justify anti-Jewish riots and disturbances; secondly, to make the participants appear to be national heroes; thirdly, to shift the guilt and responsibility for the violence onto the victim . . . ; and, finally, to minimize the unethical and criminal nature of inter-ethnic violence itself." Michlic-Coren, "Anti-Jewish Violence in Poland," p. 44.

9   Pufelska, *Die "Judäo-Kommune,"* pp. 193–94.

10   Engel, "Patterns of Anti-Jewish Violence in Poland," p. 85.

11   Gross, *Fear*, pp. 245–61.

12   Engel, "Patterns of Anti-Jewish Violence in Poland," pp. 51, 74.

13   "In Memoriam after the Holocaust," *Wierzbnik-Starachowice Memorial Book* (CD version), p. 608.

14   VHA 7366 (Naftula Korenwasser, 1995).

15   Becker, p. 801 (Abraham Gershon Rosenwald, 1967).

16   VHA 7366 (Naftula Korenwasser, 1995).

17   VHA 9113 (Hyman Flancbaum, 1995).

18   VHA 5030 (Jakob Binstock, 1995).

19   VHA 5096 (Malka Isser Perla, 1995).

20   Natan-Neta Gelbart, "We Ate Grass and Coal," *Wierzbnik-Starachowice Memorial Book* (CD version), p. 335.

21   Adam Penkalla, "Poles and Jews in the Kielce Region and Radom, April 1945–February 1946," *Polin: Studies in Polish Jewry* 13 (2000), p. 246.

22   Personal account written by Shoshana Fiedelman (Rozia Einesman), May 2008. (I am extremely grateful to Mrs. Fiedelman for providing me with a copy of this account.) Author's interview (Shoshana Fiedelman, 2008).

23   VHA: 15188 (Annie Glass, 1996), 51793 (Sally Recht, 2001). Author's interviews (Annie Glass and Sally Recht, 2004).

24   USHMM, RG-50.030*0396 (Chris Lerman, 1998). Author's interview (Anna Wilson, 2004).

25   Chava Faigenbaum (Shraga), "The Nazis' Followers," *Wierzbnik-Starachowice Memorial Book* (CD version), pp. 543–44.

26   Perele Brodbekker-Unger, "Murders After Liberation," *Wierzbnik-Starachowice Memorial Book* (CD version), pp. 541–42.

27   VHA 23533 (Jacob Kaufman, 1996).

28   VHA: 15188 (Annie Glass, 1996), 51793 (Sally Recht, 2001). Author's interviews (Annie Glass and Sally Recht, 2004).

29   Author's interview (Annie Glass, 2004).

30   VHA 43845 (Morris Spagat, 1998).

31   VHA 15188 (Annie Glass, 1996). Author's interview (Annie Glass, 2004).

32   VHA 1833 (Isidore Guterman, 1995).

33   V. H., "Kupat Cholim," *Wierzbnik-Starachowice Memorial Book* (CD version), p. 188.

34   Personal account written by Shoshana Fiedelman (Rozia Einesman), May 2008.

35   At least one Jew from Wierzbnik-Starachowice was killed elsewhere. Szaja Langleben, the most hated camp policeman, returned to Poland and was killed in a restaurant in Radom. Author's interviews (Howard Chandler and Alan Newman, 2001). He is not listed among the returning Wierzbnik Jews who perished after the war at Polish hands, apparently because he was the target of a revenge killing and not the victim of a random anti-Jewish killing.

28: Postwar Investigations and Trials in Germany

1   Becker, p. 3 (Nehemiah Robinson, World Jewish Congress, to Dr. Blank, Zentrale Stelle, April 24 and May 1, 1961).

2   Becker, pp. 193–228 (Abschlussbericht: re Walther Becker, August 28, 1962).

3   Becker, pp. 258–59 (Dr. Artzt, Central Agency, to StA Hamburg, August 28, 1963).

4   Becker, pp. 575–76.

5   Becker, pp. 578–87 (Verfügung, 147 Js 37/67).

6   Becker, p. 918 (Beschluss: Hamburg Untersuchungsrichter 5, April 3, 1968).

7   Becker, p. 1434 (testimony of Else Althoff, Ralf Althoff's sister-in-law, 1968).

8   Schroth Indictment, p. 88.

9   Becker: pp. 883–84 (Morris Zucker, 1967), p. 1271 (Morris Zucker, 1968).

10   For two key studies on how German law worked (and did not work) in the 1963–65 Auschwitz trial in Frankfurt, see: Rebecca Wittmann, *Beyond Justice: The Auschwitz Trial* (Cambridge: Harvard University Press, 2005), and Devin Pendas, *The Frankfurt Auschwitz Trial, 1963–1965: Genocide, History, and the Limits of the Law* (New York: Cambridge University Press, 2006) .

11   Ingo Müller, *Hitler's Justice: The Courts of the Third Reich* (Cambridge: Harvard University Press, 1991), pp. 252–53.

12   Rebecca Wittmann, "Tainted Law: The West German Judiciary and the Prosecution of Nazi War Criminals," in *Atrocities on Trial: Historical Perspectives on the Politics of Prosecuting War Crimes*, ed. by Patricia Heberer and Jürgen Matthäus (Lincoln: University of Nebraska Press, 2008), pp. 220–23. Müller, *Hitler's Justice*, pp. 246–49. Joachim Perels, *Das juristische Erbe des "Dritten Reiches": Beschädigungen der demokratischen Rechtsordnung* (Frankfurt/M.: Campus, 1999), pp. 210–13. The effect of this amendment produced what some have referred to as an "unintentional" amnesty, although both Wittmann and Müller suggest the authors of it knew all too well what they were doing.

13   Schroth Judgment, pp. 50–57, 76–78.

14   Schroth Judgment, pp. 64–84.

15   Schroth Judgment, pp. 111–17.

16   Schroth Judgment, pp. 140–45.

17   Schroth Investigation, p. 45 (Schroth, 1968).

18   Schroth Judgment, pp. 91–103.

19   Schroth Judgment, p. 151.

20   ZStL II 206 AR 125/68, pp. 44–45 (Staatsanwaltschaft Stuttgart, Antrag auf Ausserver-

folgensetzung in der Strafsache gegen Kurt Otto Baumgarten, January 14, 1972), and 51–52 (Beschluss, Landgericht Hechingen, February 2, 1972).

21   Becker Indictment (Staatsanwaltschaft Hamburg, 147 Js 37/67, Anklageschrift gegen Walther Becker, April 8, 1970), pp. 15–16.

22   Becker Indictment, pp. 1–3.

23   Becker Indictment, pp. 34, 40.

24   Becker Judgment (Landgericht Hamburg (50) 35/70, Urteil in der Strafsache gegen Walther Becker, February 8, 1972), pp. 21–28, 56–58.

25   Becker Judgment, pp. 29–31.

26   Becker Judgment, pp. 61–65.

27   Becker Judgment, pp. 66–69.

28   Becker Judgment, pp. 69–79.

29   Becker Judgment, pp. 80–90.

30   Becker Judgment, pp. 91–103.

31   Becker Judgment, pp. 108–11.

32   Becker Judgment, pp. 38–52, 116.

33   This is a clearly evident pattern in the interrogations of the 210 German policemen of Reserve Police Battalion 101, also conducted by the Hamburg *Staatsanwaltschaft*, that I studied in the court records upon which I based my book *Ordinary Men*.

34   Becker Judgment, pp. 32–37, 129, 132.

35   Becker Judgment, p. 116.

36   Becker Judgment, pp. 120, 122.

37   Becker Judgment, p. 136.

38   Becker Judgment, p. 125.

39   Becker Judgment, pp. 133–34.

40   Becker Judgment, p. 119.

41   Becker Judgment, pp. 117–30.

42   Becker Judgment, pp. 141–42.

43   In 1962, Mendel Mincberg briefly outlined accusations against all the major Starachowice perpetrators, including that Becker beat and shot people on the Wierzbnik marketplace. In a longer deposition in 1968, he included the accusation that Becker had struck him personally. Becker, pp. 81–85, 998–1005 (Mendel Mincberg, 1962 and 1968).

44   Becker Judgment, pp. 142–44.

45   Becker Judgment, p. 144.

46   Becker Indictment, p. 44.

47   Becker Judgment, p. 150.

48   Kaschmieder Investigation, pp. 157–58 (Landgericht Traunstein, Beschluss, March 9, 1972).

49   Kaschmieder Investigation, pp. 179–86 (Staatsanwaltschaft appeal, May 5, 1972), and pp. 196–228 (appeals court decision, March 12, 1973).

50   Kaschmieder Judgment (Landgericht Traunstein 2 AK 127/73, Urteil in dem Strafverfahren gegen Gerhard Kaschmieder, October 6, 1973), pp. 20–38.

51   Becker, p. 1736 (Bundesgerichtshof Urteil 5 St R 58/73).

52   Gunner C. Boehnert, "The Jurists in the SS-Führerkorps, 1925–1939," *Der "Führerstaat": Mythus und Realität*, ed. by Gerhard Hirschfeld and Lothar Kettenacker (Stuttgart: Klett-Cotta, 1981), pp. 361–73.

53 Wittmann, "Tainted Law," pp. 220–27. Müller, *Hitler's Justice*, pp. 201–98. Perels, *Das juristische Erbe des "Dritten Reiches,"* pp. 11–38.
54 Mitteilungen des Hamburger Richtervereins, 1/2004, pp. 42–44.
55 "Takt und Türke," *Der Spiegel* 41 (October 6, 1965), p. 78.
56 National Archives, Berlin Document Center microfilm: RuSHA files for Wolf-Dietrich Ehrhardt.

29: Conclusion

1 For a brief review and summary of the vast historiographical literature on this topic: Robert Rozett, "Jewish Resistance," in *The Historiography of the Holocaust*, ed. by Dan Stone (New York: Palgrave Macmillan, 2004), pp. 341–63; Michael Marrus, "Varieties of Jewish Resistance: Some Categories and Comparisons in Historiographical Perspective," in *Major Changes within the Jewish People in the Wake of the Holocaust*, ed. by Yisrael Gutman and Avital Saf (Jerusalem: Yad Vashem, 1996), pp. 269–99; Nechama Tec, "Resistance in Eastern Europe," in *The Holocaust Encyclopedia*, ed. by Walter Laqueur (New Haven, CT: Yale University Press, 2001), pp. 543–50.
2 Yehuda Bauer, *Rethinking the Holocaust* (New Haven, CT: Yale University Press, 2001), p. 134.
3 Author's interview (Howard Chandler, 2001).
4 Author's interview (anonymous).

INDEX